D0455225

Date

INTELLIGENT
ENTERPRISE

THE FREE PRESS
New York   London   Toronto   Sydney   Tokyo   Singapore

INTELLIGENT ENTERPRISE

A KNOWLEDGE AND SERVICE BASED PARADIGM FOR INDUSTRY

JAMES BRIAN QUINN

FOREWORD BY
TOM PETERS

The Free Press
A Division of Simon & Schuster Inc.
1230 Avenue of the Americas
New York, N.Y. 10020

Printed in the United States of America

printing number

      7 8 9 10

Library of Congress Cataloging-in-Publication Data

Quinn, James Brian.
    Intelligent enterprise : a knowledge and service based paradigm
for industry / James Brian Quinn.
       p. cm.
    Includes bibliographical references and index.
    ISBN 0-02-925615-1
    1. Organizational effectiveness. 2. Organizational change.
3. Customer service. 4. Technological innovations. I. Title.
HD58.9.Q357   1992
658.5'14—dc20   92-19384
                                                     CIP

Page 65: Quotation from M. Moritz, *The Little Kingdom: The Private Story of Apple Computer* (New York: William Morrow, 1984). Copyright © 1984 by Michael Moritz. By permission of the author and William Morrow & Company, Inc.

Page 110-111: Quotation from "Lots of Respect, Little Love," *The Economist*, July 27, 1991. Copyright © 1991 The Economist Newspaper Ltd. Reprinted with permission.

Page 421: Quotation from S. Roach, "Services under Siege: The Restructuring Imperative," *Harvard Business Review*, September–October 1991. Copyright © 1991 by the President and Fellows of Harvard College; all rights reserved. Reprinted with permission.

TO MY LITTLE FAMILY
the most delightful, challenging, supportive,
comic bunch imagination could invent

CONTENTS

PART 3
MANAGING THE KNOWLEDGE BASED SERVICE ENTERPRISE

PART 4
MANAGING THE INTELLIGENT ENTERPRISE

FOREWORD

I found my hands shaking on several occasions as I read Brian Quinn's manuscript. I was that excited. (And I had seen drafts of bits and pieces years ago.) "Revolutionary"? "Mind-warping"? Those apparently hyperbolic words are too timid.

In *Intelligent Enterprise*, Quinn pushes us to the wall, and beyond—and demands that we completely rethink the nature of the corporation, the sources of its added value, and how it is embedded with other, co-dependent corporations in the economy. If you are serious about this book's message, you will (1) take a couple of weeks off and read it; (2) put it aside for a month, then give it a second, thorough re-reading; and (3) use it as the basis for your top-management retreat in 1993.

The average manufacturing company today ain't. Seventy-five percent to 95 percent of a "manufacturing" firm's employees are in non-manufacturing activities—engineering, design, sales, marketing, information systems, purchasing, service, distribution. That is, they are in the professional-service development and delivery "business." Quinn urges us to reconceive every organization as packages of interdependent services. The consequences are enormous. First, all "industry" designations disappear. Old-line mining toolmaker Kennametal used information technology successfully in its own operation, then ended up inventing a new business: It now manages tool storage areas for several of its customers. Federal Express does much the same: Its $400 million

Business Logistics Services operation manages all logistics (including internal inventory) for the likes of Laura Ashley. These two firms took "internal" service activities (which we previously called "staff" activities) and turned them into solid-gold lines of business. So tell me what "business" Kennametal is in? And if you're a (former?) toolroom worker at a Kennametal customer, did you ever imagine you'd be "competing" for your job against a tool "manufacturer"?

Brian Quinn is a meticulous researcher, and you'll find nothing "pop" in this extraordinary book. Every comment—no matter how apparently zany—is backed up by a bucketful of incontrovertible evidence. No walking away from this troublesome message by writing it off as the latest yarn spun by a hyperactive business guru. Quinn's got you dead to rights; the detail is overwhelming.

Intelligent Enterprise goes beyond providing a brilliant analysis of what firms (of all stripes) are becoming. Quinn also gives you a running start toward figuring out how to deal with the redefined enterprise, how to manage *intellect*—the basis for virtually all of tomorrow's added value. No, you won't find any 10-step approaches. But you will discover a raft of practical ideas for thinking your way through your own firm's dilemmas and opportunities.

Oddball corporations are defining traditional corporations right out of business. Your stomach may go queasy at times when you consider these pages. Every service your company provides (engineering, information systems, financial management) may be done better by a bevy of outsiders—and that's one enormous problem in a context when virtually all your value comes from frequently uncompetitive staff services.

In short, the wise executive will read this book with a king-size bottle of Maalox at his or her side. If you don't reach for that bottle from time to time as you peruse these pages, then go back and re-read what you've just read: If your stomach stays tranquil, you haven't understood what Brian Quinn is trying to tell you.

TOM PETERS

PREFACE

This book attempts to develop a new paradigm that explains and integrates many of the massive changes we are seeing in the economy, in industry competitive structures, in corporate strategies, and in the form of many individual organizations. With little fanfare, over the last several decades the development and management of services, service technologies, and human intellect have emerged as the primary determinants of business and national economic success. In the United States, service industries account for 77 percent of all employment and 75 percent of all GNP. Service activities contribute most of the value-added in manufacturing and constitute 65 to 75 percent of most manufacturers' costs. These are not developments to be deplored or ignored. This book demonstrates how, if approached properly, they represent major opportunities for all executives and policymakers to exploit on behalf of their companies and the nation.

Contrary to popular mythologies, the United States enjoys a strong-to-preeminent competitive position in most services relative to Japan or Europe. By utilizing these capabilities to their fullest and by developing their own strategies around carefully selected intellectual and service "core competencies," virtually all companies can achieve much greater strategic focus, higher leveraging of their human and fiscal resources, flatter less bureaucratic organizations, faster response times, and vastly increased flexibility and morale in their organizations. This is true for all companies, whether in services or manufacturing. This book tries to show why and how all the key elements fit together in assembling and managing these more efficient, competitive, and flexible "intelligent enterprises" of the future. It tries to show how the frontiers of theory and practice merge today. Utilizing all of the relevant statistical databases and well over 100 interviews with CEOs, Chief Information Officers, and operating managers of major companies, it tries to present concepts in the most pragmatic and useful form for business leaders, national policymakers, and thoughtful academicians.

Research for the book began in 1983 in preparation for a conference on "Technology and Economics" sponsored by the National Academy of Engineering at Stanford University. The conference papers were later published as *The Positive Sum Strategy*, edited by Ralph Landau and Nathan Rosenberg, National Academy of Engineering (Washington, DC: National Academy Press, 1986). As a member of the sponsoring committee for this conference, I was astonished to find that, among all the papers planned for what was to become a 980-page book, not one paper addressed the subject of technology in services. Consequently, with the help of my research assistant, I put together a brief analytical commentary, which appeared in that book.

Dr. Robert White, then President of the National Academy of Engineering, became interested in that short presentation and asked me to head a committee on "Technology in Services" for the National Academy of Engineering. With the help of an excellent committee, we sponsored NAE's "Conference on Technology in Services: The Next Economy," held in Washington on January 28 and 29, 1988. Bruce R. Guile and I edited the two books that resulted from that conference: (1) *Technology in Services: Policies for Growth, Trade, and Employment* and (2) *Managing Innovation: Cases from the Service Industries*, published by the National Academy Press in 1988. Having dealt almost exclusively with the high-tech manufacturers of the world in my consulting, this effort was a major departure for me. However, I soon became intrigued by the use of technology in the services sector and came to believe that the development and use of technology for services—whether in the "service industries" or within manufacturing—was the key to future wealth and productivity in advanced industrial countries.

This has been a team effort from the beginning. Several excellent research assistants, notably Mr. Christopher Gagnon, Ms.

Penny Paquette, and Ms. Patricia Higgins, helped with a series of data studies and interviews to understand this interaction better. We first investigated the major national and private databases that contained macro economic data on services. They included the Commerce Department Bureau of Labor Statistics, PIMS, and *Fortune 500* databases. These provided some interesting insights but were very limited because of (1) the definitional problems and (2) the lack of fine-grain data collection for services. As we proceeded, however, we tried constantly to reconcile our empirical findings with those of the major databases.

As portions of the 1988 National Academy study, several succeeding projects, and a 1991–92 study for the National Research Council, we carried out extensive interviews with many leading companies developing and using service technologies. Interviews were carefully structured to sample the top four acknowledged advanced technology users and developers in each of the major service industries: financial services, wholesale trade, retail trade, transportation, communications, professional, and other services. These were exploratory studies in which we were "trying to find out what was going on" rather than establishing or testing specific hypotheses. What one can derive from such studies is a sense of the "patterns" of success and failure in the real world. This is a technique commonly used by field biologists, meteorologists, geologists, oceanographers, and other scientists dealing with macro systems. It is a valid stage in the knowledge generation process, normally followed by hypothesis formulation, hypothesis tests, development of new system technologies, development of knowledge bases, and ultimately new paradigms for further exploration. Results of these exploratory studies have been published in a number of refereed conference papers and books in such major applied journals as *Scientific American, Harvard Business Review,* and *Sloan Management Review*.

All of the personal quotations in this book have been cleared with their sources, unless they are referenced from secondary sources. On a few occasions, because of some element in the quotation, its source preferred not to be identified. In those cases, we have used the designation of the person's title and industry only. While we have interviewed primarily in companies that are considered to be leaders in their field now, time and competition can play unexpected tricks. No company can stay at the top of the list forever. And technology is moving so rapidly that some of the companies we cite as exemplars today may, for other reasons, not look so good in the future. Learning is a cumulative process. We present the examples for what may be learned from them today, knowing we cannot predict an unknowable future for each company.

As a result of these studies, it became clear that service technologies had restructured both the economy and the way in which one could and should approach strategy formulation and the organization of enterprises. Papers on these topics appeared first in 1987 and 1988, coauthored by Penny Paquette and Jordan Baruch, in *Scientific American* and *Harvard Business Review*. Then in the January 1990 issue of *Sloan Management Review* and in the March–April edition of *Harvard Business Review*, in collaboration with Tom Doorley, we published the first papers that systematically set forth the concept of strategy later called "core competencies." Expecting earlier publication of these concepts by the *Harvard Business Review*, we had disclosed them in professional conferences repeatedly during 1989. During that time we also published some of the earliest papers specifically on the relationship between service technologies and the new organizational forms described here in Chapters 4 and 5. This book is a continuation of our studies on the interactions among service technologies, economics, strategic control systems, and organization. We are convinced that this confluence is critical to the future productivity, economic growth, and quality of life in advanced industrial countries.

This book is an attempt to integrate and reformulate some of the most important themes in economics, corporate strategy, and organization theory today. It focuses on the service economy and the development of the myriad technologies which support that economy as the basic causes of many of the social and business restructurings now taking place. Rather than simply describing these changes, it attempts to explain them, link them, and provide a pragmatic framework within which managers can design and implement more effective corporate and organizational strategies. Now and in the future, effective strategies will depend more on the development and deployment of intellectual resources than on the management of physical and fiscal assets. The key concept we present here of disaggregating corporate activities into manageable intellectual clusters—called service activities—is the crux of reconceptualizing organizational structures, the management of intellect, and the interlinkage of corporate organizations with the new "alliance" modes of external competition.

We have consciously gone beyond the concepts of "core competencies" as they have been published to date and the mere use of "information technologies" as causative factors in these changes. Information technologies almost always require interfacing with other physical—materials handling, transportation, storage, health care, production, chemical, mechanical, fluid flow, or management—technologies in order to be effective. The reconceptualization and restructuring of human and technology interactions at the "service activity" level brings coherence and manageability to many other complex phenomena at the enterprise level. New technologies have made it possible to disaggregate, delegate, and manage work at much more decentralized and refined levels—not only within an enterprise but across enterprises—and at a scale and scope never feasible before.

To use the technologies and their new possibilities to their fullest extent also requires a major reconceptualization of strategy processes. Many of the prevailing mainstays of strategic analysis—including economies of scale, experience curves, industry analyses, and market share—need to be reconsidered in the light of the new competitive structures and organizational forms made possible by the dominance of services and their technologies. In this book we have tried to provide a new conceptual framework for considering these important changes at the macro economic and enterprise levels. As a first attempt, the results are, of course, incomplete. However, we hope readers will find the approach new, insightful, and provocative and will contribute their experiences and views to amplify or challenge key points. We also hope readers will discover enough useful practical examples to transform the broader concepts into utilitarian solutions for their own companies or clients. The goal is to make this a readable, pragmatic book contributing both to theory and to practice.

JAMES BRIAN QUINN
HANOVER, NEW HAMPSHIRE

ACKNOWLEDGMENTS

In any work of this scope, it is impossible to acknowledge all of its many individual contributors. However, we would like to thank those particular individuals and organizations who were especially generous and helpful. First among these are the sponsors of our research. Personally, I feel especially grateful to Mr. Hiroshi Murakami, Secretary General of the International University of Japan, and Dr. Shuntaro Shishido, President of the International University of Japan, who arranged sabbatical funding for the book. In the same generous category are Mr. Alan Taylor and Warren Bull, CEO and Vice President, Strategic Planning, respectively, of the Royal Bank of Canada. The Royal Bank helped sponsor both an earlier study of technology in the services sector and our ongoing studies of productivity in services.

Other major sponsors include Mr. John Foster, CEO of Nova-Care; Mr. Robert Clements, CEO of Marsh and McLennan; Mr. Peter Coster, President of William M. Mercer Companies; Mr. Robert Elmore, Partner of Arthur Andersen & Company; Mr. Roger Ballou, President, U.S. Travel and Related Services, American Express Company; Mr. Thomas Doorley, Senior Partner, Braxton Associates; Mr. Peter Lengyel, Vice President, Bankers Trust; Mr. Donald Frey, CEO, Bell & Howell; and Charles Zoi, President of Bell Atlanticom. Each of these executives and their companies very kindly provided support for a major portion of the approximately five years of research represented in this book. In addition to the financial support they provided, each company also made significant intellectual contributions, through exchanging ideas, providing access to case studies, and, in the case of Braxton, Tom Doorley's co-authoring several articles. In addition, we would like to acknowledge the help of the National Academy of Engineering and the National Research Council, for whom some portion of each study was initially prepared. Each group helped by providing access for interviews with key individuals in the service industries.

In this regard, we would especially like to thank those executives who generously offered their time for interviews, particularly Jon d'Alessio (McKesson), Dennis Allen (BellSouth), Roger Ballou (American Express), William Barker (retired, CBS/Fox), Gregory Berardi (Bank of America), Richard Bere (Kroger), Rino Bergonzi (United Parcel Service), Sherwood Blake (Marsh & McLennan), Mitchell Blaser (Marsh & McLennan), Wendy Brown (American Express), Mary Brumbaugh (Sysco), Raymond Caron (CIGNA), Edward Chylinski (NovaCare), Earl Dawson (Chase Manhattan), Janet Duchaine (CIGNA), Donald Dufek (Kroger), Robert Elmore (Arthur Andersen), Frank Erbrick (United Parcel Service), Lafayette Ford (United Airlines), David Fawcett (Ford), John Foster (NovaCare), Timothy Foster (NovaCare), Sharon Garrett (Disney), Theodore Gerbracht (Merrill Lynch), Craig Goldman (Chase Manhattan), John Hancock (Pacific Bell), Edward Hanway (CIGNA), Charles Hayes (Marsh & McLennan), Steven Heit (United Parcel Service), Michael Heschel (Kroger), Herbert Hofmann (Bulova), Richard Hoover (Nalco), Donald Karmazin (United Airlines), Monique Kinsolving (Chase Manhattan), Dennis Lee (BellCore), Richard Leibhaber (MCI), John Loewenberg (Aetna), James Looper (MCI), David Malmberg (McKesson), Douglas McLean (Apple Computer), John McPherson (Safeway), Joseph Michael (Avery Dennison), Michael Miller (J. P. Morgan), Randall Miller (Deloitte & Touche), Melvin Ollestad (CIGNA), Lawrence Pulliam (Sysco), Joseph Ripp (*Time*), Ralph Sarich (Orbital Engine), Thomas Sawyer (Dayton–Hudson), Garret Scholz (McKesson), Richard Seigel (Sysco), William Sinkula (Kroger), Dennis Smith (Loew's), Howard Sorgen (Merrill Lynch), Martin Stein (Bank of America), James Stewart (CIGNA), Douglas Thompson (McKesson), Josh Weston (ADP), Douglas Williams (Chase Manhattan Bank), and Peter Woicke (J. P. Morgan). These individuals have been quoted or paraphrased in this book only with their specific consent. They greatly influenced my thinking on this complex subject. Obviously, however, the author takes sole responsibility for all the conclusions expressed in this book.

In addition, we would like to acknowledge the contributions of those executives who contributed to the major cases upon which much of this study was based. These included Fred Middleton and Robert Swanson of Genentech, Inc.; Dr. Robert Noyce and Dr. Gordon Moore of Intel Corporation; Fred Smith, James Barksdale, and Thomas Oliver of Federal Express Corporation; Masaru Ibuka, Akio Morita, Dr. Nobutoshi Kihara, and Dr. Makoto Kikuchi of Sony Corporation; Nobuhiko Kawamoto, Yasuhito Sato, T. Yashiki, and F. Kikuchi of Honda Motor Company Limited; Warren Bull, Rowland Frazee, Alan Taylor, and James Gannon of the Royal Bank of Canada; Lew Veraldi and Charles Gumushian of Ford Motor Company; both Arthur H. Sulzbergers, Senior and Junior, and Warren Hoge of *The New York Times*. Each person contributed significant and valuable time to this project, and we are deeply grateful.

The people who really make such a work come into being are the competent research associates, secretaries, and professionals who undertake the major burden of the work. At the Amos Tuck School of Business Administration, Penny C. Paquette, Patricia Higgins, Suzanne Sweet, and Tammy Stebbins deserve special praise. Ms. Paquette was researcher and co-author of many of the cases and earlier articles on which the book is based. She made major research and finely honed conceptual contributions to all of these. Her efforts in coordinating the endless problems of clearances and production logistics for those works, as well as her intellectual contributions, were most important to the entire multiyear program of research and publication. Ms. Patricia Higgins has also contributed greatly as principal research associate on this project. She has collected enormous quantities of data for the project, overseen the complex relationships with the National Research Council and our various interview respondents, and managed much of the proofreading and logistics that went into this book and the NRC project. A special debt of gratitude goes to Mrs. Suzanne Sweet, who managed the thousands of pages of cases, interviews, articles, chapters, and revisions in this work— usually prepared from remote telephone dictations originating in Australia, Japan, and various hotel rooms around the United

States. We have provided significant income for the facsimile and communications industries of the United States and the world over the last several years. Mr. William Little served as research assistant on this project and contributed valuable materials in a number of background cases, government data analyses, and compilations of corporate financial information. Ms. Linda Hartson also helped enormously in the final typing and manuscript organization stages.

We all appreciate the genuine help and intellectual support of the team at The Free Press. Bob Wallace was the main champion at Free Press, counseling, editing, mentoring and arguing points—and possible titles—with me endlessly. Bob's fine hand will be felt throughout the book. Associate Editor Lisa Cuff and Production Supervisor Loretta Denner also provided continuous, professional, and cheerful help whenever it was needed. We hope the results justify their efforts.

Finally, two other people deserve special recognition. Dr. Jordan Baruch—one of the most accomplished technologists, entrepreneurs, and creative minds I have ever met—helped crystallize many of the ideas in the macro-economic and manufacturing-services chapters. He has been a unique friend and an insightful resource. But another very special friend and companion, my wife Allie, also contributed much of the energy and intellectual input for the project. She performed important library and background research in Australia, Europe, and Japan, participating in many early case studies that led to the book. She was a continuing, stalwart resource in capturing many interesting examples of service-based strategies, with a quick and sure eye that scanned innumerable publications on my behalf, and she oversaw the proofreading of endless drafts of the book. As always, she also patiently withstood the wild psychological ups and downs—and continuous drudgery—of manuscript preparation. Without her, none of this would have been possible.

To all of the above, I express my deep gratitude.

JAMES BRIAN QUINN
HANOVER, NEW HAMPSHIRE

PART 1
Intellect and Services: Restructuring Economies and Strategy

CHAPTER 1
Services Restructure the Economy

This book is about managing intellect and the services, service-based strategies, and service technologies that are revolutionizing competition in all industries, including manufacturing, today. Intellect is the core resource in producing and delivering services. Since World War II provision of services has become by far the largest component of the U.S. economy (see Figure 1–1) and dominates manufacturing in virtually all "industrialized" nations. In the United States, the service industries—as broadly defined—now account for 74 percent (or $3,345 billion) of the Gross National Product and 77 percent (or 92.6 million) of all jobs.[1] Through 1990, the services sector continued to grow during recessions and booms alike, although there were some signs that its rate of growth might be slowing and that it too might become vulnerable to downturns. Reflecting its increasing dominance in the economy, during the 1991–92 recession services employment dropped for the first prolonged period since the early 1950s.

In contrast, total employment in manufacturing had declined erratically but in a continuous downward secular trend over the past fifteen years.[2] While this represented some serious deficiencies in selected industries and a personal tragedy for many work-

NOTE: Research for this chapter was first published in J.B. Quinn, "Technology in Services: Past Myths and Future Challenges," in B. Guile and J. Quinn (eds.), *Technology in Services: Policies for Growth, Trade, and Employment* (Washington, D.C.: National Academy Press, 1988).

ers, the shift was not as radical as often portrayed (see Figure 1–1). The United States has long been the world's strongest manufacturing country, but it has never had a dominantly manufacturing economy. Figure 1–1 shows that services employment has always exceeded that of manufacturing in the United States.

Manufacturing employment remained relatively steady as a percentage of the total for a long period of time; what declined continuously was agricultural employment. Nevertheless, in recent years, some traditional and highly visible U.S. industries—such as basic steel, automaking, and electronic appliances—have experienced pronounced losses in both output volume and employment. And many others operating from a U.S. base have lost export sales since the mid-1980s.[3]

In the meantime, service industries have grown steadily in scale, technological sophistication, and capital intensity. Why have services become so important today? Steady productivity increases in agriculture and manufacturing—largely technology induced—have meant that it took ever fewer hours of work to produce or buy a pound of food, an automobile, a piece of furniture, or a home appliance. While productivity improved, demand for goods

FIGURE 1–1
Employment As Percentage of Total Labor Force

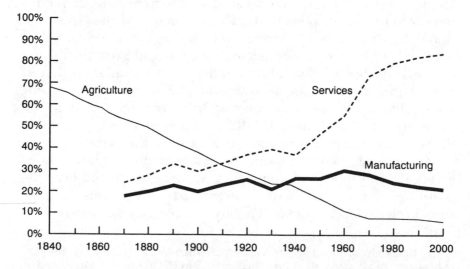

SOURCE: Prepared by M. Dingman from Bureau of the Census, *Historical Statistics of the U.S.: Colonial Times to 1970*. 1960–2000 data from Predicast, Inc., *Predicast Forecasts*, 1982.

was somewhat capped; people could consume only so many units of food, automobiles, sofas, houses, or washing machines. Meanwhile new technologies lowered services' relative costs and increased their variety and value. The relative utility of nonproduct purchases therefore went up for each individual. And in recent years, as people became more affluent, they began to seek increased satisfaction and improved life quality through more services.

The basic cause of this massive economic transformation is the emergence of intellect and technology—particularly in services—as highly leverageable assets. Leveraged intellect and its prime facilitator, service technology, are reshaping not only the service industries but also U.S. manufacturing, the country's overall economic and growth patterns, national and regional job structures, and the position of the United States in world politics and international competition.[4] They are forcing totally new concepts of strategy and organization on both the services sector and the product industries—nationally and globally. The manufacturing–services interface is now the key to most manufacturing strategies (Chapter 6). And the competitiveness of both nations and companies will increasingly depend upon carefully exploiting the new strategic potentials of better-managed intellect and service technologies. Based upon multiple years of research, this book will suggest how best to analyze and implement these new knowledge and service based strategies and the new organizations that support them.

BASIC RELATIONSHIPS: SERVICES, INTELLECT, AND ECONOMICS

What do services and managing intellect have to do with a sound economy? Economic texts barely mention either. Many executives and policymakers dismiss services as predominantly "taking in laundry" or "making hamburgers" for others. Such simplifications belie the complexity, scale, employment, and profit potentials of services in the 1990s. While there is not a complete consensus on definitions, most authorities consider that the services sector includes all economic activities whose output (1) is not a product or construction, (2) is generally consumed at the time it is produced, and (3) provides added value in forms (such as convenience, amusement, timeliness, comfort, or health) that are essentially intangible concerns of its purchaser.[5] *The Economist* has more simply defined services as "anything sold in trade that could not be dropped on your foot." "Service technologies" are technologies developed by or primarily for use in the services sector. They include not just information technologies but transportation, communications, materials handling, storage, health care, and other technologies predominantly used by service enterprises.

The "service industries" include transportation, communications, financial services, wholesale and retail trade, most utilities, professional services (like law, consulting, and accounting), entertainment, health care and delivery systems, and so on in the private sector—and government-social services in the public sector. "Service activities" include personnel, accounting, finance, maintenance, legal, research, design, warehousing, marketing, sales, market research, distribution, repair, and engineering activities, which may be performed as functions inside an integrated—manufacturing or service—firm or by a separate firm (like a market research or accounting firm). The common element among all these activities and industries is the predominance of managing intellect—rather than managing physical things—in creating their value-added. The key to productivity and wealth generation in over three-fourths of all economic activity is managing intellectual activities and the interface to their service outputs. As we shall show, this is just as true in manufacturing as in the service industries. Indeed, the lines between these two are rapidly being obliterated.

FOUR MYTHS ABOUT SERVICES

To develop a proper perspective about these changes, we first need to expunge some of the more misleading myths, held over from the past, about services.

The "Lower Value" Misconception—perhaps first stated by Adam Smith[6]—regards services as somehow less important on a "human needs scale" than products. Since services are essentially marginal (so the argument goes), they cannot add the same economic value or generate the growth potentials manufactures can. Karl Marx made this a central part of his dogma.[7] As a result, all his adherents so underinvested in services that their countries today tragically cannot store, transport, distribute, finance, communicate about, or repair the products they could otherwise produce in abundance. So prevalent are these misconceptions that many economists—particularly in developing countries—refer to services as "the tertiary sector."

In very elemental societies it is perhaps true that the first production to meet basic needs for food, shelter, or clothing do take precedence over all other demands. However, as soon as there is even a local self-sufficiency or surplus in a single product, the extra production has little value without further distribution, financing, or storage—all "service" activities. In most emerging societies services like health care, education, trading, entertainment, religion, banking, law, and the arts quickly become more highly valued (high-priced or capable of generating great wealth) than basic production. And the positive wage differentials their practitioners receive tend to be even more marked as societies grow more affluent.

Far from being inferior economic outputs, services are directly interchangeable with manufactures in a wide variety of situations. Few customers care whether a refrigerator manufacturer implements a particular feature through a hardware circuit or by internal software. New CAD/CAM software can substitute for added production or design equipment, and improving transportation or materials handling services can lower a manufacturer's costs as effectively as cutting direct labor or materials inputs. These "services" improve productivity or add value just like any new investment in physical handling machinery or product features.

Even more fundamentally, products are only physical embodiments for the services they deliver. A diskette only delivers a software program or data set. An automobile delivers flexible transportation or a personal image—both services. Electrical appliances deliver entertainment, dishwashing, clothes cleaning and drying, convenient cooking or storage—all services. In fact, most products merely provide a more convenient or less costly form in which to purchase services. Although it is a surprise to some people, on a national basis value-added in services is much greater than that in manufacturing (see Table 1–1). In fact, value-added in the services sector accounts for approximately 74 percent of all value-added in the economy, while the total goods sector (including all manufacturing, construction, mining, agriculture, forestry, and fishery outputs) accounts for only 25 percent.

Although the total value-added per employee in private services nationally is slightly lower (at $38,069 per person) than that

TABLE 1–1
U.S. Value Added and Employment by Industry *(latest date available)*

	Annualized 2d Qtr. 1991 Value-Added ($ billions)		1990 Employment (millions)	
Total economy	$4,525		119.6	
Agriculture, forestry, fisheries	105		1.9	
Mining and construction	248		6.0	
Manufacturing	784		19.3	
Total goods sector	$1,137	25%	27.2	23%
Finance, insurance, real estate	$ 655		7.0	
Retail trade	386		20.4	
Wholesale trade	266		6.3	
Transportation and public utilities	239		4.6	
Communications	95		1.3	
Other services[a]	1020		30.3	
Total Private Services	$2,661	59%	69.9	58%
Govt. and Govt. Enterprises	684		22.7	
Total Services Sector	$3,345	74%	92.6	77%

[a] Includes health care and delivery, business services, legal services, hotels, and recreation.
SOURCE: Bureau of Economic Analysis, "The National Income and Product Accounts of the United States," series in the *Survey of Current Business*. Value-added data from October 1991, Table 6.3B, page 13. Employment data from January 1992, Table 6.4C.

in manufacturing (at $40,622), in the strategic business units of the larger companies sampled by PIMS data,[8] value-added per service employee is quite comparable to that in manufacturing (see Figure 1–2.) This suggests (1) that important economies of scale and scope may be available through technology investments in larger private service enterprises, and (2) that it is the government sector's $30,132 of value-added per person that poses the major problem.

FIGURE 1–2
PIMS Indices of Value-Added

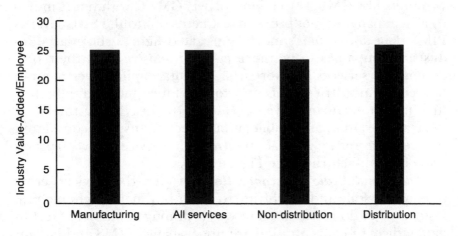

SOURCE: Profit Impact of Market Strategy (PIMS) database of the Strategic Planning Institute.

The "Low Capital Intensity" Perception asserts that service industries are much less capital-intensive and technologically based than manufacturing. While this may be so for small-scale retailing and domestic services, many service industries today are extremely capital- and technology-intensive. The prime examples have been communications, transportation, pipelines, and electric utilities. But the banking, entertainment, health care, financial services, auto rental, package delivery, wholesaling, and retailing industries also increasingly qualify.

Stephen Roach, Chief Economist of Morgan Stanley, has calculated that total capital investment—and in particular high-technology investment—per "information worker" (mostly employed in service industries) has been rising rapidly since the mid-1960s and now exceeds that for workers in basic industrial activities.[9] Similarly, Kutscher and Mark's data show that nearly half of the thirty most capital-intensive industries (of 145 studied) were services. And certain service industries—notably railroads, pipelines, broadcasting, communications, public utilities, and sea and air transport—were among the most capital-intensive of all industries.[10] Surprisingly, few service industries were found in the three lowest capital-intensity deciles. PIMS data, collected on a different basis, show aggregate capital intensity in larger service entities to be comparable to—although slightly less than—that in manufacturing. *Fortune 500* data, which often contain large service units like GM's $115 billion (asset) GMAC within an "industrial" company, do not break investments out to the SBU level as PIMS data do. *Fortune*'s more aggregated figures show large industrial companies to be more capital-intensive than their predominantly services counterparts. But total capital investment in the service industries has been growing much more rapidly than that in manufacturing. Even excluding the heavy investments of the transportation and public utilities sectors (usually considered services), aggregate annual investment in services now surpasses that of manufacturing (see Figure 1–3).

The "Small Scale" Misconception considers the services sector too small in scale and too diffuse to either buy major technological systems or to do research on its own. Although complete Herfindahl indices of concentration are not available, PIMS and *Fortune 500* data suggest that concentration and scale among larger service units are comparable to that in larger manufacturing units (see Figure 1–4). In fact, as we shall demonstrate shortly, many companies in the services sector are much larger than their manufacturing suppliers.

Large banks, airlines, utilities, financial service institutions, communications companies, and hospital, hotel, or retail chains now not only have the scale to be lead purchasers of technology, they also contribute extensively to its initial design, early financing, reduction to practice, and wide diffusion. In addition, such companies acting in intermediary roles (like distributors) often force new technologies out into smaller service and manufacturing companies (through their just-in-time systems), further assisting diffusion. Many large service institutions now also support extensive R&D activities, creating or guiding major new technological developments themselves. AT&T-Bell Labs, Federal Express, COMSAT, Arthur Andersen, Citicorp, Arthur D. Little, Microsoft, EPRI, and Rand Corporation are just a few among many such organizations.

The "Services Can't Produce Wealth" Viewpoint holds that services are not capable of producing the ever higher levels of real income and personal wealth that have been the hallmarks of the "industrial" era. This argument assumes, in part, that services inherently cannot achieve the productivity increases available through automation in manufacturing. If not, services cannot pos-

FIGURE 1–3
Plant and Equipment Spending

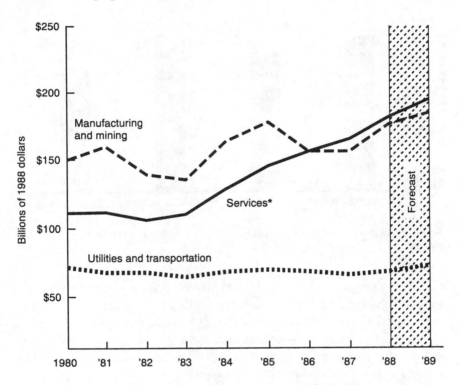

* Trade, finance and insurance, communication, miscellaneous
  personal and business services.

SOURCE: "Services are Supplying the Steam for Business Investment," *Fortune*, June 5, 1989. Copyright © 1989 by The Time Inc. Magazine Company. All rights reserved.

sibly provide the inflation-free income growth rates manufacturing can. While many past measures of productivity in services have tended to support this view at the macro economic level, there is increasing evidence that the measures themselves may have serious flaws.[11] Productivity in services is notoriously difficult to measure because of problems in numerically defining output units and quality levels.[12] For example, how does one evaluate medical procedures that may use greater resources but may substantially decrease patients' pain or morbidity levels? Of what validity are the standard economic productivity measures that ignore the output value of many public services (like sewage treatment plants or air depollution) and assume that the output value

FIGURE 1–4
PIMS Indices of Concentration

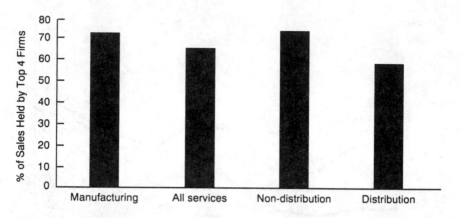

SOURCE: Profit Impact of Market Strategy (PIMS) database of the Strategic Planning Institute.

of critical services (like fire departments, police forces, some aspects of banking, and many welfare services) is equal only to their cost inputs? One should be very careful in interpreting aggregate productivity data about services and should look behind the numbers to the measurement methodologies used. Chapter 11 will deal with this issue in much more detail.

Productivity measures are more valid in competitive arenas, where customers can make direct purchase tradeoffs between one class of service and other services or manufactures.[13] Here the sales value of the service can provide a better surrogate for measuring output. In some of the more measurable service segments, Bureau of Labor Statistics (BLS) historical data—and some new measures—suggest that individual service industries can sustain productivity growth rates as high as those in major manufacturing sectors for substantial periods (see Table 1–2). As managers become more sensitive to the value-added potentials of service activities and focus on the 60–75 percent of their (nonmaterials) costs that typically lie in internal services, further growth in productivity can be expected.[14] Since in the future most of a company's or nation's competitiveness and productivity increases must come from better performance of service and intellectual functions, a central focus in this book is on managing such activities for greater productivity, output quality, and value-added.

TABLE 1-2
Productivity Changes by Industry Group: Compound Annual Rates of Change (*output per hour of all persons*)

	1950–79	1950–69	1970–79	1980–85	1979–88
Goods producing industries:					
Total-farms, mining, construction, and manufacturing	2.6%	3.4%	1.1%	2.8%	2.4%
Manufacturing—total	2.5	2.5	2.6	3.5	3.5
Durables	2.0	2.1	2.1	3.5	4.0
Nondurables	3.1	3.0	3.4	3.7	2.6
Non-goods producing industries:					
Total	2.2	2.5	1.8	1.0	1.0
Transportation	2.3	2.3	2.7	1.5	1.4
Communications	5.0	5.0	5.1	3.3	4.9
Electric, gas, and sanitary services	4.3	6.0	1.3	0.1	2.7
Wholesale trade	2.9	3.0	2.9	4.3	2.7
Retail trade	1.9	2.0	1.9	2.9	1.9
Finance, insurance, and real estate	1.3	1.6	0.7	−1.0	−0.4
Business and personal services	1.9	2.3	0.9	−0.7	−0.3
Other services:					
Eating and drinking places	N.A.	N.A.	−0.1	−2.0	−0.4
Hotels, motels and tourist courts	N.A.	N.A.	N.A.	−1.0	−0.6
Automobile repair shops	N.A.	N.A.	N.A.	−0.2	−0.1
Government enterprises	0.2	0.0	1.1	−1.0	−0.4

N.A. = not available
SOURCE: Unpublished measures, Bureau of Labor Statistics, U.S. Department of Labor, November 19, 1991.

SERVICES OFFER PERPETUAL GROWTH OPPORTUNITIES

The growth of the services sector should not be viewed with alarm, despite the comments of some spokespeople to the contrary.[15] Fortunately for the economy, until the 1991–92 recession demand growth in the services sector caused services employment gains to far outstrip employment declines in the goods-producing sectors (see Figure 1–5). And despite the problems of certain industries, the total output of U.S. manufacturers is growing in both quantity and quality. As we shall show, service technologies have actually supported manufacturing productivity in the United States and—in many sectors—have begun to cause the "remanufacturing" of the U.S. economy. Lower transportation, communications, retail and wholesale distribution, and financial service costs in the United States have presented unrecognized cost advantages to U.S. producers. As virtually all services have grown on the basis of their improved technologies over the past several decades, they have enhanced both the standard of living of individuals and the manufacturing outreach of U.S. companies. For example:

FIGURE 1–5
Employment Changes in United States, 1950–90

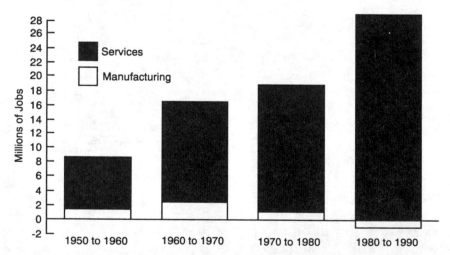

SOURCES: *Bureau of Economic Analysis, "Business Statistics," The Biennial Supplement to the Survey of Current Business,* 1979 edition, October 1980, pages 61–63. "Business Statistics," A *Supplement to the Survey of Current Business,* 1986 edition, December 1987, pages 46–48. *Survey of Current Business,* January 1992, Table 6.4C, page 66.

■ Jet aircraft have made long-haul passenger and freight handling much more efficient and convenient. New containerization, loading, refrigeration, and handling techniques for dangerous and volatile materials—by making it possible to transport virtually all goods safely and effectively—have vastly extended international trade. Electronics, information, and communications technologies have stimulated innovations in virtually all service areas, most notably in retailing, wholesale trade, engineering and design, financial services, communications, and the professional services that support manufacturing and service industries alike. In addition, new technologies have revolutionized other fields affecting U.S. quality of life, like entertainment, personal security, or medical care. The high-technology fax, cellular phone, movie, theme park, videotape, and emerging virtual image and multimedia industries of today were unimaginable a few years ago. New noninvasive imaging devices, drugs, diagnostics, genetic engineering, and life-support and surgical systems have revolutionized medical research and practice. And so on.

Note that it is not just information technologies, but service technologies developed across a wide spectrum, that have changed the entire structure of U.S. and world competition. Not only have service technologies revolutionized the U.S. economy, they have had the same impact in all other major industrialized countries (see Table 1–3). All these countries now increasingly compete as service economies. And service industries are becoming the bellwethers of all countries' future international competitiveness and standards of living.[16]

The services-produced trends in value-added in the U.S. economy since World War II (see Figure 1–6) can, with nurturing, continue to provide opportunities for unending economic growth—with fewer of the undesired environmental effects of a heavily production-oriented society. Since the value of all services (as well as service-based or high-style products) exists solely in the mind—i.e., a jewel, an opera, a Ferrari, a sightseeing tour, or a stylish coat may have little functional value relative to its high price—the growth of a service-based economy is limited only by the capacity of the human mind to conceive of activities as having higher utility. Surely a safer, healthier, better educated, or more stable society can easily be considered "wealthier" than one with more physical goods. And this wealth can be passed on to future

TABLE 1–3
Industrial and Services Activities in the Largest Ten OECD Countries[a]

(Definitions standardized for OECD differ somewhat from U.S. definition.)

Country	Value-Added in Industry[b] As % of GDP		Value-Added in Services As % of GDP		Employment % Services
	1968	1988	1968	1988	1988
United States	37%	29%	61%	69%	70.2%
Japan	44	41	48	57	58.0
Federal Republic of Germany	48	40	48	58	56.2
France	39	29	54	67	62.9
United Kingdom	38	32	59	67	68.0
Canada	34	31	62	66	69.8
Australia	38	33	53	63	67.8
Sweden	38	30	57	67	66.7
Belgium	40	31	55	67	69.3
Austria	45	37	48	60	54.5

[a] For which comparative data are available. [b] Industry figures include mining, manufacturing, and public utilities, but exclude construction and agriculture, hence industry and services do not sum to 100 percent.
SOURCES: OECD in Figures: Statistics on the Member Countries, Supplement to the *OECD Observer*, no. 164, (June–July 1990), pp. 10, 11, 28, 29. *Economic Outlook Historical Statistics 1960–1988*, OECD, Tables 5.2 and 5.4, pp. 62 and 63.

generations. Services like better education, art, music, literature, information repositories, banking, trade, transportation, scientific or design know-how, public health, and legal systems are true national assets—intellectual assets with greater value than physical assets—for posterity. In fact, such "intellectual assets" have generally been the measures of a nation's wealth throughout history (as in Florence, Athens, or Alexandria) and have proved to be the basis (as in Hong Kong, Japan, Singapore, France, or Germany) of rapid recovery from disasters.

One must hasten to add this does not suggest that the United States could or should exist without its advanced manufacturing capabilities. Instead, in a healthy economy, the two go together. Well-developed service industries upgrade and add significant

FIGURE 1–6
Real Value-Added by Sector

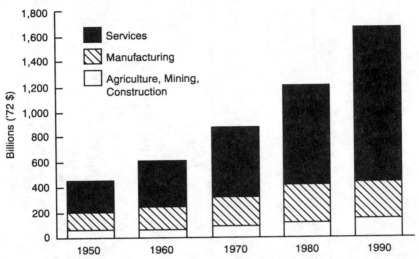

SOURCE: Bureau of Economic Analysis, "The National Income and Product Accounts of the United States," series in *Survey of Current Business.*

value to the manufacturing sector, making it more effective domestically and more competitive internationally. And they support a strong military capability, as the advanced transportation, communications, and logistics support systems of the Gulf War proved. Strategic opportunities and economic growth are maximized when services and manufacturing are developed in tandem.

SERVICES RESTRUCTURE THE ECONOMY

As services have expanded, they have restructured virtually all individual industries, the basic relationship among industries, and the total economy. First of all, the scale and power of service companies have increased markedly relative to manufacturing companies. As their economic power has grown, service companies have redefined their roles versus those of manufacturing. Table 1–4 demonstrates the relative scale of manufacturers in several consumer product industries versus that of their retailing, wholesaling, or product using partners. For example, Toys "R" Us, with its $5.5 billion sales, enjoys three times the revenues of the world's largest toy suppliers. With its greater information

TABLE 1–4
Size of Consumer Product and Health Care Companies vs. Service Companies (*1990 revenues x $ billion*)

Industry	Product Companies		Service Companies	
Toys	Hasbro	$ 1.5	Toys "R" Us	$ 5.5
	Mattel	1.5		
Health care	Johnson & Johnson	$11.2	McKesson Corp. (drug divisions)	$ 7.8
	Baxter International	8.1	Walgreen Co.	6.7
	American Home Prods.	6.8	Humana, Inc.	5.9
	Merck	7.7	Bergen Brunswig	4.4
	Bristol Myers Squibb Co.	10.3	Hospital Corp. of America	3.1
Food/	Proctor & Gamble Co.	$27.0	American Stores Co.	$22.2
general	Pepsico	17.8	Kroger Co.	20.3
merchandise	RJR Nabisco Holding Co.	13.9	Safeway, Inc.	14.9
			SuperValu Stores, Inc.	11.6
	West Point-Pepperell, Inc.	1.2	Wal-Mart Stores, Inc.	32.6
	Burlington Industries	2.0	Sears, Roebuck & Co.	32.0
	Springs Industries, Inc.	1.9	(merchandise division)	

SOURCE: Lotus One Source

about the marketplace and capacity to control the positioning, display, retail advertising, and pricing of toys, Toys "R" Us can in many cases dictate what toys make it to the marketplace, how well they sell, and even how they should be designed, packaged, transported, or presented. Within the industry Toys "R" Us packaging and marking procedures set the standard for all producing companies.

■ Because it has specialized, Toys "R" Us can sell products virtually year round, while its competitors can afford to carry significant inventories only during the short pre-Christmas season, when over 60 percent of all toys are sold at retail. Consequently, Toys "R" Us, with its high volumes and sophisticated electronic inventory and point of sale systems, has a powerful mechanism for pretesting what toys are likely to sell—and in what form—when the big Christmas sale season comes. In addition, with its sophisticated models of toy sales, toy production, and changing tastes, it can invest in its inventories with considerably less risk than other companies. Finally, it can force many of these risks back onto its suppliers—especially those for inventories—by insisting on very efficient "just in time" deliveries. Such practices further decrease markdown losses, which are as much as 25 percent of the industry's cost for other retailers, while increasing Toys' own returns on capital invested relative to its competitors.

■ Similarly, $7.8 billion McKesson Corporation's wholesale drug divisions can strongly influence the sale and distribution patterns in its field. By providing its retail dealers with analytical services that spring off its ECONOMOST inventory control system, McKesson can create a mutually beneficial relationship with retailers, making it very difficult for them to shift suppliers. As a result of McKesson's and other drug wholesalers' use of similar technological power, wholesaling's share of the pharmaceuticals market grew from 47 percent in the mid-1960s to 77 percent in the late 1980s, and is expected to become 85 to 90 percent by the end of the 1990s.

POWER SHIFTS TOWARD SERVICES

Manufacturers have had to adjust their strategies to the reality of this kind of economic power. As Table 1–4 further shows, textile companies like West Point–Pepperell, Inc., Burlington Industries, or Springs Industries, Inc., have become quite small relative to their retail customers—i.e., less than one-tenth the sales of Wal-Mart at $32.6 billion or Sears at $32.0 billion. Increasingly, these customers actually co-design the products they want, dictate precise inventory and shipment standards, and dominate manufacturers' relationships with the ultimate marketplace. This is particularly true when such retail giants source from overseas, where suppliers have relatively little direct power in the U.S. marketplace and are highly dependent upon orders from U.S. soft goods retailers for their very existence.

McDonald's fast food chain provides a dramatic example of the impact such scalar shifts can have.

■ McDonald's feeds 22 million people a day—approximately one-third the population of Britain. Each day it uses 2 million pounds of potatoes and dictates the fortunes of many farmers in that segment of agriculture. It purchases an astonishing 3,400 tons of sesame seeds a year. Its volume potentials are so great that when it sought to "lighten its menu" by introducing a shrimp line, it found that not enough shrimp could be caught in the world to supply its needs. When it tried to introduce a raspberry sorbet, it discovered that there were not enough raspberries being grown. And when it decided to go to a more healthful, low-fat milk shake, it destroyed the already weak price of butterfat in the marketplace. Now, because of this and similar trends elsewhere, a whole series of entrepreneurs are busily working on ways to use butterfat chemicals in new and interesting products.

With their combination of size, electronics, and market power, major retail chains—like Toys "R" Us—can provide *both* maximum flexibility or differentiation and lowest cost at the marketplace level, calling into serious question theories about "generic strategies," which hypothesize that low cost, flexibility, and differentiation are inherently incompatible. Because retailers have much more access to and information about the marketplace than any individual producer, they can also—with their electronics communications systems—sense and respond to detailed changes in the marketplace much more rapidly. To put it differently—and more positively from the manufacturer's viewpoint—the producing system is so closely related to customer needs at the retail level that the ultimate *customer* now dictates desired responses *throughout the entire system* in extraordinarily short time cycles. Virtually all apparel merchandising has become a "fashion" industry forced to react to the current whims of the consumer marketplace within days.[17] Most noticeably, low-cost discount, "off price," and high-volume chains are beginning to sell essentially fashion—rather than staple—goods as a result of the new flexible, worldwide marketplace that retail information, electronic communications, fast transport, and materials handling technologies have made possible.

Even extremely large manufacturing companies like GM Truck, GE Transportation, Fruehauf Trailer, Lockheed, and McDonnell Douglas Corporation's aircraft divisions have become smaller relative to their customers in the services sector (see Table 1–5). And in information services, only IBM, with its $69 billion (1990) sales, is larger than the biggest information service users in the financial service industries. Increasingly these large service users are forcing even the manufacturing giants to respond to their needs in real time. Time-based strategies[18] have become a necessity in the new service economy but are only one element in the service-based strategies now needed for success.

CUSTOMERS DETERMINE STRATEGY, DESTROY INDUSTRY BOUNDARIES

These powerful service companies, directly connected to their product producing sources, have placed ultimate consumers ever more in command of the world's production system and able to dictate responses to their individual and collective desires. Being able to sense, produce for, and service these trends is the *sine qua non* for success in the new service society. Service technologies have created both the need and capacity for such responses. They have also radically changed the sources and options one can call forth in responding.

Most importantly perhaps, the widespread penetration of service technologies has virtually destroyed the boundaries of all industries. The example of the financial service industry is often cited. But airlines no longer compete just against airlines. They also compete against travel agents, tour groups, retailers (for products sold from in-flight catalogues), financial service companies (credit cards), ground transportation providers (rental cars or buses), communications companies (network and database services), and so on. Similarly, accounting companies no longer compete just with accounting companies, or computer companies just with computer hardware companies. Instead, the software and

TABLE 1–5
Size of Capital Goods Producers Versus Service Companies (*1990 revenues x $ billion*)

Industry	Capital Goods Producers		Service Providers	
Air transport	Boeing Commercial Aircraft	$21.2	American Airlines	$11.0
	Lockheed Corp.	10.0	United Airlines	11.0
	McDonnell Douglas Corp. (aircraft divisions)	9.3	Federal Express	7.7
Ground transport	Navistar International	$ 4.2	UPS	$13.6
	Fruehauf Trailer Corp.	0.6	CSX Corp.	8.2
	GM Truck/Bus	1.7	Burlington Northern	4.7
	GE Transportation	0.8	Consolidated Freightways	4.2
	GM Electro-Motive	0.5		
Information/ financial services	IBM	$69.0	American Express Co.	$24.3
	Xerox	18.0	Aetna Life & Casualty	19.0
	Digital Equipment Corp.	13.9	CIGNA	18.2
	Northern Telecom	6.8	Travelers Corp.	11.3

SOURCE: Lotus One Source. Copyright © 1987, 1991 by Lotus Development Corporation.

computer service divisions of accounting companies compete with the software and service divisions of computer companies, as well as those of user companies. Their executive recruitment activities compete with headhunters and personnel organizations, their consulting groups compete with independent consulting firms as well as staff arms of manufacturers, and their merger and acquisition groups compete with specialists in investment banking. And so on.

As a result, managers can no longer define their corporation as being in a single "industry." Technology demands that they reconceptualize the "industries with which they compete" to include all functional and potential cross-competitors for the services and products they create. Later chapters will show how this changes the very basics of one's approach to strategic analysis, strategy formulation, organizational structure, and control systems. Those companies that do not respond could join the long list of enterprises and industry segments that service technologies have already made obsolete. Fortunately, experience has led to some very concrete and productive ways to analyze technological advance, to think about strategy in this milieu, and to organize for maximum service and responsiveness in today's more service-oriented marketplace. The remaining chapters will define in detail how to develop such service-based strategies and manage the knowledge-based intellectual resources at their core.

TECHNOLOGY'S DISTINCTIVE IMPACT PATTERNS

New technologies tend to invade and diffuse through the service industries—and the service arms of manufacturers—in more or less predictable ways. As they do, they usually initiate vast economic restructurings and important new strategic opportunities. These forces cause industries to pulse from concentration to decentralization, from economies of scale to economies of scope, from simpler product lines to greater complexities, and often from regulation to deregulation to reregulation. Fortunately, this sequence of impacts is both distinctive and relatively repetitive in pattern—and hence manageable once recognized. Each stage creates a new group of strategic options, possible organizational responses, competitive threats, and industrywide structural impacts.

New Economies of Scale generally appear first, causing centralization of key service activities into larger institutions. An initial period of consolidation ensues, in which many smaller enterprises lacking capital and expertise are driven out. Later a renewed decentralization occurs as smaller units in more dispersed locations link into networks to provide feeder operations for the larger enterprises and to deliver their services locally to widely dispersed locations. Ultimately, these networks allow both small and large units to share the lower costs and greater productivity of the new technology. This pattern has recurred in health care, air transport, insurance, communications, retailing, banking, professional and financial services—and so on. Midsize service enterprises—unable to afford the new technologies themselves yet too large to service only one location—have often been forced to merge upward in scale, niche their services radically, or go out of business. Strategists describe such pressures on midsize firms generally as "being caught in the middle."[19] For example:

■ In air transport, when the airlines moved to wide-bodied jets, their new economies of scale and improved service potentials consolidated the fragmented industry into a relatively few larger carriers that could (1) serve major trunk routes efficiently and (2) afford the enormous infrastructure investments called for by the large jets. Midsize airlines were forced out or merged. A series of small "express" airlines later emerged to serve the localized route structures these large companies and planes could not handle well. To obtain scale efficiencies, they linked their schedules and reservation systems to those of the few remaining "majors."

■ In hospitals, the expensive new technologies for PET and CAT scans, open heart surgery, organ and bone transplants, and new cancer therapies forced a centralization of such activities into fewer larger hospitals. Specialists moved to these hospitals, where they would have a sufficient patient flow to practice their specialties. Smaller hospitals withered as they became less and less able to attract patients and doctors who were willing to forgo the opportunity to practice these more complex procedures. Instead, smaller hospitals began to specialize in primary care and more routine procedures, acting as referral units linked to the large research and tertiary care centers.

■ Similarly, as the large banks and insurance companies automated their bank offices, they were able to achieve economies of scale that smaller and midsize companies simply could not afford. Their entire industries restructured as the latter either affiliated with better-endowed companies, sharply niched the services they offered, or in many cases simply disappeared.

New Economies of Scope[20] frequently provide powerful second-order effects. Once properly installed, the same technologies that create new scale economies—or the supporting technologies necessary to implement the large-scale technologies— allow service enterprises to handle a much wider array of data, output functions, or customers without significant cost increases. In fact, with proper management, unit costs actually decrease as variety and flexibility increase; and the larger companies allocate their technology development or equipment costs over a richer base of operations. For example:

■ Airlines (like American or United), wholesalers (like Super-Valu or McKesson), retailers (like Wal-Mart or The Limited), travel-bank services (like American Express), and professional service providers (like Arthur Andersen, ADP Services, or Bechtel) used their installed facilities and networks to extend their presence into a broad range of new activities. Similarly, in health care, hospitals soon found that their equipment and laboratory infrastructures allowed them to handle a much greater range of maladies and cures, eventually extending their activities even further into the realms where individual practice had dominated.

Such economies of scope generally become so powerful that competitors focusing on narrower lines can rarely provide the same flexibility, quality, or cost advantages that new service technologies allow those innovators who develop their technologies with broader markets in mind. At this stage, consolidation usually continues, while the innovating companies simultaneously reach outward with their new and varied product lines toward new customer niches. Finally, as these niches become large enough, major companies refocus into them, or whole new companies form to specialize in and exploit their potentials by designing technologies especially for them—as National Medical Care did for kidney dialysis or Lenscrafters did in optometry.

Increased Complexity then can be economically handled by the new technologies if they receive proper human resources support. Electronic systems and computer models have frequently been the main enabling technologies—but are by no means alone—in permitting the management of much greater complexity. A variety of new sensing, telecommunications, information handling, materials, and processing technologies now routinely design, build, and test radical new designs for boat hulls and aircraft; specify structures for new molecules and predict their performance; transport volatile or perishable materials worldwide; suggest and test hypotheses for medical research; access and analyze global and astronomical databases; run remote factories and processes; handle worldwide monetary and securities transactions; control effluents and water supplies; monitor environmental and political events; and manage huge transportation systems with a precision and at a speed previously impossible. Entire new service and regulatory systems often emerge—as they have in advanced medical care fields like organ replacement, severe trauma, and brain, genetic, or heart diseases—to deal with problems whose solutions were so complex they could not be imagined in the past. In many cases technology has improved probabilities of success so much that patients may have higher expectations than can yet be justified.

Disintermediation is often a consequence of this process. Given the innovators' large scale and technological power, outside parties seek to connect directly to the innovators' systems rather than go through intermediaries. For example, large corporate users of transportation systems began to demand direct access to the reservation systems of airlines. Patients and referring physicians gravitated to specialized outpatient centers to avoid dealing with big hospitals' bureaucracies, high costs, and greater complexities. Large corporations began to place their securities directly on the market to avoid substantial brokerage fees. Individual investors bypassed brokers and went directly to no-load mutual funds. And so on. In addition to increasing the efficiency of each service system, this forced small intermediaries either to develop highly specialized services or to become representatives of the larger entities. As a result of economies of scope, increased complexity of products, and such disintermediation, cross-competition among units in different service (or product) firms and industries became rampant. This then led to the vast restructuring in existing industries already noted—and to the destruction of traditional barriers among many others.

Deregulation became a more viable policy option in many areas as new technologies made extensive cross-competition possible. Policymakers began to look to market forces to control corporate actions in areas where government regulation and monopolies had earlier held sway. Such industries have included airlines, trucking, rail and intermodal transportation, hospitals, financial services, communications, and even public utilities. Decreased regulation has had an enormous impact on the strategies and strategic options of all players, customers, and suppliers associated with these industries. While costs have generally been lowered for customers—particularly airline and financial service customers—too rapid deregulation (without transitional government oversight in many cases) has allowed competing companies to externalize many costs onto the public. The savings and loan, banking, and emerging insurance debacles provide prime examples of the social costs of such badly implemented public decisions. The increased waiting, confusion, safety concerns, lateness, and unpleasantness of air travel and some communications systems provide others. Some imaginative companies have already recognized these problems as new strategic opportunities. But new government policies will undoubtedly be needed to deal with the remaining externalities. And those in turn will lead to another round of corporate strategies, essentially resulting from the initial decision to install earlier generations of service technologies.

Redispersion and Redecentralization are the final phases in this pulsing process. As centralization and disintermediation occur, there tends to be a counter-need for more localized and personalized contact in each of the service areas—Naisbitt's need for high-tech and high-touch.[21] New surrogates for the brokers, travel agents, and ticket vendors soon appear. On the one hand, local brokers and agents join into networks with the major players. On the other, new services like PRODIGY allow individual homes and small businesses to connect directly into the system, providing to many individuals and small enterprises the efficiencies of large companies. Skilled financial advisers and travel consultants replace the order-taking brokers and ticket-selling travel agents of the past. Each of the survivors has higher-power technologies locally available and is able to provide much more personal service than their counterparts did in the past. Thus the technology achieves a new level of outreach and connectivity to the marketplace. Many new enterprises appear in emerging small niches; and larger companies, in turn, must deal with these new competitors and service structures. Usually, the customer is the beneficiary.

CONTINUOUS TUMULT, BUT A NEW ECONOMIC STABILITY

These pulsings have meant continuous tumult in the service marketplace. Service companies and industries have made greater transitions in their scale and earnings in the last decade than ever before. Over half of all the companies in the *Fortune's Top 100* industrial group ten years ago are no longer there, and long protected industries have been completely restructured.

Yet services have also introduced a new stability to the total economy. A classic study by Moore[22] showed that employment in services is considerably more stable than that in the goods sector, as measured by overall percentage gains or losses during recessions. Figure 1–7 graphs similar data through 1989. From 1956 through 1988 there were net increases in average employment in services each year, as compared with the total goods sector, which

FIGURE 1–7
Services and Goods Sector Growth
(1982 dollars)

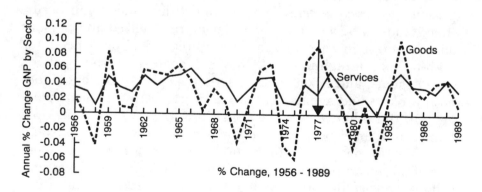

SOURCE: Bureau of Economic Analysis. Data prior to 1977 are from the *Economic Report of the President*, 1991, Table B-11, "GNP by Industry in 1982 Dollars." Data since 1977 are from *Survey of Current Business*, April 1991, Table 4, "GNP by Industry in Constant Dollars," page 27. Data for gross domestic product by industry beginning 1977 are based on a revised methodology and are not comparable with data for earlier years.

fluctuated violently. During the four recessions from 1969 to 1982 private service employment rose an average of 1.0 percent while the goods producing industries dropped an average of 7.9 percent. The 1991–92 recession is the first time service employment has dropped in a recession for a significant period, perhaps reflecting that with 77 percent of employment in services, the very word "downturn" must require a decline in service activity. Canada and Britain have enjoyed similar stability patterns.[23]

If services were really more marginal relative to products, one would expect people to give up their services first in recessions. Just the opposite happens. While people may go to the movies less often or purchase fewer personal services, they are reluctant to give up their telephone, health care, education, insurance, banking, police and fire protection, and utility services. Instead they postpone durable goods expenditures. Stability is also enhanced because there is no pause in service production while inventories—which are more important in most product industries—are depleted. Many primary services associated with population growth (like social services, personal security, health care, and education) are, in fact, likely to increase in recessions—providing both employment and purchasing stability during downturns.

Given these factors, the new "service economy" may well prove more stable than an industrial economy. In addition to reducing the depth of recessions, service industry growth has tended to make them shorter. Service industries are major purchasers of capital equipment, and the replacement of services' capital items— keyed as they are to fast-moving information technologies—tends to be more constant because the useful life of equipment is shorter there. In the past three decades (until 1991–92), the service sector continued to grow and invest during recessions and thus level out (or actually expand) the manufacturing sector's sales—especially those of capital goods producers—in bad times. It would seem that capital goods producers, policymakers, and executives seeking more economic stability and continuous growth would both praise and target the services sector for support. But, with rare exceptions, this has not been fashionable.

Even these macro level restructurings and the new industries that have emerged are far from the endpoint of services' impacts on the economy. As each company responds to these new forces in its own way—changing its own strategy, organization structure, and control systems to reflect the new realities—whole new forms of enterprises and competition are being generated. So profound are these changes that—as the next chapter suggests—the very nature of companies is changing, and a totally new kind of enterprise and strategy process is arising.

CONCLUSIONS

Although frequently scorned by economists and policymakers, services clearly dominate the U.S. economy. Service industries have become the preeminent producers of GNP and new job opportunities in all advanced industrial societies. They now account for 77 percent of all employment and 74 percent of all value-added in the U.S. economy and a majority of all GNP in other countries. Service companies have become large, capital-intensive, technology driven, and strategically powerful entities. They are and should be a major focal point of investment, employment, and capital deployment strategies. The technologies that made them possible have restructured the entire economy, created cross-competition among the individual segments and functions of many companies that used to be considered noncompeting, and forced global competition on everyone. Corporate strategists—whether in the manufacturing or the services sector—who do not understand, and most importantly exploit, these changes do their enterprises a great disservice. The continuing refusal of public policymakers to recognize the power and potentials of the services sector is also likely to lead to serious misallocations at the national level and to decrease U.S. competitiveness internationally.

The following chapters will suggest in detail how corporate managers can rethink their strategies, reorganize their structures, and best develop new relationships with outside companies to exploit the new service-based economy to the fullest extent. The book's final chapters will look at the more complex issues—of quality assurance, productivity, and human resources management—that these new structures pose for executives as their corporations move increasingly away from managing physical and fiscal assets and more toward managing service-based strategies and the human intellect that brings them into being.

CHAPTER 2

Focusing Strategy on Core Intellectual and Service Competencies

While the nation has been mesmerized by the debate about the "decline in U.S. manufacturing" and what to do about it,[1] the harnessing of intellect and its handmaiden, services, has been silently revolutionizing both the U.S. and world economies—and the power relationships, competitive structures, and boundaries of most individual industries, whether in services or in manufacturing. This reordering has profound implications for the way all managers need to think about their competitive environments, strategic options, leverageable opportunities, potential coalition partners, and the very nature of their businesses. A more systematic look at managing intellect and services forces fundamental changes in the way one approaches strategy and opens a vast array of new opportunities for competitive advantage.

What are some of the critical conclusions from our research to date?

The research for this chapter was first published in two articles by J. B. Quinn, T. A. Doorley, and P. C. Paquette, "Technology in Services: Rethinking Strategic Focus," *Sloan Management Review,* Winter 1990, and "Beyond Products: Services-Based Strategies," *Harvard Business Review,* March–April 1990. The latter was submitted under the title "Focus Strategy on Your Core Service Activities." Our published use of the concept of core strategic activities (competencies) both anticipated and went somewhat beyond that in C. Prahalad and G. Hamel, "The Core Competence of the Corporation," *Harvard Business Review,* May–June 1990, in terms of implications for strategy, outsourcing, financial, and organization structures.

• *Intellectual and service activities now occupy the critical spots in most companies' value chains—regardless of whether the company is in the services or the manufacturing sector.* Such activities, developed in depth, provide the strategic bases for both leveraging resources much more highly and creating more effective "entry and switching barriers" against competitors. As automation forces cost and physical quality standards toward a common norm, intellect and services are the crucial elements in creating differentiation and value for manufacturers and service companies alike.

• *If one is not "best in world" at a critical activity, the company is sacrificing competitive advantage by performing that activity internally or with its existing technique.* This dictates that managers consider each activity in their value chain on a "make or buy" basis and seriously consider outsourcing the activity when the company itself cannot internally achieve "best in world" status.

• *Each company should focus its strategic investments and management attention on those core competencies—usually intellectual or service activities—where it can achieve and maintain "best in world" status, i.e., a significant long-term competitive advantage.* The company must (1) develop these core capabilities in such depth that it can stay demonstrably ahead of competition, (2) surround them with strategic barriers that keep other competitors or suppliers from replicating them and thus gaining access to its markets, (3) deploy them as widely as possible across the full array of products or services it offers to customers, and (4) realign all remaining activities to serve customer needs most responsively.

• *The scale, specialized capabilities, and efficiency of outside service entities have so changed industry boundaries and supplier capabilities that they have substantially diminished the desirability of much vertical integration.* In particular, new technologies allow outside vendors to supply traditional staff or overhead services with such enhanced value and lowered costs that these activities often can be extensively outsourced.

• *All this requires an intensive reexamination of basic concepts in industry and competitive analysis—and a redefinition of what constitutes a truly "focused" company.* Each activity in a firm's value chain and within its traditional staff groups must be considered a "service," which can just as easily be purchased externally. One needs (1) to look for relative competitive advantage within each of these intellectual or service activities and (2) to analyze all the potential cross-competing sources of these functions in order to understand the true nature and dimensions of competitive advantage.

• *Strategically approached, this does not "hollow out" a corporation. It decreases internal bureaucracies, flattens the organization, gives the company a heightened strategic focus, and vastly improves its competitive responsiveness.* Properly developed, such strategically focused companies can support extraordinarily wide product lines. Indeed, contrary to many theories of strategic focus, product-line breadth can help corporate focus when a company has an especially potent set of core service skills that it can coordinate—as Matsushita, 3M, P&G, and Honda have[2]—across markets which otherwise seem unrelated.

THE POWER OF INTELLECT AND SERVICES IN THE VALUE CHAIN

How does one constructively analyze the new dynamics created by intellectual and service activities, and their associated technologies? We emphasize that such analyses apply not just to the service industries. Most of the value-added in manufacturing or product companies (like construction) is created by knowledge-based service activities such as research and development, marketing research, product design, customer information functions, advertising, or distribution. In fact, 65–75 percent of those employed in most manufacturing companies are in "service tasks" like these, plus accounting, personnel, secretarial, inventory management, legal, marketing, advertising, MIS, and similar activities.[3] Technology has created major new opportunities for improved productivity and value-added in all such areas. Let us start with activities that form part of the value chain, looking first at manufacturers to prove that service-based strategies apply to all sectors.

As automated manufacture has become more universal, the most significant contributions to value-added in a product have migrated away from manufacturing activities that simply convert raw materials into useful form—i.e., steel into an auto "body in white" or grain into edible cereals—and toward those knowledge-based service activities that provide the styling features, perceived quality, subjective taste, or marketing presentation values at many different points in the value chain. Figure 2–1 presents a typical array of such activities. At each stage, technology has increased the relative power of services. On-line databases and high-powered experimental equipment have revolutionized the research process; CAD/CAE/CAM techniques dominate the design-to-development cycle; "quick response" ordering systems slash order-to-delivery times; automatic sensing and data entry devices enable "real time" control over quality and inventories; carefully designed expert systems can plan and control the details of new product launches; direct feedback loops from customers' premises (or their electronic point of sale, EPOS, systems) provide sophisticated market research capabilities; and automated repair systems lower post-sale warranty and service costs.[4]

Harnessing the potentials at each of these points can yield enormous strategic advantage in terms of leveraging the company's knowledge content, quality, cost, timing, or flexibility advantages in their targeted markets.[5] Following are some high-profile examples of how a selective focus on knowledge-based service activities can create long-term competitive advantage for major manufacturers:

■ The strategies of all pharmaceutical companies are critically dependent on their knowledge capabilities and service functions. This is especially true of the top performers like $7.7 billion Merck and £2.8 billion Glaxo. Merck and Glaxo outperform the rest of the industry's top twenty companies in gross margins (76.8 and 82.4 percent respectively in 1990, as against an industry composite of 59.7 percent), and in profits as a percentage of shareholders' equity (46.5 and 29 percent versus an industry average of 26.4 percent).[6] The direct manufacturing cost of most patented ethical drugs is trivial relative to their sale price. Value is added primarily by service activities—first discovery of the drug through R&D, a carefully constructed patent and legal defense, rapid and thorough clinical clearance through regulatory bodies, and a strong preemptive distribution system. In recent years, Merck's strategy has focused on a powerful research-based patent position and Glaxo's on rapid clinical clearance. Both strategies rest on high value-added through services.

■ Recognizing the great value-added potentials of its many service functions, Ford Motor Company brought them all together simultaneously in optimizing the design of its Taurus/Sable cars. Not content with just engineering–manufacturing coordination, the Team Taurus project formally integrated purchasing, design, quality assurance, marketing, sales, distribution, repair, personnel, environmental relations, legal, and even insurance inputs— each a service activity—to improve all elements in the value chain. Using perhaps the most extensive "simultaneous design process" in industry to date, Ford produced the country's most profitable auto line of the last two decades.[7] The Taurus/Sable project was brought in for $250 million less than budget at a quality and price exportable to Europe and Japan. The same process was used on Ford's spectacularly successful new Lincoln Continental. Ford expects the process to reduce its design cycle from 5–6 years to 2½–3½ years in the near future and to further improve its responsiveness to customer demands.

In consumer product fields especially, value-added derives ever less from manufacturing capability and ever more from intangibles—created by service activities—like enhanced colorings and flavorings, convenience features and package design, brand recognition and reliability, advertising and distribution presentation, and finely tuned market responsiveness. In fact, the service-activity component of value-added is so great for virtually all manufacturers that fixed assets have become a relatively minor component in the valuation of most industrial enterprises, other than those in real estate, forestry, minerals, or mining. Table 2–1 shows how small a percentage the values assigned to producing assets have been in the largest and most recent acquisitions of consumer and industrial products companies. Most of the value that financial markets assign a leading edge company is due to its ongoing services competencies, not the hard assets that the buyer acquires. This is true regardless of whether the company is in a service industry or in what we think of as "manufacturing."

Looking in more detail at the "market prices" paid by acquirers over the last four years, we see, with one exception, premiums of from 55 to over 1,400 percent paid for ongoing service competencies (see Table 2–1). Although strictly speaking one should use replacement value to calculate the surplus value (as Tobin's Q demands), this surrogate measure makes the point. The true value of a corporation is not in its physical assets, but in the human competencies, databases, organization capabilities, intangible im-

TABLE 2–1
Service-Competency Values Versus Asset Values of Companies ($\times \$1,000$)

	Transaction Value	Book Value of Assets Net	Surplus–Service Competency Value	Service Value as % of Book	Date
Manufacturing Companies Acquired					
Philip Morris acquires Jacobs Suchard	$ 4,183,368	$ 813,885	$ 3,369,483	414%	1990
Georgia–Pacific acquires Northern Nekoosa	$ 3,640,564	$1,802,259	$ 1,838,305	102%	1990
RJR Holdings acquires RJR Nabisco	$25,071,000	$5,697,955	$19,373,045	340%	1989
Bristol–Myers acquires Squibb	$12,656,271	$1,485,478	$11,170,793	752%	1989
Beecham Group and SmithKline Beckman form SmithKline Beecham	$ 8,253,000	$1,590,173	$ 6,662,827	419%	1989
Philip Morris acquires Kraft	$12,891,000	$2,116,749	$10,774,251	509%	1988
Bat Industries acquires Farmers Group	$ 5,148,186	$1,671,489	$ 3,476,697	208%	1988
Eastman Kodak acquires Sterling Drug	$ 5,093,072	$1,010,530	$ 4,082,542	404%	1988
British Petroleum acquires Standard Oil of Ohio	$ 7,995,213	$3,160,163	$ 4,835,050	153%	1987
Borg-Warner Holdings acquires Borg-Warner	$ 4,174,579	$1,593,351	$ 2,581,228	162%	1987
Service Companies Acquired					
Matsushita Electric acquires 97% of MCA	$ 6,273,600	$2,340,896	$ 3,932,704	168%	1990
McCaw Cellular Communications acquires 42% of Lin Broadcasting	$ 3,800,000	$ 208,677	$ 3,591,323	1,721%	1990
Time Inc. acquires 50.6% of Warner Commun.	$ 7,000,000	$1,067,073	$ 5,932,927	556%	1989
Campeau acquires Federated Dept Stores	$ 6,520,000	2,469,697	$ 4,050,303	164%	1988

SOURCE: Compiled from "Deals of the Year," annual series in *Fortune*, 1987–1990.

ages, systems, and ongoing coalition relationships (all services) that it creates. These are measured most readily as the Service Competency Values shown in Table 2–1.

FOCUS ON CRITICAL KNOWLEDGE AND SERVICE BASED ACTIVITIES IN THE VALUE CHAIN

How can one best analyze and exploit the opportunities offered by (1) new knowledge-based services and (2) the industry and organizational restructurings these force and allow? The scale and power shifts that services and their technologies create require managers to attack strategy in a quite different way.

- *First,* all nonproduction elements in the value chain and at corporate staff levels need to be redefined as "services," which can either be produced internally or potentially be outsourced to external firms (see Figure 2–1). Note that virtually all staff and value chain activities are activities that an outside entity— by concentrating specialists and technologies in the area—can perform better than all but a few companies for whom that activity is only one of many.
- *Second,* analyzing the value chain in detail, one should ask, "In which of these activities do we have, or can we achieve, 'best in world' capabilities internally?" For each other activity, one should consider whether the company can efficiently bring that activity up to world class—or whether it should outsource the activity or form an alliance with someone who can provide "best in world" capabilities. Obviously, in all cases one must include both internal and external transaction costs.
- *Third,* the corporation itself should concentrate its own resources and energies internally on those activities where it can be best-in-world, where it can create unique value, and where it must have strategic control to maintain dominance (1) within its own selected areas of special competency, (2) over its crucial customer and supplier relationships, and (3) over the systems that coordinate the two.

Any other activities it performs internally—unless they provide a positive synergy with the core competency—will tend to reduce the company's potential competitive edge. Someone else can, by definition, perform these tasks better. Modern technologies and management techniques make it possible to outsource

FIGURE 2-1
Insource or Outsource Key Service Activities

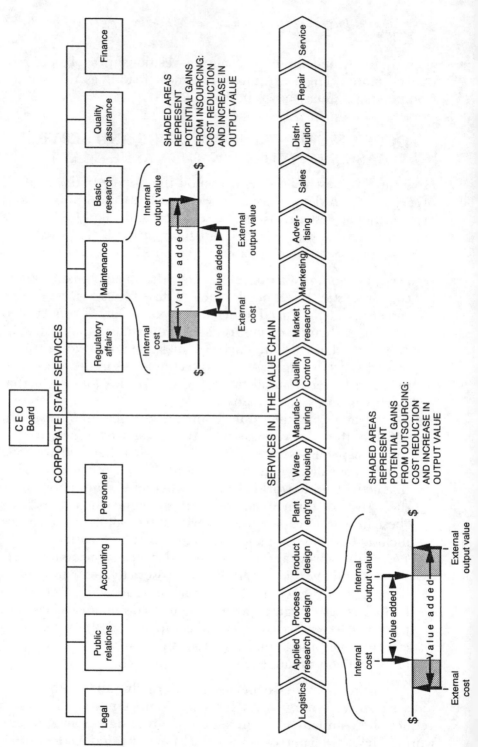

and effectively manage a range of external operations that would have been infeasible to handle only a few years ago.

Many executives query whether we really mean "best in world," not best in region or town. The answer is, "Yes, *best in world for the purpose*. If someone else can perform that function better, then the company is giving up the edge it could have if it were the best performer." Many companies have arrived at mottos that emphasize being the best. Motorola says, "We must be best in class." GE Plastics seeks places where it can have and maintain "an unfair advantage." Corning says succinctly, "If we tie, we lose." Comparing favorably against the best outsider should be the goal of every activity manager. Just as Xerox went to L.L. Bean to investigate and emulate Bean's inventory service capabilities, others need to seek out the best available service practices in the world, modify them as necessary for local conditions, and adopt them—or purchase the service from an outside entity if transaction costs don't militate against such a move.

INCREASING FOCUS, NOT HOLLOWING OUT

Such outsourcing has been disparaged in recent years as "hollowing out," leading to noncompetitiveness.[8] But for many, the real effects have proved just the opposite. The key to strategic success for many firms has been their coalitions with the world's best suppliers, product designers, advertising agencies, distribution channels, financial houses, or other outside sources. For example, for years a very profitable and fast-growing Polaroid Corporation bought all of its film medium from Kodak, its electronics from Texas Instruments (TI), and its cameras from Timex and others—while it concentrated on producing its unique self-developing film packets and designing the next generation of cameras and films. In consumer goods today, $2.2 billion Nike Inc., largest in its field and growing at 18.8 percent a year, concentrates on design, marketing, and distribution, while outsourcing virtually all production of its sporting goods lines (see "Vignette: Nike, Inc.," at the end of this chapter). And even tradition-bound, giant mining and oil companies outsource on a massive scale.

■ Many Australian mining companies, including some of the world's largest in diamonds, gold, and bauxite, outsource most of their noncritical activities. In many of these operations the leasehold is shared by a consortium of financial investors to decrease risks and to provide the initial infrastructures needed for outback mining. But almost all prospecting and aerial surveying is done by independent groups. Overall site architecture and waste disposal planning is done by outside experts, and the building of big structures like dams, lodging facilities, and crushing plants is outsourced. Most of the more modern mines contract with big earthmoving equipment companies like Leighton, which moves 150 million tons of earth a year, to remove the overburden and to haul ores to the crushers and mills. Most outsource maintenance (to companies like Caterpillar) for their permanent facilities or big equipment. Outside contractors handle all housing, food, and catering activities. Many mines outsource geophysical work, assaying, drilling, and early mineralogy to specialists. Financial houses all want independent geological assessments to support their investment estimates—plants are often leased from the banks, and the security of all debt leverage depends on estimates of reserves. Downstream companies depend on government mints and batteries to handle and market gold, DeBeers to finance and market diamonds, and in most cases outside railroads and shipping companies to move their ores to processing locations.

Although often using large sophisticated equipment, almost all these are service activities. Diamond and gold mining companies concentrate on coordinating the overall processing and marketing system and on removing their special minerals from the ore. They tap into the expertise of the best prospectors and geologists without having to maintain them full time. They gain from the scale economies, worker flexibility, and better work discipline the big earthmoving contractors can achieve. They avoid the labor clashes inherent in providing food and housing services. They lower front-end investments by a significant margin (estimated at two to three times) and can avoid losses in equipment or facilities, if the ore body requires later changes. Each form of contractor concentrates on what it does best, lowering overall system costs and risks.

CREATING VALUE THROUGH KNOWLEDGE BASED SERVICES

How can other companies best attack and exploit the opportunities systematic outsourcing allows? The process of obtaining strategic focus for each company begins by analyzing and redefining what that company really does to create value for its customers.

Most companies primarily produce a chain of services—which in some cases may include manufacturing support activities—and integrate these into a form most useful for specific customer groups. Even in manufacturing companies, typically only 10–35 percent of all activities are involved in direct production.[9] So dominant are nonproduction services in most situations that one questions whether most companies now in consumer products, computers, pharmaceuticals, clothing, oil and gas, foods, office or automation equipment, and so on should really be classified as "manufacturers" any more. When exploded to the activity level, the overwhelming majority of their system costs, value-added, profits, and competitive advantage is due to services, like those— other than "manufacturing and quality control"—enumerated in Figure 2–1.

Increasingly, successful companies, both large and small, have begun to understand this basic relationship and to target these key service activities as the core of their strategies. Merck, Genentech, Nike, Boeing, Apple, SCI, Honda, and Intel are among the most dramatic and visible current examples. Vignettes of each company's approach will appear later. But many others are equally persuasive. In fact, reconceptualizing manufacturing and service corporations alike as "intelligent or intellectual enterprises"—seeking to dominate the critical "service value" creation in their fields—is the key to long-term strategic success in most of today's rapidly changing global marketplaces. As Rappaport and Halevi point out, Microsoft and Mentor—not IBM or NEC—are the dominating players in today's computation and information marketplaces.[10] The future challenges of the computer field are principally software, not hardware, and the financial markets recognize this fact. The market awards Microsoft, with only 4,500 employees, a market value second only to IBM, with its tens of thousands.

■ Apple Computer provides a prime example of this kind of strategic focus. Its explosively successful Apple II (which retailed for about $2,000) was primarily a software and marketing triumph, costing less than $500 to build. Of this, Apple purchased from the outside approximately $350, representing 70 percent of its components, and later dropped some of those (like disk drives) it initially made itself.[11] Instead of building internal bureaucracies where it had no special skills, Apple outsourced critical activities like design (Frogdesign), microprocessors (Synertek), or printers (Tokyo Electric) and formed important strategic alliances, like the one with Regis McKenna, whose colorful Apple logo and classy ads gave Apple the image of a $100 million company at a time when it had only a few employees. In Europe Apple joined with IT&T to distribute its computers, and in the United States with Bell & Howell, whose strong reputation with teachers helped place Apple products in schools. Apple's marketing depended upon independent distributors rather than its own sales force, a channel different from what had been traditional in the industry.[12]

To avoid other major investments, Apple established more strategic alliances in its very heartland, software. While carefully focusing its internal resources primarily on its own disk operating system (Apple DOS) and the supporting macro-software to give Apple's products their unique "look and feel," it complemented these activities by being the first company to publish an "open architecture," inviting independent software houses to write compatible programs for its system (see "Vignette: Apple Computer" after this chapter). It later sought the services of Microsoft Inc. for specific portions of its operating system. The resulting software and accessories developed by independents helped Apple to further leverage its crucial relationships with dealers, who tended to push those systems having more extensive software support. By "hollowing out," Apple intensified its strategic focus and leveraged its limited management and capital resources enormously. Apple knew it could not fabricate integrated circuit boards, computer boxes, monitors, cables, connectors, or keyboards better than anyone else. It outsourced these and concentrated on concept design, software, logistics, systems integration, and product assembly to control the key elements in its value chain.

While this may have been essential in its early years, Apple's 1989–90 financial ratios still showed it to look more like a service company with an assembly activity than a fully integrated manufacturing company (see Table 2–2).

For years, Apple outperformed DEC and IBM both in sales growth and in terms of inflation-adjusted returns to its shareholders, defined by its market to book value ratio (see Figure 2–2). Tragically, Apple seemed to lose its focus in 1989–91 as it began to think of itself more as a "computer manufacturer" than a producer of value-added through intellectual processes, and lost its software preeminence to Microsoft and perhaps to NeXt. But its

TABLE 2–2

Performance Measures	Apple	IBM	DEC	Data General
Sales per employee	$369,593	$139,250	$84,972	$81,243
Net plant, property and equipment as % of sales[a]	18.4	63.0	44.6	56.7

[a] Net property, plant, and equipment figures have been adjusted to account for leased assets by multiplying the annual rental expense by 8.

recent alliances with Sony, Motorola, and IBM may indicate a refocus, leveraging Apple's core software and conceptual competencies in new ways and partnering or outsourcing manufacturing to outside specialists. Some of these arrangements key around its QuickTime software (synchronizing twenty-four different multimedia channels), and others around its Personal Digital Assistant (PDA) handheld diary and personal communicator concepts.

In a "lower-technology" field, Gallo Winery, Inc., has been able to accomplish another powerful form of service-based leveraging by focusing on its potent sales-distribution capabilities.

■ Ernest and Julio Gallo Winery, Inc., now dominates the lower-priced U.S. market with over 50 percent of the wine volume—and 25 percent of all U.S. wine volume—yet does not operate many vineyards. It outsources 95 percent of its grape production, preferring to let the farmers take on the weather and other risks of growing grapes, while Gallo concentrates on what it does best, wine production and distribution. Because of huge wine volumes, Gallo early on was able to develop new low-cost, refinery-like processing capabilities for wines. But, more importantly—using ruthlessly low pricing and the extraordinarily detailed and carefully worked-out sales controls and procedures of Ernest Gallo—it slowly began to dominate the distribution channels for U.S. wines.[13]

Because of its volume, Gallo can afford to invest more in R&D than its competitors, thus keeping its knowledge base about wines at the highest possible level for purchasing and processing purposes, while the information feedback from its huge distribution

FIGURE 2–2
Value Profile: Information Technology Companies, 1990

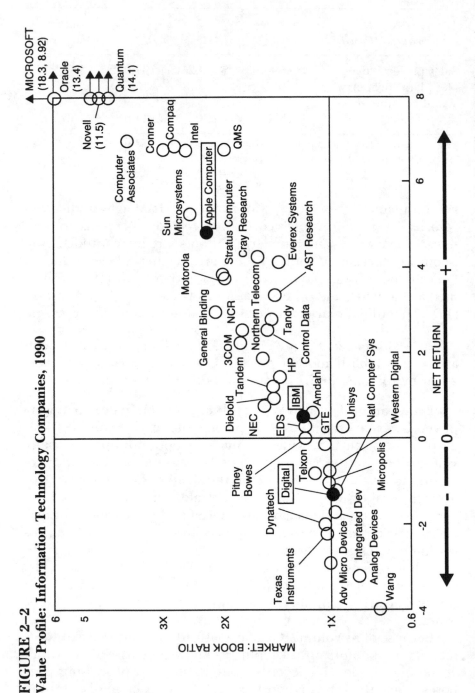

SOURCE: Original chart by Braxton Associates; reproduced with permission. Compiled from data provided by Callard & Madden Associates, July

network gives it greater information about the marketplace than any other producer could have. By combining its service-based capabilities in research, distribution, and market information, Gallo can profit by outsourcing its most essential production ingredient, grapes.

Despite the extreme market power its distribution and production capabilities have given it, Gallo still chooses to outsource not just its grapes but its advertising and promotion—and of course its retail distribution activities in most cases. In some places, it maintains wholesaling facilities to help leverage its information value even further. The secondary consequence of such careful and conservative outsourcing is that Ernest Gallo can focus his own formidable capabilities solely on the marketing-sales function and Julio Gallo can concentrate on the production function, where he has developed a specialized knowledge base unparalleled in the industry. This leverages the individually specialized skills of both to the maximum and helps create the enormous focus that has been so clearly visible in the E & J Gallo Winery strategy.[14]

Another very visible consumer products example is Nike, Inc., for whom outsourcing is an essential strategy.

■ Nike, Inc., is basically a research, design, and marketing— i.e., knowledge-based services—organization. By any accounting it has been incredibly successful, with a compound annual growth rate of 20 percent and a return on equity of 31 percent. Although it was number one in its market, selling some 70 million pairs ($2,235 million) of shoes in 1990, Nike outsourced 100 percent of its athletic footwear production and owned no production facilities. Since the early 1970s the athletic footwear industry has become increasingly both more technology-intensive and more fashion-sensitive. Both require maximum flexibility at the production and marketing levels. Nike seeks to provide its greatest value at the preproduction (research and development) and postproduction (marketing, distribution, and sales) levels, while closely overseeing the quality and responsiveness of its production units. Nike accomplishes this (1) with its "expatriate program," which keeps Nike personnel on site full time at its suppliers' facilities, and (2) by supporting and linking its suppliers as directly to Nike as possible through its "order reliability" package, which allows constant and planned production flows, and through its immediate bill paying, cooperative development, and extensive visiting and information exchange programs between headquarters and suppliers. But even in the marketing arena, Nike outsourced its advertising to Wieden & Kennedy (W & K) whose creative advertising drove Nike's product recognition and W & K's own reputation to the top of their respective fields.[15]

In the very difficult OEM subcontracting field, a similar strategy has yielded another dominating position.

■ $1.2 billion (1990) SCI, the world's largest electronics subcontractor, produces a wide variety of communications, computer, and advanced instrumentation equipment for sale both on an OEM basis and to value-added resellers. SCI has been growing at 35 percent a year in its extremely cutthroat business by outsourcing as much of its materials and nonessential service activities as possible. It concentrates its own resources on process design, joint product development with customers, logistics management, quality control, and its special expertise—low-cost assembly technology for surface-mounting components on both sides of a circuit board, often called a mother board. A key to SCI's success has been its thin overhead structure—130 managers for 7,000 employees—a condition achieved in part by its outsourcing strategies. Its flat organization structure lets it respond flexibly, rapidly, and precisely with lower bureaucratic costs than its competitors or customers can. SCI is a major supplier of subsystems for companies like Apple and IBM.[16]

Similarly, a giant enterprise like Boeing Aircraft knows full well that it cannot possibly design and produce more than a small portion of its planes' many component parts and subsystems. It relies heavily on suppliers for state-of-the-art componentry and subsystems. Although it manufactures some systems where it has special expertise, Boeing concentrates on aircraft design, relationships with its airline customers, assembly of aircraft, and managing the huge logistics systems necessary to support its worldwide sourcing. All except assembly are service activities. Bankers Trust outsources its European distribution and stock brokering for all its equity-based activities. Most of the major airlines outsource their food service activities to companies like Marriott, although in-flight meals quality is an important portion of the consumer's perception of overall service quality for the airlines. Kodak, Sun Oil, Chevron, Exxon, Merrill Lynch, and Ford have outsourced their data processing activities to major network management groups, believing the latter can perform these functions with higher quality and lower costs than they can. And so on.

STRATEGIC OUTSOURCING: NOT JUST PERIPHERAL ACTIVITIES

The point is: These are not just *peripheral* activities. Nor are they just components, parts, or fabricated subsystems. Companies are outsourcing integral and key elements of their value chains, because outsiders can perform them at lower cost and with higher value-added than the buying company.

In some cases, economies of scale have moved toward the supplier level. And service technologies make it possible to transport, store, and coordinate inputs from these sources so well that the buyer benefits more by outsourcing than producing. In others, the complexities of services and their technologies have grown so great that one must concentrate on them in order to be most proficient. In certain specialized niches, service companies have grown to such a size that they can develop and implement their technologies with economies of scale and scope fragmented individual producers cannot afford, yet provide for the flexibility and complexity new markets demand. By focusing on a few selected service activities, these firms can become "best in world" suppliers for a wide range of potential purchasers. They can focus more attention on their selected activities and develop them in greater depth than virtually any company trying to cover the complete range of services in its value-added chain or in what are considered traditional staff centers. To the extent that knowledge about the specific service activity is more important than knowledge about the end product itself, specialized suppliers can produce higher value-added at lower cost for their service than almost any integrated company.

By selectively relying on outside specialists, companies can lower their capital investments significantly—as Apple, Nike, Gallo, and SCI have done—increasing their capital turnovers to three or more times that of more integrated competitors. Strategic outsourcing provides the buyer with greater flexibility, especially when purchasing rapidly developing new technologies, fashion goods, or the myriad components of complex systems. It allows the buyer to obtain the full economies of scale and scope of the world's most sophisticated suppliers. It decreases design-cycle times for the buyer, who can have "best in class" suppliers working simultaneously on individual components of its system. Each supplier can (1) have a greater depth in knowledge about the design of its particular technologies and (2) support more specialized facilities to produce higher quality than the coordinating company could possibly achieve alone.

Such outsourcing also spreads the company's risk for component or subsidiary technology developments among a number of suppliers. By being able to switch suppliers and take advantage of new entrepreneurial or technological developments, the buyer can increase its own quality, stay up to date with more technologies, and enhance its own products' performance by incorporating the most current capabilities available. Yet it does not have to support the risk of all those development activities directly through its own R&D programs. Once production has begun, careful outsourcing decreases the risks of (1) amplified ROI losses during rapid economic downturns or (2) "chain delays" while each internal subsystem awaits the response of the slowest earlier link in an internal supply chain during upturns. By lowering such risks, the company can also lower its capital cost, further enhancing its competitiveness.

Such practices can help even the largest companies (Boeing or IBM) when technology developments are rapid or when product life cycles are extremely short (Nike or Liz Claiborne). Many forget that for years IBM regarded itself dominantly as an "assembler of product." It did very little fabrication internally. In fact, in the late 1950s it was unofficially recognized that IBM outsourced well over 50 percent of its manufacturing dollar. Even today, for its PC, IBM manufactures little internally (only ten minutes of direct assembly labor is involved) and outsources much of the rest—processors to Intel and Hitachi, printers to Epson, power supplies to TDK, disk drives to Tandem Shugart, keyboards to Keytronics or Polaroid, mother boards to SCI, monitors to Atlas, and sales to Sears and Computer Land, among others. These suppliers continuously change as new competitors are able to produce higher-quality or lower-cost componentry for IBM's purposes.

WHY OUTSOURCE NOW? DEVERTICALIZATION AND FLEXIBILITY

The key point is not just that outsourcing is feasible on a large scale. This has been true since standardization began the Industrial Revolution. More important are the facts that (1) many service elements that were once considered integral to a corporation's well-being can now be outsourced to advantage; (2) these are the activities where most value is now created, hence their correct sourcing affects the very heart of strategy; (3) services themselves are so easily transportable across national borders—and have made so many products more portable—that worldwide sourcing strategies are essential; and (4) management and electronic system technologies now make it possible to handle degrees of complexity never before possible. Effective management of such outsourcing has become perhaps the critical factor for success in many industries and companies. Logistics, contracting, and systems management have assumed a strategic significance they rarely enjoyed in the past.

As a result, strategic management must shift from concepts that presume primarily the orderly alignment of internal resources behind selected product-oriented missions. Instead strategy concepts need to focus *internally* more on developing "best in world capabilities" around a few key activities—the firm's core competencies—and *externally* more on managing a rapidly changing network of "best in world" suppliers for its other needs. Even the most powerful "manufacturing" companies can benefit from significant outsourcing when styles or technologies are changing rapidly, numerous suppliers are available and the buying company has a dominating position in some key elements of the value chain. As both product styling and technology changes become more rapid and important in all affluent markets,[17] such strategies are increasingly common across industries both in the United States and abroad. Subcontracting comprises an ever greater component of most manufacturers' costs, even in Japan (see Figure 2–3).

Economic affluence has been a major driving force behind this shift. Increased affluence means that customers pay more attention to quality details and to service responsiveness. It also means that output per person in the society must be higher. The result-

FIGURE 2–3
Value-Added: Percent of Total Manufacturing Costs in Japan

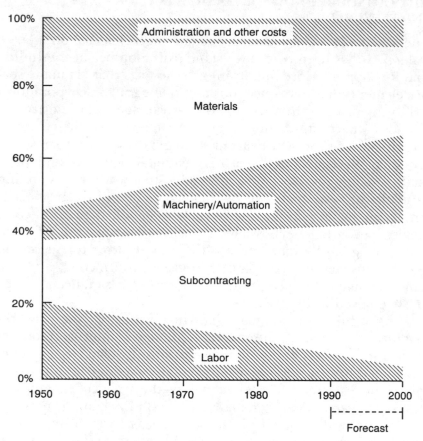

ing volume of output in turn justifies more specialization. As the total market grows, there are more discrete niches that can justify technological, production, or marketing specialization. And more specialization in other services is needed to identify, measure, and fulfill customers' desires for greater customization and personal services in each niche. "Affluence thus breeds service industries, and they in turn create more affluence."[18]

These technological and social forces—as well as the increased cost of supporting internal bureaucracies—have been central to the "disaggregation" or "deverticalization" trends in many industries. On the one hand, these more specialized suppliers—and the smaller size often required to get full scale economies—have led to a decrease in the average size of industrial firms since the late 1960s[19] (see Figure 2–4). On the other, for larger companies, substantial downsizing and decentralization (delayering and elimination of bureaucracies) have been necessary to respond more effectively to customer's demands. Chapters 4 and 5 will show in detail how some radical new organization forms support these trends. And chapters 3 and 12 will take up some of the structural issues involved in more extensive partnering and outsourcing.

FIGURE 2–4
Average Size of Industrial Firms

SOURCE: "The Incredible Shrinking Company," *The Economist,* December 15, 1990. Copyright © 1990 by The Economist Newspaper Ltd. Reprinted with permission.

A STRATEGIC FOCUS ON KEY KNOWLEDGE AND SERVICE COMPETENCIES

Outsourcing should not be regarded as a mere tactical redeployment for efficiency's sake, as the phrase "selling off the mailroom" is often used to imply.[20] Those who obtain maximum advantage simultaneously refocus their companies strategically around their own critical skills and capabilities while downsizing or eliminating those less central to the company's future. Unfortunately, this is more easily said than done. The true nature of these core capabilities is usually actively obscured by the tendency of organizations to think of their strengths in *product—not activity or service—* terms. The question usually posed is, "How can we position our products (or product lines) for competitive advantage?" Not, "What critical skills should we develop to be 'best in world' from our customers' viewpoint?" The former builds current profits, the latter builds long-term preeminence.

This error has been reinforced in most companies by organization, planning, and control structures built around products or product lines (i.e., divisional product or product-group profit centers) or SBUs that cluster activities around the products needed to satisfy a given customer class. In these circumstances almost no one sees building the overall corporation's core competencies as his or her special political domain and franchise for the future. Each decentralized entity naturally focuses primarily on the short-term profit needs it has been designed to satisfy and the special skills required for that purpose.[21] If a functional organization exists, each functional group has a psychological and political need to see itself as the company's special source of strategic strength. In neither event are there strong incentives to build the cross-divisional corporate skills that would lead to enterprise preeminence. Corporate effectiveness is undercut to satisfy personal or divisional goals.

Few internal executives can think objectively in terms of the *unique cluster of skills*—perhaps supporting multiple organizations—that the company must demonstrably dominate in order to ensure a strong *corporate* future. Usually, therefore, companies need an objective outside party to facilitate discussions and to help quantify the measurable dimensions of their presumed competencies. The process requires much careful "benchmarking" with a strong orientation toward what is important to the customer.

Many leading companies in our interviews have begun to develop customer-based metrics for benchmarking key activities. Too often, however, such analyses are entirely internally-based or subjective, when quantitative "best in world" benchmarking against outside sources is what is really needed. Most often when executives are asked, "How do you know or how will you know you are the best at that activity?" they have not thought out concretely what preeminence means or applied quantitative standards to it.

MAXIMS FOR LONG-TERM DOMINANCE THROUGH CORE COMPETENCIES

Ultimately each division—and the company as a whole—must select and define the dimensions for a *set of skills and activities* that will *give it the dominating depth* needed for competitive advantage *in serving its selected customers—both* in the near future *and* permanently. When properly selected and developed, the two sets will currently coincide or will intersect at some specified future date. Note that—as in the case of Honda, 3M, or Gallo—core competencies rarely involve only a single skill, but rather several mutually reinforcing skills that, when properly linked, others cannot surpass. Because customers' needs change over time, these selected bases of competency must not only have depth enough to prevent others from preemption but be broad and flexible enough to respond to an unknown future. Not an easy task, and not one to be decided once and then forgotten. Certain maxims seem to generate success in this kind of strategy formation.

Maxim One: For maximum long-term strategic advantage, companies focus their own internal resources on a relatively few basic sources of intellectual or service strength—or classes of service activities—which create and maintain a real and meaningful long-term distinctiveness in customers' minds. Core service competencies focus on the basics of what creates value from the customer's viewpoint and should be designed and evaluated from this perspective. In some cases, they represent a previously developed set of databases, skills, or organizational and technical competencies in which the company already has great depth or expertise. In other cases, they may require deepening selected capabilities substantially or generating new capacities the customer deems most relevant. In all cases, these must be a set of service competencies which if developed in depth will (1) be meaningful to customers and (2) provide a flexible long-term platform for strategic dominance. Despite their sophisticated dominance in their chosen realms, Federal Express and U.S. Sprint lost $0.5 billion and $1 billion respectively trying to buy increased market share with advanced telecommunications *technologies* their customers did not yet see as contributing significant value. And *The New York Times* and innumerable others have blown many more millions on videotext and prepackaged, on-line information *products* looking for markets.

With rare exceptions, products cannot be the source of competitive edge. It is too easy for some intelligent producer elsewhere to clone, substitute for, or improve upon them. Unusual situations may occur when a company has unique access to a rare raw material (as Brush-Wellman has to beryllium or DeBeers did to diamonds). Even then, substitutes are likely to abound—as the Argyle diamonds proved to DeBeers. And it becomes critical that the company's long-term competitive posture be developed more around great depth in certain key skills—such as DeBeers's diamond appraisal, financing, distribution links, and government relations or Brush-Wellman's sintering, "net shape," and pollution control technologies—which allow each company to maintain its continuing dominance. In virtually all other cases, a superior product can provide only a temporary advantage. Service-based strategies are more permanent.

Maxim Two: The key to competitive analysis and competitive advantage is to approach the company's remaining capabilities as a group of service activities that could be either "made" internally or "bought" externally from a wide variety of suppliers specializing or functionally competing in that activity. Strategists can then concentrate on whether they should produce, co-develop, or buy each specific service activity that might further support their company's intended permanent competitive edge. Rather than simply considering other direct "product" competitors in their industry, the most successful companies (and divisions within them) look at themselves systematically as being in competition with the "best in world" suppliers of each specialized service activity in the value chain. Because of service cross-competition between industries, a "best in world" activity may be found within the structures of many companies that are not direct competitors, e.g., Caterpillar or L. L. Bean (for inventory systems) or Banc One (for data center management or cash management accounts), and so on. A similar cross-industry analytical focus should apply to each division's strategy as well.

Maxim Three: For continued success companies actively command, dominate, and build barriers to entry around those selected activities critical to their particular strategic concept. Concentrating more power than anyone else in the world on these core competencies as they affect customers is crucial to strategic success. Knowing they cannot be dominant everywhere, managers pick those portions of the value chain where the company must—and with its resources can—be preeminent in serving its customers in the future. They invest their talent and resources in depth at these points and build systematic "barriers" between the company's outsourced suppliers and its chosen marketplaces. For all other activities—if the company cannot see its way to strategic superiority or if the activities are not essential to or highly synergistic with areas where it can attain such superiority—strategists consider outsourcing or partnering and actively develop "best in world" logistics and intelligence systems to oversee resulting relationships.

Maxim Four: Strategists plan and control their outsourcing so that their company never becomes overly dependent on—or later dominated by—their partners. In most cases, this means (1) consciously developing and monitoring multiple competitive sources and (2) strategically controlling certain critical process steps—whether or not the company is best in world at these—which might otherwise be totally outsourced. As the many examples cited above suggest, it is not necessary to internally fabricate a great percentage of components or parts—or to produce all value chain and staff services internally—to be able to control the key stages of an operation. *But it is essential to control some key strategic steps in the process* and to develop indepth technical knowledge bases, logistics systems, and commercial intelligence networks—about the other stages—second to none. Using this approach, companies can develop a much higher level of focus, and hence leverage, for their strategies than through traditional product-focused strategies. The Nike and Apple Computer strategies (see "Vignettes" following this chapter) present two more complete examples of how very successful companies have used these concepts for competitive advantage. Others are more briefly outlined below.

SELECTING AND DEVELOPING CORE SERVICE COMPETENCIES

Executives often ask, "How does a company select which service activities should become its core competencies?" In a raw startup, resources may be so limited that the company is forced to concentrate on those few critical activities where it has special skills that are particularly related to customer needs. In some cases, a larger company may analytically define a new set of critical skills that will be important to its customers in the future and may systematically build a set of core competencies in those new areas, as McKesson, American Airlines, DuPont, GE, and American Hospital Supply did. More often core competencies emerge from an interaction of the philosophies and interests of a few key players and a series of experimental successes in the marketplace, as those of Honda, Sony, 3M, and P&G did. Nevertheless, as they emerge, careful strategists will test these competencies against the kinds of maxims suggested above, and will develop them to avoid the problems outlined in Chapter 3.

Honda Motor Company provides a rather complete example of how such a posture can be achieved over time. While one would not claim the strategy to be based on prescience,[22] Honda Motor Company's basic strategy evolved around these principles, from the postwar period to the present (see Figure 2–5).

■ Initially, Mr. Honda's own personal commitment and engineering skills, as the company's founder, helped him create the world's finest team for designing small efficient engines, first for bicycles, then for motorcycles, and later for automobiles. When Honda Motor entered the motorcycle business, it had to counter the tremendous capital and distribution resources of Toyota and other major Japanese producers. Given its own limited capital base and the very cost-competitive nature of motorcycles, Honda concentrated its development and production resources on engines and created a very small, efficient assembly operation. It outsourced as many (nonengine) fabrication operations as possible in order to gain the economies of scale many of its potential supplier companies enjoyed. Within its manufacturing operations, Honda developed extremely low-cost capital-intensive facilities focused on those key components necessary to the uniqueness and quality of its motors. Elsewhere it developed the skills needed to manage its supplier networks, while achieving the most efficient small-scale assembly operations in its industry. These approaches

FIGURE 2–5
Core Competencies: Honda Motor Co.

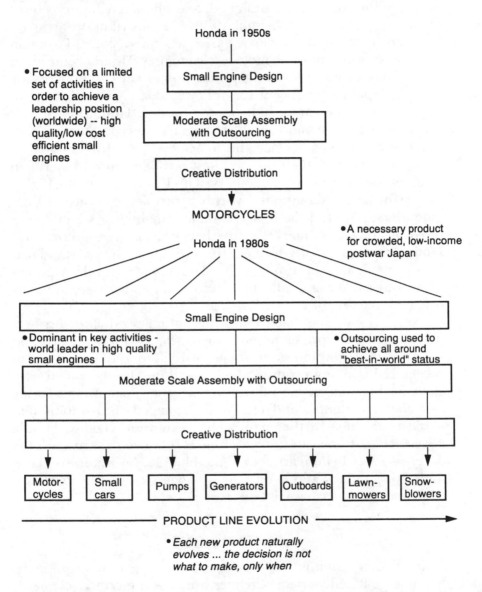

characterize Honda Motors even today. Simultaneously, Honda's President, Mr. Fujisawa, used some very innovative financing to build Japan's strongest distribution network for small motorcycles and to bypass its major competitors in reaching the marketplace.[23]

Once Honda succeeded with small motorcycles in its home

market, based on these several core skills, the company parlayed its specialized knowledge capabilities into a steadily broader line of more efficient, cleverly designed, and ultimately higher-power motorcycles sold through similarly unique distribution arrangements in other countries, particularly the United States. To obtain the most efficient possible motorcycle engines, Honda centralized all design of its motors and the production of key components for them in Japan, a practice it still follows. Leveraging off its great depth in internal-combustion motor design, Honda constantly sought to obtain the most complete possible fuel combustion, both to improve motor efficiency and to achieve Mr. Honda's goal of having the motors attain the "greatest possible external merit" in terms of their cleanliness and safety. This led directly to the highly successful CVCC (compound vortex controlled combustion) engine which powered the first Honda automobiles. As Honda entered the U.S. auto market in the late 1960s, these motors gave Honda a unique ability to meet the U.S. air pollution standards first promulgated in 1969–70. And they gave Honda a potent competitive and image edge in the efficiency and environmentally oriented markets of the early 1970s.[24]

Later Honda was able to introduce other product diversifications utilizing its core engine performance, assembly quality, and marketing-distribution skills. Increasingly, Honda's management recognized that any product which keyed on Honda's small, efficient engines, extensive fabrication logistics system, small-scale assembly operations, and creatively managed distribution networks could be a further natural line extension. Today, Honda advertises that one can fit "Six Hondas in a two-car garage," the other five not being cars, but snow blowers, lawnmowers, lawn tools, boat engines, and so on—an apt slogan to describe its knowledge and service activity based strategy.

CONCLUSIONS

This chapter attempts to develop several crucial arguments. Knowledge-based, service activities are now the critical elements in most companies' value chains—regardless of whether they are in manufacturing or the service industries. Such activities, developed in strategic depth around customer needs, provide the primary bases (1) for differentiation in today's marketplace and (2) for creating insurmountable entry barriers for competitors.

Knowledge and service based strategies are most effective when companies develop "best in world" capabilities around a few selected competencies that are important to customers, and then conscientiously maintain preeminence in these areas against all comers. By concentrating its own resources on these selected areas and benchmarking other areas to ensure that it has comparability with or access to best in world suppliers, each company can build an unassailable strategic position.

Once strategists define each activity in the value chain or in staff services as a "service activity," they will often find outside service providers who, by specializing, can provide that service with higher quality or lower cost than their internal counterparts. No company can hope to be better than all outside specialists in all the elements of its value chain. If the company is not best in world—including all transaction costs—at that activity, it is giving up competitive edge by performing the activity internally. New technologies and management systems have dramatically shifted the balance between what it pays to outsource and what it can effectively produce internally. As a result, many companies—especially in very volatile, highly customized, or advanced technology fields—find extensive outsourcing more attractive than ever before. Systematically developing this kind of disaggregated strategy offers opportunities to leverage one's fiscal and intellectual resources greatly. As later chapters will show, the same strategies can also decrease internal bureaucracies and create much higher value for customers and shareholders.

Since this kind of strategy flies a bit in the face of conventional wisdom, this chapter has tried to clearly structure, explain, and present examples of the approach without myriad caveats and cautions. The Nike and Apple Computer Vignettes amplify both the nature of successes and the realistic issues involved. However, potential gains are not achieved without risks. Later chapters will concentrate on how to manage these more disaggregated strategies and their accompanying organization forms for greatest strategic focus, minimum risk, and highest efficiency.

VIGNETTES:
Core Competencies and Outsourcing

Vignette One: Athletic Footwear at Nike, Inc.*

Nike, Inc., helped form and took advantage of the physical fitness boom of the 1970s to become the market leader in athletic shoes during the 1980s. In 1990, it sold approximately 70 million pairs of shoes, earning $243 million on gross revenues of $2.2 billion. It had been growing at a five-year compounded annual growth rate of 20 percent with a return on equity of 31 percent.

Nike is basically a research, design, and marketing company—outsourcing 100 percent of its athletic footwear manufacturing to numerous "production partners" abroad. In 1990 it owned no full-scale production facilities, although it purchased Tetra Plastics, one of its key suppliers of fabricated material, in 1991. Nike's success has depended upon its ability to manage its numerous production partners, a path that has not always been easy. Nike was formed in 1964 by Phillip Knight and Bill Bowerman as Blue Ribbon Sports Company (BRS). Based on a concept conceived by Knight when he was at Stanford Business School, BRS imported athletic shoes produced by the Onitsuka Tiger Company of Japan. Knight sold shoes at local track meets, while Bowerman worked on designs using information fed back from those sales.

When BRS's sales reached $2 million, Tiger offered to buy 51 percent of BRS and threatened to cut off supplies if BRS refused. Unwilling to sell out, BRS began a partnership with Nissho-Iwai, a large Japanese trading company, which agreed to contract with independent manufacturing sources in Japan to produce the shoes now marketed under the brand name Nike. Nissho also provided financing and import–export services for BRS. All shoes

---

* Derived from a number of secondary sources, including M. Donoghu and R. Barff, "Nike Just Did It: International Subcontracting and Flexibility in Athletic Footwear Production," *Regional Studies*, December 1990.

were manufactured in Japan until the oil shock of 1973, when Nissho decided to move production to Taiwan. Feeling it had little control over production, BRS opened a manufacturing facility in Exeter, New Hampshire, a former U.S. shoe center, to learn more about shoe production. With this knowledge, BRS began to orchestrate production in Taiwan and South Korea in the late 1970s. This began a series of production practices that Nike follows today.

MANUFACTURING PRACTICES

The first practice is flexible and extensive outsourcing. The market for athletic shoes in the late 1970s and early 80s was extremely volatile. New designs were introduced constantly, new players entered the market, heavy advertising supported new concepts, and the rapidly growing market segmented into specialized shoes for everything from football and bicycling to aerobics. Athletic shoes also became the comfort shoes for the elderly and for office workers. The number of different models of Nike shoes rose from about fifty in 1977 to 350 in 1988. Shoe design became highly technical as well as fashion-oriented. European producers like Adidas and Puma began to lose share to Reebok, Nike, and LA Gear, whose production was centered in Southeast Asia. Market shares for brands and styles fluctuated violently. Tariffs for various components—and shoes themselves—changed rapidly and with high impact on costs. Knowing it could not undertake all these risks alone, Nike responded by creating three classes of partners. Instead of the term "suppliers" or "contractors," it prefers the term "production partners," because this implies joint responsibilities, an attitude Nike carefully nurtures. The three categories, each with its special characteristics, are outlined on the following page.

Developed partners produce Nike's latest and most expensive "statement products," which can absorb higher production costs. These tend to be located in newly industrializing countries like Korea or Taiwan, where they can subcontract locally for most nonproprietary components and materials. These companies usually produce lower volumes, co-develop products, and co-invest in new technologies. *Volume producers* are above average in size (making 70,000–85,000 units a day, as against 20,000–25,000 units for developed partners). They generally produce a specific type of

Developed Partners	Volume Producers	Developing Sources
Exclusive mfg. of Nike footwear	Mfg. other branded athletic footwear	Exclusive mfg. of Nike footwear
High-quality, high-technology mfg.	High-volume producers	Primitive production methods
Technologically advanced products	Mid- to low-end products	Low-end products
Less price-sensitive products	Price-sensitive, low-cost production	Price-sensitive product, cheap labor
Monthly orders vary less than 20%	Monthly orders vary more than 50%	Orders depend on demand
20–25 thousand pairs of shoes a day	70–85 thousand pairs of shoes a day	Small capacity
Vertically dis-integrated, subcontracting	Vertically integrated, source internally	Little integration, source abroad
Cooperative development & investment	Independent absorbs volume surges	Support for "first-tier" groups

footwear (say basketball shoes) and are more vertically integrated. No development work is done with them because each company may produce for seven or eight other buyers to keep up its volume. Although Nike tries very hard to stabilize volumes for its developed partners, volume partners are expected to handle most surges in volume themselves. *Developing sources* are attractive primarily because of their low labor costs and their capacity to diversify assembly locations. They have been primarily in Thailand, Indonesia, and China. All produce exclusively for Nike, which has a strong "tutelage" program to develop them into Nike's higher-level suppliers. To help both parties, Nike tries to link developing sources (through joint ventures) with its developed partners in Taiwan and Korea. The latter assist by providing needed training, helping to finance some operations, and later moving some of their own labor-intensive activities to these units.

In addition to its "first tier" of assembly units, Nike supports a complex network of "second tier" suppliers for materials, components, and subassemblies. Some of the more specialized and technical components are made in supplier companies totally controlled by Nike—i.e., for some of its patented features like Nike Airsole's® unique airbag. Where there are no sophisticated local suppliers, many of Nike's developing sources must bring in these specialized components from outside their countries. In other cases, "second tier" control ensures Nike's control over its critical technologies and its component quality.

SERVICE COORDINATION

Nike acts primarily in a service role: as design center, production coordinator, and market interface for its system. Its key strategies are product differentiation, innovation, flexibility, and coordination of the best available suppliers (defined in cost and quality terms) for its various activities. Looking for exceptionally creative advertising talent, Nike found it in Weiden & Kennedy (W&K), whose ad campaigns soon drove Nike to the top of the product recognition list. W&K as an independent prospered too, moving to the very top ranks of recognition in its field. Desiring not just name but performance recognition, Nike also created another alliance by joining with Athletics West, the first such club to support track and field contenders for the U.S. Olympic team. Modeled after the European club system, Athletics West provided a financial and training network (including coaches, equipment, and medical support) for talented U.S. athletes—and high visibility for Nike products.

Nike developed a number of special policies to support its extensive outsourcing and partnership programs. Key among these were:

1. ***Treating partners as true partners.*** The strength of Nike's production partnership program are: (a) its "expatriate program," which keeps Nike personnel on site at all key manufacturing facilities; (b) its "order reliability" policies, which try to ensure a planned order flow to its partners to minimize their risks and costs; (c) stable financing—paying bills on time; (d) cooperative development programs, which include exchange of extensive information and plant visits with developed partners; and (e) an attempt to maintain credibility and honesty in all partnership dealings.

2. ***Participation in the manufacturing process.*** Nike "expatriates" become permanent personnel in each factory producing Nike footwear. They tend to stay with that factory for several years to know its people and processes in as much detail as pos-

sible. They function as a liaison with corporate R&D (in Beaverton, Oregon), headquarters, and the corporation's quality assurance and product development efforts worldwide. Nike jointly plans production with its partners, placing monthly orders to keep volume from varying more than 20 percent month to month. Nike's own R&D group participates in design; its corporately owned component factories give Nike a second window on production; and its corporate offices constantly scan new suppliers for better techniques. Nike's quality assurance program ensures that each factory has and enforces the most up-to-date available quality management practices.

3. *Adding significant value.* Nike adds high value through its preproduction (R&D and product development) activities, market information and image producing capabilities, and postproduction (advertising, sales, marketing, distribution, and warranty) activities. Its depth of expertise in each of these creates an effective block between the supplier and Nike's marketplace. Nike adds further value by coordinating logistics and information among its partners and their suppliers, creating another strategic barrier to partners moving downstream.

4. *Joint investment and development.* Most basic research is performed at Nike's Beaverton headquarters and in specialized supplier facilities for key materials. But development of a new product or style will be shared with developed partners. Representatives are brought to Beaverton to share information about new technologies and markets. Developed partners share development and some investment costs for new products they will make. These cooperative practices shorten development cycle times, lower costs, improve communications and shared values, and tie partners more directly to Nike.

Nike's practices are designed to give it maximum flexibility with maximum assurance to customers and suppliers. In addition to the practices noted above, Nike has (1) a "futures booking program" to give discounts and guaranteed delivery to retailers who order in advance, (2) highly automated distribution centers to lower costs and facilitate rapid, accurate response to orders, (3) an advanced worldwide logistics system to coordinate its market information and supplier data, and (4) long-term relationships with suppliers to anticipate and handle joint needs in a timely fashion. These policies have helped project Nike into the number-one position in the world athletic shoe market.

Vignette Two: Apple Computer Company

In his book *The Little Kingdom: The Private Story of Apple Computer,* Michael Moritz notes:

> Michael Scott, CFO of Apple, had unsentimental ideas about both production and finance. He had a strong dislike for automated manufacturing and expensive test machinery. He was also determined that outsiders should help pay for Apple's growth and that they should suffer the discomforts of swings in the business. His ideas about the growth of the Company were the equivalent of Wozniak's ideas about the chips in a computer. Both were talking about productivity. Scott wanted to design a company that did the most amount of work with the least number of workers. "Our business," he said, "was designing, educating, and marketing. I thought that Apple should do the least amount of work that it could and that it should let everyone else grow faster. Let the subcontractors have the problems." Scott had an undying commitment to letting outside manufacturers make anything that Apple couldn't produce more cheaply. He also felt that a fast growing business had no time to master some of the rudimentary skills needed to produce reliable components. It was easier, for example, to expand the quality tests for printed circuit boards stuffed by outside suppliers than to contemplate expanding the work force and mastering all the techniques needed for production of decent boards.
>
> So for help with board stuffing, Scott relied partly on Hildy Licht, a Los Angeles mother and the wife of one of Wozniak's acquaintances from the Homebrew Club. Licht operated a cottage industry. Parts were delivered to her home and she distributed them to hand-picked assemblers scattered around the neighborhood, tested the finished work, and returned it to Apple in the back of her brown Plymouth station wagon. She was flexible, could make revisions on boards, and offered overnight service. Scott also turned for help to a larger company that specialized in turning out larger quantities of printed circuit boards. Both were the sort of services designed to relieve small companies of time consuming chores.*

* M. Moritz, *The Little Kingdom: The Private Story of Apple Computer* (New York: William Morrow, 1984), pp. 200–201.

A central element in Apple's growth plan was having the smallest number of employees producing the largest possible amount and value-added of goods, a condition accomplished largely through subcontracting. In 1977, ten employees averaged about $77,000 in sales each; in 1981, 2,400 employees averaged $139,500 each. By 1990 the ratio had reached $370,000 per employee.

APPLE'S PROSPECTUS

In its December 12, 1980, prospectus, Apple stated its manufacturing approach as follows:

> The Company's manufacturing operations consist principally of the purchase, assembly, and test of the materials and components comprising its products at facilities located in Dallas (TX), Cupertino, San Jose, and Los Angeles (CA); and, since October 1980, in County Cork, Ireland. The principal materials and components used in the production of Apple's products include semiconductors, plastic and metal parts, and certain electromechanical subassemblies purchased from independent suppliers. Although most are standard parts, certain items, such as metal and plastic parts and circuit boards, are fabricated or assembled by independent vendors to Apple's specifications. Apple manufactures certain components such as disk drives and keyboards. Apple strives to qualify multiple sources of supply for all of its materials and subassemblies. Certain components, such as power supplies, integrated circuits, and plastic housings, are obtained from single sources, although the Company believes other sources of such parts are available. To date the Company has not experienced any significant production problems or delays due to shortages in material or components.
>
> Quality control and final system testing and inspection are performed by Apple at its production facilities. In the testing process, the Company utilizes its own computers with specialized software to perform diagnostic testing to isolate and identify defective components. As part of the final testing process, all systems are subjected to a four-day continuous "burn-in" to provide assurance of electronic and mechanical functions.
>
> Apple anticipates that as it develops more complex products, it may be required to use custom integrated circuits. There can be no assurance that the required custom circuits will be

readily available or available from more than one source. . . .
The Company also intends to lease additional office facilities
aggregating approximately 130,000 feet in Cupertino, California, which are currently under construction and anticipated to
be completed in August 1981.

APPLE'S MANUFACTURING APPROACH

The "Apple Computer, Inc." case by William H. Davidson notes
the following:

> Apple's operations were oriented toward minimizing cost and
> maintaining strict quality control. Significant emphasis was also
> placed on just-in-time inventory management. Since the Dallas
> plant was primarily an assembly operation, Apple relied heavily
> on external suppliers. Printed circuit boards were assembled by
> subcontractors in Singapore. Apple sourced microprocessors
> from Synertek, other chips from Hitachi, Texas Instruments,
> and Motorola, video monitors from Hitachi, power supplies
> from Astec in Hong Kong, and printers from Tokyo Electric
> and Qume. Reliance on outsiders is an Apple trademark.
> Michael Scott, Chief Financial Officer, stated: "Fast growing
> companies should rely on outside help for the manufacture of
> non-proprietary components and systems. As long as cost-
> efficient outside alternatives exist, we won't worry about being
> innovative in such areas as production procedures. As long as we
> are protected in terms of quality assurance, there are better
> things to do with our time here. Our scarcest commodity at
> Apple isn't cash, it's time."*

The Apple II, which retailed for about $2,000, contained
about $350 in purchased components—a large portion of the
$500 it cost to build.

MARKETING PLAN

Jobs and Markkula used their initial $600,000 in venture capital
equity funds not for product development but mainly for promotion. Regis McKenna created the colorful Apple logo and the
four-color glossy ads that began appearing in magazines. These

---

* W. Davidson, "Apple Computer, Inc.," Case UVA-BP219, University of Virginia, 1984, Darden School Foundation. Reprinted with permission.

gave Apple the image of a $100 million company at a time when it had twelve employees. Markkula later described this effort as critical, because "We had to gain recognition in the market fast. We could not start small. We had to dominate the business or go bankrupt trying."

Markkula's marketing plan depended on independent distributors rather than Apple's own sales people. Apple encouraged electronics retailers to carry its computers by offering high margins, dealer training, cooperative advertising, and point of sale displays. This distribution channel, consisting of specialized retail stores, developed simultaneously with Apple. And Apple relied on third-party wholesalers until 1981, when the Company took over its own distribution service operations.

Personal computers were distributed through channels different from those traditionally used by the industry. After attempting to use a direct sales force, such other companies as Atari, TI, and Commodore had sold through mass merchandise outlets. Although Apple, IBM, and Tandy did not authorize sales of their products through the mail, a large amount of software and peripheral equipment, crucial to Apple's success, went through mail order. Accessories and availability of software were considered important to dealers, because a prospective customer would often approach a retailer with several applications in mind and would rely on the salesman's recommendation in his or her purchase decision. Margins on software products tended to be higher than for hardware, and thus dealers would tend to prefer systems with extensive software over a machine with more limited software. Apple concentrated on software dominance to maintain its position. This was particularly true of its Apple DOS (Disk Operating System). The broad acceptance of this system inhibited development of new operating systems by others and encouraged new entrants to build their systems around one of the accepted operating softwares. As of late 1982, software could be written to be used on only one operating system. Translating programs to another operating system was expensive and time-consuming, although some developers (like Microsoft) were using languages transportable to other operating systems. Apple's DOS was proprietary to Apple and not available for license. CP/M and MS-DOS were written by software firms who had financial incentives to promote the use of their systems by other hardware and software developers. Recognizing the necessity of extensive support software, Apple was the first company to publish an "open architecture," allowing all independent software houses to write compatible software for its system. This enormously leveraged Apple's internal capabilities.

STRATEGIC ALLIANCES

Markkula is credited with guiding the formation of many alliances at Apple. Under his tutelage, the Company allied itself with larger concerns to give it a more mature, stable image. It joined with IT&T to distribute computers in Europe (although the relationship eventually foundered) and with Bell & Howell, which had a strong reputation with teachers, to help place Apple products in schools. Markkula contacted Dow Jones about the possibility of jointly developing software that would pull quotes off the Dow Jones News Retrieval Service. Apple was the first to recognize the importance of user groups and organized the first international users group to help it in positioning its product. Three and a half years after the introduction of the Apple II, 130,000 had been sold. Revenues had risen from $7.8 million in 1977–78 to $17.9 million in 1980. In the fall of 1980, just thirty-one months after the thirtieth employee had joined the Company and just twelve months after the 300th employee arrived, Apple's payroll topped 1,000.

Other important network relationships include the development (by Don Breklin) of Visicalc for Apple II. Apple II was the only computer to support Visicalc for over a year. That was a part of a strategy to develop easily usable programs for the Apple. The name Apple itself was chosen to symbolize a friendly, nonthreatening, non-high-tech image. Regis McKenna was Apple's public relations agency. It was crucial in establishing Apple's image at a time when Apple was a struggling company with little or no sales. Apple gave Ben Rosen, the electronics analyst, well-debugged Apple products and supported them with highly personal service, so Rosen became a big Apple supporter and heavily influenced Apple's share prices and venture financings.

UNIQUE FEATURES

Much of Markkula's original $91,000 investment was used for tooling the high-quality, attractive-looking outer case (designed in large part by Frogdesign and made outside Apple) that Jobs insisted was crucial to the image of the computer. The Apple II was the first personal computer with a built-in operating system. The operating system manages the computer's internal operations and executes software programs. This freed users from personally having to program the computer. Instead, they could buy outside software programs and run them without the intermediate help of experts.

In 1978 Apple was the first personal computer manufacturer to offer a floppy disk and disk drive. The written documentation that accompanied the Apple II and its software represented major innovations in the computer industry. The graphics were attractive, the type large and well laid out, the text friendly, humorous, and (most importantly) easy to understand. Previously, computer documentation had been written in the arcane language of computer professionals, usually incomprehensible to the uninitiated. By the end of calendar 1982, more than 650,000 Apple II units had been sold. The Apple II continued its phenomenal sales growth despite some obvious technical shortcomings, like a keyboard limited to uppercase letters and lacking the full set of characters used in computer programs, and a video monitor capable of displaying only forty columns while eighty columns was the standard. But the core design was so effective that Apple II placed Apple Computer on the high road to success.

CHAPTER 3

Leveraging Knowledge and Service Based Strategies Through Outsourcing

As strategists carefully develop a long-term focus around those selected knowledge or service based activities the company alone can
perform best, and as they aggressively upgrade or outsource those
where it cannot excel, they create a much more precise and enduring strategic focus for the company than product-oriented
strategies can achieve. As a major side benefit, they simultaneously
forestall takeovers by others who might identify such missed potentials as opportunities to lower costs or raise post takeover yields substantially. But to develop such an offensive and defensive posture
effectively, they need to deal with some major strategic concerns.

- How does one select and develop knowledge areas or service
  activities to achieve an enduring and dominating activity share
  in present and future marketplaces? Is outsourcing just as
  valid in the service industries as it has been in manufacturing?
- What kinds of problems should one anticipate in a more disaggregated strategy that uses greater outsourcing? How can
  one avoid the loss of key skills that may be needed for future
  success? How can one prevent overdependence on suppliers
  or forestall them from bypassing the company into its marketplaces?
- Does concentration on a few key knowledge and service activities decrease a company's capacity to diversify in the future, weaken its innovative capabilities, or increase its vulner-
  ability to swings in its markets and hence its risk?

71

- Is development of core service competencies just a new strategy for increasing market share? Or does it significantly redefine the basic nature of a company and its essential relationships to customers and suppliers?
- How does one pragmatically approach the problems of benchmarking knowledge and service activities to ensure adequate performance in areas chosen for focus, upgrading, or outsourcing?

As a company focuses ever more on its own internal knowledge and service skills and those of its suppliers, it increasingly finds that managing shifts *away from* the overseeing and deployment of fiscal and physical assets and *toward* the management of human skills, knowledge bases, and intellect both within the company and in its suppliers. In fact, its *raison d'être* becomes the systematic coordination of knowledge and intellect throughout its (often highly disaggregated) network to meet customer needs. This chapter will pose the most relevant problems in defining strategies for such disaggregated knowledge and service based entities and will offer illustrations of successful techniques some managers have found useful.

ACTIVITY SHARE, NOT JUST MARKET SHARE, FOR DOMINANCE

A beginning point is to reconsider one of the presumed pillars of strategic dominance, "high market share." Although it is important in some situations—especially in achieving experience curve effects in certain manufacturing industries—too much strategic attention has been paid to market share *per se.* Unless market share is converted into dominating depth in selected key support activities, it may have tenuous strategic impacts. Market share can be bought, as it was in the U.S. auto and television industries by inappropriate pricing strategies or other short-term practices. The Japanese, by contrast, tended to develop overwhelming depth in the critical skills underlying design, production, and quality maintenance that later *led to* long-term lower costs and higher market penetration. Those U.S. companies which have been successful in international competition—like Motorola, Merck, and Boeing—did the same. Market share, unaccompanied by superior depth in selected knowledge or service capabilities the *customer deems critical,* will soon disappear, as the tragic declines of

US Steel, GM, Pillsbury, RCA, TWA, and innumerable conglomerates based mainly on financially driven strategies so thoroughly demonstrate.

High share and high profitability together come from having the "dominating activity share" of importance in a selected market segment. The key is to think in terms of dominance—being able to bring more talent to bear on an issue critical to customers than anyone in the world. This occurs when (1) a company has the most effective presence in specific service activities a segment of the market most desires, and (2) it can capture and defend some special experience or specialization benefits accruing to that activity share. This may or may not involve a high market share, as that factor is usually measured.

■ For example, Honda and Intel have not had a high total market share relative to their larger rivals. But they have such depth in small engine design (Honda) and complex chip design (Intel), combined with intermediate-scale manufacturing knowhow and fast design-cycle capabilities (both companies), that they are very competitive in industries where scale economies once seemed central to success.

In service-dominated marketplaces—which most are—competitive analyses need to focus on the relative potency of the "activity" or "service" power a company has at each critical point in the value chain underlying its market positions. The company's own power has to be compared with that of each present or potential competitor that might provide this function. This does not necessarily mean that the company spends more money on the activity than all others, but that it focuses more talent on it, as Cray did in large computers, Microsoft or Lotus did in software, Sony did in miniaturized electromechanical systems, or Honda did in small motors.[1] All faced competitors who could make much larger fiscal investments in these activities. To achieve dominance using fewer resources, these and many other companies have depended on leveraging the intellect of key people by constantly reforming high-intensity task or innovation teams and systematically reusing these key people in different adhocracies or "skunkworks" specifically focused on customer needs. When one is leveraging intellect rather than facilities, superior selection, training, acculturation, networking capabilities, databases, flexibility, fast response, and motivation systems—not increased invest-ment—are the usual keys to success.[2] How best to develop these internally at low cost is a central subject of Chapters 8 and 9.

This kind of knowledge and service based strategic focus le-verages resources in a number of ways. It lowers absolute costs by rigorously seeking out the most cost-efficient supplier of each activity and capturing the higher efficiencies and investment sup-port the best outside suppliers can provide. It avoids dilution of internal efforts and helps prevent (or reverses) the buildup of internal bureaucracies with all their inefficiencies. As it peels out nonessential activities, a management can focus its own attention more on those activities the company alone can perform best—and where it can build an ever increasing competitive edge. As activities are eliminated, it is easier to flatten the organization—an essential ingredient in most "time-based," fast-response, or customer-oriented strategies.[3]

At the same time, well-managed outsourcing places the world's best talent from other spheres at the enterprise's disposal, offering it both higher quality potentials and much greater flexibility than internal groups could possibly achieve. By harnessing the creative potential of many suppliers in parallel, it shortens both "design" and "build" cycles—and lowers new product risks by creating prod-ucts closer to the time they are presented to customers. If one sup-plier in the system underperforms, the firm can quickly substitute another competitor's components or services. If new technologies suddenly appear, it is easier to switch among outside sources than to turn one's back on internal investments and psychological com-mitments. If there is a cyclical or temporary drop in demand, the coordinating firm is not saddled with all the idle capacity and in-ventory losses of the entire production chain. By avoiding invest-ments in vertical integration and by managing intellectual systems (as Apple, Genentech, and Nike have done), firms can move from a preoccupation with overseeing workers and machines to a posi-tion where they can leverage their true assets—intellect, knowledge bases, and human skills—much more substantially, simultaneously avoiding undesired costs and risks. These are major benefits of a knowledge or service based strategy with outsourcing.

NOT A BED OF ROSES

Extensive outsourcing is, of course, hardly risk-free. The main concerns are (1) a possible mismatch between the skills selected for emphasis today and those needed for dominance in the future; (2) the loss of skill bases that could prove to be essential in the future; (3) the loss of critical functional skills needed internally for simultaneous design projects or for cross-functional, joint-development teams with outside parties; (4) the potential loss of control over crucial suppliers; (5) the possibility that a supplier may master needed skills, then move into the marketplace, bypassing the buying company; (6) overdependence on a supplier who, for totally exogenous reasons, may become unreliable; and (7) conflicts between the buyer's and seller's priorities at disastrous moments. Other high-profile concerns are the implications of less control and greater volatility in a "smaller size" company and the loss of those "accidental" innovations that come from the random or synergistic interactions of people with different skills and outlooks encountering each other on a daily basis.

While all are important considerations, careful strategic management can deal with most of them.

• *Loss of critical skills* or ***developing the wrong skills*** for the future is perhaps the most often mentioned concern. Many U.S. companies have, unfortunately, outsourced manufacture of what, at the time, seemed to be only minor componentry, like semiconductor chips or a bicycle frame, and taught suppliers how to build them to needed quality standards. Later these companies found their suppliers were unable or unwilling to supply the company as required. Yet the buying company had lost the skills it needed to reenter manufacture and could not prevent its suppliers from either assisting competitors or entering downstream markets on their own. In some cases, by outsourcing a key component, the company can lose its own strategic flexibility to introduce new designs when it wishes—rather than when the vendor permits. For example, few manufacturers can afford to design a new laser printer engine to obtain a slight timing edge, rather than waiting for Canon (with its 84 percent market share in such engines) to move.[4] The activity share Canon has in the design function for this field—or Matsushita now has in drives for CD players—gives each company such an overwhelming competitive advantage that it can control other characteristics of its industry, limiting the strategic options of others.

In selecting which key service activities to emphasize, managers must take a very long view of competition. Those activities developed in depth must also have wide generality and long-term validity (as do Honda's engine design, small-scale assembly, and innovative distribution skills, or Merck's basic research capabilities). They are invariably rooted in the *basics* of a business and not in activities with a particular time or product reference. For a long time IBM prospered because of its strong "marketing-assembly-systems" orientation despite a shift from mechanical, to vacuum tube, to integrated circuit technologies. Intel survived its industry's shakeout because of its emphasis on the frontiers of integrated circuit design, its unique innovation system and organization, and its highly developed "maximum-freedom-with-maximum-measurement" culture. If Intel instead had maintained a product focus on its early strengths in computer memories, it probably would have failed.

Since the specific skills needed for long-term dominance cannot always be accurately forecast, most companies tend to build incrementally around a set of skills that have contributed to their early successes, as did 3M and P&G. Occasionally, a company like AT&T-Bell Labs, NEC, Citicorp, or DuPont may foresee a broader generality and consciously build up whole new sets of competencies, which let them proactively design the future, as these companies did (respectively) around fiber optics (AT&T), computers and communications (NEC), ATMs (Citicorp), and complex polymers (DuPont). More often skills or knowledge bases are built step by step around a core set of competencies needed to dominate a particular market need. Procter & Gamble (P&G) grew into today's $15 billion corporation largely based on two central sets of service-intellectual skills: (1) its R&D capabilities in five core technologies and (2) its superb marketing-distribution skills. P&G's development of special knowledge-based skills around fats, oils, skin chemistry, surfactants, and emulsifiers was a natural outgrowth of its early success in the bar and flaked soap fields. Later, as these technologies and P&G's marketing-distribution skills interacted, it saw new opportunities in mouth-washes and skin care. P&G's research depth in surfactant chemistry provided the central linkage among products as diverse as its soaps, detergents, and acne or bone disease drugs. Matching these two core strengths with clever and continuous upgrading of advanced high-production packaging equipment has given P&G opportunities to introduce myriad new products in related fields for decades. In turn its multiple products, constantly improved by incremental innovations, have given the company more shelf space (added market share) and greater sales and financial stability than many of its competitors.

• *Loss of cross-functional skills* is frequently cited as a potential problem. The interaction between skilled people in different functional activities often develops unexpected new insights or solutions. Companies fear outsourcing will make such cross-functional serendipity less likely. However, if the company consciously en-

FIGURE 3–1
Procter & Gamble: Technology Activity Profile,
Household Products

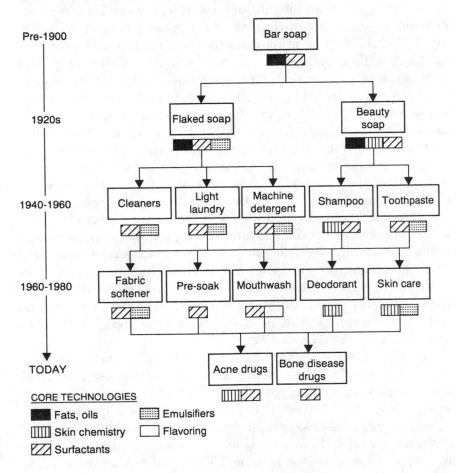

SOURCE: Original chart by Braxton Associates; reproduced with permission.

sures that its remaining employees interact constantly and closely with its outsourced experts, its employees' knowledge base can be higher than if production were in-house, and the creativity benefits can be even greater. For example, companies using TI's or Intel's design capabilities can literally have these suppliers' design experts—with their much greater technical expertise and access to support technologies—in house to co-design chips along with their own design teams during the development process. This puts the buyer's employees in contact with much more skilled integrated circuit people than the buyer could possibly have itself. It is well known that a high percentage—about two-thirds in the industries studied—of all innovation occurs at the customer–supplier interface.[5] Since by definition outsourcing increases the buyer's own presence (as the customer) in such interfaces, it can increase total innovation potentials (including the supplier's greater technical inputs) substantially if it manages the joint relationship properly.

More difficult, however, is the problem of forming fast-moving, closely integrated, cross-functional teams for innovation within the company. The fact that outsourced expertise is generally at a different location may make such close teamwork much more difficult. In entering a long-term outsourcing relationship that may involve future innovation, many managements specify that the outsourced partner's personnel can be "seconded" to the buying partner's premises when necessary for special development projects. They then ensure that close personal relationships are developed between their own and the partner's technical personnel at the bench and operating levels. Contractual prearrangements are usually necessary to have access to selected personnel from the outsourced partner when needed. But the buying company must also be close enough to its partner to evaluate or name the specific key people desired. Otherwise the agreement may be worthless when it is most needed. Much more detail on this interface appears in Chapter 12.

• *Loss of control over a supplier* is another major concern. A large buyer dealing with a small seller has fewer difficulties. Nevertheless, real problems can occur when the supplier's priorities do not match those of the buyer. The most successful outsourcers find it absolutely essential to have both close personal contact and rapport at the floor level and political "clout" and understanding at the top management level of the supplier. This is why Nike both has its "production expatriates" on the premises of its suppliers at all times and frequently brings the suppliers' top people to Beaverton, Oregon, to exchange details about future capabilities and prospects. When conflicts occur, the supplier's CEO and the relevant operating personnel can be pressured to break the log jam. Even then, serious difficulties can occur if the buyer does not have sufficient market power relative to the seller. Some buying companies go to the extreme of owning key pieces of equipment used by the seller to make the components they are purchasing. If priorities conflict too badly, the buyer can pull out its equipment and shut down the whole line of the seller. These buyers say that such arrangements "ensure we can get the seller's attention when we need it."

As a component of this problem, some suppliers, after building up their expertise with the support of the buyer, will use that expertise to bypass the buyer directly into the marketplace—as Giant Manufacturing of Taiwan, a supplier of bicycle frames, did to Schwinn. Alternately, the seller may learn as much as possible from the buyer and its engineering groups and then attempt to resell this knowledge in different product configurations to the buyer's competitors. Careful definition and limitation of such relationships has now become critical in any but the most routine outsourcing arrangements, and companies that have outsourced extensively have generally found satisfactory legal and operational ways to deal with the problem.

Bypassing becomes most complex when the supplier is a division within a diversified company seeking new markets itself. Frequently, the selling division will enter a partnership relationship in good faith as a supplier, only to have a sister division later decide to exploit the broader market opportunities the supplying division has helped to open—and try to use the supplying division's capabilities to facilitate its own entry. When such strategic conflicts occur, the buyer can both lose its supplier and be in the incongruous position of having helped to start its own competition. Similarly, a producer selling downstream to a distribution partner may find that, after opening the marketplace with its product, the distribution partner seeks out new sources in order to whipsaw its original supplier for better prices, features, or services.

Such problems are very real. However, in many situations there are strategic and management options for overcoming them. This is particularly true when the buyer is large and suppliers are fragmented. Outsourcing and joint venturing have been common practices in most mass production, resource exploration, real estate–construction, and finance–insurance businesses for years. Models from these industries can be most useful to others. With forethought, key relationships can usually be managed if executives analyze their own company's relative power positions— and monitor their suppliers' strategic capabilities and potential future moves—in detail and take adequate precautions. The Japanese have clearly prospered by using long-term outsourcing strategies and have developed management techniques appropriate to the purpose. Chapter 12 will develop specific useful management approaches in more depth, but the strategic point is clear. Outsourcing can work well in the right circumstances, if it is properly managed.

The Boston Consulting Group, which has studied more than one hundred major companies doing extensive outsourcing, has concluded that most Western companies outsource primarily to save on overheads or short-term costs.[6] The result is a piecemeal approach that "results in patches of overcapacity scattered at random throughout the company's operation. . . . [These companies] end up with large numbers of subcontractors, which are more costly to manage than in-house operations that are individually less efficient."[7] Worse still, the buying companies, by not providing adequate monitoring and technical backup, often lose their grip on key competencies they may need in the future. The Japanese, by contrast, outsource primarily to improve the efficiency and quality of their own processes, focus on a very few sources, build close interdependent relationships, and hold on tightly to high value-added activities that are crucial to quality. For systems they contract out, Japanese companies do not let go altogether; they usually advise closely on manufacturing and cooperate in process and product R&D on supplier premises.

These practices suggest a strong caution. This kind of outsourcing must be approached not as a short-term fix but as a major component in a long-term strategy. And new internal structures— notably, vastly improved logistics systems, information systems that extend in depth into suppliers' operations, sophisticated technical and strategic monitoring capabilities, and improved top-level expertise to craft and manage contractual relationships in detail— become crucial. Combined with the kind of practices described in Chapter 12, these moves can make systematic outsourcing a powerful extension in the use of a knowledge or service based focus for strategic advantage.

DIVERSIFYING FROM A SERVICE COMPETENCY

As companies develop sufficient depth in a specific knowledge or service activity to dominate a segment of their industry, they often find they can sell that capability to new customers in ways that increase profits, absorb costs, or support diversification. Thus companies like TRW, AMR (American Airlines), and Lockheed often make more profits from selling information services than they do off their "main product" lines.

■ TRW has an information base for making credit checks (which contains 145 million records usable for "credentialing" credit references) springing off TRW's computer bases for other needs. This enormous base, often known as "Big Mother," is now adding real estate, title search, medical, demographic, and other service capabilities that make TRW a formidable participant in each of several other "industries." So powerful are its databases that it has recently been the target of some landmark lawsuits that may redefine privacy rights through court actions.

In a different vein, TRW's Customer Service Division alone employs more than 2,400 professionals providing independent maintenance, repair, and support services for information-handling and computer systems customers. Although not a major computer producer, TRW has used its depth in computing systems to design unique software/hardware units (SLEUTH) to diagnose system problems quickly and accurately, SLATE software to update field information constantly, and an advanced artificial intelligence (AI) system used with an "inference engine" to guide field service people through their test procedures. These allow TRW to effectively service a wide variety of customers with varied computer-communications systems. Like many others, TRW has diversified into new industries without departing from its central skill base.

Chapter 6 will present numerous examples of how other manufacturing companies (like 3M and Matsushita) have utilized depth in their selected core competencies to diversify successfully into extremely broad product lines. These often have distribution channels, customers, and production processes very different from the company's original products, and are linked only by the centrality of a few selected core service activities developed in depth. Within the service sector, such examples are very common. For example:

■ *In the transportation and lodging industries,* AMR, Inc., the holding company of American Airlines, has recently created a sister company known as AMR Information Services (AMRIS). AMRIS is developing a coordinated reservation system for travel, hotel, and car rental companies, slated to go on line in the first quarter of 1992. None of the hotel or car rental companies involved could have undertaken such an ambitious project alone. Costing its partners some $125 million, AMRIS's CONFIRM reservation system will link Marriott Corporation, Hilton Hotels, and Budget Rent-a-Car initially. Later it may add other partners and sell entirely new data services which derive from the databases it accumulates about the activities of its partners and their customers. CONFIRM is intended to run on every airline's computerized reservation system, giving virtually all travel agents access to bookings through it. Through this vehicle, AMR can potentially enter a host of new service fields using the distinct competencies it initially developed through SABRE.

■ *In the professional services realm,* ADP Services, Inc., has developed a great depth in flexible software for handling payroll systems. Its processes became so low-cost that it soon processed payrolls for more than 10 percent of its potential client base in the regions it served. From this initial service, ADP expanded into routine bank accounting and tax filings for its customers and their employees. Next ADP moved into ERISA reporting, then into personnel records and further cost accounting and financial services, and finally into personalized communications like printing slogans, messages, or logos on employee checks or distributing information with employees' paychecks. While lowering its customers' costs substantially, ADP eventually created a totally new set of value-added services. By analyzing and aggregating the information in its files, without violating any confidences, ADP could later create detailed regional or industrywide analyses of cost structures, compensation plans, and other important cost parameters. Thus, ADP's customers (1) had access to expertise they could not afford in-house, (2) lowered their overhead costs thanks to ADP's substantial economies of scale, and (3) had an objective check on their own costs for various services they decided not to outsource. ADP became both a supplier for its customers and a potential competitor for their other poorly performing departments.

REDEFINING THE BASIC NATURE OF THE COMPANY

More powerful than these diversifications, however, is the fact that *once a core service capability is developed in depth, it often redefines the very nature of the company's business* in its original industry. Some examples from the financial service sector will make the point most dramatically:

■ In the early 1980s, after the very successful automation of its back-office functions, Bankers Trust found that it could handle many wholesale banking operations with a sophistication much greater than most of its competitors. As Bankers Trust increased its wholesale volume, it began to sell off its credit card operations and its New York retail and upstate commercial banking operations. It scrapped its earlier hierarchical organization and formed a partnership. Finally, it mutated almost totally toward wholesale banking and trust operations. The core of its business became proprietary trading in bulk capital market activities. Bankers Trust became so sophisticated that it could invent complex and lucrative products—like global master trusts for its large clients—which gave it a temporary edge over competition. Within the wholesale markets it understood so well, it could also take higher risks with newer, more complex instruments, making much higher margins. Once new instruments became more liquid or even turned into a generally accepted commodity (for example "swaps"), Bankers Trust changed its approach to a more standard trading format. In efficiency terms its automation enabled Bankers Trust to cut its staff by two-thirds, while increasing its volume three times. But more importantly, Bankers Trust had redefined its total business concept.

■ Similarly, Bear Stearns developed its back-office capabilities to obtain very low processing costs for bond clearances. Although in 1990 Bear Stearns did only 4.5 percent of the volume in its bond markets, it cleared accounts for one thousand outside institutional and retail clients. By capturing the information from these trades, Bear Stearns had a much better sense of the market than its competitors and had the knowledge to lend to very sophisticated investors interested in buying or selling debt on margin accounts. By 1990, Bear Stearns handled some 13 percent—three times its bond market share—of the market's margin debt, and gained very high profit margins on the business. In early 1992, despite the recession, it posted record profits in its field.[8]

■ Banc One, a Columbus, Ohio, super-regional bank, has used its sophisticated back-office processing capabilities to become a major service center for nonbanks. As its relationships with these groups grew, Banc One became increasingly a producer of bank services for distribution by nonbanks. Starting with BankAmericard, Banc One began back-office processing of credit cards. It soon added M Corporation, Southwest, and others. It quickly found its processing profits to be greater than the profits it made on issuing its own credit cards. Buoyed by its experiences, Banc One began providing processing services for Merrill Lynch's cash management accounts (CMAs) in 1977. By the late 1980s it had more than a million CMA customers and processed 80 percent of all CMA automatic NOW accounts.

Banc One then developed special software to integrate check- and card-handling activities. It took over credit card processing for a number of credit unions, many of which were too small to set up efficient systems on their own. From this base Banc One expanded into affinity cards for electronic shopping (the CompU-Card). It then took on Northwest and Holiday Inn, and provided the American Association of Retired Persons' national credit union with CD processing and access to automatic teller machines. Now Banc One has created a dedicated center for such activities, which can develop major one-stop M2-level programs (application development and processing software) quickly for new clients and can connect these into the large distribution systems of such clients, when they are available.[9]

In other branches of the financial services industry, Morgan Stanley used the common information-processing infrastructure it had developed to handle transactions from trades-through-clearing to sell services to other financial houses. Now it uses its core system to clear others' trades. With its vastly improved information base derived from these more extensive trading activities, Morgan Stanley has a better sense of the market, has cut back its client numbers substantially (to about two hundred) and focuses on the more complex and profitable aspects of their needs. Salomon Brothers used its extensive program-trading capabilities to invade the Japanese market. Investing $400 million, it was able to build its arbitrage penetration in 1990–91 to about 20 percent of all Japanese paper traded at auctions, although it held a much smaller (though respectable) 2 percent share of stock market turnover.

Such examples suggest how, by developing its service technologies strategically, a company can first enhance its own internal efficiencies; then, by selling its new capabilities to external parties, it can leverage its investments to obtain even greater competitive advantage. Selling its services externally, of course, lowers costs by absorbing development and spreading overhead costs over a broader base. However, the company obtains even greater competitive advantage by having more information (derived from its customers' transactions) about the total marketplace. This information can be used to develop either more highly specialized niches where margins are higher or totally new activities where its broader information base provides it with a unique competitive advantage. For example:

■ Linking databases to downstream services for manufacturers has been one such opportunity. Mead (with LEXIS and NEXIS) and Lockheed (with Dialog Information Services) have found it natural to connect their electronic technologies to printers and to move downstream into publishing from their extensive databases. Similarly, Chase Bank leases customers access to its own extensive Information Intelligence System, with hourly and daily updates of business information from every part of the world. This system, connected to a CD ROM, provides the customer with updated information on economic events, new economic data, individual company activities, and so on, from most major countries in the world.

Another example has implications at several levels of the production–distribution process:

■ SuperValu, a $9.4 billion distributor to independent grocers, initially developed an inventory and cost control system to lower its own costs and to provide better service for customers. But SuperValu also saw the advantages of segmenting and integrating the data from its ever increasing volumes to provide its customers with data and services they otherwise could not obtain.

SuperValu's extensive development of inventory control and product handling technologies has allowed it to manage thousands of product lines and to move its control of distribution and product functions upstream, downstream, and geographically. SuperValu's growth and expertise helped eliminate many of the specialized and regional wholesalers that once dominated its industry. It also helped redefine U.S. grocery wholesaling in a way that has consolidated the function from 1,400 to 300 participants in the last ten years. SuperValu uses its purchasing power and electronic systems to guide its suppliers more effectively and to provide the widest possible range of packaged foods at lowest prices. It also offers extensive host-support services for the EPOS systems of its supermarket customers, permitting them to manage their operations better through instant access to price files, shelf tag printing, and detailed reports about their products' turnover, gross profits, category profits, and so on. No single food product manufacturer could compete with these services. This is even more true for farmers, for whom SuperValu handles the complex functions of coordinating field produce contracting and transportation, fresh meat delivery and marking, and in-store shelf price verification.

Through its Plan Mark and Studio 7 programs, SuperValu also performs architectural design and manages construction projects for its customers. So effective is SuperValu in providing a full variety of products and services that several major supermarket chains now buy from SuperValu in order to obtain its system economies.

OUTSOURCING IN FINANCIAL SERVICES

Financial service firms—like the many manufacturing and mixed service entities described previously—provide especially interesting examples of the process of investigating the value chain with a view toward profitable outsourcing. In the best study of this phenomenon to date, T. Steiner and D. Teixeira have found the distribution of noninterest expenses in banks to be as indicated in Figure 3–2.

With almost three-quarters of all noninterest expenses lying in marketing and distribution, credit approval, and funds movement, it is not surprising that outside suppliers have found ways to achieve economies of scale in the technologies underpinning these activities and to sell their services to many customer institutions. Figure 3–3 illustrates the types and names of vendors who have moved into these openings.

Much of the outsourcing is in data network activities. But this is only a portion of the massive data network outsourcing going on throughout American industry. Input, a computer research firm in Mountain View, California, has estimated such activities to

FIGURE 3–2
Distribution of Banks' Noninterest Expenses

	Marketing and distribution	Credit approval	Funds movement (debits and credits)	Customer service	Collections	Investments and trading	MIS
Major elements	Calling officers	Credit officers	Check processing	800 numbers	Workout	Trading	Accounting
	Direct mail	Scoring models	Operations	Corre- spondence	Retail collections	Foreign exchange	Manage- ment reporting
	Branches	Databases	Cash management	Branches	Legal	Treasury	
			Branches (tellers)	Calling officers			
			Networks	Statements			
Percentage of non- interest expense	(19%)	5	(49)	13	8	3	3

Source: T. Steiner and D. Teixeira, *Technology in Banking* (Homewood, IL: Dow Jones–Irwin, 1990), p. 43.

be approximately $7.2 billion in 1990, growing to more than $15 billion by the mid-1990s. Others estimate even higher activity levels. Of this, 36 percent is in facilities management, 24 percent in systems integration, 30 percent in contract programming, and 10 percent in other services.[10]

A large number of major players have become suppliers of total networks, network management, and partial networks. Such players include IBM, Arthur Andersen, AT&T, EDS, MCI, DEC, and ITM. These suppliers have even greater depth and more experience in network development and management than their largest customers—which, in addition to banks, include sophisticated product companies like Chevron, General Motors, Exxon, Ford, American Standard, and Kodak. Even these companies have found that they can profit by looking outside to find "best-in-world" suppliers for their highly technical information and logistics system needs.

Sometimes by checking outside sources, however, companies discover the uniqueness and power of their own capabilities.

■ One of the largest PTTs recently approached Citibank with a proposal to run its whole global network. Citibank soon found the PTT did not have the skills to handle its 36,000 PCs and 830

FIGURE 3–3
Functional Disaggregation:
Outside Suppliers for Crucial Services

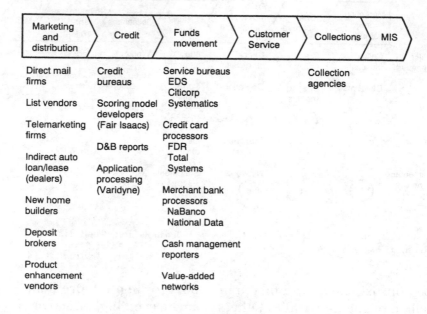

Marketing and distribution	Credit	Funds movement	Customer Service	Collections	MIS
Direct mail firms	Credit bureaus	Service bureaus EDS Citicorp		Collection agencies	
List vendors	Scoring model developers	Systematics			
Telemarketing firms	(Fair Isaacs)	Credit card processors			
	D&B reports	FDR			
Indirect auto loan/lease (dealers)	Application processing (Varidyne)	Total Systems			
New home builders		Merchant bank processors NaBanco National Data			
Deposit brokers		Cash management reporters			
Product enhancement vendors		Value-added networks			

SOURCE: T. Steiner and D. Teixeira, *Technology in Banking* (Homewood, IL: Dow Jones–Irwin, 1990), p. 56.

mainframes connected by networks to ninety-four countries. While wanting to unburden itself of the problems of dealing with innumerable national communications companies, Citibank saw no evidence that the outside supplier could handle its system needs with the reliability Citibank enjoyed in its remaining internal network. Until some supplier—maybe eventually a consortium of telecommunications companies—can demonstrate that capability, Citibank will probably keep its network in-house.[11]

Activities other than data processing have also been widely outsourced in financial services. Major banks, like Bankers Trust, frequently outsource their international distribution to others, especially in the early stages of internationalization. Antonson Securities of Sweden even found that setting its sales people up as individual entrepreneurs allowed it to make 3-to-1 gains in its sales volume-to-cost ratios. Many large banks, of course, outsource their cleaning and maintenance activities, their plant security operations, their food services, marketing, and advertising. Few would deny that such outsourcing lets bank managers focus on what they do best and thus leverages the bank's critical intellectual assets. Other examples abound.

Interestingly, the entire mortgage-processing activity has mutated into a highly dispersed—heavily outsourced—industry. In many mortgage transactions the originator, the broker, the credit reviewer, the banker, the syndicators, the secondary market holders, the processors, the escrow groups, the title searchers, and the insurers can all be different parties. A similar set of multiple parties handles credit card transactions—through the cycle from sale, to transaction capture, processing, authorization, payment, collection, clearance, and customer service. The bank is now only one small element in the total value chain. Specialists fill all the other niches.

UNBUNDLING OVERHEADS

All industries have found that overhead activities can provide an especially potent case for service outsourcing. Overheads are merely services the company has chosen to produce internally. Instead of blindly building self-owned, integrated complexes and internally producing all overhead support services, companies are much more effective if they carefully benchmark, reengineer, and seriously consider outsourcing those where they are not best in world. When this isn't done, corporate staff or overhead activities slowly and relentlessly tend to build into major bureaucracies. Many companies consider activities like product design, planning, accounting, legal, personnel, MIS, or maintenance functions to be integral parts of their businesses. Yet these are little different in kind from any component, part, or subsystem the company might choose to outsource. If outside producers can do the job better, the company is giving up competitive edge by producing the service internally, unless the function is critical to its strategy.

Managers too often spend inordinate amounts of time, psychic energy, and resources dealing with "overhead support" functions and other bureaucracies, most of which decrease their attention to the company's truly crucial areas of strategic focus. When they selectively outsource these and other noncritical value chain activities to independent specialists, managers can not only focus their own talents more on value-adding activities but generally can expand the range of crucial activities they oversee. As the firm's internal personnel numbers decrease, there are fewer levels of management, faster response times, and more opportunities for personal management of the remaining employees. And it becomes easier to form the highly motivated and focused cross-functional teams that best provide low-cost, innovative responses to customer needs. With the time delays and frictions of bureaucracies greatly decreased, a company can substantially leverage its most critical resources—intellectual and managerial talent. The next two chapters will show how some remarkable new organizations augment the flattening, restructuring, and disaggregation new technologies now allow.

STRATEGIC OUTSOURCING

When implementing an overhead and operations unbundling strategy like those illustrated here, a company will undoubtedly focus first on what are considered the company's less critical activities. Over time, however, by creating new strategic partnerships the company may find it extremely profitable to outsource much more critical activities to *noncompeting* companies that can perform them more effectively. Whenever this is done, of course, the contracting company must rigorously control carefully selected, strategically critical interrelationships between its suppliers and its customers. For example:

■ Seagate Technology, one of the world's leading manufacturers of hard disk drives for personal computers, concluded that one of the best ways to stay ahead of its Japanese rivals was (1) to guarantee the delivery dates of its products and (2) to pay for the cost of delivering them to its customers. At the same time, it decided to switch its manufacturing to Singapore. To handle its inbound logistics, Seagate contracted for space on Flying Tigers four times a week from Singapore. For outbound logistics from its one U.S. distribution center in California, Seagate partnered with Skyway Freight Systems as the sole vendor serving the entire United States for Seagate's new "guaranteed four-day delivery, freight paid program." Neither Flying Tigers nor Skyway, of course, had any interest or capability in disk drives *per se*. Seagate's payments to Skyway on a per unit basis amounted to less than 1 percent of the total cost of each disk drive for this strategically critical service. Yet in the first six months—during which thousands of shipments were handled—

the program experienced only three customer service "incidents," all of which stemmed from a misunderstanding of what "four business days" really meant.[12]

■ Commodore Business Machines recently outsourced its customer service response activities to Federal Express. Said James Reeder, Commodore's VP of Customer Satisfaction, "At that time we didn't have the greatest reputation for customer service and satisfaction." But this was FedEx's specialty, handling millions of packages weekly and more than 300,000 calls for service each day. Commodore arranged for FedEx, which was trying to leverage its communications infrastructure, to handle the entire telephone customer service operation out of FedEx's hub in Memphis. Commodore provided the technical training needed for a special team of operators, called Commodore Express, operating in FedEx's facility twenty-four hours a day, seven days a week. The team handles 88 percent of all customer problems over the phone, eliminating virtually all the unnecessary and expensive returns to distributor outlets. If a machine is defective or in need of repair, FedEx's delivery service will pick it up and leave a replacement or a loaner at no charge. FedEx has a return and repair operation that fixes the repairable hardware, eliminating Commodore from this portion of the service loop. Commodore Express does everything from answering general inquiries to arranging bulk shipments of sales literature and telemarketing. Handling 16,000 calls a month, Commodore Express tripled Commodore's positive responses in its customer surveys in its first year of operations.

Partnerships do not work well when the partners' interests are not quite congruent. In early 1991 the ACE consortium, led by Compaq, Digital Equipment, and MIPS, sought to create the technological standard for the next generation of PCs. However, in arriving at the standards, the consortium's members forced so many compromises that ACE may now be at the point of irrelevance. Various ACE members have refused to abandon solutions in which they had large previous investments. They ended up agreeing to a standard that failed to guarantee that all machines built to its specs would (1) run on the same software as all other ACE machines or (2) allow similar upwardly compatible hardware changes from all of its eighty-plus members. As *The Economist* said, "This amounts to no standard at all."[13]

Still, strategic partnering arrangements are increasingly common. They are especially useful for newly forming or high-growth companies that cannot afford the investment in all aspects of their value chains and do not threaten their larger partner's existence. To expand on a briefly noted example:

■ Polaroid Corporation, during its early growth stages, concentrated its own limited talents and investment resources on developing, producing, and improving the "peel-apart" film processing package that was the core of its instant photography system. For years, it outsourced seemingly critical aspects of its business.[14] Kodak produced virtually all of the film media used by Polaroid until it began its revolutionary SX70 instant-color-film product, which had to be made in a single integrated process and became the core of Polaroid's business. Polaroid also outsourced its cameras to Timex, and it developed its electronics components with Texas Instruments during the critical early stages when it lacked mass production skills and was first introducing electronic capabilities to its cameras.

During this period, Polaroid maintained a very flat corporate organization, operating with no formal organization chart and a number of fast-moving "teams" assembled to solve specific problems. Yet Polaroid kept absolute strategic control over the core "instant development" technologies of its product line and over the crucial integrating interfaces between the products produced by its suppliers and the marketplace. Only when the SX70 system came along and outsourced components and systems became so integral to its core technologies that they could not be separately produced did Polaroid begin production internally. Similarly today, many major producers of magnetic and thin film memory buy their substrate materials from outsiders and concentrate on the incredible complexities of developing, producing, and maintaining quality on their rapidly advancing core technologies of coatings and surfaces.

Similar approaches have helped build a number of world-class companies, including Honda, Sharp, Casio, and Sony among major Japanese producers. Today, realizing that no one of them is "best in world" in all needed skill areas, Sony, Motorola, and Hitachi—all very large companies—are entering a partnering arrangement to develop "multimedia systems" for that most complex and challenging new marketplace.

HOW TO APPROACH SERVICE BASED
STRATEGIC ANALYSES

All of the above examples suggest the advantages of undertaking a carefully structured analysis of one's value chain as a set of service activities, then seeking out the best-in-world potential providers of those services, whether they be internal or external. But, in a practical sense, how does one approach the analysis process? For multidivisional companies, the best way to start is by comparing the cost and effectiveness of the same activity between various divisions, using the best comparative output measures available. This usually can highlight some stark differences. Next one can exchange information and benchmark specific activities against a few high-performing noncompetitors, who are friendly and feel they can benefit from such an exchange. These steps will develop some initial techniques and useful information.

Since it is admittedly difficult to obtain objective numbers to compare the costs and outputs of service units, companies often seek out other companies believed to have "best in world processes" for handling a specific function—as Xerox did in investigating L.L. Bean's inventory control and customer response systems. Having done their homework in earlier analytical phases, they have some information to exchange. At a minimum, they can evaluate whether their internal processes are meeting their customers' needs—or their own needs—with greatest efficiency. Most potential benchmark companies would rather share process information than specific numerical cost and output measures they fear might slip inadvertently into competitors' hands. This is the key to IBM's "Best in Breed" process comparison studies. Many outsiders actually welcome the informed questioning and exchanges with visiting teams as a way to evaluate and hone their own processes further.

Finally, potential outside suppliers of services are much more willing to provide numerical price and performance data that can be used directly for benchmarking. Using these data, the often abused "internal customers" for the company's own services can be asked to evaluate internal service providers' cost and output versus the quotes from outside suppliers. This tends to lend another degree of objectivity to evaluations. Even a series of relative performance rankings of different activities within a service function (versus those of outsiders) can help point up areas for improvement. Numerous scaling techniques exist to calibrate relative evaluations when objective numbers are impossible to obtain. Many companies join groups that allow an outside consultant to analyze each company's processes and compare their effectiveness and costs, reporting results (with company names removed) back to the group. For example:

■ Mr. Martin Stein, Vice Chairman of Bank of America, said, "We have worked a lot with The Royal Bank of Canada on benchmarking because our sizes and philosophies are comparable and we're not direct competitors. We have had some particularly good exchanges with them on processes. We can also benchmark through the Research Board against an array of companies reported in a disguised fashion. What these do is highlight anomalies. You can't get down to a unit cost or the systems task level. But if a comparable company has twenty-two people and I have sixty, we can sit down and try to figure out what's going on. It's not as precise as I would like, but it will highlight things. . . . We have also hired Booz Allen to look at the overall effectiveness of our investments in technology. This is based on a comparison with other institutions' performance. The combination is very helpful in calibrating us."

Independent service sources are much less commonly used directly for benchmarking, although for specific make or buy decisions about data system outsourcing many companies explicitly do so. For example:

■ Mr. d'Allesio, formerly Staff Vice President and Chief Information Officer of McKesson, said, "We don't do much [software or data system outsourcing]. Occasionally, we'll do it where they've got some specific expertise we need, and it is too expensive to create internally. The trick is to manage the process thoroughly. We basically manage them the same way we manage internal people. They become part of the team. We're looking to them for technology. But we've got to bring the applications understanding to the project, control the interface to our client, and integrate it to our system. You've got to look at and compare the total costs of such outsourcing, not just the programming costs."

The ultimate test, of course, is to have the units using internal services pay for them on a direct purchase basis, while being free to buy any service outside, as they can parts or components in product decentralized companies. A combination of internal and external benchmarking, "best in breed" process analyses, and some elements of these "gestalt" methodologies—which essentially create internal "markets" for services—seems to offer the most thorough, yet acceptable, method of analyzing and testing one's own service capabilities. Chapters 10 and 11 develop in depth these and other customer-based techniques for benchmarking and appraising service performance.

EXPLICITLY INCLUDE TRANSACTION COSTS

As the McKesson example points out, any analyses of the company's internal capabilities in service activities, or the relative positioning of these against the best of all external providers, must include the "transaction costs" of managing *both* the outsourced operation and its internal counterparts. One must be especially careful not to assume that internal service activities lack important transaction costs. Many companies outsource individual activities largely because internal sources have become so bureaucratized, conservative, difficult to move, and time-consuming for management that outsourcing becomes almost an obvious solution.

A classic example is a large New York bank with extensive worldwide operations. It wondered why its Federal Express costs were soaring and found that it took two days more to get a letter or package delivered from the third floor of its building to the fortieth floor by its internal mail than it did to send the material FedEx. Similarly, both GM and Ford have found that their reliance on in-house suppliers was one of their main barriers to competitive costs, investment control, and quality achievement. For them—as for many others—noninnovative, ineffective, captive in-house suppliers had proved one of the major plagues of vertical integration. Fortunately, services technologies—principally new information, communication, logistics, and materials-handling systems—now offer opportunities to break away from these constraints into more flexible, competitive, disaggregated structures.

The mere process of going through a service-based strategic analysis can have many side benefits. At a minimum, each activity reviewed feels under increased pressure to assess and improve its own productivity and to evaluate the outputs it is creating. This alone often leads to internal innovations. When threatened with outsourcing of its data centers, UTC decided to consolidate its fourteen mainframe installations to four, and Avon merged six centers, with multiple millions in annual savings. Metropolitan Life, startled by the benchmark data it generated, decided to try to meet the outsourcers' costs and capture benefits internally.[15] The internal and external analyses used for benchmarking also help the company develop more useful and objective performance measures for these functions on an ongoing basis and help to bring their costs under control, even if outsourcing does not take place.

FINDING THE TRUE BASES OF COMPETITIVE ADVANTAGE

At least as importantly, the company begins to look in a sophisticated fashion at the true bases—and not just the results—of its competitive posture and future sources of competitive advantage. Higher profits and growth are merely results of performing some activities better than everyone else. Service based analyses force strategists to ask which internal activities are really up to world-class standards and which are not. They are forced to regard competition not just as their traditional "product competitors" but as all those who can produce similar elements of service anywhere in the world. Such analyses also quickly reveal where direct competitors' true strengths and weaknesses lie. Too often, managers are allowed to think about their division's or company's relative positions in terms that are not meaningful on a longer-term basis—i.e., "We have the highest-performance computer in the marketplace," "We have the lowest-cost manufacturing facilities," or "We have the best-known brand in the industry."

None of these descriptions explains *why* the company has achieved these positions or *why* it is likely to continue to be ahead in the future. As mentioned earlier, the author has often asked top executive groups, "How do you *know* you are best in the world at that activity? What *makes* you best in world? By what measures do you know you can *continue to exceed* competitors' performances?" Repeatedly, there is no serious analysis behind their responses. Rarely have multidivisional companies even attempted to benchmark their service activities seriously against the "best in class" within their own companies. This should be a routine starting point. But it needs to be extended systematically to evaluate outstanding noncompetitors' capabilities as well as professional outside sources of the activity as a service. Most companies can do this to their advantage.

CONCLUSIONS

Old "industry analysis" tools no longer fit the realities of the many diverse forms of competition service technologies now allow. Instead of looking at product-focused strategies, managers need to look beyond these to those knowledge and service based activities which actually produce competitive advantage for them—versus their direct or functional competitors. To do this properly, they need to break down their company's value chain and staff support activities into those service activities that actually generate the company's value-added. By defining each value chain or staff activity as a "service" that could potentially be outsourced to a wide variety of suppliers, and by making appropriate internal and external benchmarking comparisons, managers can obtain a much better sense of their company's true competitive capabilities. Because of improved service technologies, they may now profitably outsource many activities that were long considered integral to operations. Whenever the company insources an activity where it is not "best in world"—unless there are compelling synergies or strategic considerations in continuing the activity—it gives up competitive edge.

Through various morphologies, managers can determine strategically which activities are most crucial to the company's future and which it can (and must) dominate in order to be successful in the future. If they focus their resources and talents on these high-leverage activities—and upgrade or selectively outsource the rest to achieve world competitive levels—they can avoid management and resource diversions that actively decrease their competitiveness. By linking their core competencies and remaining support activities as directly as possible to customers, they can achieve much greater value-added and profitability with their limited resources. By developing a few strategically selected core service activities in greater depth than any competitor, carefully surrounding these with strong barriers to entry, and constructing an effective strategic "block" between suppliers of outsourced services (or products) and the downstream marketplace, a company can create a genuinely focused strategy and the most effective possible maintainable competitive edge.

PART 2
Knowledge Based Services Revolutionize Organizational Strategies

CHAPTER 4
Revolutionizing
Organizational Strategies

The preceding chapters have shown how knowledge based service systems and technologies have radically reordered the power relationships, competitive environments, and leverageable opportunities in most industries—whether in services or in manufacturing. Such major restructurings have inevitably led to revolutionary changes in organizational forms within companies. The adage that "organization follows strategy" has never been more true.[1] One should also recall the second adage, "structure follows technology."[2] We should add to this a third: "service-based strategies focus on customers." When consistently implemented against these principles, services technologies have obliterated long-held precepts about the management process—along with many of its more ancient artifacts. They now present a host of entirely new strategic, organizational, and control system options for achieving competitive advantage. What are some of the more important insights from our research?

- Contrary to much popular dogma, well-managed service technologies can simultaneously deliver *both lowest-cost outputs* and *maximum personalization and customization* for customers.
- In accomplishing this, enterprises generally obtain strategic

The research for this chapter was first published in J. B. Quinn and P. C. Paquette, "Technology in Services: Creating Organizational Revolutions," *Sloan Management Review,* Winter 1990.

advantage not through traditional economies of scale, but by *focusing on the smallest activity or cost units* that can be efficiently replicated—and then *cloning and mixing* these units across as wide a geographical and applications range as possible.

- Instead of the dehumanization often experienced in other realms, properly managed service automation usually *increases the independence* and value of lower-level jobs and *empowers contact people* to be much more responsive to customer needs.
- Such systems, when well implemented, frequently drive organizations toward entirely new conceptual configurations. These may assume *"infinitely flat," "spider's web," "shamrock,"* or *"inverted pyramid"* characteristics in order to deliver their particular outputs most effectively and flexibly to a widely distributed customer base. Which form is most effective depends on the company's strategy.
- When properly conceptualized, these organizations can *eliminate or disintermediate costly organizational bureaucracies*, dramatically *lower overhead costs, support rapid execution of strategies*, and substantially *increase the learning rate of employees and their responsiveness to customers*.

Creative implementation of technology in leading-edge companies has converted these concepts from theoreticians' fantasies into realistic strategic options that virtually any company can consider. For this to occur, one needs to conceptualize the organization in new terms. In many knowledge or service based strategies, the person in contact with the customer—the "contact person" or "point person"—becomes perhaps the most important person in the organization. Most services are produced, in large part, at the instant that they are delivered or consumed. Consequently, they must be right the first time through, every time. Although significant value-added may be created anywhere in the service chain—from the back room to the contact point—if the point person does not perform his or her job correctly, the benefits of all the company's preceding investments in research, systems development, product conception, marketing positioning, advertising, and image-building will be obliterated.[3]

The best performers in this contact role need three things: the personal competence, the organizational empowerment, and the psychological motivation to deliver the service in its most effective form during the brief interval they are in contact with clients.

Achieving this conjunction at the contact point should be an overarching goal for almost all service strategies. Optimizing the contact person's capacity to deliver a complex product, while minimizing systems costs, is then the critical challenge. Unfortunately, implementing this concept calls for a mixture of technological, multifunctional, and organization skills that few individual executives span. This is why transitions to more effective service-based strategies are often so painful. They involve both the scrapping of many traditional management concepts and the creation of much unwanted pressure for existing managerial personnel, particularly middle managers. The key to unlocking these new organization capabilities usually lies in imaginative integration of the company's knowledge-producing (intellectual), electronic (information and control), and personal interaction (communications and authority) systems. How does one approach this integration strategically?

OBTAINING BOTH CUSTOMIZATION
AND LOWEST COST

At the outset, we need to set aside some widely accepted strategic dogmas about "generic strategies." These pose an inherent—and in the case of services, false—conflict between obtaining "lowest cost" and offering highest "differentiation" (through flexibility and customization) within the same strategy.[4] Many well-run service companies *do both;* they optimize flexibility at the customer contact point *and* maximize the "production efficiencies" that flow from repeatability, experience curve effects, and integrated cost and quality control. They accomplish this by (1) seeking the smallest possible core unit at which activity or output can be "replicated" or repeated, (2) developing micro measures to manage processes and functions at this level, and (3) mixing these micro units in a variety of combinations to match localized or individual customers' needs. This approach has been the touchstone of some of the most successful service strategies. With properly implemented systems, many outstanding service companies—including Bankers Trust, AT&T, Toys "R" Us, Domino's Pizza, ServiceMaster, Wal-Mart, Federal Express, American Express, McKesson, and American Airlines—have achieved both maximum flexibility and lowest cost in their market segments.

What do these "smallest replicable units" look like? "Replicable" simply means "repeatable with a small variation" in response to local conditions. The nature of the particular unit that will be most useful, of course, varies by industry and by strategy.

■ For Mary Kay Cosmetics or Tupperware, the elements of a sales presentation provide such repeatable core units. For accountants, audit check procedures, inventory control processes, unique problem solutions, or tax preparation subroutines may be critical. For hotels, it is information about customers' preferences, past service selections, special personal needs, travel patterns, and so on. For lawyers, prepackaged documents, paragraphs, phrases, court opinions, or case briefings may be the leverageable units. In financial services, elements of individual "transactions" (buy/sell information about names, units traded, prices, times received and transacted, customer codes, opposite parties' positions, and their relationships to total market movements) are the core units. For information retrieval businesses, it is the "category" or "key word"; for communications, it is the "packet" or even the "bit"; and so on.

SEEKING THE SMALLEST REPLICABLE UNIT

Early in the life cycle of many service industries, the smallest truly replicable unit seemed to be an individual office, store, or franchise location. Later, as volume increased, it often became possible for the headquarters to develop and replicate greater efficiencies within locations by managing and measuring critical performance variables at individual departmental, sales counter, activity, or stock-keeping unit (SKU) levels.[5] Then the successful reduction of key activities to their most refined elements allowed McDonald's, Federal Express, Wal-Mart, Citicorp, Mrs. Fields, Pizza Hut, and even the New York Stock Exchange (NYSE) to push the repeatability unit to even smaller "micro management" levels. Replicating precisely measured activity cycles, delivery times, customer query sequences, personal selling approaches, customer data, inventory control patterns, ingredients, freshness and cooking cycles, counter display techniques, cleanliness and maintenance procedures, and so on, in detail became keys to service and financial success. Lapses led to difficulties.

The concept of seeking the "minimum replicable level" of information for more flexible and precise management now goes even farther in many industries—like transportation, banking, communications, structural design, or medical research—where it has become possible to disaggregate the critical units of service production to the level of data blocks, packets, or "bytes" of information. Accessing and combining such units on a large scale are emerging as the core activities in achieving flexibility, quality and cost control, and economies of scale on a level never before envisioned. So precise are many large enterprises' (AT&T, Fed Ex) and many nationwide chains' (Mrs. Fields, General Mills Restaurants Group) measurement and feedback systems that their headquarters can tell within minutes—or even seconds—when something goes wrong in the system, at a client contact point, or in a decentralized unit, and often precisely what the problem is. Broadcast, power utility, or transmission networks, of course, must know of problems within split seconds and have on-line electronic monitoring devices for the purpose. CNN, for example, has found that a pause of more than five seconds is a complete disaster, causing massive audience tune-outs, and all employees and systems are keyed to preventing such catastrophes. In these cases, on-line monitors signal the problem immediately; people throughout the system are trained to anticipate possible sources of interruption and are empowered to move instantly to take whatever action is necessary to avoid or correct an aberration. Most problems end up being fixed before the customer ever knows there is an issue—the ultimate goal of quality control in services.

How does disaggregation of data and control at the appropriate minimum replicable level work in practice? Most of the successful large service systems in our study (many named earlier) first analyzed their processes into the smallest measurable details. Then, through careful work design and iterative learning processes, they both reengineered their processes to use this knowledge and developed the databases and feedback systems to capture and update needed information at the micro levels desired. Only then did they automate repeated or difficult processes—usually in sequence to avoid unnecessary risks and disruptions—within an overall system design that maintained compatibility and interface control among the subsystems. The best systems were flexibly designed with a five-to-ten-year time frame in mind, allowing new modules and data comparisons to be added as needed in the future.

Wherever possible, automated processes were interlinked to market-based feedback systems that provided up-to-date or continuous quality measurements and allowed mixing and matching of data in new ways to create greater value-added for customers. Unfortunately, insufficient attention to the feedback loop between customers and the company's own information/control systems has led to the failure of many strategies. When systems were automated properly—as in the cases of AT&T, McKesson, ADP Services, Mrs. Fields', Federal Express, and so on—the systems and their associated organization concepts became the core of the institution's strategy.

■ For example, in the early 1970s the New York Stock Exchange (NYSE) recognized that its hand-entry trading procedures would soon constrain its growth and threaten its capacity to maintain its status as the world's premier securities trading institution. To automate properly, NYSE had to understand clearly the many different values its customers expected it to produce. It undertook extensive customer interviews with all its stakeholders to secure this understanding. In addition to merely handling "transactions," NYSE found its systems had to (1) be seen as "fair and objective" by buyers and sellers, (2) maintain detailed control over each party's interest in a transaction, (3) generate the data all parties need to analyze the total market as well as individual securities, (4) connect individual buyers and sellers with common interests at remote points, (5) report transactions accurately to all interested public and private groups as required by law, (6) be absolutely reliable despite totally unforeseeable shifts in volume, new products, and external contingencies, and yet (7) meet all the needs of their NYSE owners and brokers for business information.[6]

NYSE ultimately was able to break each transaction down into the microscopic pieces of information that were common to each transaction yet when aggregated could meet all those other needs. Individual pieces of the system, like data input devices, were extensively pretested with their users. To ensure adequate capacity, NYSE built the system to handle fifty times the volume of transactions it anticipated, which saved the system on Black Monday in 1987. Yet despite its complexity, the system was brought up to complete operational levels over one weekend to ensure the market never closed—meeting a most important criterion for the customer: reliability. Its advanced automation system allowed NYSE not only to survive the vicissitudes of the 1980s but to lead the world in permitting the new trading practices that reshaped financial services in the 1980s.

Service management was not always based on minimum replicable concepts. In the past large transportation companies (airlines or railroads), utilities (AT&T and electric power grids), and large department stores (Macy's and Gimbels) relied more on traditional economies from large-scale facilities and purchasing power. In pioneering micro techniques, however, railroads were among the leaders. They installed completely automated switching and safety feedback systems that used micro measures to locate and control entire trains and individual boxcars. Airlines soon found they could not realize the benefits of their large-scale equipment investments—especially filling all the seats in a fixed-cost flight network—without learning to manage customer relationships at the micro level. Once identified and structured in detail, these micro units permitted the individualized routing, pricing, seating, baggage handling, special services, frequent flyer incentives, minute-by-minute scheduling, massive operations coordination, and interconnected reservations, billing, and payment systems that are now the key to competitiveness. In fact, many credit SABRE, the leading automated system, with moving American from being one of the weakest airlines in 1978 to its 1980s preeminence, while other previously prominent airlines—notably TWA, Pan Am, Braniff, and Eastern—fell into oblivion during deregulation.

MANAGING CUSTOMIZATION AT THE MICRO LEVEL

Ted Levitt, in a classic article, long ago recognized the mass production analogy in some service operations.[7] The ultimate purpose of focusing on the smallest replicable unit of operations, however, is not just the mass production benefits that standardization allows. There are much more interesting strategic benefits. Effectively combining these micro units permits one to achieve the highest possible degree of segmentation, strategic fine-tuning, value-added, and customer satisfaction in the marketplace. Interestingly, the larger the organization, the more refined these replicability units may practically be—and the higher their leverage for creating value-added gains. Greater volume allows the larger company to (1) collect more detail about its individual operating and market segments, (2) efficiently analyze these data at more disaggregated levels, and (3) experiment with these detailed segmentations in ways smaller concerns cannot. For example:

■ American Express (AmEx) is the only major credit card company with a large travel service. By capturing in the most disaggregated possible form—essentially data bytes—the details of transactions that its 22 million traveler, shopper, retailer, lodging, and transportation company customers put through its credit card and travel systems, AmEx can mix and match the patterns and capabilities of each group to add value for them in ways its competitors cannot. It can identify life-style changes (like marriage or moving) or match forthcoming travel plans with its customers' specific buying habits to notify them of special promotions, product offerings, or services AmEx's retailers may be presenting in their local or planned travel areas. From its larger information base AmEx also has the potential to provide more detailed information services to its 2 million retailer or transportation customers—like demographic and comparative analyses of their customer bases or individual customers' needs for wheelchair, pickup, or other convenience services. These can provide unique added value for both its consumer and commercial customers (see "Vignette: American Express" at the end of this chapter).

The key to high-profit micro management is to break down both operations and markets into such compatible detail that managers can discern, by properly cross-matrixing their data, how a slight change in one arena can affect some critical aspect of performance in another. The ability to micro manage, target, and customize operations in this fashion, using the knowledge base that size permits, is fast becoming the most important scale economy available in services today. For example:

■ In its now classic strategy, Benetton was able to develop such detail in its information base that it could fine-tune the offerings of each individual store to the specific demographics of the customers in its immediate shopping area. Thus colors, styles, and sizes could be adjusted to the specific characteristics of customers for stores only a few blocks apart, allowing Benetton a much denser store location strategy and offering customers greater selection of those garments they most desired.

Critical to effective system design is conceptualizing the smallest replicable unit and its potential use in strategy as early as possible in the design process. Summing disaggregated data later, if one so desires, is much easier than moving from a more aggregated system to a greater refinement of detail. Further, highly disaggregated data often capture unexpected experience patterns that more summary data would obscure. Much of the later power and flexibility of American's SABRE, McKesson's ECONOMOST, and National Rental Car's EXPRESSWAY systems derived from making this choice correctly, while less successful competitors' systems did not. The latter usually chose a larger replicability unit in order to save initial installation costs. In the process they lost crucial detailed experience and segmentation data that could have become the core of their later strategies. An unfortunate example was in car rentals, where Hertz, despite its larger size, allowed Avis and National to steal the early march with their more detailed and flexible Wizard and Expressway systems.

MOTIVATING AND EMPOWERING THE POINT PERSON

One may easily see how the micro unit approach addresses issues of efficiency and potential flexibility. But what about the necessity to motivate and empower service people? Do such systems empower employees to be able and activated to perform their jobs better? Or does the opposite happen? If they feel denigrated or frustrated by the company's control systems, contact people will tend to abuse, rather than assist, customers. So much of a service's perceived value is created at the moment and point of contact that it is crucial to the entire enterprise's success that such people handle the customer interface with both diligence and flair. This point is especially critical in retail or consumer sales, but it affects many other service activities as well. IBM, for example, found that the way the receptionist answered the phone predetermined much of its customers' reactions to the company even after they had reached the person they were seeking. Many other studies have found that "pleasure" in buying—especially interactions with the contact person in consumer sales—is at least as important to customers as price, efficiency, or other aspects of quality.[8]

Companies as diverse as Steuben Glass and Honda have also found that the salesperson's handling of a customer carries over to the later perceived quality of the product. Consequently, both place elaborate emphasis on dealership selection and personal training of contact people. Quality hotels set up their communication systems to call customers by name and to track their preferences and perceptions of service to treat them better on the next visit. Portman Hotel, for example, says that its most valuable asset is its capacity to manage such information to individualize and optimize its service presentation to clients. Such hotels also teach their employees to develop eye contact, to use customers' names, and to smile when delivering services—and to prevent the buildup of queues like the plague. Such simple acts, easy to check and costing little once other elements are built into the software system, are often as important to quality perceptions as are elaborate building or facilities investments. One need only note the long, customer-satisfying survival of old eastern U.S. and European spas with outmoded facilities but finely developed personal services.

STYLE, PERSONALIZATION, AND EFFICIENCY

In commercial markets, a company's style can also be a major influence on purchases of more technical services. EDS, the leader in the huge independent network management business, is admittedly technically competent and a very low-cost operator. But, *The Economist* notes, EDS

> . . . badly needs a change of image. Electronic Data Systems may be number one in the $30–40 billion market for information-technology services, but its hard driving, starched-shirt style makes even rival IBM cuddly. That, despite its daunting competence, is costing EDS business it needs if it is to escape the influence of its major shareholder and main customer, General Motors.
>
> EDS does one thing for its more than 7,000 customers, big or small: it runs their computer networks on contract more cheaply than they can. EDS makes its money by achieving economies of scale (in both buying equipment and running systems, and in keeping up with technical advances) that are beyond the scope of most individual customers. The ever-falling cost of computer power means ever-widening margins on its fixed-price contracts. . . .
>
> Just how much the firm needed to change was brought home when [EDS] lost—to IBM—the highly publicized battle to take over Eastman Kodak's data processing. . . .
>
> Under its new boss, Les Aberthal, a 47 year old whose school-

masterly manner wins friends in Detroit, EDS responded by reorganizing its top management into customer groups, and set about trying to look more friendly. The changes aimed to flatten the hierarchy, to keep the company hard driving and entrepreneurial. . . . The company's biggest challenge in managing its rapid growth is people. When it takes over a firm's data processing, EDS also takes over its staff, not all of EDS's own choosing. [Smaller firms especially] have to feel comfortable that EDS understands their businesses, as they will necessarily rely on [EDS] for the development of software applications as well as bulk data processing.[9]

Properly designed service systems will simultaneously deliver both a personalized feeling and efficiency.

■ Federal Express's DADS computer system for automated pickup and delivery allowed sophisticated real-time truck routing, eliminated input errors, provided a basis for monitoring service cycles, and freed the contact person to interact with customers on a more personal basis, a key to the FedEx strategy. It is fascinating to see the pride and confidence the hand-held scanner/computer (tied to the DADS and COSMOS systems) gives to a relatively untrained individual operating at the customer contact point for FedEx. It allows the point person to feel and behave essentially as an individual agent taking time to personalize the service, yet be linked to a huge network whose goal is to deliver "absolutely, positively on time" with a strategy of personalized customer contact. (See "Vignette: Federal Express Co.," at the end of this chapter for further details.)

■ Domino's Pizza, perhaps the fastest-growing food chain in history, encourages its local store managers to regard themselves as individual entrepreneurs. First, for each of its 4,500 highly decentralized outlets, industrial engineering and food research automated the making of a pizza to as near a science as possible, eliminating much of the drudgery in such tasks, yet ensuring higher quality and uniformity. Then, finding that its store managers were still spending fifteen to twenty hours a week on paperwork, Domino's introduced NCR "mini-tower" systems at its stores to handle all of the ordering, payroll, marketing, cash flow, inventory, and work control functions. This freed store executives to perform more valuable supervisory, follow-up, menu experimentation, public relations, or customer service activities—expanding and elevating their management roles and focusing them even more on founder Tom Monahan's goals of (1) making them independent entrepreneurs and (2) supporting the company's strongly held customer service philosophies.

Some strategies, of course, call for more education, motivation, or empowerment; some for more standardization of activity. Some specific service situations even require that technologies be used primarily to obtain uniformity rather than flexibility. In such services—e.g., bank accounting, letter sorting, film processing, systems programming, or aircraft maintenance—one may actively discourage too much independence. Repeated exactness and tight tolerances, not creativity, are required. Great service successes, however, generally exhibit a unique blend of (1) a distinctly structured technology system and (2) a carefully developed management style and motivation system to support it. The subtle development and timing of the balance between the two can lead to quite different strategic postures in the same industry. Amplifying the FedEx example above and contrasting it with another well-known company, UPS, will make the point quickly. The rest of this chapter will develop in detail how new organization forms can support specific empowerment strategies.

■ Federal Express (FedEx) has historically emphasized the use of a friendly, people-oriented, entrepreneurial management style in conjunction with "state of the art" technology systems as the basis of its competitive edge. Its DADS (digitally assisted dispatch) and COSMOS II (automated tracking) systems give FedEx maximum capability to be responsive, while its training programs, colorful advertising, decentralized operating style, and incentive systems emphasize the need to "go to the limit" personally in responding to customer needs and ensuring reliable on-time delivery. By contrast, UPS long utilized old-style trucks, hand sorting, detailed time and motion studies, and tight controls for its drivers. A hard-headed cost control system gave it a lower-cost—but considerably less customer responsive—market position. Both companies have been successful, FedEx by emphasizing "highest reliability and customer service" and UPS by emphasizing "the most efficient ship in the shipping business."

Neither approach is right in the abstract, or for all parties. But with better technological capabilities, customers' demands for more flexibility and responsiveness are driving more and more companies toward decentralization and empowerment at the contact level.

NEW ORGANIZATION FORMS FOR BOTH EFFICIENCY AND FLEXIBILITY

In their efforts to harness these two principal service drivers— maximum technological efficiency and flexibility at the micro level along with personal empowerment for customer contact personnel—some service companies have developed strikingly new, and much more effective, organizational models for all businesses. In this respect, service company managements have often moved well ahead of their manufacturing counterparts. Some of the basic concepts are also appearing in service activities within manufacturing companies, where they often prove to be remarkably easy to apply. Although some suggest that all organizations are moving—or should move—toward some predetermined new form,[10] we found a rich new variety of organizational strategies available. Each seems most suitable in certain circumstances, and not others. But all seem to embrace similar themes and to call for somewhat comparable technology and management support. First, what are some of the more important new organizational forms and where can they best be used? Later we shall develop their common themes.

"INFINITELY FLAT" ORGANIZATIONS

When technology is creatively implemented in service activities, there appears to be virtually no limit to the potential reporting span—the number of people reporting to one supervisor or center—that a service organization can make effective. While spans of 20–25 have become relatively common, spans of hundreds exist in some service organizations. Even the term "span of control" seems an anachronism. Perhaps a better term would be "span of communication" or "span of coordination." In most of these "very flat" organizations, few orders are given by the line organization to those below. Instead, the central authority becomes an information source, a communications coordinator, or a reference desk for unusual inquiries. Lower organizational levels more often connect into it to obtain information for the purpose of performing better rather than for instructions or specific guidance from above.

Many examples exist. It is common for twenty to forty fast food operations to be connected to a single logistics support or order coordinating center. Domino's Pizza is moving toward two hundred connections per center. A single conductor often coordinates a hundred or more people in a symphony orchestra.[11] And two, or even more, symphony orchestras in different locations could easily play together simultaneously, if linked by fiber optics. A single communications and satellite tracking system can coordinate and direct innumerable aircraft or container ships worldwide. And so on. In other fields:

■ Shearson American Express's 310 and Merrill Lynch's 480 domestic brokerage offices each connect directly into their parents' central information offices for routine needs, yet can bypass the electronic system for personal access to individual experts in headquarters. Merrill Lynch has a PC-based workstation for each of its "financial consultants" (brokers) linked through LANS and SNA to its central mainframe computers. Although regional marketing structures exist, business is conducted as if each of Merrill Lynch's 17,000 branch office contact people reported directly to headquarters, with their only personal oversight being at the local level. Computers extend Merrill Lynch's system capabilities to the level of individual customers, printing 400 million pages of output a year, largely customer reports captured directly from online transaction data. In effect, technology permits the company to compete in a coordinated fashion with the full power and scale economies of a major financial enterprise, yet local brokers can manage their own small units and accounts as independently as if they alone provided the total service on a local basis. From an operations viewpoint, the organization is absolutely flat; 17,000 brokers connect directly into headquarters for all their needs.

■ Federal Express, with 42,000 employees in more than three hundred cities worldwide, has a maximum of only five organizational layers between its nonmanagement employees and its COO or CEO. Typical operating spans of control are 15–20 employees per manager, with only 2.1 staff employees per $ million in sales— about one-fifth the industry average. As many as fifty couriers are under the line control of a single dispatching center. FedEx's DADS and COSMOS II computer-communications capabilities allow it to coordinate its 21,000 vans nationwide to make an average of 720,000 "on call" stops per day within a few hours' time.

Because of its leading-edge flight operations technologies and avionics controls, as many as two hundred FedEx aircraft can be in the air simultaneously, but under the control of a single authority, should it become necessary to override flight plans because of weather or special emergencies.[12]

DESTROYING HIERARCHIES

There is no inherent reason that organizations cannot be made "infinitely flat"—i.e., with innumerable outposts guided by one central "rules-based" or "computer controlled inquiry" system. As the above examples suggest, these need not be simple repetitive activities. Functions as various as personal sales, brokering, piloting aircraft, captaining ships, running railroads, playing music, reporting news, and performing research also qualify.

Nevertheless, most executives immediately think of harnessing routinized activities like those of fast food operations into the "infinitely flat" form. This should also quickly suggest its applicability to many equally routine manufacturing operations, where spans of control are often still tragically held to the seven-to-nine-person level, dictated by concepts that date back to Frederick Taylor. Once production jobs have been adequately analyzed, and real-time electronic measurement systems have been put in place, manufacturing can be an ideal place for 20–100-person spans of coordination. In fact, GM's Nummi joint venture with Toyota operates with an average span of twenty now.

By routinizing and automating operating parameters at their finest replicable level, both manufacturing and services companies can also develop the detailed cost and quality controls they need for system coordination and productivity at each of their many highly decentralized operating nodes. Under proper circumstances, the scheduling, order-giving, and information feedback functions normally provided by hierarchical structures can be completely automated. And if retained the hierarchy itself becomes a costly artifact. General Mills Restaurant Group found that as it automated more of its restaurant operations, it could double its spans of control, eliminate whole layers of management, and save tens of millions in administrative costs alone (see "Vignette: General Mills Restaurants" at the end of this chapter). Union Pacific removed six layers of its organization after it automated operations and delegated responsibility for on-time performance to small front-line teams.

Technology naturally supports several of the major trends that lead to empowerment and flatter organizations. New technologies permit today's burgeoning number of less-trained employees to perform to much higher quality and output standards than they otherwise possibly could as beginners.[13] Then they encourage these new workers to learn further skills and with these to take over many of the traditional functions of middle managers.[14]

■ High school trained typists or accounting clerks—given word processors, spell-checks, and spreadsheet software—can quickly achieve better output volumes and finished work quality than all but a few executive secretaries or senior accountants used to attain. Then they begin to tinker with their computers, seeking more interesting things to do, expanding their skills and range of services into areas their supervisors used to handle.

As the software system takes over most of the quality checks middle managers used to perform, it becomes natural to extend the latter's spans of control. Since front-line people can do most of the work actually needed (and cost less), this leads naturally to the elimination of intermediate management and the "delayering and flattening of organizations" so widely observed today. In the past, the lowest ranks were the most vulnerable persons in an economic downturn. In the 1991–92 recession it has been the middle managers made redundant by the empowerment of lower levels.[15] Repeatedly, our respondents noted that re-engineering of contact jobs—followed by automation and reorganization of tasks to empower the point person—had led to the elimination of 2 to 6 layers of administrative management.

FREEING PEOPLE FOR MORE HUMAN TASKS

Properly installed technology and management systems, however, do more than simply destroy management bureaucracies. By studying and automating repetitive tasks down to the minimum replicable production unit, companies eliminate much of the routine in jobs and free up their employees for more interesting and human tasks. For example:

■ Marshall Field & Co. has developed a computer-based employee scheduling system "to maximize sales potential at the point-of-sale, increase managerial effectiveness, and improve expense and productivity controls." Yet the same system sets higher standards for customer service quality by ensuring an adequately sized, better-trained, and more customer-focused sales force on the floor at all times. Marshall Field automated most check approvals, sales slip writeups, and stock reorder procedures. It simplified its package wrapping and checkout procedures to let sales clerks give faster checkouts and have more time for customer attention. By eliminating these "task-interfering duties," it enabled salespeople to concentrate on customer-related interactions and to decrease customer waiting times substantially.[16]

In more routine settings, one can completely automate most manual steps in baggage handling, cleaning services, fast food preparation, or car wash operations. One can also "informate"[17] most checkout, reservation, point-of-sale, bank teller, or similar systems that require much routine activity combined with interactive human inputs. Since the people who handle or oversee these tasks no longer have to spend their time on dull mechanical routines, they can be empowered to undertake more personal or sales-oriented—and higher value-added—activities, which enhance perceived quality in the customer's eyes. As people move up into these more personally rewarding and responsible tasks, companies frequently find them ready to act more as managers than as hourly employees. Repeatedly, our respondents said that even the least skilled people quickly began to set their own goals responsibly and to monitor their activity levels against agreed-upon goals. In many cases, the same micro measurement systems that permit maximum efficiency and flexibility can also be expanded to monitor both productivity and service quality at the point of contact. For example in the ephemeral realm of service quality measurement:

■ Airlines can ensure reliable delivery of a variety of customized services for those who are physically impaired, need special meals, are premium customers, or are first-time or nervous passengers. They can also monitor gate delays, on-time departures and arrivals, overbookings, stockouts on meals or drinks, maintenance delays and failures, baggage handling times, and many other measures of service quality. Communications companies have dozens of on-line measures of signal quality, connection times, interrupts, wrong connections, billing errors, special service needs (and so on) that they review daily. In chain restaurants or food outlets, like Mrs. Fields Cookies, systems can monitor sales at fifteen-minute intervals and suggest needed product mix changes, promotional moves, or operation changes to improve customer response. In other settings, like Toys "R" Us, micro measurements can improve quality of service indirectly by allowing the operation to have the broadest, deepest inventories available for customer selection. Because of higher volumes, they can also support product guarantees and provide installation help—at lower fees—than any other competitor.

Well-designed information systems can *both* offer greater flexibility in responding to customer needs *and* simultaneously ensure maximum efficiency. In these circumstances, the supposedly inherent conflicts between "generic" *low cost* strategies and generic *differentiation* strategies cease to exist. And anyone who does not pursue both strategies simultaneously is likely to become a loser.

■ Recognizing these verities, the Royal Bank of Canada, operating more branches than any other bank in North America, has instituted a Customer Reference File for use by contact people in most of its branches. With the Customer Reference File, the contact person can quickly seek out details about all of the relationships the bank has with a particular customer. These enable the customer representative to offer more services to customers, yet optimize the Royal Bank's own positions with more accuracy than its competition. While offering more flexibility to contact people, necessary controls are built into the system to ensure the security of the Bank's own portfolio. From the customer's viewpoint, with greater knowledge at their fingertips the Royal's point people appear to be much more cognizant of the customer's situation and thus assume an aura of greater professionalism. To leverage the potentials of this greater empowerment, the Royal Bank is experimenting with extremely wide spans of control in its Waterloo, Ontario, branches and in numerous self-directed customer service teams. To date, these experiments have led to decreased hierarchies, greater enthusiasm from the staff, and a much more flexible orientation toward customer service in the Waterloo branches. The bank is currently considering how far and how best to roll out this experience to its other branches.

WHEN TO USE "INFINITELY FLAT" ORGANIZATIONS

When combined with well-designed information systems, extremely wide reporting spans work most easily—but not exclusively—in situations where (1) localized interactive contact is important, (2) each ultimate contact point or operations unit can operate essentially independently from all others at its level, (3) the critical relationships between decentralized units and the center are largely quantitative or informational, and (4) the majority of the relationships with the information center can be routine or rules-based. Although service companies—because of their communications–information intensity and localized delivery needs—have generally pioneered such organization forms, some manufacturing enterprises are beginning to implement similar approaches. The immediate economic impact of such systems is that they (1) justify making major investments in extremely sophisticated systems at the center, (2) deliver this sophistication in highly customized form at remote points, (3) eliminate administrative hierarchies, and (4) add value at lower unit costs both at the center and in the remote nodes. The Federal Express Vignette provides an excellent, somewhat expanded example of managing these seemingly conflicting relationships (see "Vignettes: Revolutionizing Organizations" at the end of this chapter).

Although "infinitely flat" organizations are now most often used for somewhat more repetitive and routine, rules-based situations, this is likely to change rapidly in the near future. As has been noted, many successful professional service examples already exist. Others are appearing constantly as the full power of information and service technologies becomes more apparent. The need for highly localized independence, within some specified, limiting rules or constraints, is probably the only critical characteristic for this organizational form.

■ Perhaps the most interesting example of an "infinitely flat" organization with extremely independent action at the operating nodes was the bomber deployment system utilized in the Gulf War, where each bomber was targeted to an individual point, and many even carried bombs designed and built specifically for that target only a few days before. This was a triumph of logistics, communications, transportation, and information (service) technologies working in tandem with just-in-time production and design systems 7,000 miles away. Hundreds of aircraft were in the air simultaneously, operating almost completely independently to accomplish very specific missions and yet maneuvering flexibly in combat as needed. Although the bombers had to comply with certain flight rules, timing, and communication codes (to avoid damage and to ensure their effectiveness), more than a thousand aircraft were coordinated simultaneously around the clock from a few communication centers.

In this situation, as in most others, the common characteristic of infinitely flat organizations is that interactions within the organization are predominantly *either* at the local contact point *or* with a communications center. Knowledge intensity is also concentrated at these two points, and leveraging of the center's expertise is critical. Direct lateral interactions are considerably less important or nonexistent.

"SPIDER'S WEB" ORGANIZATIONS

When the highly dispersed nodes of service operations or customer contact must interact with each other directly and frequently, another type of organization and communications–control system generally emerges, often called a network—but best described as a "spider's web" because of the lightness yet completeness of its interconnection structure (see Figure 4–1).

The "spider's web" organization operates essentially without—or with only minimal—formal authority or "order-giving" hierarchies. Individual units would operate entirely independently if it were not essential to capture certain information economies of scale or scope that benefit the total organization. The bomber example above is very close to this, but its strong direct authority linkages to command centers differentiate it. Some say university faculty members—bound mainly by common library and plumbing systems—have achieved this result. Among larger commercial organizations, international cooperative ventures for research, legal actions, investment banking, auditing, consulting, technology development, intermodal product transportation, or management of trusts or charitable contributions come closest to true spiders' webs. The independent nodes of such organizations contain essentially all the accumulated knowledge of the organization and work to a great degree without formal authority inter-

FIGURE 4–1
Spider's Web Organizations

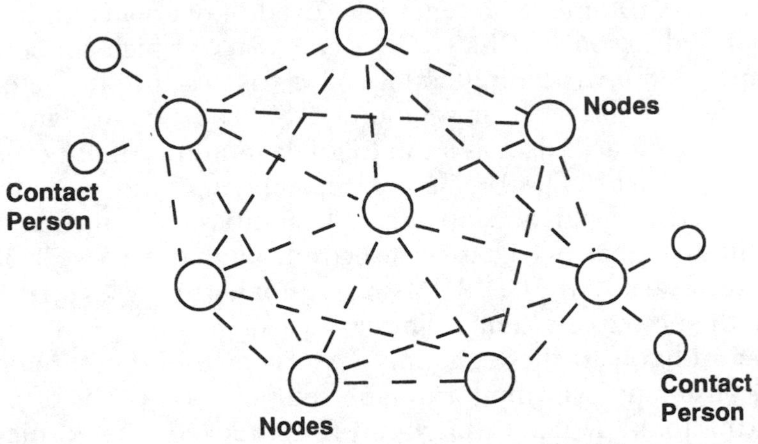

actions most of the time. The center, if there is one, collects and transfers information from and for the nodes, instead of generating it. There may be hierarchies within the nodes, but these tend to be quite limited. When authority interactions are necessary with the center, they tend to occur through single-level task forces, *ad hoc* committees of peers, or an agreed-upon coordinating committee for a special purpose like capital allocations. Arthur Andersen & Co. provides an excellent example.

■ Arthur Andersen and Co. (AA&Co.) is a leader in applying technology to professional services. It has to link more than 51,000 people in some 243 offices in 54 countries. The offices try to keep internal hierarchies to minimal levels. Its clients have a mix of operations around the United States and in up to two hundred other countries. The AANET, a T1-level private all–fiber optics system, links most AA&Co. offices. The system is intended to carry data, voice, and video.

All AA&Co. partners (approximately 2,400) own part of the total firm and make investments on a firmwide level, based upon a plan agreed to by an investment committee of the partners. The company's cumulative experience, virtually all at the operating nodes, is growing so fast that executives say, "Even those in the know may not have the best answer to the totality of a complex question." In order to benefit from its experience, however,

AA&Co. tries to link its highly independent offices in a number of ways that can exploit the firm's extensive know-how. On the one hand, it tries to capture the history of its contacts with major clients in a Customer Reference File. In addition, on its Audit Reference and Resource Disk (a CD-ROM system which connects to Compaq 386 microcomputers) it collects as much up-to-date tax, customer, special problem solution, FASB, court ruling, and professional standards data as it can to guide its auditors and consultants in the field. The ROMs are kept updated and periodically distributed to all partnership offices. In addition, the offices can tap into the headquarters database directly through the AANET. Field auditors who take the CD-ROM onto customer premises carry with them the power of a central library on a single disk.

In addition to these routine performance updates, auditors and consultants who find a unique solution to a problem introduce this to the system through carefully indexed "subject files" in the Chicago headquarters. These let other units share their unique solutions. However, any field professional who encounters a new problem can also query the entire system on an "electronic bulletin board." Anyone in the AA&Co. system who has an answer to the query can notify the inquirer. Communications then ensue either in person or through the network. Arthur Andersen also spends very large sums to allow its people to meet for personal exchanges on important problems.

The firm operates in a highly decentralized, real-time information mode. Because of the company's size and complexity, individuals in AA&Co. can no longer rely on their personal knowledge of whom to call for information. Yet with its information system, partners say the company's distinctive competency has become "empowering people to deliver better quality technology-based solutions to clients in a shorter time." Because of the personnel skills AA&Co. has built along with this system, customers now look to AA&Co. to deliver computer-based solutions to systems problems in the same league as EDS or IBM, and the nature of AA&Co.'s core business has shifted accordingly.

"Spider's web" formats can also be used within individual portions of a larger company. For example, a research division might very well operate in this mode, although other divisions might not. Researchers may interact with other scientists in labs throughout the world as collaborators working on particular segments of a problem, with few formal authority linkages—and little more than their personal integrity, their project's goal, and the disciplines of their science to manage their work. Unlike the units of "infinitely flat" organizations, each of the nodes in a "spider's web" needs, for effectiveness, to be intimately in touch with the information or resources all other nodes may contain. Within wide ranges, each node may function quite independently in servicing a particular client base.

However, in certain circumstances, the individual nodes may need to operate in a highly coordinated fashion to achieve strategic advantage for a specific purpose, like coordinating an audit for a multinational client or syndicating a complex capital restructuring for an acquisition or private placement. To deal with such problems, the approach used by companies with traditional organizational structures will usually be a complex matrix organization which allows a project leader to coerce resources, as needed, from otherwise decentralized divisions. But this often creates very costly motivational, priority, turf, and transfer pricing issues. Many more creative firms have found the flexibility, fast response, and opportunism of the spider's web concept so attractive that they have established entirely new management modes to let it operate.[18]

THE "SKUNKWORKS SPIDER'S WEB"

The most common such new management mode in large organizations is the cross-functional design group—or a genuine "skunkworks"—which in many ways typifies the organization and management structure used in larger "spider's webs." Here we find a very organic structure, little formalization of behavior, and numbers of highly specialized individuals working on an *ad hoc* basis toward a common interest. Why is this form so often used for innovation? To innovate means to break away from established patterns, to move rapidly and creatively in new realms; hence the most effective innovation groups often abandon the trappings of formal organizations and their planning and control systems. Interacting in a way that maximizes contacts among individuals and with knowledgeable individuals outside the core also maximizes learning, potential knowledge gains, and progress through what are called "network externalities." If a number of individuals (n) work in parallel, but individually alone, on a project, their expected knowledge output would be n times the output of one individual. If they share information and don't duplicate work, and if the information of each person is of importance to the others, the potential output relative to that of an individual should approximate the function $2^{(n-1)} - 1$, the number of interconnection channels among the n nodes.[19] This is a powerful multiple, limited only by the capacity of individuals to absorb information.

When operating on the frontiers of knowledge, authority is vested in those who have the most information; hence there is little need for formal authority structures. Successful research or innovating adhocracies tend to break the boundaries of conventional specialization, since no specialist can solve the whole problem alone. Advance occurs as disciplines and functions interact. A team forms for each project and usually for each subsystem within the project. Control comes not from the watchful eye of an all-knowing formal authority or conformity to established "milestones," but from a commonly felt urgency to solve a particular problem and to receive the psychic and material rewards of having "done it."

So closely knit is the interaction cycle in these situations that administrative and operating tasks blend into a single effort.[20] One person becomes subordinate to another for a particular task, and roles reverse for the next. Outsiders may have more temporary authority than insiders. Solutions flow not linearly but organically, as pieces of the solution drive other pieces, only to be replaced in turn by still others; and the organization's power centers flex and flow around these partial decisions. But at the end, the customer for the service—an outside party—decides its ultimate configuration in use and hence becomes the true decision-maker. Consequently, all the formal apparatus of goal-setting, progress measurement, and rewards should focus on results from the customer's viewpoint. Later chapters present numerous detailed examples of how to do this. This paradigm is equally useful whether the spider's web is used for a new product design or for a complex financing, a consulting project, or a promotional campaign for a charity client.

Perhaps the most important key to managing a spider's web—after selection and development of people and the information system itself—is to make sure the incentive structure focuses on the customer and that the organization's internal structures are designed around the twin goals of sharing information and adding value for customers. For example:

■ In Arthur Andersen & Company, a conscious effort is made to deemphasize localized profit centers and performance measures that do not contribute to sharing information. Partners share in total firm profits instead. People seeking promotion to partner are evaluated, in part, on the number of "case solutions" they have submitted to the system for sharing. The frequency with which a person is sought for a team or to solve a complex problem and how well that person cooperates in team endeavors are also important components in performance evaluations. The ultimate considerations are that the entire firm's resources can be concentrated on a particular customer's need when necessary and that profitability is calculated and shared worldwide—not primarily on a local office or specialized functional basis—by partners. The entire culture is managed to develop and share new information and solutions. And the technological system—by allowing interactions that often cut research time and routine calculations on projects from days to minutes—increases opportunities for adding intellectual value to audits and consulting, yet lowers costs for the client.

What concepts seem to be most useful in managing these organization forms? No generalizations, of course, suit all situations. But many observations suggest that organizations operating in this mode create their greatest value by increasing (1) the levels of information shared among members and (2) the motivation of individual members to solve customer problems. To maximize these effects, network managers often consciously leave the formal organization somewhat ill-defined, but establish well-defined, customer-oriented control and monitoring systems centering on individual client or segment activities, such as market penetration, call and service frequency, postservice interviews with customers, and other customer satisfaction measures. They often use team, overlapping, or shared responsibilities to increase the number of people among whom information is communicated. Rotating tasks and locations, pooling resources, and mixing membership on various ventures further enhance information sharing and personal ties within the web. With vague hierarchical goals—yet with well-defined output measures directed toward customer outcomes—

individuals focus on ends and are free to adopt the organizational and technical means most appropriate to accomplish them.[21]

To encourage lateral coordination further, many such organizations no longer try to allocate profits among cooperating groups. They either use simple fee-splitting rules—like equal division among the departments—or multiple counting systems that give full credit to all contributing groups. This eliminates conflicts among groups but enables managers to give selective bonus rewards to contributing individuals and teams at the end of the year. To make the whole system work well, managers stay very close to ongoing operations, spend a great deal of time on personnel evaluations, and are willing to give substantial bonus differentials for outstanding versus mediocre performance. Any of these can represent a shocking change for organizations operating in traditional hierarchical or profit center modes. Yet, as will be seen later, they are only the beginning of the changes needed to implement true network organizations well.

LEADING TO "SHAMROCK" COMPANIES AND INDUSTRIES

Chapter 7, "The Intelligent Enterprise," shows how entire industries and companies are restructuring as spiders' webs, creating whole new sets of opportunities and strategic issues for those associated with these industries. Industries as diverse as software development, publishing, biotechnology, construction, investment banking, movie or video production, and resource exploration and development now operate largely in this mode.

■ For example, semiconductor chips may be designed almost anywhere, have their photo masks made in Silicon Valley, and be water-etched in Japan, diced and mounted in Korea, assembled in Malaysia, encapsulated in Singapore, and finally sold through independent distributors anywhere in the world. The same approach works for much larger products. A company like American Standard has designed its structures to allow architectural specification of products to local tastes near the point of sale, product design from these specs in Italy, product engineering in Germany, mold-making in France, and production in Germany, Mexico, or Korea, depending on production and shipment costs to the pertinent marketplace.

Knowledge within these networks is concentrated at the nodes. Units operate as essentially independent units, connected primarily by information and market needs. Within the network, each producing or design unit can be much smaller and more specialized, more flexible, and more personally motivated than in most large integrated companies. Each unit can be financed either locally or centrally to maximize the coordinator's or investor's leverage. While most such networks remain highly decentralized, each consortium will vary in form and can establish any desired degree of coordination or control its members want for the overall process.

Some provocative thinkers see this kind of highly disaggregated organization as the dominant form for the future. Charles Handy refers to it as the "shamrock,"[22] with a very small permanent core of highly qualified professionals, managers, and technicians surrounded by three "leaves" of activity—the leaves of the shamrock. The small central group is primarily a coordinating body, perhaps with a major operating unit attached, that embodies the core competencies of the company or the project. These are the organization's only permanent employees. All other essential work is outsourced to people or companies who specialize in it. This is the second leaf.

In the third leaf of the shamrock are all the part-time and temporary workers—the fastest-growing part of the workforce—who contribute to the production or sale of the good or service the shamrock creates. They handle the off-hours and seasonal surge loads no one can afford to accommodate through permanent staffing. Some of these may be part time, some full time. For example, Rank Xerox Ltd. in the United Kingdom has seventy former employees working full time as contractors to its central office. As the cost of maintaining a staff person in a headquarter's office rose, Xerox found it could profit by setting up people with special skills as independent companies selling services to Xerox on demand, but free to sell their skills to others as well.[23] In Handy's structure, this third leaf also includes the increasing number of professionals who work from their homes, connected to the main organization by computer, and the consumers who voluntarily assist (by pumping their own gasoline, emptying their trays, or preparing their garbage) for those who are paid to do work. Such "free outsourcing" has become a powerful component of strategic design for many companies. While Handy's vision was intended to be provocative—i.e., to cause what he calls "upside down thinking"—it is becoming ever more prevalent.

WHERE DO "SPIDER'S WEBS" WORK BEST?

When creatively harnessed, these smaller, highly independent, flexible structures can generate significantly increased returns on lower investments. Formal consortia now seem to work most efficiently when targeted toward a single clear goal, like developing an oilfield, a book, a gold mine, a new biological entity, or a complex new electronics system. But increasingly, these organization forms are becoming strategic models for companies seeking to leverage limited investments—but very high talent levels—at their center through significant outsourcing to other specialists. High-fashion, high-technology, and knowledge enterprises have led the way to date—for good reasons. All live in worlds dominated by fast response times, high value-added, and significant risk, making it essential and less costly to harness the parallel capabilities of multiple suppliers rather than make all investments and take all risks internally. As more companies realize they too must live in these worlds, the trend will grow apace.

Spider's web companies are very different from infinitely flat enterprises. All the nodes of a spider's web are directly connected by communication links, and the interconnections are relatively frequently used. Nevertheless, the nodes of spider's webs tend to be quite independent, operating largely on the basis of agreed-upon goals or performance contracts related to specific projects. Rules, limits, or constraints set up by the central group are less important in managing performance. In fact, there may be no formal authority lines between the center and the nodes, and the nodes may be so independent that they can raise funding locally and serve many customers who are direct competitors of some units in the coordinating company.

Spider's webs serve best where a high degree of expertise is needed at the nodes, where relations between the nodes themselves or between nodes and the center are intermittent and largely informational—or where local flexibility and creativeness are more important than central efficiencies. These are the dominating features of most knowledge-based webs. In most cases, the nodes enjoy economies of scale, special access to resources, or unique facilities that it would be prohibitive to recreate centrally. Such are the characteristics of most resource- or manufacturing-intensive consortia today. As these enterprises begin to realize that their competitive edge depends ever more on service or knowledge capabilities, they are increasingly looking outside to find best-in-world suppliers of these capabilities.

A major driving force is customers who demand increasing flexibility and responsiveness in the supply of ever more complex products and services. When great knowledge depth, technological competency, and response capability are required, the best way to obtain the requisite combination at lowest cost is to develop and tap a network of best-in-world sources. This is especially true when a wide variety of specialized inputs is necessary. As these conditions continue to grow, so too will the incidence of "spider's web" companies. And the only way specialized internal staff and service groups will survive is to become either best in world sources themselves or the internal nodes coordinating this process for the company and reaching out to other external nodes to leverage their expertise.

THE "INVERTED" ORGANIZATION

A confluence and extension of these forms is appearing in another radical type of organization most often seen in the service sector—the "inverted" organization. The reason this form has emerged first in service activities is fairly straightforward. To the service customer, the most important person in the company is usually the one at the point of contact. What happens in the limited moments of that contact personifies what the company is to the customer. It verifies or invalidates all the value the rest of the company so expensively seeks to generate through its many research, product, facilities, quality, distribution, and advertising investments.

For some companies the contact person is so important that, rather than operate merely in a flat or network mode, they will literally invert their organizations, making all line executives, systems, and support staffs in the company "work for" the front-line person. They recognize that the contact person—normally considered the organization's lowest tier—is the one on whom everyone else depends to deliver the company's full capabilities at the moment of customer contact. Managers in such enterprises try to conceptualize relationships and make their organizations perform as if they were "an inverted pyramid," with the contact people at the broad top level and the CEO at the pointed bottom. Some companies, like Toronto Dominion Bank and AIG, have gone

FIGURE 4–2
The Inverted Organization

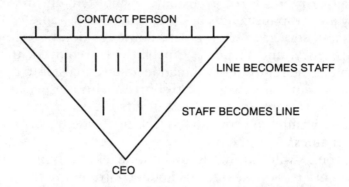

farther and created formal organization charts with customers at the top and the contact people reporting to the customers.

■ NovaCare, Inc., the largest provider of rehabilitation care in the United States, with net sales of $152 million as of June 1991 and growing at 50 percent a year, is another excellent example. In its industry, trained physical, occupational, and speech therapists are in short supply, yet the elderly population needing their care is growing rapidly. NovaCare has prospered by providing the business infrastructure for its 3,500 therapists, arranging contracts with nursing homes and chains, handling accounting and credit activities, providing training updates, and stabilizing and enhancing the therapists' earnings. Chairman John Foster says, "The key to this business is our therapists and the quality of service they deliver. They drive the business, and the rest is set up to support them. They are my bosses, and all our area and regional managers' jobs are there to support them and to solve problems for them." Throughout the organization one hears executives refer to the therapists as "the people I report to."[24]

NOT JUST A GIMMICK

Where this concept works, as it does in NovaCare, it is not just a gimmick. All executives genuinely regard those closer to the customer as "their bosses" and regard their jobs as those of coordinators and supporters. All systems and procedures ensure that intermediate-level personnel genuinely respond to orders from the contact people. In fact, the people closest to the customer rate those "lower" in the hierarchy during performance, salary, and bonus reviews. Until this happens, those in more traditional organizations attempting to shift to the "inverted organization" often cannot achieve the responses they seek.

The other aspects of such an inversion are also quite interesting and require major role reconceptualizations and attitude changes. Although line managers must specify major performance parameters and must assist in the system design process, it is usually the software or planning personnel (ordinarily considered "service or staff") who code and hence interpret "line" decisions—in the usual order-giving sense—for the system. Their actions determine much of the form and content of the information intended to answer routine questions and to run day-to-day operations. But in the process of developing the code, programmers' interpretations built into the software also implicitly make the subtle judgments in expert systems that mimic the more sophisticated decisions line managers would ordinarily undertake. Thus software or other information technology "staff" specialists provide many of the human judgments "line" managers ordinarily would.

To complete the inversion, those who were intermediate "line" managers (in the old organization) instead of being order-givers now become essentially analysts of special problems, expediters or enablers, information sources, and performance observers—roles normally assumed to be "staff"—supporting the contact people. In these roles, they can support many more front-line people than in the past, delayering or flattening the organization in the process. Their other substantive line roles—particularly those as arbiters of last resort for front-line personnel and as sensors of situations beyond the scope of the technological systems—nevertheless persist. In fact, these become of even greater relative importance as formerly routine activities decline for those who remain in middle-level positions. By automating and delegating as many tasks—and removing as many organizational levels—as possible in their inverted systems, top executives can, in time, achieve much more efficient, more responsive, flatter organizations. In these organizations, the few remaining "line" executives have even more important roles and greatly expanded scopes for opportunity. They can manage much wider ranges of organizational contacts, yet simultaneously concentrate on those more complicated issues where interpretation, intuition, creativity, and human motivation really count.

APPLICABLE IN MANY SITUATIONS

While the concept of inversion at first seems radical, it has actually been used in well-run professional organizations for years. Doctors are treated as the key people in hospitals, pilots are the crux of flight operations, on-site project teams lead major construction engineering tasks, and "principal researchers" and "creative personnel" are accorded privileges as the most important people in research or advertising concerns. Most hierarchical elements in these situations are subordinated to this fact. All others in these organizations are best conceptualized as "support," not managerial personnel—and often get in trouble when they don't recognize the fact. When sufficient professionalism is inculcated in the point person, inversion can work in other situations as well.

It usually takes both sophisticated technology and a genuine inversion in traditional roles and attitudes to make the concept work in mass service organizations. The point person often has the desire and needs only information plus hierarchical empowerment to function properly in this environment. Technology and a willingness to share information in a new way can provide the former. The point person (for example, a bank's customer service representative) often cannot possibly internalize or keep up with all the system details (investment options, differential interest rates, future value potentials, customer information, etc.) necessary to deliver the organization's full power to the customer. The first problem in successfully inverting such mass service organizations, therefore, is to capture—and then continuously organize, update, and monitor—as many relevant information elements as are necessary to make the point person thoroughly *au courant* in a professional sense. NovaCare, for example, is setting up its Nova Net system to help it identify new therapeutic approaches any of its specialists may develop for faster rehabilitation and then to feed these back to its other therapists to improve the quality of care throughout the system. NovaCare's incentive systems, keyed both to internal productivity and to patient progress, then reward the professionals for adopting better solutions quickly.

Companies operating in this mode structure all internal and

external databanks, "expert system" models, and interactive feedback and communication systems to make as much as possible of the firm's (and the world's) relevant professional expertise available instantly to the front-line person. When well-developed, the network's technologies allow front-line personnel to call forth and cross-matrix whatever details their customers' specific needs may require, using collected micro units of information either directly as data or indirectly to build unique solutions for customers even at the most remote locations. For example:

■ The Royal Bank of Canada can use its pace-setting position in automated corporate cash management to add portfolio management, payroll services, international exchange, and other services for clients at minimal incremental cost. And its Customer Reference File lets it provide other rapid and specialized commercial and private banking services, yet keep up with all its transactions with the customer to ensure the bank's own interests are protected.[25] Within the data limits and clear decision rules and checks defined by the system, nonroutine decisions are left as much as possible to contact personnel.

In inverted organizations—which Royal Bank does not yet claim to be—these individuals then call for their "subordinates" to help on those specialized issues they cannot handle themselves. And each person in the (former) management hierarchy is expected to respond to this "order" for support. How best to achieve this response from middle managers is the subject of much of later chapters on managing professional and intellectually dominated companies.

NEW SYSTEMS ARCHITECTURES NEEDED

Unfortunately, many companies' information systems have not been designed with this kind of flexible response capability in mind. The optimum system would be a fast-acting "database system" with the contact person able (1) to move easily from one specialized data source to another and (2) to mix and match data in an optimum fashion for each customer. For historical reasons, companies have usually developed their internal systems separately around their old organizational configurations and around computer architectures that are more suitable for calculations than for database callups and comparisons. Many banks, for example, started their automation around accounting system structures keyed to personnel records and cash control needs, customer account numbers, specific types of banking transactions, or other specifications for required regulatory reports—rather than designing them for information segmentations appropriate to full customer service or to new product introduction and marketing needs.

Over time, these systems often became internally incompatible and very difficult to access from other points in the enterprise. So difficult can later readjustments be that one British bank estimated that it would take $2 billion to reverse the historical constraints built into its systems by happenstance.[26] Such problems are common, to a greater or lesser degree, for all but the foresighted few (like ADP Services, SABRE, or McKesson) who developed more flexible systems early. Increasingly, however, object-oriented software systems, more powerful and flexible parallel processors, and the improving compatibility of network-interfacing systems will enable many others to achieve the capability to call up, mix, and match databased details as desired. This may well be the most powerful early application of massively parallel computers, rather than the artificial intelligence applications that have been so highly touted. As the Chief Information Officer (CIO) of one of the four largest insurance companies said, "Powerful parallel computers to access our databases through object-oriented programs are exactly what we need, but our systems are a long way from that now."

In all but the smallest systems, until new technology is installed to enable the point person (or point team) to access all the information needed to serve the customer completely, implementation of a fully inverted organization is unlikely. But units within a company can proceed to do so incrementally. American Express offers an excellent example of the attempt to develop internal technologies for maximum flexibility and strategic power. It has already obtained significant economies of scale in its back-office operations and is currently developing extensions of these technologies to utilize advanced interactive databases to serve its multiple customer groups with greater flexibility than its competitors can achieve (see "Vignettes: Revolutionizing Organizations" at the end of this chapter).

CONCLUSIONS

New service technologies and knowledge-based management systems have created totally new organizational needs and capacities. As service enterprises grew in scale and complexity, they needed both to manage operations in detail at the most localized level and to obtain the full economies of scale and scope the new technologies permitted. By focusing on the minimum replicable unit of service production, expanding companies found they could simultaneously maximize both local flexibility and scale economies.

Further, as they developed their management systems around the smallest replicable unit, they found that they could disaggregate their organizations, eliminate administrative bureaucracies, yet control operating costs and quality at the contact level better than ever before. The key was empowering the point person—with better information, training, and motivation systems—to take over more responsibility. This led to the several remarkable new organization forms described here: the infinitely flat, spider's web, and inverted forms, as well as others to be discussed in the next chapter. These organization forms—and the strategies they permit—have called into question many traditional management concepts and have forced a complete rethinking of relationships between the executive structure, the contact person, and the customer.

A surprising number of industries and companies can now operate effectively in these new organization formats. Yet it is equally surprising how few companies realize the real potentials these organizations offer for eliminating bureaucracies, delayering, improving response times, and lowering total costs while improving service quality. This chapter has only begun the discussion. Later chapters will develop key management and strategic themes in much further detail.

VIGNETTES:
Revolutionizing Organizations

Vignette One: Federal Express Corporation*

Federal Express's (FedEx's) technology—along with its creative organization practices—allows the company to provide the flexible dispatching capabilities of a nationwide taxi service, the sorting capacity of a postal service with a two-hour turnaround time, the full logistics of an airline whose passengers cannot move themselves, and the responsiveness of a bank whose customers can demand immediate confirmation of every transaction's status. For years the combination has allowed FedEx simultaneously to fulfill three seemingly conflicting criteria: lowest system cost, maximum service flexibility, and highest output reliability.

Because of FedEx's capacity to track performance at detailed levels and its strongly reinforced culture, it can operate with an extremely flat organization. Despite having over 45,000 people in more than 300 cities throughout the world, FedEx has a maximum of five layers of management between any nonmanagement employee and its COO or CEO. Typical operating spans of control are 15–20, with only 2.1 staff employees per $1 million in sales—as against an average of 5 per $1 million in the typical service company.

It is primarily FedEx's technologies that allow such high degrees of decentralization yet ensure the flexibility, coordination, and quality control to individually service about 750,000 customers at highly dispersed locations each day. As many as fifty couriers are controlled by a single dispatching center through the radio-based DADS (Digitally Assisted Dispatch System) units in their vans, allowing FedEx to optimize routings for both best customer service and lowest cost. As FedEx's 2,000 service representatives feed their 241,000 daily calls into the COSMOS (Customer,

* "Federal Express Corporation" (case), in H. Mintzberg and J. B. Quinn, *The Strategy Process*, 2d ed. (Englewood Cliffs, NJ: Prentice Hall, 1991).

Operations, Management and Services) system, the computerized information allows the DADS system to coordinate 21,000 vans making an average of 720,000 stops per day.

When a package is picked up, a computer wand reads the packet's bar-coded airway bill number, and the courier inputs detailed information on the package's source location, sender code number, destination zip code, courier identification, time of pickup, type of package, number of related packages, and type of service desired. This information goes directly into the COSMOS master system either through the DADS unit or through a "smart box," which works where radio transmissions are impossible. At each transfer point thereafter, the information is updated by reading the most disaggregated possible piece of information, the package identification number, into the COSMOS system. This enables FedEx to ensure reliable delivery and to respond instantly to the 20,000 follow-up inquiries customers make on the average day. In addition, FedEx supplies its major customers with direct access to follow-up information, as well as billing and inventory management assistance, if they install its PowerShip computer system on their own premises.

FedEx's two primary service products are time advantage and reliability. Technology and unique organizational management are at the core of both. To ensure reliability, FedEx operates its own weather analysis, ground control, and flight simulator facilities. It equips its planes with the most sophisticated inflight electronic systems available for commercial aviation. If necessary, each plane can be flown and controlled by onboard computers from shortly after takeoff to touchdown at the Memphis SuperHub. As many as two hundred aircraft can be in the air simultaneously, but under the control of a single authority, should it become necessary to override flight plans because of weather or emergencies. The COSMOS system plans flight operations, monitors activity levels of ground personnel, manages workflows throughout the system, and coordinates the entire FedEx ground and air network in real time to ensure minimum time delays at lowest cost.

To maximize reliability further, FedEx systems eliminate as many sources of error as possible. To eliminate sorting errors, FedEx originally kept its sorting points to one—the Memphis SuperHub—and heavily automated that. To reduce errors there, its equipment is keyed around the simplest possible unit of data input, a single data block of destination zip code information. From this one input, automated handling systems enable temporary and part-time people at the SuperHub to capture instantly FedEx's entire history of experience curve effects, and thus provide maximum value-added at lowest cost for their function. To eliminate courier errors FedEx's DADS and computer-wand systems remove much of the interruptions, uncertainties, and misinterpretations of voice transmissions and manual data input. But all this technology also has a more important ancillary benefit: it allows FedEx couriers to concentrate their attention on the friendlier aspects of customer service.

Many of FedEx's technological features can be duplicated by others. But it is FedEx's uncommon attention to people and motivation that gives the company much of its uniqueness. The Federal Express Managers Manual states "People-Service-Profit [in that order] are the very foundations of Federal Express. . . . There is no acceptable reason . . . for failing to perform in accordance to our commitments—all the time." This is the company's official statement; and all managers are expected to exemplify, inculcate, and reward the values and actions that reinforce it. They do this through an elaborate system of training, MBO measurement (of outcomes), performance reviews (of work habits), and reward systems keyed to individual and team performance. But FedEx's management of service efficiency and employee quality performance goes well beyond this.

Involvement is encouraged at all levels; top executives hold regular bag lunches to answer employees' questions and listen to their suggestions; awards of up to $25,000 are given for productivity or quality improvement suggestions; top executives spend an entire morning each week on FedEx's Guaranteed Fair Treatment Program, often handling what many other companies might consider minor grievances through this process. Self-managed work groups take over many of the tasks of front-line management, such as scheduling, training, and performance appraisal. Group incentives encourage teams not to add people, because the per person share of their bonuses would drop. And sunset rules exist to terminate—rather than perpetuate—all temporary task forces. These techniques result in attitudes, levels of motivation, and a lack of bureaucracy that have made FedEx a formidable competitor. For many years considered one of "The Ten Best Companies in the U.S. to Work For," FedEx finds its employees—

even those at routine SuperHub tasks—work at a pace professional industrial engineers consider to be extraordinary.
Technology and careful people management, in coordination,
long provided the company its premier position as the lowest-cost,
most flexible, and most reliable supplier in the industry.

Vignette Two: American Express Company

American Express Company (AmEx), was the first financial services company to earn more than $1 billion in a year. With its
17,000 representatives, its Shearson Lehman unit has the nation's
largest retail securities sales force. Its four banking units hold
more than $50 billion in assets. With more than $200 billion under management, AmEx is probably the nation's largest money
manager. AmEx exemplifies several important ways in which service technologies can affect organizations. The extremely flat organization of its Shearson Lehman division has more than 300
domestic brokerage offices connected directly into its central information headquarters. Each of the division's far-flung representatives can serve its local community with all the benefits of a
small private firm, yet compete with the full power of a major
financial enterprise—simultaneously offering customers (1) lowest potential costs from economies of scale and better information
sources, (2) maximum product diversity, and (3) highly personalized local responsiveness.

TECHNOLOGY AND EMPOWERMENT

Elsewhere AmEx utilizes other aspects of technology's power.
AmEx is the only credit card company with a large travel service.
AmEx's Travel Related Services (TRS) Division has been growing
at 17 percent a year, its $800 million dollars in profits making
TRS, by itself, the third largest financial services company in the
United States. Technology has enabled AmEx's First Data Resources division to become the world's most efficient processor of
credit and charge transactions—so much so that it is now the
largest processor of its competitors' (Visa and MasterCard's)
transactions. More importantly, however, through its Genesis experiment TRS has been developing unique internal and customer
databases to revolutionize both its own strategies and the ways its
individual customers relate to each other. By capturing in suffi-

ciently disaggregated form the details of transactions that its various traveler, shopper, retailer, lodging, and transportation company customers put through its credit card and travel systems, TRS seeks to mix and match the needs and capabilities of each group and to add value for all in new ways. The key to the process is standardizing and classifying each transaction's components to a level of detail that, without disclosing inappropriate individual information to others, makes that component relevant not just for the particular transaction but for other purposes.

If fully implemented, Genesis can allow users to capture and temporarily store data on smart cards for their own travel and entertainment reports or records to facilitate later reports and analyses. The card itself could be used directly—through telephone or computer interfaces—to make reservations, obtain money, or buy goods and services. Genesis technology could also allow many inquiries on account status to be handled through ATMs or other remote terminals. It seeks to structure data access so that decentralized "800 number" operators can answer almost all inquiries by using "expert system" rules coded into inquiry banks and the individual customer's records. Responses to each inquiry then can be facilitated by experience-based decision rules allowing much more delegation with reduced risks. The target is to be able to train operators in a week to service more products more effectively than those with six months' training could previously handle.

In test runs, AmEx found its expert systems actually increased the quality and consistency of responses versus human operators working alone. The system reduced the number of questions referred to supervisors and concentrated their managers' attention on higher value-added questions. Simultaneously, the increased decentralization allowed by the system enhanced the importance and interest of lower-level jobs, their productivity, and their potential pay levels. In time the more highly decentralized, distributed processing approach Genesis is delivering may also dramatically redefine the skills relevant for AmEx's computer, software development, and intermediate management activities.

NEW NETWORK OPPORTUNITIES

The greater disaggregation of data created for AmEx also generates a whole new set of opportunities and services for AmEx's network of customers, who are otherwise completely independent. For credit card customers or retailers who are reliable, good credit risks and rarely have disputes, AmEx can quickly resolve 98 percent of disputed billings in ways that assist its customers and cost AmEx much less than prolonged negotiations. From captured data it can identify individuals' life-style changes, such as marriage or moving, and can match forthcoming travel plans with individual consumers' specific buying habits. This allows AmEx to target special services on behalf of both those customers and AmEx's retail customers located near the customers' home or travel destinations. AmEx reportedly now sells about $500 million a year in high-quality direct mail items to its cardholders and hopes to move into other service products as a result of its expanded data capabilities. Because of the personal services it provides, AmEx already charges a premium over other credit cards. Greater disaggregation can also allow AmEx to provide its 2 million retailers with more sophisticated and specialized services, like demographic or comparative analyses of their customer bases, data for negotiating with travel agents or hotels for better rates, or such other helpful information as needs for wheelchair or pickup services for handicapped customers.

Because of its more complete and detailed data structures, AmEx can segment markets and target its promotions with more selectivity, precision, and yield than ever before. By capturing even more details from its databases, TRS hopes to introduce its future new products much more rapidly and over a broader geographical base, both keys to its future competitiveness. By providing data in new ways, the Genesis project (even though not completely implemented) can enable TRS to add value well beyond current levels—including such special services to selected customers as electronic mail, travel planning, comparison shopping, local travel information, product warranties, and responses on inquiries about items not yet billed. All this, in turn, should increase AmEx's differentiation as a high-status, higher-priced alternative in the charge card industry.

Vignette Three: General Mills Restaurant Group*

General Mills Restaurant Group's (GMR's) unique "dinner house" chain concept (which includes Red Lobster, Olive Gardens, and Bennigan's) has enjoyed a long-term annual growth rate of 15–16 percent in volume and 17.5 percent in profits. GMR's sophisticated use of new management concepts and technology at both the strategic and operations level has been its key to providing simultaneously both a friendlier, more responsive atmosphere and lower competitive prices. GMR has approached technology in the broadest possible terms and has implemented it on a very wide geographical and cross-organizational basis. While the individual components of its various systems are often not completely new or unique, the systematic way GMR has implemented its technologies and the impact they have had is extraordinary.

At the strategic level, by tapping into the most extensive and disaggregated databases in its industry, GMR can break down available operating, logistics, and marketing data to the most detailed levels possible. It then uses conceptual mapping techniques to define precise unserved needs in the away-from-home eating market. GMR's technologies can determine not just whether people want Italian food, but whether they want Italian fast food, dinner-house, midpriced, or upscale food; what ambiance packages they might desire, what price points they associate with each combination; and what value contexts are likely to influence the success of the most attractive concepts. Using these inputs, a creative internal and external team of restaurateurs, chefs, and culinary institutes arrives at a few concept designs for test. Using other models derived from its databases, GMR can pretest and project the nationwide impact of the selected concepts and even define the specific neighborhoods most likely to support that concept. Within these areas other technologies combine to designate optimum restaurant sitings and to create the architectural designs likely to be the most successful. Once a decision has been made to build a restaurant in a particular location, PERT and other operations research technologies are used to optimize site development and construction plans, and to keep building costs as low as possible. Al-

* Interview by author with Joe Lee, President of General Mills Restaurant Group, summer 1988.

though not foolproof, these systems decrease the likelihood of costly strategic positioning errors and specify the design and location features most likely to increase volumes for individual outlets.

At the operations level, by mixing and matching very detailed performance data from its own operations and laboratory analyses, GMR can specify or select the best individual pieces and combinations of kitchen equipment to use in light of investment considerations, performance characteristics, operating costs, repair needs, flexibility for different menus, systems fit with other pieces of equipment, and so on. For a given restaurant concept it uses its own experience and other data to create a facility layout that will demand the minimum personnel, walking distances, cleanup times, breakdown costs, and overhead costs to operate. Using its lab data, GMR works with equipment manufacturers to optimize their designs for its needs, thus obtaining a further competitive edge.

Once a restaurant unit is functioning, GMR has an integrated electronic point-of-sale and operations management system directly connected to headquarters computers for monitoring and analysis. Because employee time cards are really computer cards—coded by employee number and task category—which are read into the EPOS computer rather than a time clock, a restaurant manager can monitor and manage labor by the fraction of the hour, job classification, task, etc., against preset schedules and standards, ensuring that local quality and cost controls meet GMR standards. An inventory, sales tracking, and forecasting program automatically adjusts plans, measures, and controls for holidays, time of day, seasonality, weather, special offers, and promotions. But the local manager overrides for temporary local events, like conventions or street repairs, that the system could not anticipate. These programs not only minimize operating costs and wasted food but also ensure that inventories are balanced to provide customers with the freshest possible food—in the proper stage of preparation—for rapid service with the fullest possible menu selections.

At the logistics level, using one of industry's most sophisticated satellite, earth sensing, and databased systems, GMR can forecast and track fisheries (and other food sources) worldwide. For example, by tracking the acidity, salinity, and temperatures of U.S. and other river systems entering the Gulf of Mexico, GMR can predict short- and long-term shrimp and fish yields, species availability, and prices, and can plan its menus, promotions, and purchases accordingly. With raw materials costs being a high percentage of operating cost—but able to vary as much as 70–80 percent in a short time—this is critical to GMR's low-cost strategy. It also knows its menu needs in such detail that it teaches suppliers exactly how to size, cut, and pack fish for maximum market value and minimum handling cost to GMR, while achieving minimum waste and shipping costs for the supplier.

With the increased control and flexibility its systems provide, GMR has been able to flatten its organizations significantly, eliminating regional headquarters, doubling the number of restaurant managers reporting to a single supervisor, saving tens of millions of dollars a year, and shortening decision cycles from the field to headquarters. Overhead cost savings have been dramatic. When GMR recently acquired a smaller chain, it found that to manage the acquired twenty-seven outlets with that chain's existing cash register system would have taken as many people as it did to manage all of GMR's 400 other outlets with its advanced systems. Technology provided an ROI on personnel costs alone of 15 to 1, with improved quality and responsiveness. But perhaps the technology's greatest personnel benefit is that instead of working restaurant managers 6 to $6\frac{1}{2}$ days a week—with 10–12-hour days being routine—GMR can promise managers 8-hour days and 5-day weeks. Instead of struggling with reports and statistical details, managers can spend their time motivating employees, handling special problems, providing personal attention to customers, getting subtle feedback from them, and carrying out special community and promotional activities designed to increase volume. All this has made it easier to attract higher-grade employees and restaurant managers, who in turn help to ensure that intended quality and service levels are delivered. By using videotape updates, carefully implemented training cycles, and recertification of its restaurant managers, GMR makes sure that all its outlets share the entire system's experience curve benefits.

To ensure quality and customer responsiveness, GMR monitors output quality continuously. Its system allows it to "poll" the restaurants' sales and operating patterns each night to see if undesired trends are developing. Incentive systems reward managers for hitting targets, not for cutting costs too tightly. These are tied to 50,000 "satisfaction tracking surveys" performed each month to monitor GMR and competing chains on eight measures that consumers use as quality indicators. The computer automatically flags any unusual performance in measured variables, three times a day, for the restaurant manager and central office. From the marketing standpoint, GMR has such detailed and up-to-date sales information that it can tell within a few days how well an advertising campaign or promotion is working—and adjust it in midcycle. As a result of their coordinated and thorough application of technology, GMR's dinner houses have consistently been able to supply quality food at 10–15 percent lower prices than most competitors, yet provide a 15–20 percent return to investors.

CHAPTER 5

Service Based Disaggregation with Strategic Focus

Services and service technologies have opened a wide variety of new organizational options for managing intellect on a much more disaggregated basis. The infinitely flat, spider's web, and inverted forms embrace the most common structures. But there are many other configurations, the most significant being "starburst," "cluster," and "voluntary" organizations. All these radical organizations enjoy certain common characteristics and similar problems.

- All tend to be flatter than their hierarchical predecessors. All assume a constant dynamic rather than stasis in their structures. And all support greater empowerment of people closer to the customer contact level.
- All develop around a maintainable set of core service competencies at their center. These competencies—typically consisting of special depth in some unique technologies, knowledge bases, skills, or organizational-motivational systems—are then radiated outward toward customers by information technologies or through organizational dynamics that enable mixed clusters of people, with greater knowledge access, to work directly with customers.
- All recognize intellect, motivation, and knowledge bases as the most highly leverageable assets of a company. They use the new organization forms and their supporting systems as improved ways to attract, keep, and leverage key people as knowledge resources.

146

- Successful companies use their new organizations as both aggressive and defensive strategies. Most companies look to these forms initially to lower costs, decrease cycle times, and ensure more precise implementation of strategy. At the same time, they allow the companies to bring more energy, focus, and responsiveness to bear on customers than ever before. But companies have also found that these organizations make the firm a more exciting, personally challenging, and satisfying place to work.

Like earlier decentralization or SBU concepts, some of these new organization modes have often been touted as cures for almost any management ill. They are not. Each form is useful in certain situations, and not in others. But more importantly, each requires a carefully developed infrastructure of culture, measurements, style, and rewards to support it. When properly installed, these disaggregated organizations can be awesomely effective in harnessing intellectual resources for certain purposes. When improperly supported or adapted, they can be less effective than old-fashioned hierarchies. What are some of the more interesting applications?

"STARBURST," "FEDERAL," AND "CLUSTER" FORMS

Some highly innovative companies have found a special form of disaggregation—best described as a "starburst" organization—to be very effective. These companies constantly "split off" and "sell off" units like shooting stars peeled from the core competencies of their parents.[1] Rather than extinguish their innovative fires with the constant dousing of internal bureaucracies, Cypress Semiconductor, Raychem, and Thermo Electron create whole new enterprises, partially owned by the parent, but free to grow as entrepreneurially as they wish with outside capital infusions. MCI constantly seeks to grow by finding and developing associations with small companies having interesting services it can hang onto the MCI network. 3M and HP continuously sprout freestanding new product lines from their core technology and innovation skills. And all seem to run into trouble only when they lose faith in their freestanding "shooting stars" and try to consolidate functions in the name of efficiency. 3M, Raychem, and HP all went through this unhappy phase and later (happily) reversed again.

FIGURE 5–1
The Starburst Organization

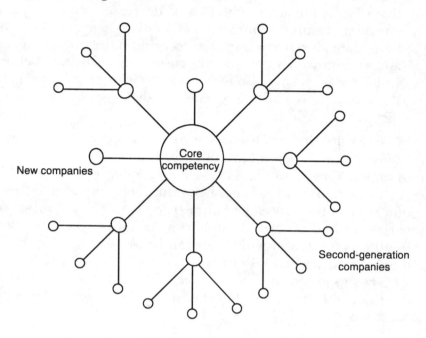

How long can these starbursts continue? As long as the core competency is maintained in depth and the corporate center has the capacity and faith to attract, trust, and oversee the venturers who entrepreneur small-scale technologies into product lines. The same could be said for any venture capital firm. And the formula for success will be much the same—a very few knowledgeable risk-takers at the core who know they cannot micro manage their diverse entities and don't try to do so. In the "starburst," the corporate center primarily raises resources, seeds the core competency, manages the culture, and sets priorities by selecting people and letting them bid for resources. The body and glitter of the company—like the skyrocket after its burst—is not in the center, but in its surrounding clusters of activities. While very useful in the proper circumstances, not all entrepreneurial companies should operate in this mode. Our research suggests that it does not work well for large-scale, heavy-investment, very long-term, or heavily mass-produced items.[2] The reasons for this and ways to adapt this mode for other situations are developed in Chapter 9.

"FEDERAL" AND "CLUSTER" ORGANIZATIONS

Charles Handy has identified other companies as operating in "federal" organizations (or what he calls "donut" organization modes) for other purposes. Federal organizations have moved beyond decentralization, because decentralization ceases to work effectively as they become sufficiently diverse and dispersed. Information needs in each of their operating divisions become so highly specialized and profuse that the center cannot possibly make composite sense of what is going on, much less manage activities better than the individual activity centers. As such organizations grow, says Handy, "Managers [try first] to run them all from the core at the center, relying on the new technologies to provide all the information needed. The new technologies do not fail, but information to be useful still has to be interpreted by its human masters. . . . In the end they have to stop asking for the information, they have to stop trying to run everything from the center, have to begin to let go. Then decentralization turns into federalism."[3] Agglomerations of discrete high-technology medical products or instrumentation companies provide excellent examples.

D. Quinn Mills goes a step farther. He states that what we have always accepted as formal hierarchy is actually disappearing in many larger, formerly bureaucratic settings. He says these institutions are shifting toward what he calls "cluster" organizations. Hierarchies, he notes, may have been appropriate when workforces were unskilled, uneducated, and often unmotivated to perform repetitive factory work. But they are often not effective for highly trained, better-motivated people doing the constantly varying tasks many office-based knowledge workers now perform. Mills concludes:

> Communications and technology are the great sources of productivity advances in the future. [In factories] automation has proceeded very far, and there are few people left in the plants. But there are enormous gains to be made in offices. . . . The real question is: How is this to be achieved? Technology alone is not the answer. Advanced communication and information networks contribute to enhanced productivity only if people are able to utilize them fully. This is a management, not a technical, issue.[4]

Instead of operating like independent (but more permanent) starbursts, Mills says organizations should form loosely related clusters or teams to carry out specific tasks. Unlike true adhocracies, these organizations form around some relatively permanent activity classes, which then lend their people temporarily to form (as needed) into task-oriented units. Some clusters work primarily on selected continuing activities, for example dealing with external customers, handling internal customers' needs for staff services, managing alliances, or generating longer-term innovations (see Figure 5–2). However, each team will form and re-form into smaller task clusters within the unit to solve specific problems that affect that cluster's own activity. In addition, people cross from one cluster to another as needed to solve particular problems that require multiple groups' skills.

Cluster organizations are neither traditional adhocracies nor committee organizations. While generally focusing on one specific activity set, people are expected and trained to participate in solutions for the whole entity. Although giving the highest profile to adding value through team solutions, clusters enhance individuals as well by letting them participate in varying and higher-level opportunities. As Mills says, "Playing for the Boston Celtics doesn't destroy Larry Bird's individuality; instead it gives him the support of others to maximize his own potential." Large companies as mature and diverse as Volvo, GE, DuPont, GM, IBM, and BP have used cluster organizations in specific situations to delayer and to obtain greater customer focus, motivation, and responsiveness. Smaller high-tech companies often start in this disaggregated mode.

FIGURE 5–2
The Cluster Organization

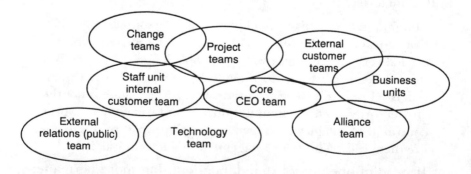

SOURCE: Adapted from D. Q. Mills, *Rebirth of the Corporation*, (New York: J. Wiley & Sons, 1991), p. 31.

Like all the other new organization forms, clusters seem to work well in certain circumstances, i.e., when there is a base load of common but variable activity yet a high incidence of completely new, cross-specialty problem-solving needed. They flourish when skills for problems of a certain class can be geographically centralized but move more to a network mode for more dispersed problems. Like all the other disaggregated modes described, they require a great deal of trust and mutual respect to operate well. Although cluster groups can solve some problems in short order, they typically take a long time (two to three years) to create the acculturation needed for people to operate continuously in their unstructured environments. Like the other modes, they are very dependent on the quality of leadership and the breadth of training and motivation of those who participate.

Clusters tend to sacrifice some benefits of specialization but substitute a learning environment, which may be even more helpful in the long run. While clusters provide another interesting model for many more geographically or operationally centralized organizations, they do not fit as well for highly dispersed, more repetitive, or highly individualized and localized activities like brokerage, retail chain, or telephone services, where repeated fast action and operating cost efficiencies are dominant considerations. Nor do they deal as well with professional specialist activities like medical care, where a very skilled practitioner delivers the same basic limited set of procedures over and over again and needs a highly coordinated team that performs just those functions well—not necessarily creatively, but proficiently.

THE "VOLUNTARY" ORGANIZATION

How far can these various modes of disaggregation go? The answer is: to the stage that the hierarchical organization almost ceases to exist or be meaningful—except as a means for lowering resource costs, periodically bringing people together, and setting overall priorities. In today's knowledge-based industries, the best people (i.e., those most capable of creating value-added) don't *have* to work for a particular company. Unlike the "wage slaves" of the past, they are where they are because they want to be there. For them, the corporation has become a "voluntary" organization to be joined because it can let them achieve more of their personal goals than any other institution can. Such people will only be part of any enterprise if it lets them achieve what they could not aspire to on their own.

ATTRACTING AND KEEPING VOLUNTEERS

Executives who manage with this in mind can more successfully attract, motivate, and keep the very best talent. If not, they consciously create their own competitors. The best talent gravitates to companies like Microsoft, Genentech, Bankers Trust, Intel, Davis Polk Wardwell, Bell Laboratories, Marsh & McLennan, and so on, because these firms work on the largest and most exciting problems. And the best talent will only stay for the long run if the company provides the most advanced technologies, management concepts, and facilities to support them. In product companies, like Analog Devices, special functions like design, manufacturing engineering, and customer-intensive activities are also managed as "voluntary organizations." In fact (to the author's knowledge), Analog's CEO, Ray Stata, coined this term.

To be "best in world" in any of the activities where specialist groups dominate, a firm has to conceptualize a combination of technologies and management techniques that make it the most attractive place in its field for key people to "volunteer," to perform, and to stay. For example:

■ The Orbital Engine Company of Perth, Australia, is an interesting example. Orbital is designing state-of-the-art small engines for automobiles, using extremely advanced fuel injection and combustion control systems. Its announced mileage performances show 40–50 percent gains over standard engines, with 0.08 ppb (parts per billion) of NOx emission. Its engines are in verification tests by EPA, the National Academy of Sciences, and all major manufacturers. CEO Ralph T. Sarich notes:

> We are dealing with the best-known design people in the world as customers, and we must be better. Since people come here to work in a small company environment on the most exciting problems and concepts that exist, we can attract almost anyone who can work in our unique environment. We throw people into deep water fast. We give them the feeling that the company depends on them, and they learn to respect that responsibility. No single engineer can outdesign the ten good people our competitors could put on the same project. So we always work in

teams, and people are willing to put in long hours whenever it is necessary.

At Orbital the attitudes of the people you work with are as important as their technical knowhow. So they are always interviewed by both specialists in their field and their team peers. We pay reasonably, but no more than anyone else, and the pay of the top people is not above average. People are here because of the technology and the task. Once here we try to stimulate all our people. For example, we gave an executive secretary the task of putting together a major "due diligence" report. She found out what was needed, who had the information, and how to package it. She did a terrific job, increased her value to the company, and gained enormous self-confidence. When you give good people a chance, they don't let you down.

We combine trust with a heavy dose of discipline. Lunches here are simple. Alcohol or drugs mean dismissal. In our flexitime system, if you are two minutes late, it costs you fifteen minutes. Five minutes late costs you thirty. One of our professional staff was unreasonable and disrespectful with our office staff. As a result he was severely reprimanded because the company operates on the principle that all staff are treated fairly and respectfully, no matter what position they hold. The person was warned of dismissal if he failed to effectively work as a team member. If the phone rings three times, someone answers it. We don't care who; I'll answer it if I'm there. To be best in our field, you have to make no errors, you have to be honest, and create trust among everyone. If you don't have trust, you waste enormous amounts of time. And if you're not honest, you'll be wrong. We can't afford any errors.[5]

The need for a "voluntary organization" is most apparent in professional services—such as accounting, law, consulting, entertainment, research, design, engineering, finance, marketing, or public relations—where key people can move so easily. The best-qualified professionals naturally seek out and stay with firms that provide the most advanced technologies and exciting environments for practicing their art. Interestingly, therefore, strategic management of technology in professional firms provides a dual leverage. On the one hand, it enhances the professionals' personal capabilities within the firm—expanding their salary potentials and enabling them to receive higher billing rates. Yet at the same time it creates a dependency that ties key people more tightly to the enterprise. Thus used, technology serves both a crucial offensive and a crucial defensive role.

■ Well-managed accounting, legal, consulting, and financial services houses—recognizing the competitive significance of their information resources—use technology as a multi-edged weapon. They continuously capture, catalogue, and store updated regulations, legal opinions, client and industry data, and professional practice rules in automated systems in order to ensure the highest quality for their services. In some cases they capture and reproduce judgmental aspects of intellect in "expert" or artificial intelligence systems. For efficiency they also automate routine audit, client analysis, and other repetitive operations (like contract clauses and audit procedures), enabling staff members to concentrate on the unique aspects of each client's situation. This has progressed so far that some activities—like basic audit functions in CPA firms or the portfolio and bubble chart analyses that used to be core offerings of many consulting firms—have become commodities with such low margins that they are often used primarily as promotional activities to obtain other business.

Freed from overseeing these routine tasks, key people gain the excitement of solving more challenging problems and earning the higher revenues these allow. Many professional service firms now find that the core of their distinctive competency lies in the accumulated knowledge of their databases and the expert software systems that capture the firm's most advanced analytical thinking—and their members' capacity to access these resources and to devise entirely new solutions from them. Their technologies create formidable entry barriers for competitors, switching costs for clients, and (perhaps most importantly) barriers to exit for their own key personnel, who would lose access to the firm's databases and analytical software if they left.

THE BEST OFFENSE IS ALSO A GOOD DEFENSE

Strategic use of technology in these situations revolves around certain imperatives. *First,* the technology must be "enabling," i.e., designed to enable key users to leverage their personal skills and to enhance their value to the greatest possible extent. *Second,* it should capture the "maximum complexity possible" in repeatable solutions, allow for constant updates of data, and provide flexible opportunities to segment and aggregate the data in the "most refined detail possible." *Third,* to realize the maximum value from the technology, other infrastructures need to change—for example, quotes, billings, internal controls, and incentives may need to shift from a "time spent" basis toward a "value-added" concept. While being simple to access, the technology's innards must be sufficiently complicated and well protected that it is nonportable and so unique that its loss will genuinely inhibit key individuals from leaving.

To reinforce their systems' security, an increasing number of firms follow defense industry practices of encrypting key elements in the system and sealing off access to these sections to all but a few technical specialists tied to the firm by golden incentive chains. Such defensive considerations are especially critical in independent professional partnerships but are becoming increasingly common in divisions of product-oriented companies—for example, in research, design, or marketing—where value-added from services is high and an individual's personal knowledge or contacts may be central to the enterprise's success.

EMPOWERING "VOLUNTEERS" IN MASS SERVICE ORGANIZATIONS

While emphasizing the voluntary nature of professional organizations, the same view holds to a large extent for more mass-produced services. Perhaps the most important strategic differences between large-scale services and manufacturing operations are (1) the fact that most services are consumed in the very moment they are produced, (2) the high degree of geographical dispersion often separating headquarters from the service's production and delivery points, and (3) the dependency of the entire system on the attitudes and skills of individual people, particularly those at the contact point with the customer. Companies, of course, may differ radically in where the bulk of the value-added is created. In financial services, for example, analysts in the back rooms may be critical. In medicine, the doctor or caregiver dominates. In most cases—however heavily skewed the balance may be toward the center or the contact point—the best service results only if all elements do their jobs well. The customer may most immediately feel the influence of the point person. But back-office competency (in financial services) or the maintenance, nursing, and sterilization support teams (in hospital operating rooms) determine at least as much of the long-term success of the transaction.

Those people who create the greatest value in these situations are genuinely "volunteers"; their skills, attitudes, and knowledge are such that they rarely have to stay with a particular company unless they so choose. They often have been described as "critical assets who walk out the door every night." All those in key service positions, but especially the people who deal directly with customers, need an environment where they *want* to perform well and are trained and empowered to do so. In mass service organizations, such people—often numbering in the thousands—tend to be at the most remote locations from the corporate center. Customers want these people to be friendly, responsive, and sometimes creative. Yet they must deliver the company's special competency with assured quality and efficiency, each time, every time.

This requires empowerment with control. To deliver against this standard, the most successful mass service producers focus on two things: (1) providing the point person, in a timely fashion, with all the empowering details—including information, supplies, instant system access, and clear, specific performance measures—that make quality performance possible, and (2) paying special attention to values and attitude management—i.e., selection, indoctrination, skills training, and incentive systems—for the people who actually create and deliver the service. Values management is crucial both to ensure maximum responsiveness at the contact point and to be as certain as possible that the point person will intuitively respond in the proper way when unique situations occur.

To accomplish this, the premier service companies not only train and retrain constantly, they reinforce values repeatedly with slogans (like "absolutely, positively, on time"), with extensive cheerleading sessions, and with inculcation and dissemination of myths. All remember the FedEx employee who saved Baby Jessica from the well where she had fallen. Another myth surrounds the FedEx courier who voluntarily spent his Labor Day getting a supply of matched blood to a child who needed it for surgery the next day in Boston. More importantly, executives who take values leadership seriously constantly retell such myths internally, back the myths with their own personal commitment—for example, Fed-

Ex's CEO, Fred Smith, personally calling my secretary for details about an overseas package that was late—and support desired values with the full power of the incentive systems of the company.

■ American Express Company (AmEx) identifies and enshrines its heroes of customer service in a series of "Great Performers" booklets. One of these was the Boston service representative who rose in the middle of the night to deliver a card to a stranded customer in Logan Airport. "Great Performers" is distributed to all of AmEx's 45,000 service employees worldwide as a constant target and reminder of expectations. But AmEx also reinforces the personal service message constantly in other ways. AmEx surveys its customers endlessly and uses over 40 customer-based metrics to measure its customers' perceptions of each service it offers. Then CEO James Robinson presses the message home with constantly repeated slogans like "membership has its privileges" and his favorite, "quality is the only patent protection we've got." The result: employees and customers respond. The Nilson Report, which monitors the credit card industry, describes American Express's service image as "incomparable."[6]

The best people will not stay if a company culture does not actively support high performance and quality values. Hence the inordinate attention leading companies like American Express, Bell Laboratories, Microsoft, Merck, Federal Express, Intel, Sony, The New York Times Company, and Genentech spend on reinforcing enterprise values that will attract top people. All enjoy long lists of talented applicants at all times. Technology and values management are the keys to job satisfaction at all levels of service organizations.

The best employees initially come to a firm where they can work most productively and pleasantly. How well the company and its technology systems then support them—whether they are actuaries, researchers, lawyers, skilled technicians, expensive professionals, or sales clerks and baggage handlers—will ultimately be reflected in their creativity, responsiveness, and efficiency, and most importantly in how well they treat customers. Since managing values and culture is one of the most important concepts contributing to quality and productivity in today's service-based "intelligent enterprises," this topic will be developed extensively in

Chapters 8–10. What are some of the other central management themes leading to success with these new organization forms?

COMMON MANAGEMENT THEMES

First, any new organizational form selected—and its performance evaluation, incentive, and management support structures—must reflect the special balances management is seeking in its overall strategy. This will almost always involve some intermixture with more traditional structures. Thus a company may have a predominantly market, region, product group, or function oriented macro structure. Yet within any given group, it may be desirable to implement an infinitely flat, spider's web, starburst, cluster, or inverted form. Conversely, a management may choose to emphasize one of these forms across the entire enterprise—if strategic prerequisites dictate—yet have individual divisions or departments operating in more traditional structures. In many places good old-fashioned hierarchies will probably work quite well. Our research does not lead us to espouse one organizational form in preference to another, only to encourage managements to consider much more radical solutions than they may have in the past.

The three elements needed to implement these concepts—adequate supporting technologies, appropriate management techniques, and new methodologies for influencing employee attitudes—as well as exemplary success models, are widely available to those who wish to go ahead. Each organizational mode presents its own fascinating prospects, but none fits all situations. Each is useful for some purposes and not others. Yet as different as these organizations appear, they all share certain common characteristics and goals. A few are summarized here. The remainder of the book will develop these and other issues in greater depth.

DESTRUCTION OF BUREAUCRACIES

Perhaps the most striking common characteristic of these new organization forms is their dramatic and immediate capacity to reduce management layers and organizational bureaucracies. While this goal is widespread among all enterprises, it is especially critical in providing effective services. Delivering reliably against the customer's demand for as much personalization, responsiveness, and customization as possible at the point of sale is usually paramount. This means the maximum possible purge of all intermediate levels of interpretation, decisionmaking, or processing between the service's producer and its user. The direct costs of bureaucracy are obvious enough. But each transfer or intermediary point in the service chain also introduces unintended errors, distorts intentions, and creates costly though unmeasured delays, which can outweigh such direct costs by a substantial margin. Because the outputs of service activities are so difficult to measure, without great care their costs can balloon uncontrollably over time.

Yet most companies do not approach the problem correctly at the outset. As their first attack point, companies usually try to automate what their bureaucracies are already doing. Generally this does not help much. Our respondents repeatedly noted that when they mechanized only existing functions, unless they were just simple transactions, their companies generally failed to achieve expected efficiencies—or measurable productivity improvements of any sort. Transaction costs might drop, but transaction rates or other support overheads often rose more than proportionately. To make real productivity or quality gains, they found they needed to eliminate whole tasks and to think carefully about redesigning the entire work system and its many outmoded individual practices before they automated. There are many horror stories, but a few well-documented examples will point up the problem.

■ One insurance company attempted to automate its extensive Rolodex files of customer contacts only to find later that the computer system was used only to print new Rolodex cards for the old file system, at a net loss in total efficiency. Like many others, another insurance company, Mass Mutual, put PCs on every desk at headquarters, but the staff there grew from 3,300 to 4,300 in five years as it thought up new things to do. Overall, technology investments by major financial services houses grew in the 1980s at 15 percent a year, but the number of employees on Wall Street grew even faster as transactions and volumes soared. And so on.

Stephen Roach of Morgan Stanley has repeatedly displayed macro data showing investments in service sector technology doubling per worker every eight years, but with essentially no gain in productivity as measured by government data sources. As a later chapter will indicate, much of this effect is caused by definitional and measurement problems in the government data. However, there are some very real problems that need to be attacked with vigor, as many of our respondents noted:

■ Mr. Raymond Caron, Chief Information Officer (CIO) of the CIGNA companies, said,

> With the emergence of the electronic spreadsheet, we suddenly have hundreds of financial types who are wizards at spreadsheet work. You have to ask the question, however, "How many times do you have to display this kind of data, and who cares?" People get into "making it look good" when they have all this computing power at their disposal. Executives start to question: "Are all these technology tools having any value in terms of the bottom line?" When CIGNA began automating straight clerical activities, we achieved very high payoff, demonstrably, on our investments. However, as we moved beyond clerical automation, the effectiveness of our investments became less clear.
>
> For example, when we began automating some of CIGNA's agents, the theory was that if we gave the agents better tools, we would have less work coming into our office for the underwriters to do. Naturally, there would be an improvement in service, as well as a shift in the workload. For the most part, the shift in workload didn't happen primarily because we underestimated the amount of effort required to change traditional underwriting practice. Because there wasn't a design change in the basic underwriting process, we really did not achieve our goals. As we push further into the managerial ranks, we're finding that just automating activities that managers do doesn't produce any direct payoff. It seems that as you eliminate work from their queue, they find other work to replace the eliminated activities.
>
> Now the question is: "Does the original or replacement work have value?" At the bottom line of the company, I think the answer was no. Employees will create new work if they perceive you're threatening their jobs. We found examples where the underwriting processes were tied so closely to traditional techniques that underwriters could redo what an agent had done just to validate the agent's accuracy.

Mr. Melvin Ollestad, Senior Vice President, further noted:

As you break organizational barriers, change and redefine some of the functions of the organization, there is a certain amount of pain involved. But it is better to do the re-engineering and re-organization first, then do the automation. The second big problem was in not involving the real users enough in the automation process, and getting people who are actually building the system together with the people who were doing the work. In the past we tended to use a bunch of "go-betweens" so that the people actually building the system might never have seen the people who were doing the work.

Now as we've established self-directed teams, we try to bring in some representatives from the customer, especially if it's just one customer being served by a team. The customer companies all have their ideas on what we ought to be automating—and how it ought to be done—so that we get so much advice we can't really deal with it all. But you want to get as much of it as you can.

RE-ENGINEER PROCESSES, THEN REDESIGN ORGANIZATIONS

Our respondents noted quite consistently that they attained neither significant organizational changes nor efficiency gains if they either (1) installed new desktop computers, LANS, or elaborate workstation software without totally re-engineering their processes or (2) preannounced de-layering or new organization structures as their goals for automation. The most successful approached the problem from the opposite direction. They first re-engineered all tasks in a given activity with the help of both professional work analysts and the workers themselves. After getting the task flows designed right, they automated those steps that made sense. Then with worker participation, they redesigned the organization to perform the remaining tasks most efficiently. Many paraphrased, "We could have achieved most of the productivity gains by just re-engineering processes and rethinking our organizations. But the new technologies often gave us the excuse for making changes and the basis for next-generation capabilities. When implemented together the results were very impressive."

Efficiency gains of 60 to 90 percent were not uncommon. In fact, most leading users said they routinely used 6–18-month paybacks as hurdle rates for these kinds of projects. Even more impressive were the genuine morale gains achieved as people began to operate with their new systems in a self-directed way. This was especially true when displacements were absorbed by attrition or growth throughout the company. As later chapters will indicate, however, disillusionment, frustration, and recriminations could develop if other elements of the organization failed to respond to the new efficiencies of the redesigned process. All was not sweetness and light.

As Roach says, the problem of reducing overheads is daunting and needs a systematic attack by all companies.[7] But our interviews show clearly that using a zero-based—anything can go—attack in a classic industrial engineering fashion can work wonders when combined with sensitive organizational change procedures. The steps are straightforward: (1) Analyze the total task and its interfaces. (2) Try to simplify or eliminate a total system first. (3) Then analyze each activity within the system with an eye toward totally eliminating it or any of its discrete parts. (4) Simplify the rest. (5) Then automate the most onerous, most burdensome, least creative remaining activities. (6) At each stage, ask whether the company can or should be "best in world" at that activity in order to serve its customers optimally. (7) If not, consider outsourcing it. (8) Interactively co-design and reorganize all personnel activities and systems around what remains. Chapter 11 develops relevant issues and approaches in detail.

Targeting both internal and external service activities in this way can lead to startling competitive gains, but only if organizations and support systems are changed at the same time. Most companies reported that de-layering and new team-based or flat structures were effective only if re-engineering and personnel planning were properly performed. When this happened, overheads often dropped precipitously, while customers received more rapid response times and much better quality service. For example:

■ In the order-processing section of GE's circuit breaker division, the elapsed time from order receipt to delivery was an excruciating three weeks. With a target of no more than three days for the cycle, GE consolidated six production units into one, reducing a variety of former inventory and handling steps. It automated the design system to replace a human custom-design process. The technology saved a week while maintaining 40,000 different product configurations to meet customer needs. But it took a major organizational change—cutting the organizational layers between managers and workers from three to only one—to achieve the remaining time gains. Productivity went up 20 percent in one year, and manufacturing unit costs went down 30 percent.[8] Motorola cut order-processing times from two days down to four minutes. And American Express cut out three layers of hierarchy when it developed self-managed teams to handle all types of customer inquiries in a single-call, quick-resolution mode.

Our interview respondents offered numerous other examples of organizational flattening. Some of the more interesting were:

■ Mr. Richard Liebhaber, Chief Strategy and Technology Officer of MCI, noted:

> There isn't a lot of paper here that isn't electronic messages. We manage our business through MCI mail; we don't have a lot of staff meetings, a lot of committees. We have a few things that come to us on paper, but that only takes four or five pages of printout. That is how we manage our company. We get boiled-down reports that we call "flight controls," so we have the ability to correct things quickly. Electronic mail has helped us flatten the organization. We do about 1 million internal e-mail messages a week. We have only five levels of organization between operations and my office. That is a policy. With about 4,000 people in five tiers, the average span of control is about 11.8

■ Mr. Raymond Caron, CIO, CIGNA companies said:

> We have flattend the Systems organization dramatically. I have 15 direct reports, and that kind of span of control is becoming common. This is a far cry from the "1 over 3 or 1 over 5" designs we had in the past. You just don't need them. As we flatten organizations, it doesn't take a rocket scientist to figure out who gets flattened. That's where middle management resistance starts. The second area is in the first line . . . When employees become part of work teams they have to learn a lot of new skills such as team leadership and group dynamics. It takes a lot of energy and hard work. Some people just don't get there.

The New York Times offers a major example of the kind of significant restructuring technology can cause in knowledge-based services:

■ In major newspapers, like *The New York Times,* electronic technologies now enable editors and reporters to go directly to printable copy in final format at their electronic work stations. While still in contact with their field sources, they can pretest spacings, enhance picture quality, and lay out entire pages without handling any hard copy. Through eliminating make up, typesetting, and multiple proofing stages, they cut costs, shorten cycle times, and deliver more current news to their customers. But to accomplish this *The New York Times* had to revise its entire structure of page preparation and editing. Editing often is done on line with the reporter, and elaborate software has been developed to track all changes made in copy. Instead of passing the paper's preparation linearly across many different functional divisions, multifunctional teams from the editorial, art, advertising, and layout groups make up each page simultaneously, avoiding errors, rework, and lost time of earlier sequential processes. In order to accomplish needed work changes, there had to be extensive union negotiations and task rearrangements to eliminate many typesetting and production operations and to reabsorb people, where possible, into new tasks. Without these reorganizations and the elimination of whole sequences of operations, *The Times* would not have realized measurable productivity gains despite its $450 million in investments for new flexible makeup and production processes.

Nor could it have used the technology as it has to target its news to the multiple geographic, income, and demographic units it has segmented in its marketplaces. In addition, *The Times* is moving its databases over to electronics as rapidly as possible to ensure the thoroughness and quality of its background information on stories and special analyses. All these steps enable *The New York Times* reporters to do the highest-quality possible job, filing news as late as possible compatible with deadlines, and maintaining *The Times'* reputation for top-quality reporting and attractiveness as "a reporter's paper." Although substantially increasing the efficiency of news for its readers and the effectiveness of advertising for its sponsors, and most of these quality improvements, while very real and perhaps even crucial to maintaining high-quality readership and advertising revenues, do not show up in any measurable productivity figures for *The New York Times*, other than in the printing areas. Most have been passed through to customers as lower prices and more timely news. But they have changed *The Times'* value and output structures immeasurably.[9]

PRECISE, FLEXIBLE, AND SWIFT EXECUTION

Another common goal and result—as in *The New York Times'* experience—is the capacity to obtain faster cycle times in meeting new strategic challenges and in implementing major operating or systems changes. By breaking service production down to the smallest replicable units consistent with customers' needs and having this information available at the contact level, managers can signal and implement both strategic and tactical changes across the system quickly and precisely. If they install proper monitoring and feedback mechanisms, they can maintain targeted goals for productivity, quality, and product mix even as demand fluctuates randomly or new products are introduced in a rapidly changing environment.

■ While insurance companies used to rewrite their offerings and rate books once or twice a year, they now must adjust almost daily to the constantly changing interest rates and offerings of other direct and functional competitors, like Treasury, bank, money market fund, or single premium annuity offers of brokerage houses. Insurance executives state flatly that their agents could not possibly understand or present the complexity of their current products without their responsive, on-line information connections with headquarters. From the company's viewpoint instant communication capabilities are essential to calculate, update, and monitor the company's margins on each product, to maintain desired spreads, and to motivate agents to sell the most profitable product mix. From the agents' viewpoint, such instant access means more satisfied customers, a more professional appearance, and higher profitability for themselves. As rapid changes occurred in the 1970s and 1980s, those who could not hook up to such systems were literally driven out of business.

Respondents in our study often paraphrased that "*in services, execution is everything*. If you can't deliver what customers want, when they want it, with the personal touch they like, all your strategic thinking and investments won't amount to much. Our technology is one key factor in execution. Also key are the management systems and culture that cause our people to react quickly and favorably to our offerings and to our customers' needs." The General Mills Restaurant Group offers an interesting example of the combination of benefits an organization can obtain by using a well-integrated set of technological, structural, and facilitating management techniques. Key among the benefits that General Mills Restaurant Group attained were much lower costs, higher flexibility, flatter organizations, lowered overheads, increased motivation, and much higher profitability.

■ General Mills Restaurants systematically used technology throughout its system to leverage its corporate knowledge base and buying power and to increase both its productivity and flexibility. Like most chain restaurants, it automated all its food production processes and had extensive programs for optimizing restaurant locations and layouts. But it has also tied its systems into LANDSAT and other ground and water monitoring systems that help it predict the location, timing, and size of fish and shrimp yields in the Gulf of Mexico to optimize its purchasing and long-term marketing programs. At the strategic level it can monitor programs in such detail and react so quickly to operating changes and to actual consumer responses that within a few days it can adjust a many-months-long preplanned national promotion campaign to optimize results. At a tactical level, its programs allow it to sense needed changes within hours at each outlet and to signal appropriate corrections in local managerial patterns or to provide special local support promotions. For more details, see "Vignette Three: General Mills Restaurant Group" preceding this chapter.

EMPOWERMENT AND AUTOMATED KNOWLEDGE CAPTURE

Although often derided as being strategies to "control people," service technology systems are usually used to empower both professionals and less experienced personnel. They play an especially vital developmental role in permitting relatively inexperienced people to comprehend and perform very sophisticated tasks quickly—vaulting them over normal learning curve delays and giving them confidence in their new roles. Later, technology adds even more value by constantly updating these individuals through automatically capturing and incorporating into the system knowledge from the best-performing areas of the entire company. Even the newest employees can exploit the total organization's constantly expanding total experience base and problem-solving capabilities, including capturing knowledge about advances or events at remote points where few could possibly be involved in changes first-hand.

This kind of automated knowledge capture is especially important in leveraging knowledge into those service operations which must rely heavily on entry-level, part-time, or relatively inexperienced workers to meet personnel needs at lower costs. By having extremely simplified input and display units featuring color coding, pictures of objects, and simply sequenced "help" codes, companies like McDonald's, ServiceMaster, Wal-Mart, and Pizza Hut can, in short order, make relatively unskilled people into full-fledged managers of a local activity. By increasing the value-added of each employee, such technologies open possibilities for higher wage levels, and even opportunities for previously untrained employees to become proprietors of profitable enterprises or to manage multimillion-dollar franchises on their own. Although there are some exceptions, effective service automation generally will encourage greater, rather than less, empowerment and decentralization at the contact level. This is true of both professional firms and more "product-oriented" service organizations, like restaurants, retailers, or postsale product support units.

By routinizing the detail that it once took great effort to master, professional managers and associates can concentrate their attention on the more creative, conceptual, and personalized tasks only humans can perform. As was noted, the routines of client analysis that used to occupy most of the junior staffs of auditing and consulting firms are often completely automated now, as are legal case precedents and many medical records. Instead of spending time on these details, professionals can move quickly to the creative, interpretive tasks of dealing with clients and patients.

One can easily say, "Of course, empowerment works with professionals, but what about the great bulk of other service jobs?" Examples from a variety of different institutions will suggest how technology also helps decentralize and empower personnel in what we think of as much lower-skilled organizations.

■ In manufacturing services, Shoshana Zuboff's book *In the Age of Smart Machines* describes the fears versus realities of automation in a paper mill. Before automation, workers had said, "In fifteen years time there will be nothing for the workers to do. The technology will be so good it will operate itself." Instead, once the

workers got used to running the mill by remote means and reading screens instead of physically handling the pulp or reading
in-line gauges, they literally became staff managers treating small
deviations in operations or quality as puzzles to be solved. One
operator is quoted as saying, "With all this information in front of
me, I began to think about how to do the job better. And being
freed from all that manual activity, [I] really have time to look at
things, to think about them." The plant manager said, "We are
depending on the technology to educate our people in abstract
thinking. . . . You have to drive decisions from the interrelation-
ship among [many] variables."[10] In short, workers had to start
thinking and acting more like humans—or staff executives—and
less like sensors, gauges, or robots.

■ Supermarket chains like Kroger and other high-volume retail
stores like Kmart have discovered that technologies can change
the attitudes and demeanor of people in many tasks that are considered routine, yet in reality require extensive learning. Well-
installed bar-code scanning systems with price look-up features
can, for example, enormously improve the morale and effectiveness of checkout personnel. On the one hand, such scanning systems make customers feel there is less likely to be an error in the
checkout process. They are therefore less suspicious in monitoring the checkout person. On the other, checkout personnel are
not constantly embarrassed by having to look up current prices or
to call out to other "experts" when they do not know prices. Instead, they can concentrate on faster data entry, package handling, and wrapping, while dealing with each customer in a more
pleasant, personal fashion.

Well-designed systems allow mass merchandisers to lower
costs and increase values to customers by rapidly and selectively
changing prices across their entire inventory structures to meet
competition. Yet, reportedly, they also find that their error rates
and turnover ratios for checkout personnel plummet after installation of automatic scanning systems. Since checkout personnel
are among the very few personal contacts a customer has in most
self-service stores, checkout agents are critical members of the
team conveying the desired storewide image to customers. This is
carried to pleasant extremes at stores like Stew Leonard's ac-
claimed food store in Norwalk, Connecticut, where store clerks
suddenly converge for a brief celebration whenever a sales slip

exceeds $100.[11] One of the critical concepts in modern retailing is that it appear not just efficient but "fun" to the customer; and the checkout clerk's attitude is the centerpiece in this relationship.[12]

IMPROVING RESPONSIVENESS TO CUSTOMERS

One of the most important consequences of empowerment is an increasing responsiveness to customers. If service personnel are frustrated by lack of information or poor operation of the up-stream technical system, this will be conveyed quickly to the customer. Including contact people in the systems design process, actively observing their personal responses during alpha or beta tests, and constantly monitoring their attitudes and behavior patterns during operations would seem obvious keys to services productivity and quality. Yet, with rare exceptions, this critical later psychological and information loop is played down or ignored. For example:

■ The author was recently shown a large bank's new, about-to-be-installed automation system. Top managers, regional managers, and branch managers had all been included in specifying the design parameters for the system. But the "lowly" clerks and tellers who would operate it had not been included. In the same bank, one of the most automated in its field, middle and top managers all had PCs on their desks. Yet few used them for anything but "electronic mail." The system had been designed to provide what the professional *staffs* thought these managers should have, and some selected managers—the most computer literate—had been included on the system design team. But involvement of other managers and personal support to them at the time of installation had been limited. Planned follow-up as to actual use was almost nonexistent.

The typical cost of bringing in a new customer is five to ten times as high as retaining an existing customer, and unhappy customers tend to complain on average to eleven other people.[13] Companies should therefore be able to devote substantial sums to assuring adequate professional support during technology or systems installation and to monitoring the attitudes and behaviors of contact people after installation. Yet these are the investments most often cut back in the development cycle of installing information technology.

Strong counterexamples include SAS and American Express (see the "Vignette" preceding this chapter). In the former, Jan Carlzon's crucial vision was that the contact person's few seconds of contact with customers was "the moment of truth" in which the customer either experienced SAS's desired service image or was irreparably antagonized. Carlzon and his team followed through with almost propagandistic fervor on all aspects of empowering SAS's point personnel and on providing the support systems needed to change behavior at that level. John Reed and Walter Wriston at Citicorp followed a "let 1,000 flowers bloom" philosophy, encouraging innumerable champions to actively help develop the systems they would use themselves. Users became designers. While Citicorp's systems were not as elegant as those developed by competitors, these practices minimized installation risks, shortened the design cycle, and gave Citicorp significant competitive advantage for years. Despite the high $900 million cost of being the first innovator, Citicorp's success came from the quality of its thinking and the leading time advantages it accrued.[14]

ADDING VALUE FOR CUSTOMERS THROUGH KNOWLEDGE FEEDBACK

A final common feature of these new organizations—although too often overlooked in planning stages—is the longer-term payoff potentials from the knowledge-building feedback loops the decentralized nodes and customers can receive from the center. By sophisticated segmentation, analysis, or synthesis of data from all its decentralized nodes—and all the detailed customer information of the network beyond those nodes—the "information center" or corporate office can create a knowledge base with a power no single internal or smaller external outlet can achieve. By aggregating and comparing detailed information from these sources, the center can often develop new higher-value, knowledge-based services and even "sell" them back to its own nodes (or the latter's customers) to further increase profits and those units' competitiveness. The most publicized example of this is perhaps AMRIS, mentioned earlier.

■ American Airlines' parent recently created a sister company, AMR Information Services (AMRIS) to leverage off the managerial knowhow, staff, facilities, and technologies its SABRE reservations system had built. Along with an offshore data entry business, AMRIS is entering a partnership with Hilton, Marriott, and Budget Rent-a-Car to handle critical reservations and property management activities worldwide for its clients. This system (called CONFIRM) will provide a single source with hundreds of remote nodes—i.e., a very flat organization—through which travel agents can confirm all such arrangements.

But CONFIRM, by combining the inputs it receives, can also provide its client industries with a broad enough and deep enough data base to micromanage their yield strategies, for example foreseeing unexpected shortfalls or special surges in occupancy or demand in time to target short-term promotional and pricing strategies. In the future, comparative data collected from and fed back in analyzed form to client companies may enable AMRIS to develop industrywide decision support models, further amplifying its own and its clients' competitive advantages. Yet each of the participants in this consortium (and their individual outlets) can operate as independently as they wish, creating essentially a network company with a starburst of new service opportunities.

Properly developed, these kinds of network gains can ultimately outweigh the direct efficiency benefits the system was originally designed to produce—as they did for Bankers Trust, Banc One, McKesson, Bear Stearns, and other winning innovators. Designing for such flexibility at the start is the key to developing major new opportunities and the support organizations they demand. For example:

■ Time-Warner Inc., with its many different magazines, books, and entertainment products, has more than 20 million customer files that are a gold mine of market information it can use to introduce new products or to fine-tune the positioning of existing products. With its numerous magazines, *Time, Life, Sports Illustrated, People, Fortune, Money, Southern Living*—as well as the 100 million pieces of mail the company processes each year for the American Family Publishers (Ed McMahon) Sweepstakes—Time-Warner can distinctively profile many of its readers in terms of demographics, life-styles, particular interests, and so on. By combining this information with other economic and location-specific data that come from zip codes and SMA sources, the company can further segment its customers. Combining this information with flexible production equipment in the bindery, Time Inc. can now target individual ads and article contents to each household. Using "targeted ink jet" technologies, advertisers can even send messages to individual customers. The result is that each customer can receive a publication tailored to his or her specific interests, and advertisers do not waste money on broadsides to the wrong customers. Time Inc. can target its own products—i.e., books, videos, and other services—to those most likely to respond and can fine-tune the content and editorial styles of its media offerings to maintain maximum reader interest.

To take advantage of such constantly changing knowledge based opportunities, each company must be able to sense new needs early through its electronic systems, staff for these needs in a timely way, then form flexible teams to develop and introduce the new products called for. The result is a constant organizational dynamic and fluidity that old organization modes simply could not satisfy. Both manufacturing and service organizations must now be able to respond to their customers so rapidly that the concept of product cycle times is almost obsolete. Responses need to be continuous, fluid, and organic—yet targeted ever more precisely on customers' needs and desires. How to do this most effectively will be a central topic in the remaining chapters.

CONCLUSIONS

Services and service technologies have opened a wide variety of new organizational options for managers. All of these tend to push responsibility outward toward the point at which the company contacts the customer. All tend to flatten the organization and to remove layers of hierarchy. All seek faster, more responsive action to deal with the customization and personalization an affluent marketplace demands. All require a breaking away from traditional thinking about lines of command, one person–one boss structures, the center as a directing force, and lower levels as mere tools for the delivery of wisdom derived from above. Such structures are unwieldy in the fast-changing worlds of services and technology.

These two chapters have summarized many of the causes,

structures, and effects of these new configurations. Each has its particular utility and its own problems. Managing these organizations will be very difficult for people trained in traditional organizational theory and settings. And transitions to such organizations will be exceptionally difficult in many mature settings. Nevertheless, the potential gains—only suggested by the examples in this chapter—are substantial. Chapters 8 through 12 take up in depth many of the more interesting complexities of making the transition to these new organization forms and managing in them. Nothing presented here is intended to suggest that managing such organizations is either easy or a panacea. Instead, we have purposely tried to pose both the reality and the challenge of these fascinating new structures. They do indeed represent a "revolution in organizational thinking" for most companies. Yet these new organization modes seem to fit well with the emerging realities of the marketplace, technological capabilities, worker and social attitudes, and—most importantly—the demands customers are making on virtually all organizations, whether they be in manufacturing or in service industries.

As Peter Keen has noted, service technologies have reached a stage similar to that of manufacturing when electric motors were introduced.[15] If managers merely replicate past practice, as companies did when they installed electric motors in multilevel mill factories, they will miss the power of new technologies to redefine the entire business in relation to all its environments. To achieve maximum benefit takes a thorough reconceptualization of the business as a series of interconnected knowledge based and service activities—and a willingness to reorganize and refocus management around these activities in ways the technologies now permit. The processes of change will be very uncomfortable, but the payoff can be extremely high. And the cost of not changing may be comparable to that exacted from manufacturers who did not make the transition to electricity properly or in time.

CHAPTER 6
Exploiting the Manufacturing–Services Interface

In recent years many have expressed concern over the decline of U.S. manufacturing.[1] Some have blamed the nation's shift toward services as a major contributing cause. Few perceptions could be farther from the mark. If anything, the nation's growth and competitiveness in services have helped manufacturing by lowering costs, creating major new markets, stabilizing markets particularly for capital goods, and forcing manufacturers to be more responsive to markets. Further, as the nation's primary engine for long-term economic growth, despite the current slowdown, services will continue to offer manufacturers their most important new opportunities for future growth in value-added, productivity, flexibility, and product sales. Services and manufacturing are now so intertwined and mutually supporting that, increasingly, success in either goes to those who effectively utilize the combined technological potentials of both. This chapter will discuss how this integration can best be achieved.

A FLUID BOUNDARY

The interactions between services and manufacturing are very large-scale and complex. Some of the principal interactions are

Research for this chapter was first published in J. B. Quinn, J. J. Baruch, and P. C. Paquette, "Exploiting the Manufacturing–Services Interface," *Sloan Management Review,* Summer 1988.

174

suggested in Figure 6–1. As the arrows indicate, economic benefits flow both ways between all the activities. While most of the structure seems self-evident once disclosed, the role of the "services intermediary" may not be. Not all products can be used by a consumer without the intermediation of professionals who can (1) harness those products' more arcane possibilities for use or (2) control their potential hazards. "Do-it-yourself brain surgery kits" or "home hazardous waste disposal units" would seem unlikely product successes. Yet specialized service intermediaries have created very large markets for sophisticated technical equipment and supplies by handling such problems. At every exchange point in the diagram, service entities create new opportunities that manufacturers otherwise would not enjoy. However, the boundary between manufacturing and related service groups is very fluid and can be expanded at any moment by one side or the other to its advantage.

Data collection anomalies and the way terms are used often obscure just how liquid the boundaries are between services and manufacturing. Specialized services (like product design, research and development, market research, accounting, or data analyses) are usually considered "manufacturing" activities if performed within manufacturing concerns, but "services" if performed externally. Internal salesmen are a part of "manufacturing" employment, but external sales representatives and wholesalers are in the service sector. If farmers harvest their own grain, the costs become "production costs"; if the same farmers hire a professional combine operator, the activity is considered a service. Home cooking and clothes washing are not measured as service activities, but restaurants and automatic laundries are.[2] And so on. Rather than dwell on such meaningless differences, we have referred consistently to the actions that create service outputs as "service activities"—whether performed in a "manufacturing" or a "services" company as defined by government statistical classifications.

Even more fundamentally, products themselves are only physical embodiments of the knowledge and services they deliver. Ted Levitt's famous paraphrase notes that millions of quarter-inch drill bits are sold "not because people want quarter inch drill bits, but because they want quarter-inch holes. People don't buy products, they buy the expectation of future benefits."[3] A diskette delivers a software program or a data set (knowledge-based services); an automobile delivers flexible transportation (a service).

FIGURE 6–1
Some Mutual Interactions Among Manufacturing and Service Activities

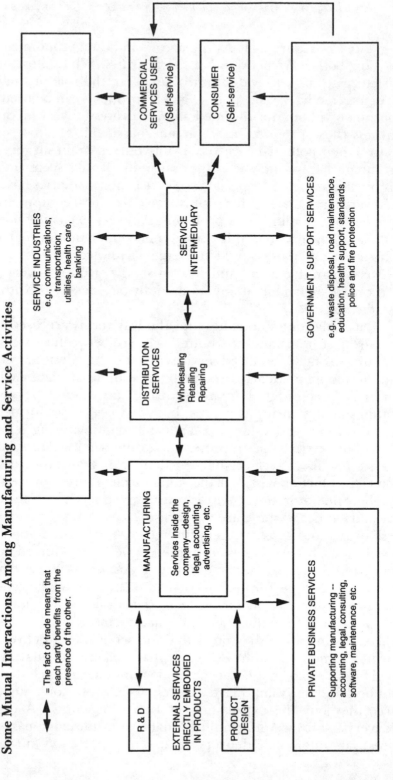

= The fact of trade means that each party benefits from the presence of the other.

SERVICE INDUSTRIES
e.g., communications, transportation, utilities, health care, banking

COMMERCIAL SERVICES USER (Self-service)

CONSUMER (Self-service)

SERVICE INTERMEDIARY

GOVERNMENT SUPPORT SERVICES
e.g., waste disposal, road maintenance, education, health support, standards, police and fire protection

DISTRIBUTION SERVICES

Wholesaling
Retailing
Repairing

MANUFACTURING

Services inside the company—design, legal, accounting, advertising, etc.

R & D

EXTERNAL SERVICES DIRECTLY EMBODIED IN PRODUCTS

PRODUCT DESIGN

PRIVATE BUSINESS SERVICES

Supporting manufacturing -- accounting, legal, consulting, software, maintenance, etc.

Electrical appliances deliver entertainment, dishwashing, clothes cleaning and drying, garbage disposal, convenient cooking, or food storage—all services. In fact, most products merely provide a more convenient or less costly form in which to sell knowledge or services. Thus "services" and "products" are both means of providing satisfactions to customers and should always be considered potential substitutes for each other in a strategy.

Because new knowledge and technologies constantly create new options and substitution potentials, which can quickly modify or eliminate unneeded features or processes, the boundary between services and manufactured goods is not only extremely fluid but it varies substantially over time. Recognizing this, manufacturers can often extend the scope of their operations, lower their costs, and expand their margins by leveraging their knowledge bases through services—and by eliminating or taking over adjacent service functions. Targeting these opportunities sometimes opens up whole new industries for the innovators themselves—and support industries for others. In a classic example:

■ "Permanent press" and "crease-resistant" fabrics—both knowledge-based manufacturing innovations—significantly restructured the white goods, apparel, and personal service industries. They also shrank the commercial laundry business, eliminated many domestic service jobs, increased the attractiveness of home washers, dryers, and "touch up" irons, and freed domestic workers and homemakers for more rewarding tasks. To support permanent press markets, totally new detergents, whiteners, and home laundry equipment designs soon appeared, changing the scale and nature of competition in those fields as well.

Similarly, the increased quality of home appliances and automobiles has decreased the time, cost, and frustration consumers expend on maintenance and repair. Prepared gourmet foods, convenience mixes, and microwave dinners have substituted for restaurant sales and home-cooking time. The converse—substitutions of services for manufactures—has also been widespread; CAD/CAE/CAM software systems have substituted for costly machine capacity used in setup and prototyping. Cable network services have replaced home antenna sales and movie films—providing more of what the customer really wants, increased flexibility and quality in home entertainment. And so on. At the extreme, many "manufacturing" firms are beginning to regard the factory itself as a service. For example, Mr. Ge van Schaik of Heineken's breweries has said, "We are just a marketing company with a production facility as a service."

STRONGER MARKET LINKAGES

One of the most powerful relationships between services and manufacturing is the development of stronger, more flexible, more direct relationships with distribution channels and ultimate customers. The immense and growing scale and power of manufacturers' service customers (and their technologies) present a host of highly leverageable new opportunities. Among the more interesting are (1) using service companies as major knowledge sources and as lead customers or co-developers of new products; (2) locking in customers and suppliers to decrease lead times, improve service levels, and create switching barriers for customers; (3) obtaining more rapid, flexible, low cost, and powerful distribution through downstream coalitions with major distribution networks or buyers; and (4) utilizing service companies and technology-based market analysis mechanisms to obtain more instantaneous and highly segmented knowledge about marketplaces. Some detailed examples will suggest how individual manufacturers have effectively modified their strategies to harness the increased knowledge power that technology and services offer.

AS LEAD CUSTOMERS AND CO-DEVELOPERS

Because of their scale, knowledge capabilities, and aggregate economic power, service companies have become the principal customers for many manufacturers. For example, in the mid-1980s chain discount stores handled an incredible 72 percent of all full-line general merchandise sales in New England and 48 percent of such sales for the entire country.[4] With the size of major retail chains being 20–30 times larger than the biggest textile firms, they obviously drive this industry and determine what reaches the market. The same is true for most consumer goods. But what about high-technology products? In the late 1980s over 80 percent of all communications and information processing equipment went to the services industries.[5] By 1990 over 85 percent of all installed information technologies were in services.[6] And these companies' complex information infrastructures were driving the shift of all computer companies away from hardware manufacture and toward becoming primarily providers of software, system integration, and support activities.[7]

In many situations service companies have become the primary lead customers and co-developers for major technologies. In some cases such collaborations have opened whole new industries. For example:

■ Federal Express essentially put NEC into the "facsimile copier" business. In 1978–79 Fred Smith, CEO of Federal Express, worried about the impact electronic communication would have on his market for overnight delivery of documents, started a project, code-named Gemini, to put FedEx into the instant document transmission business. Working from specifications developed in its Colorado communications laboratories, FedEx contracted with NEC to produce the ZapMailer. This was the first computerized "store and forward" facsimile machine to offer a high-quality (160,000 pixel per square inch) output, high throughput, and complete telephone system compatibility.[8] FedEx wanted to provide (1) instant connectivity to large and small users through a private satellite network, (2) pickup and delivery services for those without their own fax machines, or (3) direct faxing services from its local offices with delivery through its existing ground network to those who lacked their own machines. NEC's costs per unit dropped by a factor of five within two years as FedEx transmission volumes grew. When FedEx withdrew from the ZapMail business—because the unexpectedly high volume of faxes and the collapsing cost of fax machines made it a natural for AT&T and others to provide interconnection services—NEC had a large experience curve lead over all comers.

There are many other co-design possibilities for those who are prepared to work with service groups. Textile manufacturers often get retail buyers to redesign or fine-tune product lines to their specific tastes. Based on direct electronic connections to retail stores, ski boot producers can build individualized ski boots to fit each customer's feet. Artificial joints for hip or knee replacements can be customized from x-ray or other scans to fit each individual precisely in nontrauma replacements. Many larger-scale opportunities exist in other industries for manufacturing–service company co-design projects to provide greater customer value. For example:

■ As the number of major trunk airlines (service providers) declined with deregulation and the introduction of wide-bodied jets, aircraft manufacturers had to modify their strategies. The number of U.S. lead customers for a firm like Boeing shrank to a handful of large "megacarrier" airlines, each with a more powerful bargaining position than before. The military no longer provided the necessary "first order" volumes to launch a commercial aircraft. To obtain essential economies of scale and yet satisfy each customer, Boeing invested heavily (more than $800 million) during the late 1970s and early 1980s in flexible automation, allowing it to modify internal seating, baggage, storage, maintenance system, and customer convenience patterns to suit virtually any configuration its major (airline) customers might demand over the useful life of the aircraft.[9] To secure its $5 billion bet on its new 777 aircraft Boeing has set up some 235 "design build teams," each including customer engineers to make sure it taps the knowledge of its key users. By carefully listening to customers' needs, Boeing shifted its concept from an extended version of the 218 passenger 767 to a 320+ passenger "family" of 777 aircraft with common parts, maintenance, and operating procedures. United Airlines, which placed the first order for 34 aircraft, worth over $3 billion, has its own full-time project head at Boeing's Renton facility and its engineers directly on the Boeing design teams, as do other major carriers.

Hospital chains like Humana (with its $4 billion in revenues, eighty-five hospital care units, and total of more than 17,500 beds) have become important standard-setters in medical care and major targets for manufacturers introducing medical products or equipment. To attract doctors to practice in its system, Humana must have the most up-to-date equipment and at the same time must meet the requirements of state "certificate-of-need" processes and the government's Diagnostic Related Group (DRG) payment system (which sets the amounts that can be reimbursed for individual procedures). To meet these conflicting specifications, hospital equipment manufacturers have had to undertake much more targeted development strategies than they pursued in the past. To assist them in its own interest, Humana has created a corporate-level group to work with manufacturers, using its knowledge capabilities to specify and develop new products, sometimes providing clinical testing facilities, and occasionally even taking a venture capital position in newer companies. When a new technology proves effective, Humana can quickly roll it out to all its hospital and outpatient facilities, and—with its volume—require the producer to provide needed educational, training, or supplies support.

LOCKING IN CUSTOMERS AND SUPPLIERS

Large manufacturers can also use service technologies and coalitions to gain leverage in much more decentralized marketplaces—and in the process lock in customers or suppliers to its own systems. Otis Elevator Company moved its activities downstream by providing its OtisLine service to coordinate its maintenance efforts on a national basis. Highly trained operators took all trouble calls, recorded critical information on a computer screen, and dispatched repair people directly via a beeper system to the local trouble spot. From the computer inputs, problem patterns could be identified nationally and designs changed if necessary. Information to designers was more complete and more precise than ever before, and much of the needed information for repairs could be provided directly from the elevator itself through microcomputers, further lowering error rates.

In addition, recognizing that architects specify elevator systems, Otis is reportedly creating downstream coalitions directly with these intermediaries by making its design software accessible to major architects' offices. Otis may have no inherent cost advantages over foreign firms in manufacturing the elevator boxes, cables, or motors of an elevator system. But it can capture the competitive advantage its greater depth of knowledge, longer history, and larger volumes allow. By putting its design software at the architects' disposal and offering further design consulting services, Otis can lower the architects' costs and convert these savings directly into higher margins for these important intermediaries. Since architects' design fees depend not on their own costs but on the total costs of construction and systems installed, their internal cost savings drop straight to the bottom line. Using this software should also increase the likelihood of the architects' specifying either Otis systems or establishing specifications on competitively bid systems for which Otis will have an excellent competitive position.

American Hospital Supply (AHS) was, of course, among the first to use direct linkages to customers to lock in their orders. For the low cost of a computer terminal and some software—its Automated System for Analytical Purchasing (ASAP)—AHS virtually assured itself of a continuing stream of orders. Once hospital supply buyers became familiar with the AHS system, it became much easier and less costly to order from AHS than from others. American Hospital Supply could update its prices constantly, bringing it 50 percent larger orders on average than its competitors and lowering its own transaction costs accordingly. And it could soon offer inventory control, billing consolidation, accounting, and other special services over the same system to tie the customers ever closer to AHS. Strategically, it applied technology to capture its customer base, then used its new knowledge bases to provide even more services to its customers. This link and the potential leveragability of its knowledge bases were the key assets Baxter purchased when it acquired AHS for $2.3 billion over its book value. When Secom of Japan bought Hospital Corporation of America in 1988, it was primarily seeking direct links for its product lines to America's hospital floors, instant access for its product lines to U.S. markets, and an information base about the U.S. market that it otherwise would have taken years to build.

This is the "camel's nose under the tent strategy," which has been widely used by service companies—like McKesson, ADP Services, SuperValu, and others—to expand their downstream scale and scope of operations. Once customers begin to feed the camel a little bit, they find it can provide more and more service until it grows large, and they come to depend on it ever more extensively. Both the customer and the camel prosper together until the camel becomes an integral part of the customer's activities. The keys to this strategy are (1) being the first to provide an integrated interface system, usually a PC or workstation today, to lock in the customer and discourage use of competing systems; (2) having a sufficiently detailed and flexible software structure to grow with customers and provide them with feedback information and new services matched to their developing needs; and (3) using data derived from the system to segment and serve the markets ever more precisely. This is an important application of the "minimum replicable unit" concept developed earlier. The company that has longer experience with the customer—and has accumulated more detailed information about the customer and its markets—can provide better segmented data and more finely tuned future services than anyone else possibly can. And the company that can aggregate and analyze information from many such customers has a knowledge base others cannot equal.

Downstream service "lock ins" take many forms. On a small scale, it is becoming relatively common to insert an integrated chip into office equipment, appliances, or product-dispensing machines to signal when supplies or repairs are needed—and thus ensure optimum service and decreased downtime losses for customers. Stratus Computers, for example, has built into its computers special circuits that diagnose a failure or developing fault and send a signal back to Stratus headquarters with the diagnosis and location of the computer. Often before the customer is even aware of the problem, a Stratus customer representative or a Federal Express package from Stratus will arrive to correct the fault. Similar systems can be installed in soft drink or other dispensing machines to keep the machines constantly in stock, a key service factor in this business. By linking the data from the dispensers to routing computers, distributors can also optimize their truck drivers' routes to lower total costs.

On a larger scale, IBM and AT&T have long used their systems software to lock their customers into their equipment. As long as IBM could maintain upward compatibility on proprietary software and standard interfaces on its equipment, its customers faced cost barriers that made it prohibitive to switch over to other manufacturers. Only as these broke down did IBM begin to lose its overpowering share of market. Similarly, AT&T has found that it can use an increasing array of software-based services—like UNIX or its Dial USA Direct service—and special billing and accounting capabilities to lock customers into use of AT&T's huge operating equipment networks, even while traveling overseas.

DISTRIBUTION POWER FORCES ORGANIC RESPONSE PATTERNS

In addition to these downstream service strategies, other service entities—in the form of chains like Wal-Mart, Sears, Computer-

Land, Businessland, IKEA, Toys "R" Us, and Home Depot—have changed the very nature of manufacturing competition for many consumer or commercial products. On the one hand, by the weight of their purchasing power they have forced all manufacturers into global competition. On the other, they offer manufacturers instant access to any of the world's major marketplaces—with immediate mass distribution, instant knowledge about the market, powerful presentation capabilities, and large-scale financial support for any consumer product, specialty, or innovation they choose to carry. Some large industrial wholesalers can do the same in their markets. As a result, both overseas and domestic innovators can now access advanced U.S. and European markets without creating the costly information and distribution bases they once had to build for themselves. By substantially decreasing distribution time lags, entry costs, and new product risks for producers, these distributors have made a major contribution to the increased rates of innovation and product proliferation now appearing everywhere. Clearly, access to large distribution chains has created the basic opportunity that many Asian and LDC computer product "clones"—or furniture and clothing manufacturers—have exploited.

Enhancing the interface between manufacturer and market has irreversibly heightened the intensity of competition and shrunk the available response times for virtually all advanced-country manufacturers. The relative power of big distribution companies and their knowledge-technological sophistication is forcing everyone to look at production as merely one part—often a declining part—of a value-adding continuum. Beyond just "competing in time"—i.e., seeking competitive advantage through timing—manufacturing and distribution must often be organic, i.e., changing simultaneously and interactively together. For example, Panasonic estimates that its average product life cycle for a typical new electronic consumer product is only ninety days. There is no way a competing producer can discover Panasonic's moves, redesign its product, respond, and flood its distribution channels in this time period. Instead, a manufacturer must "design through" its present product line to at least two more models, providing itself and its products with a structured fluidity—beyond flexibility—for continuous incremental changes as the market dictates. Instead of product life cycles, one needs to think in terms of continuous product evolutions.

■ Perhaps Tektronix was the first company to use this strategy to seize dominance in its marketplaces. During the 1950s, while its major competitors, RCA, GE, and DuMont, continued to design and present ever more complex oscillographs in their lines, Tektronix modularized its designs. By merely substituting a new circuit board or plug-in module, the customer could modify a basic Tektronix oscillograph to meet its particular needs. And Tektronix could keep up with the rapidly changing technical demands of its marketplace by designing and releasing only circuit modules, rather than whole oscillograph systems. Today Motorola has set up its factory in Boynton Beach, Florida, to be able to produce any of several million different electronic pagers within two hours to the exact specifications of its individual customers. From receipt of an order to beginning its production is only twenty minutes. Yet Motorola's products are so engineered that as new components or features become available, they can be automatically incorporated as options.

In such cases, because *customers* can essentially design their products themselves, product redesign can be a continuous organic process, and design cycles become essentially meaningless. Lenscrafters, a division of U.S. Shoe Co., has accomplished much the same thing by bringing the factory to the customer. Before, eyeglass wearers had to make at least two trips to the optician and wait one to two weeks while someone else produced and shipped their lenses. Now they can see an optician and within about an hour receive their customized lenses in the frame of their choice. In this case production and distribution are truly organic, taking place in the same unit interactively with the customer. As in all companies that follow this strategy, Lenscrafters' technical concerns move away from a focus on its end product and toward a focus on maintaining a competitive edge in its knowledge-based production and communications services.

To carry out this kind of organic design and response strategy, many Japanese companies simultaneously design the next two or three iterations of a new product along with its initial introduction. This ensures that the product can be migrated upward while maintaining any available scale economies. To adapt the product successfully, a manufacturer must be able to detect early market signals as soon as possible. This is where large companies that use their own or a large partner's distribution power—as MCI, Matsushita, and Gallo do—have major advantages. Through their greater contacts with all segments of the market they have the potential to sense detailed changes before their competitors and to test and mutate their new product offerings, if necessary, before competitors are even aware of trends. Others achieve organic response patterns in different ways. For example:

■ Procter & Gamble (P&G) codes the 900,000 call-in inquiries it receives annually on its 800 number. Along with extensive continuing market research, P&G uses these as early warning signals of product problems or changing tastes. Honda targets a portion of each new car line for redesign each year, based on engineering potentials and an elaborate customer follow-up questionnaire and tracking system. By the time the external design of the car is ready for a face lift, it already embodies a whole generation of "under the skin" subsystem and componentry changes, which lower costs and improve quality in the next generation product the customer sees. Ford, for its Taurus/Sable line, has linked its dealers' repair shops directly to its factories and its suppliers' production floors so that persistent problem patterns can be sensed and fixed continuously—instead of waiting for Ford Marketing to accumulate complaints or a new design cycle to trigger changes.

It has become almost a cliché to say that design cycles have to be shortened and that companies must "compete in time" or "compete against time."[10] Making design changes organically upon receipt of reliable market information is becoming the target and perhaps the ultimate mode of such competition. In an interesting approximation:

■ GE has begun to implement this concept as part of its "Best Practices" program. To develop a new product, GE makes a "multigenerational technology-product plan," which generally calls for a first generation product primarily using known technologies. This allows GE to get the product to market faster, start an interactive learning cycle with users, and avoid taking the dual risks of having to cope with new markets and new technologies simultaneously. GE tries to introduce newer support technologies as they are developed and to insert them whenever possible into modular "concept openings" predesigned for future flexibility. In actual production, it tries to avoid "guessing" the mix of features the customer will actually order. By designing models to have as many common parts as possible, concentrating inventory controls on the 5 percent of unique parts that are complex and have long production cycles, and using buffer stocks on the rest, GE can manufacture most appliances to order, has cut inventories by 20 percent, and can respond in half the time it used to need.[11]

STRATEGICALLY OFFSETTING DISTRIBUTOR ADVANTAGES

Since large retailer-distributors generally now have more information about marketplaces than most manufacturers, they can dominate design decisions to their advantage. How can manufacturers offset this scale and information advantage? The toy industry provides an interesting example of the opportunity and the problem.

■ With its $5.4 billion volume, Toys "R" Us has more than a 20 percent share of its market, is 3.5 times the size of the largest publicly owned toy manufacturer (Hasbro), has more information about the market than any single producer could have, and will give producers information only about their own company's sales. While this is very helpful to individual producers in predicting some feature preferences and product trends, it does not allow manufacturers to fine-tune their positioning against other competitors' products. As a result, the industry formed the TRIST group, getting eight other major toy retailers to aggregate information from their EPOS systems. This flows directly to a market analysis group, which combines the sales data with national panel interviews to give each manufacturer an aggregated analysis of more subjective responses to its products. Although not perfect, such information is critical to manufacturers when their principal customer—by ordering with its superior information, at their most vulnerable times—could force them to invest in impossibly high capacity levels to handle surge needs. In an industry that sells 60 percent of its product at retail in the few weeks before Christmas, producing margins clearly depend on the relative market information capacities the retailer and each of its suppliers can muster.

In some cases, direct interconnections to downstream outlets can solve the problem in a way that benefits both manufacturers and retailers. For example:

■ In its LeviLink system, Levi Strauss was able to cut its cycle time for production to delivery from three months to only one week. Its system allows Levi Strauss to take electronic orders directly, provide tailored product marking for its retailers, tag merchandise for them, perform electronic inspection to ensure quality, and supply them in minimum times. In addition to slashing inventory and direct personnel costs, the LeviLink system has eliminated multiple management layers inside Levi Strauss and passed enormous benefits on to its retailing customers. Approximately 25 percent of the latter's costs for clothing sales were in markdowns. With orders now more closely approximating sales, retailers can avoid most of that cost. Overall, the industry has reduced typical cycles from fiber, through fabric and apparel creation, to distribution and display to only 15 percent of what elapsed times used to be. Savings for the U.S. textile system are estimated at $25 billion per year.[12]

Automated direct linkages to customer showrooms have become major competitive weapons for consumer durable manufacturers. The Buick Division of General Motors has announced it will allow customers to design their own car in the dealer's showroom; and in selected areas, Buick will guarantee delivery of that customer's "personalized car" in ten days to the dealer's floor. Buick has automated its electronic credit analysis to further shorten waiting times and eliminate credit clearance frustrations for its customers. In Japan, Toyota provides an even more closely linked and responsive system. An automobile designed in the showroom and ordered on Monday can be delivered on Friday. As they become available, high-definition television systems will further amplify the impact of this kind of marketing by allowing customers to see in pictorial detail and in color-print quality the effects of their decisions as they design their own personalized vehicles. Soon customers may require all manufacturers to do what a few have proved they can do.

In some cases the market power of intermediaries has become so great that a company's only option is to work closely with them and use the intermediaries to decrease cycle times, handling and inventory costs, and investments on a systemwide basis. As one manufacturing CEO said, "Wholesalers are no longer simply inventory break points in the downstream system; those with powerful information/product-handling systems can own the relationship between you and your ultimate dealers."

Their continuous interconnections with retail customers have made some wholesalers like Super Valu (in foods), McKesson (in pharmaceuticals), and some large retailers like Toys "R" Us (in toys) into true "channel commanders" controlling the interface between their suppliers and large components of the retail marketplace.

■ SuperValu, a major grocery wholesaler, is an interesting example. SuperValu can provide full support for a grocery store's point-of-sale scanning system, its shelf-price verification needs, and its receiving functions—even for goods from direct-delivery suppliers like those for local vegetables or produce, and so on. These are functions no single manufacturer could possibly provide. Instead, SuperValu offers a wide range of suppliers sophisticated and immediate access to a broad segment of the retail marketplace they otherwise could not access effectively. By performing its distribution task so efficiently that even chain grocers can save more than by buying direct, SuperValu offers small independents the same advantages of scale that major chains have. Using similar approaches, McKesson and other drug wholesalers in the last two decades have increased the percentage of pharmaceuticals going through their distribution systems from 45 percent to over 75 percent (with more than 85 percent penetration estimated for the late 1990s). Manufacturers increasingly are finding that such groups are essential links to the market, simultaneously serving retail customers more efficiently and able to share their distribution efficiencies upstream and downstream to the benefit of both manufacturers and their ultimate customers.

Even when buyers have not consolidated into large individual units, service technologies allow them to aggregate bargaining power through coalitions. Participating with these groups at a minimum provides significant further market exposure for a manufacturer. When such coalitions also evaluate each supplier's service quality—in addition to merely tracking prices—they can provide important additional market leverage for reliable, quality-oriented producers.

■ For example, a team of airline and manufacture–supplier experts, coordinated by the Air Transport Association, has created an automated parts procurement system (Spec 2000) that can save buyers millions of dollars a year, yet is accessed simply from a personal computer. Spec 2000 was originally designed as a computerized compendium of manufacturers' catalogues, including more than a million part numbers and an automated computer-to-computer ordering system. But as the system developed, it not only allowed an airline to get comparative specification and quotation data but also gave information about how vendors meet specified delivery and performance criteria, thus increasing information leverages for all potential purchasers and the market leverage for the best-performing producers.[13]

STRONGER MARKET LINKAGES CAUSE THE "REMANUFACTURING OF AMERICA"

It is well established that as personal affluence and the sheer size of markets grow, there is an increasing demand for differentiated, individualized, or customized products.[14] These characteristics dominate most of today's rapidly growing markets, making the fastest possible response time with lowest possible costs a prerequisite for success. Although highly touted in many quarters, producing technical quality—i.e., holding tight specifications consistently—is no longer a sufficient basis for differentiation or premium prices for most products. Instead, in many fields such quality is assumed; it is a *sine qua non*. Technical quality, in short, is fast becoming a commodity. Increasingly, premiums will go only to those who can sense and fulfill needs for new product features before the market for these features is saturated and customers move on to the next "fashion."[15]

U.S.-based manufacturers who can link flexible production systems directly to the world's best market intelligence networks will have very real competitive advantages (in terms of timing, currency of features, and lower inventory and transportation costs) compared to offshore producers. Since the United States is still the world's largest truly integrated market—although this may change if an integrated Europe becomes a reality—U.S. companies should enjoy an important competitive advantage (versus foreign sources) provided they use it properly. Light, storable, high-value goods can be produced anywhere and shipped to the United States on a competitive basis. But for heavy, bulky, or complex products like automobiles, it may become impossible for overseas producers to compete against responsive, tightly integrated, domestic manufacturing–distribution systems. The same may later become true for outsiders trying to sell similar systems in Europe.

Neither a strategy of mass producing a few standardized lines nor one of supporting a very broad line of such products from abroad will work in these situations. If one produces standardized lines, the customer will soon become bored and move on to other products. Note the Nike example. If one tries to ship a broad line across an ocean barrier, inventory costs become prohibitive. Already, foreign manufacturers of such products are investing heavily in U.S. production capacity—as well as in distribution systems here—to get closer to the nation's huge, highly variable marketplace. This process is helping generate a genuine "remanufacturing of America" for certain products. And the number and range of goods it pays to produce in or next to the U.S. or other major markets will continue to expand.

■ Such considerations seem to be an important factor in Honda's rapid proliferation of automobile models and options, its increased emphasis on U.S. production, and the importation of its own "just-in-time" suppliers to the United States (when U.S. manufacturers proved unwilling or unable to meet Honda's service and quality demands). Like other Japanese manufacturers, Honda initially limited the variety of styles and options on its cars quite strictly. In the mid-1970s, it had only some thirty options available. Now it offers a much wider variety of options (several thousand in total) and faster delivery to the U.S. marketplace than it ever could have provided economically from a solely Japanese base. Increasingly, Honda will have to source more of its components and subassemblies from nearby, U.S.-based producers to obtain the response times it needs without escalating inventory costs. And other Japanese competitors have been forced reluctantly into U.S.-based manufacturing.

The U.S. textile and apparel manufacturing industries, which were decimated by foreign competition, have begun a resurgence through the use of technologies that allow them much closer linkages to their customers than foreign sources can achieve.[16] "Quick response reordering systems" linking stylists and producers allow fabrics designed from original fibers to be delivered from domestic sources to U.S. customers in one-third the time it takes from Taiwan. And direct CAD/CAM linkages between specialized cutters on Seventh Avenue and southeastern mills further cut in half the time to design, order, and deliver a specific cut or style. Both are critical elements in reducing the investment costs and market risks of fashion merchandising, as Levi Strauss did so well with its proprietary LeviLink system. Unfortunately, however, as global communications improve, distant producers of lightweight or high-value products will be able to offset much of this advantage, forcing domestic manufacturers to find new ways to differentiate once again. Knowledge-based competition and service technologies thus create a constant dynamic of new opportunities for some, major threats for others. For example:

■ Federal Express Company has exploited new electronics and materials-handling potentials by becoming essentially "the logistics arm" for its customers. By storing high-value and time-sensitive materials (like medical supplies or perishables) at its Memphis SuperHub, Federal Express can offer delivery in a few hours for customers whose products have a high time value. Digital Equipment Corporation (DEC) has been able to substantially simplify shipping of its complex of computers, peripherals, software, connections, and so on, to its customers on an "a la carte" basis. Its system allows DEC to input each order electronically and then to check the order—assembled from multiple points within the company—carefully on an automated basis, before shipment, to eliminate errors, time delays, and ill-will costs. TI and Intel have put their designers directly onto customer premises, linked electronically to their own formidable in-house capabilities, to provide instantaneous interactive customer design services.

MANUFACTURERS AS SERVICE COORDINATORS

Well-integrated links to downstream service institutions offer high potentials for manufacturers almost anywhere. But use of other specialized external service providers may generate even higher payoffs. New technologies now allow a large specialist firm to achieve greater value-added, economies of scale, or flexibilities in production of any specific service than virtually any integrated manufacturer can achieve internally. By concentrating its attention solely on a particular activity, developing its supporting technologies in depth, and allocating costs across many users, some outside specialist can perform almost any overhead or value chain activity better than any manufacturer for whom that activity is not a core competency. Many successful manufacturers therefore become primarily coordinators of these outside sources, integrating their suppliers' activities by controlling a few key steps in the value chain. Knowledge-based planning, logistics, market information, technology, finance, and coordination (service) skills become their core competencies. For example:

■ With crude oil reserves primarily in the hands of foreign nations, the oil majors have largely become service intermediaries connecting huge networks of facilities—like drilling platforms, pipelines, ships, or refineries—often owned or shared by others. Their profits increasingly depend on their ability to find, track, deploy, trade, transport, finance, and distribute energy efficiently. All of these are service activities and are technology driven. These companies' most important strategic weapon often becomes their capacity to effectively manage the worldwide logistics of finding, trading, mixing, transporting, pricing, and distributing energy supplies. Competition and shared technologies have driven refining and retail operating margins to such low levels that exploration technologies and logistics management systems have become the vital sources of value-added for virtually all energy companies today.

These and other huge product handling companies have become prime examples of enterprises which outsource—or partner—many important elements in their value chains with others who can find, assay, drill or cut, transport, process, or distribute in specific regions more effectively than they can. Complex production joint ventures and long-term contracts for financing, exploration, assaying, equipment operation, development, drilling, lodging, catering, or transport services have long been commonplace in the natural resources industry. Major players in the great mining industries of Australia and South Africa operate with this logic; most of their activities are outsourced to specialists and remotely coordinated.

■ When a new mining area is found by prospectors, a holding company in one of the major cities orchestrates the financing and acquisition of a lease. To offset risks, the holding company usually arranges the financing with multiple financial sources—with shareholders in South African mines often being direct competitors of the mine's majority owners. Further exploration and geophysical work are usually outsourced to other professional firms, aerial photographers, and analysis groups. As samples come in, chemical assays go to other outside groups for objectivity. Once operations begin, large equipment contractors may oversee open pit mining activities, coordinating tens of millions of tons of earthmoving a year. Other subcontractors may transport the ore to processing plants, where power or other minerals may be more available. Professional contractors may design and build the processing plants. The owners (or other contractors) may operate the initial ore-processing plants. After further assaying by other independent parties, the purified metal usually goes to refineries for final upgrading. In the case of gold, these may be government-owned batteries or mint refineries. Then the gold goes to state-run market outlets or independent professional distributors. In some cases, it goes to other independent marketing firms, which convert the gold into coins for international sales. The whole enterprise tends to be a series of independent service activities coordinated almost completely by a relatively small central core of people managing mainly information activities and contracts.

Auto companies (from Mazda and Honda to Toyota, Ford, or GM) have also become largely service intermediaries, coordinating enormous design, supply, logistics, distribution, and financing services worldwide.

■ Mazda, then Toyo-Kogyo, was one of the most successful early developers of a Kanban (just-in-time) logistics system that turned its suppliers—and the highway leading into its plant—into "an extension of Mazda's production line." Even the largest producers—recognizing that they can only excel in fabricating a few subsystems themselves—concentrate increasing attention on managing their design, system integration, marketing, distribution, and logistics activities. Ford's and Honda's integrated design systems illustrate one aspect of this coordinative focus; Ford's new IMKA software illustrates another. All three will be described shortly. IMKA is just one of Ford's many attempts to develop and monitor "best in class" suppliers worldwide and to leverage quality for its entire system.

Ford's total logistics system coordinates more than 1 million parts—most made externally—and deals with 500,000 queries per day. It has to coordinate daily production scheduling and design shifts for more than a thousand suppliers in Europe alone. Yet if exchange rates suddenly reverse, Ford must be able to reoptimize its sourcing instantly. For example, having co-designed a new compact car with Mazda, Ford suddenly found that it could not source from Mazda as planned because of sudden exchange rate reversals. To have continued with existing plans would have hurt both Mazda and Ford, and would have priced the car out of its market. Within a few weeks' time, Ford was able to completely restructure the car's sourcing to suppliers whose component costs were now more favorable than Mazda's. Ford's rapid, flexible logistics system alone saved Ford and Mazda from disastrous losses and let them bring in the car at targeted costs.

In addition, these companies' service activities have become major revenue sources. In 1991 Toyota made three out of every eight yen of its profits from nonoperating sources, while Ford and GM had become the country's largest private holders of consumer credit. With $105 billion in financial assets, GMAC's profits frequently outpaced those of GM's manufacturing operations. Ford Financial Group held $123 billion in assets, and, like virtually all other auto companies, Ford used its financial service capabilities as a direct substitute for its inability to lower prices through further production efficiencies. Special financing deals for customers and the service capabilities to make these pay off have become as much a part of manufacturing competitiveness as auto production on the factory floor. Nonproduction service activities have reshaped the structure of manufacturing profitability everywhere. Table 6–1 shows the extent to which some of the most powerful Japanese manufacturers depend on service-based profits.

Unfortunately, however, positive gains are not guaranteed. Westinghouse recently wrote off $0.75 billion after losses of more than $1.5 billion on its financial services venture—with more losses perhaps imminent. Unlike GE (America's biggest equipment lessor) and GMAC or Ford Financial (mostly auto loans), Westinghouse's financial services diversified into areas substantially removed from the company's traditional knowledge base in the fields it had served well for years.

For manufacturers in other fields, integrated knowledge and

TABLE 6–1
Services Profits

Company Name	Nonoperating Profits (¥ Billions)	As % of Pretax Operating Profits
Toyota Motor	149.6	37.6
Matsushita Electric	109.2	58.8
Nissan Motor	89.4	65.3
Sharp	28.0	73.2
Sony	27.2	62.8
Honda Motor	22.7	26.1
Sanyo Electric	21.5	134.2
Mitsubishi Corp.	20.8	29.8
Isuzu Motors	16.4	1,962.4

SOURCE: "Japan Inc.'s Most Profitable Factory," *The Economist,* June 25, 1988. Copyright © 1988 by The Economist Newspaper Ltd. Reprinted with permission.

service based capabilities have become the dominant components of value-added and profitability.

■ At IBM, for example, service and software have always been keys to success. This was especially true in the early years when software was "bundled" into IBM's products and list prices, and the "Big Blue" salesforce was crucial to sell, explain, and maintain productive hardware systems for customers. Now, as many types of computer hardware become extremely low-cost and competitive—approaching a "high-tech commodity" status— IBM is shifting its focus ever more toward software, network design and management, specialized customer services, training, and communications activities as its bases for adding value and improving profits. All are services. As machine speeds and interfacing complexities grow exponentially, networking capabilities, new application programs, constant upgrading of system software, and retraining of computer personnel become the keys to better performance. Software becomes the critical cost element in both product design and operations. Reportedly software is some 90 percent of a new product's development cost at IBM and about 60 percent of an average customer's system cost once installed.

Meanwhile the profitability of manufacturing "computer

boxes" has been dropping steadily relative to the value of embodied operating software, applications programs, or network services. Ultimately, one wonders whether U.S. companies can—or should—compete with lower-wage countries for box manufacture.[17] IBM has tried to offset the impact of wage differentials as much as possible by driving direct labor costs to minimal levels through automation. Still, external groups estimated that as much as 90 percent of IBM's profits currently derive from its software and service capabilities, although these are closely related to the company's huge installed equipment base. During late 1990 and 1991, published reports indicated that IBM's CEO, John Akers, had recognized the implications and was attempting to refocus the company on its knowledge-based software and service capabilities in moves that could represent the most significant restructuring of IBM since its integration around the 360 architecture in the late 1960s.[18]

SERVICE BASED STRATEGIES FOR MATURING MANUFACTURING COMPANIES

For companies in maturing product markets, a shift toward knowledge-based services can be especially strategic. As their products move toward maturity, most companies need to seek new bases for differentiation and new ways to conceptualize and leverage their special competencies. Many have to find new growth vectors for higher profitability. In many cases, knowledge-based activities or service substitutions become the critical vehicle. Foods companies moved downstream in the value chain to produce more convenient, then ready-to-microwave, then gourmet foods, substituting product-embodied conveniences for household services—adding value to their products that mere packaging and better-quality processing or ingredients could not. But these extensive substitutions for home services were not enough. Following the trends toward away-from-home eating, major food companies began operating restaurant chains in the late 1960s, moving first into fast food chain concepts, then into family dinner restaurants, and finally into upscale bars or pubs (like Bennigans).[19]

Other manufacturers have initially created major service ventures to support their main product offerings, and then found the services to be attractive, independent revenue producers. For example:

■ Because of the extremely high costs its customers incurred when their equipment went down for repair, Caterpillar developed one of the largest fast-response, global parts systems in existence. Around 1980, hearing of Caterpillar's success, some of Caterpillar's customers began asking for help in managing their own parts control and distribution functions. Caterpillar responded and now has a lively business providing worldwide logistics and transportation services to large manufacturers interested in efficient warehousing and delivery of their own parts.[20] By 1989 Caterpillar had twenty-three warehousing centers, occupying 10 million square feet and handling more than 350,000 SKUs of inventory for customers. As in its own operations, Caterpillar tries to provide twenty-four-hour response time for all comers.

Manufacturers of complex production, test, or measurement equipment—like that used in the nuclear power or chemical industry—frequently find that they can make as much money by locating and training personnel for their customers as they can from equipment sales. Polaroid, finding that the key to profitability is increasing film use for its camera, has experimented with photography training and "photo experience" excursions at major resort areas.[21] Argyle Diamonds of Australia produces a large number of yellow, pink, and other "off-white" diamonds because of the structure of the fissure it mines. Instead of confining itself to mining and selling the less desired colors as "seconds" through DeBeers, Argyle has bypassed the distribution syndicate for about 30 percent of its production. For this output it has taken over the service tasks of cutting, polishing, and direct-marketing its yellow diamonds as "champagne diamonds," browns as "cognac diamonds," and pinks as "premium diamonds."

ELIMINATING FIXED OVERHEAD AND SERVICE COSTS

A service activity-based analysis of strategy improves manufacturing capabilities in other ways, one key contribution being the reduction of unnecessary overhead costs. On average, some 65–75 percent of all nonmaterials costs in manufacturing enterprises are in this category,[22] and the percentage is growing as automation eliminates direct labor. Many CEOs have been startled by this statistic when mentioned in lectures. Not infrequently, after they investigate their cost structures, they telephone back saying, "Our percentage turned out to be ____ percent, a much higher number." One surprised CEO found out it was over 90 percent of his internal nonmaterials costs.

Unfortunately, overheads have been among the most difficult costs for manufacturers to control. Their traditional cost accounting, performance measurement, and reward systems have been ill-suited to the purpose. Despite substantial investments in office and professional-support automation, the measured productivity of manufacturing's white-collar workers—mostly in "overhead activities"—has risen very slowly,[23] unlike direct labor productivity, which has grown substantially in recent years. While diligently driving down direct labor costs (and, more recently, materials costs), most companies have only faintly dented the greater costs— and exploited the value-adding potentials—of overheads and services.

Overheads are usually just services the company has chosen to produce internally. What is needed is a much more structured and aggressive attack on all overhead groups' costs and their value-added potentials. The attack begins by defining all internal overhead and staff functions as "services," which can be either produced internally or purchased externally. Then, using techniques described in Chapters 2 and 5, each activity needs to be benchmarked to ascertain the relative effectiveness and cost of its processes and outputs. For many overhead activities, new service technologies and organizational strategies make it possible to achieve major economies by (1) purchasing selected services externally and (2) effectively managing outsourced services on a global basis. Almost any manufacturer can benefit by comparing each service activity in its value chain and staff functions (see Figure 6–2) and asking whether the company is really "best in world" in that activity relative to outside providers. If it is not "best in world"—including internal and external transaction costs[24]—the company is giving up competitive advantage by not upgrading or outsourcing at least those portions of the function where it is least effective.

At a minimum, careful benchmarking against outsiders will introduce a new objectivity into overhead evaluations and will create some strong competitive pressures for internal productivity improvements. But other benefits are also quite likely. As manufacturers begin to outsource portions of their overhead activities (for example, payroll), other overhead groups realize that (1)

FIGURE 6–2
Industry Analyses Comparing All Functionally Competing Sources

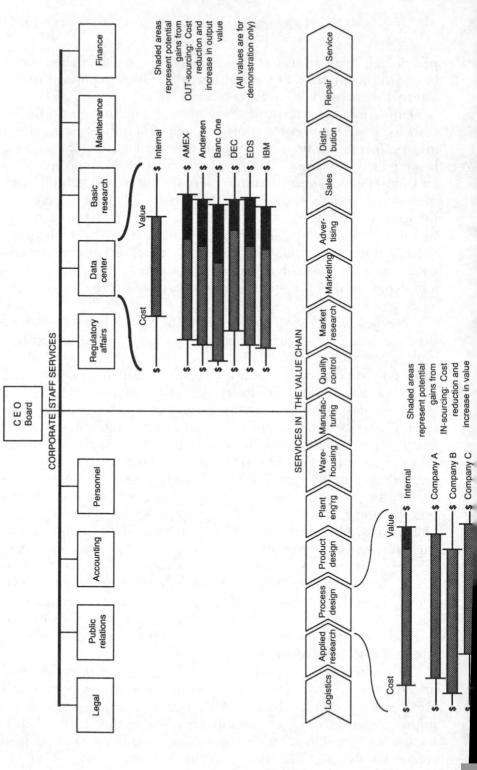

they are not exempt from justifying their productivity levels, (2) they too can be benchmarked against outsourcing providers, and (3) they must seek new ways to innovate and improve productivity. In some cases internal groups can be stimulated to reach world-class performance levels. In many cases, however, top managers find specialized outside service sources are much more cost effective, and switch to outsourcing for lower costs and improved value-added. For example:

■ As was noted earlier, ADP Services has developed a flexible payroll-handling system that is so low-cost that it now processes payrolls for over 10 percent of the potential client base in its geographical sales areas. Outsourcing these service activities has allowed ADP's customers access to (1) expertise they could not afford in-house, (2) substantial economies of scale and lowered overhead costs, and (3) a check on their own costs for these and other accounting functions. In 1991 ADP processed checks for more than 11 million employees in 200,000 firms. With check-processing costs in companies varying between about $3.00 to more than $22.00 in a survey made by KPMG-Peat Marwick, there are substantial opportunities for direct cost savings by outsourcing.

Starting initially with payrolls for small companies, ADP expanded its services into routine bank accounting, tax filings, ERISA reporting, personnel records and analysis (its HR Partner program), and even personalized communications functions— printing slogans, messages, or logos on checks or notes included with payroll checks to employees. By standardizing the small elements of payroll in a more complex total system, ADP could offer much lower costs and greater variability. Using similar techniques, it developed an Automatic Teller Machine network service, a collision repair estimating service for automobiles, and back office and reporting services for stock exchange houses— clearing, account maintenance, and general ledger capabilities. From these it moved into market data quotation services and branch office automation systems. Once ADP's database systems were installed with the proper breakdowns of data, the greater their use, the lower their unit costs became. Step by step, clients found they could outsource critical overhead activities at minimum risk and achieve both higher quality and lower cost.

■ Similarly, the $1.8 billion ServiceMaster Company has taken over many of its customers' equipment and facilities maintenance functions, simultaneously improving quality and lowering costs for these activities through its system economies and specialized management skills. With its sixteen years of experience in managing maintenance systems and its database covering more than 17 million pieces of equipment in thousands of locations, Service-Master has a computerized, sophisticated, analytical basis and management system for determining objectively just how each maintained unit should perform, when equipment purchases and preventive maintenance will pay off, and when subsystem or parts replacements should take place. So effective are its systems that ServiceMaster can not only lower absolute maintenance costs and ensure maintenance quality but also often jointly invest in new equipment (for those classes of equipment where it specializes) with its customers, sharing productivity gains to the benefit of both parties.

PRODUCTIVITY FOR EACH ACTIVITY, NOT JUST "DOWNSIZING"

The simple act of defining overheads and value chain activities as services that can be outsourced changes the context and focus of overhead analyses. Overheads are no longer just cost centers with unmeasurable benefits to be attacked with "cost reduction" or "downsizing" programs. Because outside sources of these services are available, internal activities can be individually calibrated against them, tested for value and cost, and outsourced if desirable. This does not imply that all overhead costs are "bad" and should be eliminated. Many of the most essential activities of a modern manufacturing company are in these service categories. The objective, therefore, is not simplistically to lower costs but to produce or buy each needed service activity as effectively as possible.[25]

Another high-payoff area for inquiry in competitive analyses is the relatively lower cost of U.S. service providers versus those in foreign countries. A significant portion of any manufacturer's competitiveness depends on externally purchased services like communications, transportation, financing, distribution, health care, or waste-handling activities. Controlling the quality and cost of these activities can be far more important than controlling costs on the production line itself. External services are one area where U.S. manufacturers enjoy some unique, and unrecognized, structural advantages in international competition. U.S. service industries are generally much more efficient than their foreign competitors, including Japan. A 1991 study by the Japan Productivity Center found that, largely because of its lagging services productivity, Japan ranked only tenth in the world in measured output per person.[26] The United States, Canada, and Belgium were the top three. Because they have been smaller-scale and often have been managed as government monopolies in the past, the transportation and communications systems of most other G7 countries have been more costly than those in the United States. American wholesale and retail distribution systems have also been more aggressively managed and competitive, as have its professional and financial services.

Health care services are a mixed bag where heavy subsidies and different social goals make comparisons difficult. U.S. productivity in health care is admittedly quite low and costs are rising dramatically. But even here American manufacturers can at least choose among different suppliers to improve the value they receive for the costs they do incur. In other countries such costs, being socially administered, show up as a less controllable tax burden. In virtually all service areas, U.S. manufacturers enjoy a greater range of choices and greater competition among their service suppliers. And U.S. service producers, with few exceptions, have led the world in driving new technological innovations. Properly utilized, these producers currently offer manufacturers important opportunities for competitive advantage, and their capabilities should be carefully benchmarked and exploited by those in international competition.

To obtain greater effectiveness from all service activities, companies can now outsource some most unusual and high-margin-producing activities—for example, renting their Chief Financial Officers or even CEOs. Firms like Arthur Andersen and IMCOR will provide a Chief Financial Officer or Chief Executive Officer, respectively, on request. Through such services, many smaller companies find they can obtain the capabilities of a superbly qualified individual—temporarily or part time—they could never afford otherwise. Larger companies in transition also find such services invaluable. In other arenas critical to large producers, companies like Microsoft, Novell, Lotus, and Ashton-Tate provide crucial software for computer manufacturers, and do so more efficiently and effectively than most major manufacturers can. Chains like Businessland, ComputerLand, Iancomp Computer Centers, and Sears have proved to be much more efficient distributors for some computer and electronics products than have manufacturers. And so on. With careful scrutiny, producers can potentially outsource virtually any activity—no matter how crucial it once seemed—to outside suppliers who can provide it more effectively.

INTERNAL TRANSACTION COSTS

Many executives are reluctant to outsource because of legitimate fears that coordinating a vendor's activities may be harder than coordinating similar units internally. However, in intuitively making such evaluations, they often do not include the very substantial transaction costs of dealing with the activity internally. A great deal of management time goes into overseeing internal overhead functions. In his classic studies of managerial work, Henry Mintzberg found that most of a top manager's time (78 percent) was spent in conversational contacts, mostly fragmented, with individuals—the most frequent being conducted near his or her office. Of these verbal contacts, 93 percent were *ad hoc*, most dealing with relatively current issues. Half lasted an average of less than nine minutes. Inevitably, a high percentage of such contacts are with those functional and staff units that surround the CEO.

A major portion of an organization's inflexibility and delayed response times is usually caused by the need to negotiate transactions on a personal basis across a number of functional or specialist departments—one of the major costs of "insourcing" overhead functions. Elimination of these bureaucratic interfaces is why self-directed teams so often lower costs by factors of 3 to 5 and decrease response times by orders of magnitude.[27] When one adds in the operating inefficiencies and ineffectiveness of unbenchmarked internal services—especially those that have been long entrenched—the balance can shift strongly toward outsourcing. If one includes the additional benefits of strategic focus and capital reduction obtained from outsourcing, the total benefits can be formidable.

The critical mindset is this: *When a company internally produces a service—whether in the value chain or in a staff function—that others can produce more effectively externally (including transaction costs), it sacrifices competitive advantage.* Given the power of service technologies, specialized external providers can frequently surpass the capabilities of manufacturers trying to "do everything" internally. Conversely, the key to strategic success for many firms has been a set of coalitions with the world's best service providers—as Apple Computer had with product designers (Frogdesign), software groups (Microsoft and Visicalc), advertising and promotion groups (Regis McKenna), distribution channels (IT&T and Computerland), and industry analysts (Ben Rosen).

FORCED LATERAL INTEGRATION

For those services which remain, manufacturers can look for even further gains through forced lateral integration. Many of the bureaucratic losses staff units cause are a result of their being organized as specialist or elitist groups whose power depends on their expertise and the defense of their private realm from the expertise of others. They naturally look inward for colleague approval and the nurturing of their skill base.[28]

As a result, most service staffs become fragmented enclaves of experts, operating like guerrilla bastions through which progress can be gained only by fighting or submission. Fragmenting these units' power by forcing them to contribute their expertise directly as team members on projects has become a key in dealing with their xenophobic attitudes. This is clearly the effect of the self-directed team and cluster organizations described earlier. Without going to such extremes, many manufacturers have found they can achieve huge gains by forcing lateral integration through reengineered work flows and team relationships, especially in their design-development processes, where much of their value-added is created. For example, in the automobile industry the multibillion-dollar service processes used to design, develop, and introduce new car lines generate a major portion of the value the customer perceives in the car. And they constitute a major component of the car's cost.

■ Honda Motor Company used a unique structure. Recognizing that neither he nor Mr. Honda would have prospered in a pyramidical organization, Honda's first outside chief operating officer, Mr. Fujisawa, developed what became known as Honda's "expert system." He wanted a flat or "paperweight" organization in which a promising person was not dependent on or restrained by his immediate superior. Honda's researchers could define their own project themes and—working in small teams of two to ten people—pursue them in an unstructured environment.

Once development began, projects were managed across research, design, product design, and early production stages. Few risks were taken once a product or process was prototyped. Honda operated on a 2–2½-year design cycle for a new car, with constant system updates after its market entry. A very specific schedule for release was set, and no deviations were allowed despite problems that might develop. Every three months an SED (Sales-Engineering-Development) oversight group reviewed progress. Each group was to argue for its position as vigorously as possible with what was called "mutual aggression."[29]

In development there were two ranks, engineers and chief engineers. Fujisawa described the organization "as a kind of web with engineers lined up sideways instead of top to bottom." The newest engineers were to "argue frankly" with senior people, including VPs who might be on their teams. Engineers were taught to "think like customers" by constant rotation of tasks and by the SED process. Professor Robert Guest, a world authority on automobile organizations, described the keys to Honda's organization this way: "Almost all members of Honda's operating management started in the shop itself, as did 65 percent of its Japanese sales personnel. There is frequent movement laterally and through promotions. Everyone understands that automation will be targeted at the most onerous tasks first. Much of Honda's special machinery is built by Honda's engineering subsidiary, which was set up because of the many new ideas originated by the workforce itself. No one fears problems of technological unemployment, as growth continues."[30] Harnessing its assembly knowledge to the maximum, workers could suggest and implement process changes themselves, and worker teams were often seen on the factory floor designing and implementing their own prototype processes. Mr. Honda by skill and temperament was a "shop man," always concerned about product, production details, the role played by people on the shop floor, and their potential contributions.

■ In Ford Motor Company, as in other U.S. auto firms, the new product design cycle had traditionally taken 5–6 years—and generally cost several billion dollars for a totally new car or line as the design moved sequentially through product design, process design, plant engineering, manufacturing, environmental, regulatory, financial approval, marketing, sales, and distribution staff interfaces. In the early 1980s, Ford's new CEO (Caldwell) and President (Petersen), frustrated at the lack of creativity and low productivity of this process, agreed to undertake a new "simultaneous design" process for a complete "clean sheet" redesign of Ford's upper-middle car line, then the Ford LTD and the Mercury Marquis and Crown Victoria lines. The new line would ultimately be called Taurus/Sable.

Under the direction of Mr. Lewis Veraldi, they decided to laterally integrate the full power of all the knowledge-based service activities involved in Ford's car design process. To integrate the new auto's design from research through postsale service activities, they established a core "Car Product Development Group" (CPDG), later called Team Taurus, that had a full-time representative from all the critical service groups within Ford—including purchasing, product design, component engineering, manufacturing, sales, marketing, postsale service, North American Auto, legal, environmental and safety engineering, and corporate headquarters. Virtually all were service activities, which reported through different functional divisions to the centralized top management of Ford. Team Taurus unified these activities for the first time across what had become known in Ford as the functional groups' "chimneys of power."

Ford later included its major suppliers, factory workers, insurance companies, and external repair people in the process. Instead of moving the design step by step along these groups toward the marketplace—or simply limiting its coordination to design, engineering, and manufacturing groups as other companies had—Ford was able to harness the full value all these service activities could contribute. And it avoided the numerous conflicts and design reworks that sequential movement through the old design process normally entailed. Team Taurus broke the design of the car into four hundred subsystems, for each of which there was a multifunctional design team. Each team sought out the "best in class" design features and producer for its subsystem—anywhere in the world. To release their creative juices, Team Taurus did not set rigid cost—or cost reduction—constraints on each subsystem as Ford had in the past. Instead, Veraldi asked each team to justify all its proposals on a value-added basis and to seek out the "tremendous trifles" that so enhanced quality perception—hence perceived value—in the customer's eyes.[31]

By involving all service activities from the beginning, Team Taurus gave the U.S. car industry some of the most original design features of the early 1980s. And yet Taurus/Sable's introduction costs were some $250 million *less* than its design budget. The process developed the most profitable single car line produced in the United States in the 1980s.

As the potentials of such "simultaneous design" processes have become recognized, more manufacturers have moved to laterally integrate the service activities in their design systems. On its 777 aircraft, for example, Boeing is including customers, pilots, suppliers, mechanics, plant representatives, computer designers, and marketing and finance people. But few have dared to be as complete in their lateral integration as Ford and Honda, or consequently as successful to date. Cross-functional integration can be very potent. However, it is only one of many management techniques needed to increase the effectiveness and decrease the costs of what have been considered "overhead activities" in the past, but now often provide the service power and "intellectual core competencies" of what a modern manufacturer produces. To exploit to the maximum all their overhead and staff service potentials, companies need a whole new mindset—that they are no longer so much managers of physical assets as fiduciary holders of knowledge and managers of intellect.[32] This is the subject of much of the rest of this book.

CONCLUSIONS

Discussions concerning America's manufacturing competitiveness have consistently overlooked an area that offers major productivity leveraging possibilities: the manufacturing–services interface. On the one hand, service companies have become some of the most important customers, suppliers, and coalition partners for many manufacturing concerns. U.S. service enterprises are both near at hand and are among the world's most efficient performers—surpassing the services productivity of virtually all other advanced industrial countries, especially Japan. Major opportunities exist for manufacturers to exploit U.S. service companies as major customers, as lead companies or co-developers for new products, as potential suppliers, as value-adding advisers or market intermediaries, and as sources of invaluable information and distribution clout in their markets.

But more importantly, internal service activities are both the greatest producers of value-added for most manufacturers today and also the cause of burgeoning overheads for many. Each manufacturer needs to evaluate every service activity in its value chain and in its staff overheads, determine if it is "best in world" at that activity, and, if it is not, consider outsourcing the activity to the best-in-world supplier. As it does this, each manufacturer will focus more of its attention on what it does best and less on activities where it is not as effective. As it selectively outsources its less efficient activities, it may leverage its own unique resources and talents to a much greater extent. It will flatten its organization, improve its response times, and lower its overheads. By refocusing on how it can best link its unique skills to customer needs, it can get closer to its markets, increase its value-added, and increase its quality. As the firm progresses through this transition, it becomes ever less a holder and manager of physical assets and more a repository and coordinator of intellectual assets. Like many of the world's most profitable performers—from Merck to Microsoft—it becomes an "intelligent enterprise" managing the highly leverageable outputs of knowledge and service based activities worldwide. In a world where products are moving more toward commoditization and where services and intellect are increasingly the bases of differentiation, leading manufacturers are moving ever more toward service-based strategies and concentrating on developing and managing that most leverageable asset of all: human intellect.

PART 3

Managing the Knowledge Based Service Enterprise

CHAPTER 7
The Intelligent Enterprise:
A New Paradigm

At their core, most successful enterprises today can be considered "intelligent enterprises," converting intellectual resources into a chain of service outputs and integrating these into a form most useful for certain customers. Clearly, enterprises providing law, accounting, financial, architectural, applied research, health care, education, consulting, design, and most forms of entertainment services primarily sell the skills and intellect of key professionals. But in manufacturing as well, most of the processes that add value to materials derive from knowledge-based service activities. In the past, investors—and particularly venture capitalists—shied away from companies with a strong service base, "because their assets could walk away any night and leave you with nothing." They wanted "solid assets to offset downside risks." Now that view is rapidly changing.

REWARDS COME FROM INTELLECT, NOT BRICKS AND MORTAR

In manufacturing today, most venture capitalists recognize that investments in bricks and mortar provide little security and warrant only mortgage rates of return. They make their money by (1) investing in the special skills and intellect that only highly motivated, knowledgeable people can provide, and then (2) leveraging this intellect in the marketplace through a few "best in world" internal systems and the integrated management of many out-

213

sourced activities. Virtually all high-technology startups work in this fashion today. Venture capitalists try to keep conventional plant and equipment investments limited—in part because they can be so quickly supplanted by new technologies—and focus their client companies' management talent and investments on effectively building the intellectual assets and personal attitudes most important to the needs of a selected customer group. Unless the facilities and manufacturing technologies are themselves part of the core competencies of the company, strategy dictates that they *should* be limited—and be selectively outsourced—whenever feasible. This is not an argument against facilities investment *per se*. It does suggest, however, that those fixed facilities that the firm retains should themselves embody as much of the firm's uniqueness and critical intellect as possible.

Every few years *Inc.* or *Venture* magazine runs a special article in which they feature the garages in which today's great companies started, as a reminder that companies start small and that ideas and intellect, not physical assets, build great companies. TA Associates, one of the longer-running and more successful venture capital groups with high-tech manufacturing firms, now actively looks for service companies "having good cash flows, low overheads, and steady revenues from service customers." One venture capitalist summarized the issue clearly, "We don't want to invest in hard assets. They are too short-lived and risky. We certainly don't want to invest in bureaucracies. We want to invest in people who have a clear viable concept, who can manage outside contracts with the best sources in the world, and who can concentrate their internal energies on that small core of activities which creates the real uniqueness and value-added for the company. That's where the action is today, but it's a tough sell against traditional thinking."

■ Novellus Systems Inc., the most profitable and fastest-growing company in the semiconductor production equipment field, provides an interesting example. With only twelve shop floor personnel, Novellus concentrates on design and engineering of advanced chemical deposition equipment. It disdains internal "metal-bending" activities in favor of long-term strategic relations with a few trusted and specialized parts and subsystem producers. In addition to design, Novellus controls all assembly, test, customer contact, and postsales service work and uses partners and suppliers to leverage its inhouse capital and design resources. In a notoriously cyclical industry, Novellus's profits grew 20 percent during the 1991–92 recession on sales of $350,000 per employee —almost double the industry's average.[1]

Many large manufacturing companies (like Sony, Nike, Honda, Apple, Matsushita, Polaroid, Liz Claiborne, Genentech, and IBM) initially succeeded by following the intelligent enterprise model quite closely. At first, they purposely invested limited amounts in plant and standard equipment, produced as few components internally as they reasonably could, and leveraged their limited resources by sourcing externally. The approaches of Nike, Apple, Honda, and Polaroid were described earlier. In Japan, Mr. Konosuke Matsushita simply assembled his bicycle lights and portable electric lights using standard parts made by others, but fitted into his own unique designs. Sony first rented a bombed-out corner of a department store in Tokyo. Its first permanent quarters were some old warehouses in Shinagawa, whose roofs were so leaky that experiments had to be run under umbrellas. Knowing it could not design and make all the needed parts for its miniaturized electromechanical devices, Sony outsourced major portions and taught suppliers how to produce to world quality standards. Genentech rented warehouse space in South San Francisco and bootlegged other space from its researchers' university-related laboratories. Genentech primarily performed research and coordinated the complex processes of early scale production, clinical trials, regulatory clearance, and patenting. It essentially maintained a home for advanced researchers and networked worldwide with university researchers to stay on the frontiers of its remarkable new technology. It licensed the large-scale production, marketing, and distribution of its early "high-volume" products to others like Eli Lilly and Kabi.

As these and many other successful manufacturing companies grew to large sizes, they continued to focus on a selected set of intellectual or service skills and to leverage these against multiple products to develop dominating product-market positions.

CORE INTELLECTUAL AND SERVICE COMPETENCIES SUPPORT BROAD LINE STRATEGIES

The broad lines of all these companies—and some other even more remarkable examples—demonstrate that strategic focus lies not so much in narrowing or limiting one's product lines and product-market scope as in focusing strategy around a uniquely developed set of core intellectual and service capabilities important to customers. A broad or mixed product or service line may not signify a loss of focus at all. In fact a broad line may add to strategic focus—when one can coordinate the deployment of an especially potent set of service skills against numerous marketplaces.

In strategic circles it has recently become popular to seek increased "focus" by concentrating only on fewer and more closely related product lines. After a prolonged period in the 1960s and the early 1970s when ill-conceived financial strategies drove companies to overextend their product lines through conglomeration, a reverse fad developed. Those who had made fees from the acquisition programs of the 1960s and 1970s found that they could make further fees by "deconglomerating" and selling off divisions of companies that had followed the preceding fad too far. These narrowing (or divestiture) strategies were often justified as giving the company "greater strategic focus." Unfortunately, as many have sadly learned, such strategies make the company considerably more risky, because it is subject to much more violent responses when the total economy turns down, or its particular segment of the economy goes sour.

By contrast, looking beyond mere product lines to a strategy built around core intellectual or service competencies provides both a rigorously maintainable strategic focus and long-term flexibility. Once a company develops sufficient depth in a few such activities, these can become linchpins for a consistent corporate strategy and competitive edge lasting for decades. Innumerable new products or services can spring off of these core activities over the years, providing the company with constant refreshment for its line and with enough diversity to stabilize earnings and offset downturns, unlike many traditional product-focused strategies. The concept has worked well for companies as diverse as Merck, Sony, Intel, Motorola, Pilkington Bros., Moulinex, Matsushita, Sharp, Texas Instruments, Nike, and the myriad other companies already noted, whose widely diversified product lines have been powered by a few core competencies, mostly knowledge-based service activities. 3M Corporation provides probably the classic U.S. case.

■ 3M's extensive growth has been founded on its R&D skills in three critical related technologies: abrasives, adhesives, and coating-bonding. In each of these areas, it has developed knowledge bases and skill depths exceeding those of its major competitors. To these core technologies (referred to as historic in Figure 7–1), 3M has attempted to "add" four other compatible sets of core technologies, at least partially from acquisitions. When combined with 3M's remarkable "entrepreneurial-innovation system" and with a strong, broad-based distribution system, its "historic technologies" let 3M develop a wide variety of products internally and sustain continuous growth for six to seven decades (through 1980) at a compounded annual growth rate of 10 percent. From time to time, 3M identified a specific application area, for example small labels, which offered an opportunity to leverage its core technologies or distribution skills by acquisition. Sometimes it needed the complementary skills of a small manufacturer to realize strategic timing goals or to attain a full product presentation in a key area for its "wave front" of products. But for decades 3M's growth basically exploited its core knowledge-based and service competencies in its three or four "historical technologies," its unique innovative system, and its broad-based distribution system.

However, as 3M began to see its growth rates fall in the early 1980s, it tried to acquire new core technologies well beyond its origins—i.e., in imaging and instrumentation. Acquisitions to support these markets were no longer gap-filling but moved the company into new business areas with less connection to its core competencies. As 3M moved farther from its well-developed competencies, success became harder to achieve. Despite strong efforts to diversify further, businesses built off 3M's adhesives, coatings, abrasives, and nonwoven technologies continued to generate a return on assets, on average, about 50 percent higher than the new areas.

As product cycles become shorter, technological performance or style becomes more important and product-based experience curves recede in importance. As a consequence, many sophisticated long-term strategists no longer look primarily to market share and its associated cost-reducing potentials as the keys to strategic planning.[2] Nor do they try to build vertically integrated empires to achieve ephemeral scale economies. Instead they concentrate on identifying those few core service activities where their company has—or can develop (1) a continuing strategic edge and (2) long-term streams of new products to satisfy future customer

FIGURE 7–1
3M: Technology Driven Strategy

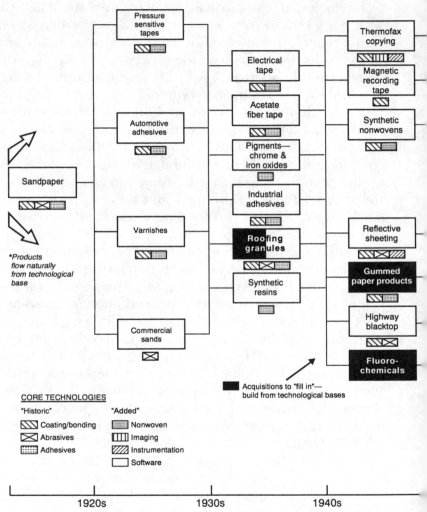

SOURCE: Original chart by Braxton Associates; reproduced with permission.

Acquisitions "add" new technologies/ businesses

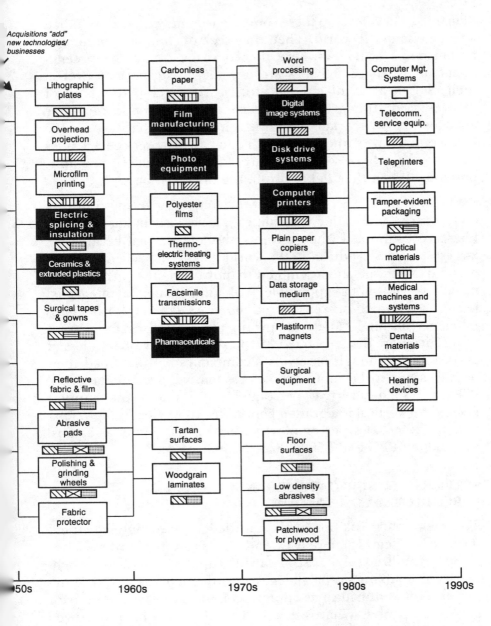

demands. They develop these competencies in greater depth than anyone else in the world. Then they seek to eliminate, minimize, or outsource activities where the company cannot be preeminent—unless those activities are essential to support or protect their chosen areas of strategic focus. To develop this kind of service-based strategy, managers concentrate their competitive analyses not on market share but on "activity share"—i.e., the relative potency of the key knowledge-based or service activities underpinning their own and all direct and functional competitors' positions. When they fail to do so, the price can be high.

■ Pilkington Brothers PLC, after thriving as a growing company on its process innovation capabilities (particularly in flat glass and fiberglass), stumbled when it forgot this adage. As it became the largest flat glass producer in the world, Pilkington relied more on economies of scale and attempted to move into other areas where its skill base was not as applicable. It also maintained an integrated posture as competitors outsourced more. As demand for flat glass fell 4 percent in 1990–91, its profits plummeted 52 percent, as against its more disaggregated European rival St. Gobain's loss of 20 percent. Although other glass companies had flattened their organizations to be more market responsive, a combination of Pilkington's conservative personnel policies and the support needed for vertical integration kept its fixed overheads high. Pilkington's 1990 sales per employee were only $83,000, as against $171,000 at PPG and $500,000 at Nippon Sheet.[3]

SERVICES DISAGGREGATE ORGANIZATIONS, FORCE GLOBAL COMPETITION

To develop their full potentials, knowledge-based "intelligent enterprise" strategies generally extend across national borders. They try (1) to utilize truly "best in world" suppliers or (2) to benchmark the company's capabilities against them. Some global sourcing or joint venturing has always been an important option for larger companies. What is new is the extent to which improved knowledge bases along with service technologies now facilitate—or force—companies to think globally.

Improved telecommunications, air transport, financial services, storage, and cargo-handling technologies mean that virtually all manufacturers (regardless of size) must consider supply sources, markets, and competition on a worldwide scale—or lose their competitive positions. About one-fifth of the total capital invested in U.S. manufacturing firms has now moved outside the United States.[4] The knowledge-based activities of coordinating production, sourcing, and value-added services among these overseas investments have become critical to multinational profitability. In addition, the places where the greatest value-adding economies of scale exist are usually in knowledge-based services (like R&D, marketing, design, information systems, etc.) and not in plant economies of scale. As a result many of the profits, royalties, and intracorporate sales these enterprises remit to the United States rest on these service-based activities. The cash flows from these transactions are among the few strongly favorable "net balances of trade" U.S. manufacturing has provided in the late 1980s and early 1990s. In addition to the royalty fees and profits these companies remit to the United States—primarily due to their knowledge-based capabilities—they also account for a major portion of the goods shipped into the country. Their sales from overseas divisions to the United States are significant components of U.S. imports from abroad (see Table 7–1).

Through large importers in certain sectors (like Nike, IBM, or Exxon), U.S. manufacturers strongly shape the design, specification, and location of much of the world's trade. The country's powerful wholesaler–retailer systems, however, direct even more of the world's manufacturing trade. With their purchasing power and superior knowledge of U.S. markets, these "service" companies often now specify both what will be made and how it will be produced. In addition to the substantial direct influence these capabilities give the United States in world trade, they exert other powerful impacts on world competitive structures. Through their relative efficiency, these companies increase U.S. workers' purchasing power, giving them higher real wages and higher living standards compared to foreign workers. For example, because distribution channels are so much longer and less efficient in Japan, Japanese workers must pay a multiple of the (exchange-weighted) price a U.S. worker pays for the same item. One of the few ways the U.S. can prosper against countries with lower wages and subsidized manufacturing industries is to have a more efficient service sector and to integrate its service and manufacturing sectors better than competitors do. To date its "intelligent enterprises" have accomplished this.

For mass-produced consumer goods, large-scale distribution en-

TABLE 7-1
U.S. Services Trade Balances, 1982-90
(*$ millions*)

	1982	1983	1984	1985	1986	1987	1988	1989	1990
Selected business services, total	12,873	10,534	10,188	4,077	10,703	11,373	17,369	30,052	35,141
Travel	(1)	(2,202)	(6,255)	(7,492)	(6,473)	(6,656)	(4,163)	625	1,908
Passenger fares	(1,598)	(2,393)	(1,864)	(2,327)	(1,209)	(545)	839	1,987	3,288
Other transp.	607	368	(1,034)	(969)	(1,257)	(805)	(520)	9	(1,056)
Fees & royalties	4,560	4,553	4,674	5,104	6,192	7,644	8,721	9,776	12,647
Other priv. serv.	9,305	10,208	10,188	9,761	13,450	11,735	12,492	17,655	18,354
Selected income transactions, total	43,415	37,868	39,322	33,639	28,627	27,609	28,814	32,904	39,870
Direct investment	21,562	21,224	20,755	22,216	25,521	33,390	36,810	42,484	52,662
Other private investment	21,853	20,360	18,567	11,423	3,106	(5,781)	(7,996)	(9,580)	(12,792)
Selected U.S. gov't transactions	(15,936)	(15,226)	(18,895)	(22,426)	(23,656)	(25,009)	(30,492)	(37,853)	(36,690)
Services, income, & government	40,352	36,892	26,136	15,290	15,674	13,691	15,691	25,103	38,321

SOURCE: Bureau of Economic Analysis, "U.S. International Transactions," Table 1, *Survey of Current Business*, June 1991.

terprises and the power of service technologies to link manufacturing entities are the key factors making worldwide coordination of integrated manufacturing, global product and process development, and functionally segmented manufacturing–distribution joint ventures effective. Although services drive globalization at many levels, perhaps nowhere else is their effect as great as in the retailer–manufacturer relationships that interconnect world economies so tightly today. These leverage knowledge bases about U.S. customer demands directly into foreign producers' plants on a daily updated basis. For example:

■ Virtually all retail chains—like Kmart or The Limited's group of companies with their 2,250 and 3,860 retail outlets and their sales of $29.5 billion and $4.8 billion respectively—aggregate their day's sales each night from their EPOS systems. These systems break down sales to the minimum replicable level of detail, such as type of item, cut, size, material, color, style, number sold, price, margins, and so on. Forecasting programs at corporate headquarters then convert the day's sales into a cutting order for Southeast Asian fabric suppliers on the next day. Within a few days, a wide-bodied aircraft takes off from Southeast Asia for the distribution depots of The Limited or Kmart in the United States. A few days later, the merchandise is on their shelves. Thus, stocks are aligned to current demands, markdowns are limited, and inventories are kept to a minimum. Other programs keep track of experimental sales on new items being sampled throughout the system. Customers and retailers dictate what is stocked, and manufacturers are linked as directly to their order givers as possible.

For intermittently produced or specialty products, other manufacturing-service arrangements dominate. For example, VTI Inc. has a flexible worldwide sourcing network to obtain least-cost product design and production of its high value-added, applications-specific integrated circuits (ASICs). Through electronic interfaces, its designers can work with customers anywhere to create a new ASIC design upon request. Its software in Silicon Valley converts these designs into photo masks. The photo masks go to Japan, where others etch the chip. Chips then go to Korea for dicing and mounting, and then to Malaysia for assembly. From Malaysia they are shipped directly to customers by overnight parcel delivery, if desired.

For continuous production operations, global sourcing networks have long offered advantages. Overhead and direct costs
tend to drop markedly with offshore manufacturing. On the other
hand, logistics costs tend to *increase* by a factor of about 20 percent
and tariffs and exchange rates become increasingly significant.[5]
In these circumstances, global information concerning local costs,
suppliers' capabilities, transportation possibilities, *en route* location
of materials, and financing potentials becomes a crucial competitive weapon for manufacturers—and a critical component of
strategy. So important are logistics costs in worldwide manufacturing networks that before Toyota began its Nummi joint venture in the United States with GM, it set a target of having "the
most cost-efficient inbound-outbound logistics system in the
world." Since its own costs for production in Japan would be
essentially fixed (excluding exchange rates), its capacity to control
the relative costs of its Nummi versus Japanese sources depended
mainly on logistics. Without very sophisticated capabilities, Toyota would have been largely competing with itself. Another Japanese group, Mitsubishi, has recognized that its combined
financing and logistics functions will be so important to its future
profitability that it is currently planning to spend multiple billions
(some estimate over $10 billion) on its new MIND logistics system
to provide worldwide manufacturing and distribution support for
its broad line of manufactures.

For economies of scale, multinational manufacturing operations
today tend to look more to their knowledge-based service capabilities—i.e., their research, technology development, marketing,
market intelligence, financial, or logistics functions—than to plant-
scale economies which are dropping in most industries.[6] Many of
these services can flow duty-free across borders, offering new strategic flexibilities, if the multinational can handle cross-border data
and services flows more effectively than its competitors. Since it is
the service and knowledge components of a multinational's capabilities that a host country can least easily reproduce, these become
the company's bargaining points in dealing with host nations, with
suppliers, and with customers in each country. Unfortunately, host
countries increasingly see these data flows as potential tax sources
and as threats to their companies' competitiveness. Maintaining the
freedom of data flows has thus become a critical strategic and del-
icate political issue affecting the future international competitiveness of both manufacturing and service enterprises.[7]

International simultaneous development of products has become a *sine qua non* for most manufacturers if they hope to develop the most competitive available products or processes. But potential suppliers and partners must be intimately and continuously coordinated throughout the design process. In fact, some companies find that they can obtain a competitive edge by using the differences in time zones between countries to obtain a twenty-four-hour-a-day workday during design cycles. A design team begins working on a product in the Eastern United States in the morning, transfers its status to the Japanese team after eleven hours of coordinated work in the United States (an eight-hour day across four time zones). Its Japanese partners then pick up the design and carry it forward through the next 8–12 hours, before it is passed along to European design teams. By the next morning, when the U.S. designers return, two full eight-hour days of further work have advanced the design. However, even without such sequenced design capabilities, many firms are coordinating worldwide development with different supplier groups to obtain "best in world" design capability as a matter of competitive necessity. Ford Taurus/Sable and Boeing have already been cited as outstanding examples.

WHOLE INDUSTRIES RESTRUCTURE

In some cases, these types of "intelligent enterprises" are so pervasive that whole industries are restructuring to achieve global simultaneous interactions on a variety of projects. These industries are becoming merely loosely structured networks of service enterprises joining together (often temporarily) for one purpose, and being suppliers, competitors, or customers in other relationships. This phenomenon is common in the financial services world, where cross-competing consortia constantly form and reform to finance different projects or to spread risks worldwide. But the same is true for enterprises in the mineral resources, construction, publishing, entertainment, or software development fields, among others. Publishers, for example, have become primarily coordinators of intellect, outsourcing virtually the whole process of book creation to independent authors, copy editors, art work groups, compositors, printers, binders, advertising agencies, distributors, retailers, and so on anywhere in the world. Biotechnology provides another interesting global example. Almost all biotech products are developed by intelligent enterprises which coordinate a number of different specialist teams joining together temporarily for the sole purpose of creating and introducing a particular biological entity to the marketplace. Different types of highly specialized enterprises have developed at each level of the industry to perform individual functions.

■ Many biotechnology research groups—for example at universities—only seek to identify and patent active biological entities (or proteins) at the laboratory level. Others develop and license the cell lines that are used to reproduce promising entities. The availability of identified and cultured cells containing the genes to "express an entity" is often as important as knowledge about the active protein and its effects *in vitro*. Still others—companies like Verax and Celltec—have developed pilot-level processes that utilize cell lines owned by others to produce the desired entities in sufficient quantity for clinical tests and early commercialization, but not at full-scale "fermentation" or "flow process" levels. Medical centers handle the highly technical problems of actually administering and running clinical trials. Other enterprises or professional groups may oversee regulatory relationships and FDA clearances. Then other companies—usually major pharmaceutical companies—may take over the large-scale market introduction, detailing, production, and sale of the products, while still other service companies may handle their wholesale or retail distribution. Once the product is in the marketplace, another wider group of doctors prescribe and administer it to patients. And so on. In essence a unique consortium of specialists, intentionally tapping "best in world capabilities," forms for each stage of research, development, product introduction, or full-scale production.

■ The semiconductor, ASIC, and electronics industries are becoming similarly structured. Independent design, foundry, packaging, assembly, industrial distribution, kitting, configuration, systems analysis, networking, and value-added distributor groups do over $15 billion worth of customized development, generating almost $140,000 of revenue per employee.[8] Even the largest OEMs are finding that these groups' specialized knowledge, flexible production facilities, and fast turnarounds decrease investments and increase value at all levels of the value chain.

In advanced technology fields particularly, a single company often cannot effectively span the full chain of activities needed—because of the specialized expertise, high risks, and varying time horizons required—at each level of the development process. As a result, many high-tech industries, from biotech and ASICs to oil exploration, dam building, nuclear power, or commercial aircraft, are developing as multiple-level consortia, with each consortium and enterprise having its own network of contract and information relationships embracing a variety of research, development, production, finance, and marketing groups around the world. Although biotechnology and ASICs are commonly thought of as "manufacturing industries," most of the units that make up these industry consortia are essentially "service centers," performing specialized activities for each other.

NEW METHODS OF FINANCING

These kinds of networks present financial opportunities that are very different from financing a single company. One can participate at any risk level desired. For example, at the university level one can sponsor research seeking individual patentable biological entities with very low probabilities of any specific project's succeeding—but with generally low investments required and potentially high royalty payoffs if the project is successful. Alternately, one can invest larger amounts in companies like Genentech, Biogen, or Amgen (or a new biotech startup), which are pursuing multiple projects at the research level. At the next stage, financing independent pilot-scale processors (like Verax) allows one to average somewhat higher investments—but with lower technical risks—across a number of projects, yet potentially participate in individually large upside licensing incomes if the investments pay off. Clinical limited partnerships have been developed to spread investments and risks of failure at the more costly clinical trials stage, while sharing partially in still larger benefits if they are successful. Full-scale production and marketing investments—usually undertaken by more integrated companies—are quite large, but probabilities of success are much higher.

Each level has developed some creative new forms of financing. Only in rare instances has a single enterprise financed the complete development of a new biotech entity from research through volume production and marketing. The combination of risks with the huge amount of capital required and the industry's long time horizons makes such an integrated undertaking too risky and unwieldy. Alliances are common in biotech, with more than 170 formed just between pharmaceutical manufacturers and other independent biotech groups in 1990. Given the rapid technological advances throughout such industries, companies can lower their risks substantially by specializing, by *avoiding* investments in vertical integration, and by concentrating on managing highly disaggregated intellectual systems instead of workers and machines worldwide. Because of their high value-added and easy portability, the knowledge and service based inputs to such systems can come from anywhere in the world. The core strategy of participating companies becomes: "Do only those things in house that contribute to your competitive advantage, try to joint venture others, or source the rest from the world's best suppliers."

Interestingly, this opens up opportunities for myriad smaller companies. By concentrating on a few selected intellectual skills and attracting best-in-world talent to the company, they can become the suppliers of larger companies for whom these are not specialties. This is the core cause of the dramatic growth in the number of smaller companies—and the changing and increasing outsourcing expenditures of large companies—noted in earlier chapters. Price-Waterhouse looked at five hundred software start-ups with an average age of eight years. Two-thirds got some form of financial help from partners, in the guise of marketing assistance, equipment support, or guarantees from customers or computer builders. Only one-fifth used venture capital. Many such companies become part of the second leaves of "shamrock" companies or the nodes of "spider's web" companies described earlier. If they develop their core competencies in sufficient depth, their small scale, flexibility, and responsiveness make them ideal partners for "intelligent enterprises" with other core competencies.

GLOBAL FINANCING AND MANUFACTURING STRATEGIES

Another change in the financial realm has also been of prime importance in creating more disaggregated "intelligent enterprises" in manufacturing. The integration of world capital markets (service institutions) through electronic communications (service technologies) has forced almost all manufacturers into some form of globalization, much greater disaggregation, and major shifts in sourcing strategies. While the total of all measured goods and services sold in international trade was only $4.5 trillion in 1990, the Clearing House for International Payments (CHIPS) alone handled almost $250 trillion in international financial transactions. Euromarkets and world bond markets added more than $1,000 trillion in further transactions to this sum. Instead of following goods or trade, money now flows toward the highest available real interest rates or returns in safer, more stable economic situations.[9] These factors are generally influenced more by government policies than by trade. As money flows have sprung free of trade, exchange rates have fluctuated wildly at times— ±50 percent among major trading partners within a few months in the late 1980s—principally because of fiscal or monetary, not trade or management, decisions.[10] Such fluctuations change the relative costs of production or importing from a particular location enormously in a short period of time.

Manufacturers cannot cope with changes of this magnitude by vertically integrating and rapidly adjusting their internal productivity rates, no matter how responsive they may be. A manufacturing firm now needs to manage several groups of global portfolios, comprising (1) its financial positions, (2) its market outlets, (3) its assembly sites, (4) its supplier sources, and (5) its subassembly units in different geographical locations, among which it can switch its resources and product deployments rapidly and flexibly. Given such high cost variabilities, few firms can afford to own all of their producing entities themselves, hence the increased need to form the kind of worldwide coalitions noted above—through purchasing arrangements, long-term contracts, alliances, or joint ventures. These are inevitably linked more by information, communication, and mutual interests than by ownership (vertical or horizontal integration) ties. Because of their high value-added potentials and the ease with which their outputs can be transferred, knowledge-based service groups are the central entities in many of these coalitions.

SERVICES CREATE DISAGGREGATION . . .
AND GLOBAL NETWORKS

Why have these disaggregated global ventures suddenly become so much more common? First, new service technologies in the communications, information, storage, distribution, transportation, materials-handling, and similar fields have made it possible for manufacturers to compete directly over much wider geographic ranges. Second, the fact that more of the value-added in products comes from intellectual inputs and service outputs means that one can afford to seek out the best providers (for design, finance, etc.) wherever they exist, especially since services can be shipped across borders at very low cost and tariff-free. In addition, most manufactured products now function in conjunction with some other systems from which they obtain specialized inputs, components, software, distribution, or repair services. And it is frequently far more effective to obtain such capabilities by forming coalitions with exceptionally strong external units than by developing all needed activities internally or acquiring and owning a total vertically integrated operation.

The purported benefits of vertical integration—greater control, faster response, and profit capture at each level of production—may work well in stable or predictable industries (as glass once was) with long time horizons. But there are few such industries today. Technology, worldwide competition, and extreme (design and cost) variations among different suppliers' and customers' capabilities and needs have destroyed the potential benefits of such infrastructures for most companies. Why? Mainly because vertical integration forces companies to be expert in more areas than they can possibly sustain as "best in class." Unless transaction costs are very high, integration is unlikely to offset the costs of having units with lesser expertise and a higher total investment base in a highly variable marketplace.

■ For example, liquid crystal displays (LCDs) are crucial to the next generation of computers and perhaps televisions. Color LCD sales (probably made from thin films) are expected to exceed those of memory chips by the year 2000. But exploitation requires multiple skills. One set supports the thin films themselves, another is for the special glass needed for displays, another is for the advanced testing equipment to control defects, and another is for the equipment that uses the displays. As a result, a number of consortia are forming to link the crucial skills various specialized companies have, and to reduce investment risks during the expected prolonged development cycle.

■ Silicon Graphics, a leading manufacturer of 3D workstations, has been one of the most rapidly growing companies ever in Silicon Valley. Its high-powered computers sell for around

$200,000. Recognizing the need to increase the volume and to lower prices for its complex technologies, it introduced a $10,000 IRIS Indigo workstation. Then it entered licensing agreements with Compaq and Microsoft and opened its software to third-party licensees. Silicon Graphics is relying on its accumulated knowledge base about 3D and an enforced fast-response culture to keep it ahead. Without such alliances, its CEO, Ed McCracken, felt others could eventually force competing technologies to become the industry's standard.

■ By contrast, two electronic home equipment giants, Sony and Matsushita, saw their basic entertainment hardware products moving toward a commodity status in a few years. Instead of entering alliances, they vertically integrated. Each purchased a major software (film and distribution) company to capture the higher margins and more stable revenues there. It remains to be seen whether their strong consensus-type core "design and manufacturing" cultures will be compatible with the creative, risky, egocentric world of movies, television programming, and rock concerts—or whether alliances would have lowered risks and investments.

Vertical integration exposes the company to all the risks at each activity level in which it participates and amplifies the "systematic risks" of the volatility in its own industry. Whenever there is a downturn, such companies must absorb not only the losses in their own final marketplaces but also those in each of the supplier marketplaces in which they are vertically integrated. Outsourcing lets companies spread these risks upstream to suppliers and downstream to distribution networks. Proper outsourcing and managing of supplier networks allows the company to concentrate on what it does best, to surround that activity with enough value-added services to give it uniqueness and depth, to avoid the investments and risks in areas where it is less expert, and to tap the innovation and expertise of best-in-world suppliers in the latter areas. As the COO of a rapidly growing telecommunications company said, "You know how many advanced technology people I have working for me now? About 19,000! Less than 1,000 on my staff and over 18,000 in my suppliers' shops. And they are the best available anywhere in the world. We basically plan, design, and oversee what these people can do for our customers."

DISAGGREGATION WITH A STRATEGIC FOCUS

Such potentials change the entire concept of strategic focus in manufacturing, from a focus on product classes to a focus on those activities (usually knowledge-based services) that the company can perform and link uniquely well to customer needs. In some cases, this may mean a single-minded focus on certain aspects of manufacturing itself, as it does in SCI or Honda. More often it means integrating the company's product skills with a complex of knowledge-based service activities in ways that give the company a unique capacity to serve selected customer needs.

■ Despite current admonitions to "stick to one's knitting," for a Xerox to have stuck to manufacturing and selling reprographic machines or an IBM to have been only a computer manufacturer would have been a strategic disaster. Xerox became a huge success primarily because it created an invulnerable patent wall around its product, found a unique way to finance purchases by smaller customers so they could pay for their units as they used them, and coped with the product's early erratic performance with the best field service force then available. Xerox later extended broadly into support software and systems to give its customers the flexible image-reproducing qualities and network interconnection capabilities they began to demand. Both before and after Xerox's products went off patent, the sum of its profit contributions from such "service activities" were at least equal to its value-added from in-house manufacture.

IBM also has long received over one-third of its gross profit from direct sales of software and services. When one takes into account the value of the system software and design services traditionally "built into" or associated with the equipment IBM sells and the value of the equipment sales it would lose without its awesome service support activities, most of IBM's profits during its long period of success were truly due to its service-based focus on its customers' needs. Both IBM and Xerox had built up a service core that best delivered its carefully defined "document handling" (Xerox) or "information management" (IBM) capabilities as a system to its customers. Yet as large and as capable as these companies were, each increasingly found it could not internally create and control the full range of design, hardware, software, communications, and networking capabilities it needed.

Hence, both moved steadily away from their earlier attempts to vertically integrate—and toward a wide-ranging and constantly changing set of coalitions with outside service and support groups that let them compete globally against similar networks of other companies.

■ Given the rapid changes in technologies and world marketplaces, IBM in the late 1980s began dismantling the insularity and self-sufficiency that dominated it in the 1970s and early 80s. Even its huge multibillion R&D program—largest in the industry—needed to be leveraged externally. In addition to partnering with Apple on (RISC, UNIX, and Taligent) software and helping the MCT consortium to do basic computer technology research, IBM began teaming with Siemens to launch the next generation of 16-megabit DRAMS and to design the 64-meg DRAMS that will replace them. Siemens will sell the chips in Europe. IBM is also trying to forge partnerships with Disney, MCA, Spielberg, and Warner to exploit the multimedia worlds of industrial and personal computers. Its traditionally strong skills in industrial marketing, information, and distribution should give it advantages in that market, but it will need coalitions for success in the consumer-entertainment segment of multimedia.[11]

Networks—like those illustrated in Figure 7–2—have become the basis of competition in many industries.[12] These arrangements look much like the Japanese keiretsu structures, but with a real difference. For years, combined production–service integration (of banks, producers, and export-distribution companies) has been at the heart of Japan's keiretsu-based trading power. Although some large manufacturing groups may wield enormous economic clout within a keiretsu, the Japanese generally have been wise enough to practice "quasi-integration," not complete vertical integration. Most keiretsu operate largely through multiple, carefully interlocked coordination and decision structures based on common interest, rather than on orders from some formal central authority. Given the Japanese success, it is not surprising that similar coalitions—extended on a worldwide basis—are providing a discussion model for improving other countries' competitive postures today.

However, the keiretsu's interlocking boards would be illegal in most countries. In any event, companies in those countries can

FIGURE 7-2
Competing Global Networks: IBM and AT&T

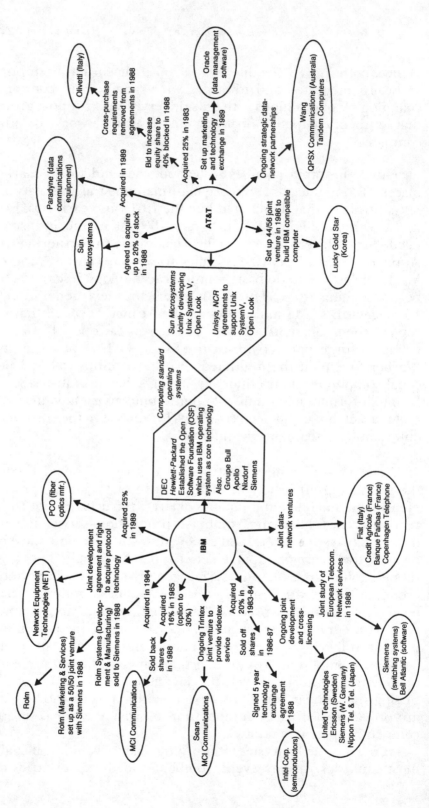

SOURCE: Original chart by Braxton Associates, J. B. Quinn, and P. C. Paquette.

probably gain greater competitive advantage by jumping beyond the mutual, partial-ownership ties of the keiretsu and directly into more flexible contract partnership-oriented structures. They can avoid much of the bureaucracy and inflexibility that keiretsu relationships are now causing the Japanese. There are numerous challenges in managing the more disaggregated Western "intelligent enterprise," which we shall take up in later chapters. But the form provides very real competitive advantages for those who use it effectively.

MAINTAINING STRATEGIC FOCUS IN THE "INTELLIGENT ENTERPRISE"

The key lies in maintaining strategic focus while disaggregating. This does not necessarily mean a tight focus on a limited set of products. Products rarely provide a maintainable competitive edge today. They can be too easily back-engineered or cloned. True strategic focus means developing a selected set of knowledge factors, databases, and service skills—of particular importance to customers—in such depth that the company becomes "best in world" at providing these to customers. It then concentrates its resources on those activities and seeks best-in-world partners (or performance parity) in other areas by careful benchmarking, process updating, and outsourcing to others when it cannot reach best-in-world status internally.

To maintain its position from a strategic viewpoint, the company's selected focus *must control some crucial aspect(s)* of the relationship between its suppliers and the marketplace. The company must block its suppliers from bypassing it to the marketplace, as Giant Manufacturing of Taiwan, originally a bicycle frame subcontractor, did to Schwinn. And it must defend itself from big purchasers attempting to vertically integrate into its turf. The best way to do both is to control some key knowledge-based segment(s) of the value chain. Just as Apple Computer defended its position by controlling the "look and feel" of the personal computer's operating software and the knowledge about computer demands that it generated from its well-developed user network, even smaller companies can develop formidable barriers to others invading their turf.

■ For example, Excel Industries of Elkhart, Indiana, had developed a better method for making auto windows. When Ford tried to bring that production in-house during a recent recession, it could not master Excel's complex process. Ford ended up having to give Excel a multiyear contract as well as investing in the company. Excel's sales grew by four times, as it reinvested in a faster, more efficient process, cutting design cycles by a year. Ultimately both companies gained by the new relationship.

The company's depth in its selected core activities and their importance to its customers must be such that customers cannot destroy the company by short-circuiting it directly to its suppliers, and suppliers cannot simply assemble components and sell clones to the market, as Sony's imitators have often attempted with its products.

This approach radically shifts the basis of strategic analysis in manufacturing. Strategists must analyze all present and potential (direct and cross-) competitors able to perform the *critical activities* in the company's value chain. Because there is so much cross-competition among most such activities, managers cannot simply look at the companies in their own "product industry." In particular, they must strategically analyze all those companies that cross-compete in providing the particular function(s) they have chosen as their core competencies and make sure they focus more talent on these areas than anyone else in the world, while benchmarking other crucial service activities to ensure that they maintain sufficient parity there not to be overtaken by cross-substitutions.

As companies begin to simplify internal operations and outsource nonstrategic activities—particularly overheads and peripheral activities—they often discover secondary benefits. The overhead cost leverages can be very impressive. For example, Black & Decker found out that as it eliminated steps in its own manufacturing processes, simplified its designs, and consolidated its suppliers, it dramatically decreased the service activities needed to support its product line. It ultimately obtained $3 in benefits from overhead cost reduction for each dollar of direct cost it eliminated from production activities.

A MORE MARKET-DRIVEN STRATEGY

For almost all firms, focusing strategy on a few core service competencies will lead to a more compact organization. The firm usually ends up with fewer hierarchical levels and a much sharper focus on recruiting, developing, and motivating the people who can create most value for the company. Knowing that it can be potentially outsourced, each activity in the company becomes more "market-driven" to provide better and lower-cost service for its internal users. Some companies establish their overhead service units as small private business units, which must sell their services to operating groups on a continuing basis, just as component divisions must sell their products in competition with outsiders. In many cases, the market-driven process can be extended to providing such services directly to outside customers—for example, selling one's own accounting or personnel services to outsiders. Some authorities even suggest that if an internal staff group cannot sell at least one-third of its output to outside users, this is a sure sign that the internal activity is not world competitive and ought to be outsourced.

Some companies go beyond this to link services directly to defined and prioritized customer needs in a strategic mode.

■ Although it is a relatively smaller company (versus its competitors, the "Baby Bells"), United Telephone of Ohio (UTO) provides an excellent example. UTO is attempting to match up the level of services it offers to customers in a profile that is much more congruent with the pattern of its customers' true needs—first understanding in depth what customers most want and need from UTO, then specifically allocating its internal resources and scaling its organizational units' sizes to fit the defined service balance (see Figure 7–3). UTO tries to benchmark the best available competitive sources for each service and to match or beat that performance. To make sure that it is "best in class" in the right places, UTO consciously patterns its organizational elements and resource commitments to be "overstaffed" relative to those needs its customers define as most critical and those in which it is attempting to achieve its own competitive edge. Conversely, those services which are less essential or less desired from the customer's viewpoint may be consciously "understaffed" or eliminated to lower overall costs. All systems and organizational elements are aligned to ensure that those activities most valued by customers receive most attention.

Such approaches help achieve a much greater and more consistent strategic focus. They also shift management's attention away from an internal or functional orientation—and the capacity to manage these functions' associated bureaucracies—and toward

FIGURE 7–3
Example: Activity Analysis Matrix—Support Activities versus Customer Needs, Large Business Segment

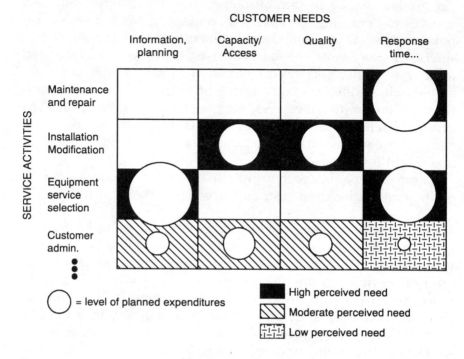

SOURCE: Original chart by Braxton Associates; reproduced with permission.

those more coordinated, strategic, and conceptual tasks that add greater value for customers. The skills needed at the top level shift strongly toward (1) coordinative interfunctional skills, (2) logistics and contract management skills, (3) specialist skills at the forefront of their fields, and (4) leadership skills that can conceive, implant, and coordinate a broad vision across the much more geographically diffused activities of a company. With fewer bureaucracies, the company can become much more quality- and customer-focused. Subsequent chapters will demonstrate in detail how successful companies manage their internal organizational, control, and reward systems to achieve these goals.

CONCLUSIONS

True focus in strategy means the capacity to bring more power to bear on a selected sector than anyone else can. While this once meant a manufacturer's owning the largest production facility, research laboratories, or distribution channels supporting a single product line, this is no longer desirable or sufficient for most companies. Physical positions like a raw material source, a plant facility, or a product line rarely constitute a maintainable competitive edge today. This is especially true of manufactured products. They can be too easily bypassed, back-engineered, cloned, or slightly surpassed in performance. A truly maintainable competitive edge usually derives from developing depth in skill sets, experience factors, innovative capacities, know-how, market understanding, databases, or information-distribution systems— all knowledge-based service activities—that others cannot duplicate or exceed.

As a company does this it needs to concentrate on those particular skills, service activities, or knowledge elements in the value chain where the company is, can be, or must be "best in world" in order to have a competitive advantage its customers deem to be critical. The company must ensure that it is and remains measurably better in its selected core service activities, developing them in greater depth than anyone else can. Then it must seek to achieve at least parity—either internally or through external arrangements—in most other key elements of its value chain. In pursuing this parity, it must seek out, join with, purchase from, or try to match the best in world performance in each activity. Finally, it must surround its selected core competencies with defensive positions, both upstream and downstream, that keep existing or potential competitors from taking over or eroding its selected positions. As it moves toward such a posture, the company tends to become an "intelligent enterprise," developing and coordinating intellectual activities worldwide.

Many companies fear that in following this approach they may not be able to maintain sufficient knowledge at the core to manage their specialist suppliers. This can be a real problem if not properly handled. To avoid losing control in the areas they outsource, successful companies maintain a small cadre of very specialized and talented managers at the top to oversee their outsourced relationships expertly. As later chapters will suggest, this often actually means upgrading the top line of people for their new activities. When this is done, despite some initial fears, many companies have found that their new activity coordinators, by riding circuit on all potentially "best in world" outside suppliers, can generate an even greater knowledge of the outsourced activities than the company had when its internal bureaucracies were producing these outputs on a proprietary basis. For example, as a portion of its Taurus/Sable project, Ford installed a "must see before" contracting policy, which forced its teams into the field to investigate alternate suppliers in detail. This led to greater understanding of suppliers and design problems, new ideas for the car, and a higher level of internal understanding about possibilities than the old processes allowed. Later chapters will outline how to manage this and other critical aspects of the knowledge and service based strategies leading to the "intelligent enterprise."

Fortunately, new knowledge-based service technologies—especially on-line systems for remotely monitoring research, design-logistical activities, quality, and cost relationships—can markedly reduce the "transaction costs" and improve the effectiveness of managing highly disaggregated systems. Most companies find their other internal costs and time delays drop as long-standing bureaucracies disappear or are reduced in power, and as their managements concentrate more of their time directly on more coordinative activities and the important core strategic activities of the business. None of this is easy. Implementing this kind of strategy is a complicated undertaking, and it usually must be approached incrementally, as Chapter 12 will suggest. However, when successful, the changes in the company's competitive posture can be very impressive.

CHAPTER 8

Managing Knowledge Based and Professional Intellect

With rare exceptions, the economic and producing power of a modern corporation lies more in its intellectual and service capabilities than in its hard assets—land, plant, and equipment. Similarly, the value of most products and services depends primarily on the development of knowledge-based intangibles, like technological know-how, product design, marketing presentation, understanding of customers, personal creativity, and innovation. Generating these effectively in turn depends more on managing the company's intellectual resources than on directing the physical actions of its people or the deployment of its tangible assets.

Virtually all public and private enterprises—including most successful corporations—are becoming dominantly repositories and coordinators of intellect, i.e., "knowledge-based" or "intelligent enterprises." Intellect and services create value-added. The capacity to manage human intellect—and to transform intellectual output into a service or a group of services embodied in a product—is fast becoming the critical executive skill of this era. There are many challenges in developing this new management perspective. Among the most important are:

The concept of the "knowledge-based enterprise," or "intellectual holding company," was published first in J. Quinn, T. Doorley, and P. Paquette, "Technology in Services: Rethinking Strategic Focus," and J. Quinn and P. Paquette, "Technology in Services: Creating Organizational Revolutions," *Sloan Management Review*, January 1990.

241

- How to think about, identify, develop, and measure intellectual assets and the outputs they produce? How best to capture this value internally and convert it into shareholder wealth?
- What management processes to use to generate greatest output value and productivity from the more specialized professional and creative service activities that are the heart of many large enterprises?
- How to guide and motivate people in knowledge-based or mass service-producing enterprises to maximize their productivity and the quality of their outputs?
- How to select and oversee those activities the company can most effectively produce internally, outsource, or create through strategic alliances?
- How best to manage the dramatic new organization forms (described earlier) for strategic focus and higher profits—and how to make the transition to such organization forms?

These are complicated and profound issues that cannot be neatly separated for discussion. Part 3 of the book basically attacks the first three; Part 4 concentrates more on the latter three. Mass services will be addressed in both sections. While not pretending to lay all questions to rest, these two sections of the book hope to structure relevant problems in a new light, provide some pragmatic insights, and lay out some key issues for further research. McKinsey & Company estimates that by the year 2000, 70 percent of all jobs in Europe (and 80 percent of those in the United States) will require primarily cerebral skills rather than manual skills.[1] The percentages are probably low, but the message is clear. The Japanese have already recognized that they cannot maintain a higher standard of living for their people than Southeast Asia's LDCs will enjoy, if they employ their people in the same manufacturing jobs. Japan knows it must convert the greater intellectual capital its educational system and social infrastructures generate into higher-value services or knowledge-based outputs. It is time the United States concentrated on the same factors.

MEASURING INTELLECTUAL ASSETS

What is involved in managing intellect and its output function, service production, as value-generating systems creating measurable assets? A phenomenon to be understood or managed must first be delineated and measured.

Despite the preponderant contributions of intellect and services in creating the value and growth of modern companies and nations, with few exceptions our management control systems, economic models, and social measurement devices focus on physical assets and their physical (or physically measurable) outputs. We measure and compare the wealth and economic prosperity of nations primarily in terms of the autos, televisions, kilowatt hours, miles of road, and tons of food or materials they produce—and the capitalized value of the tangible things their people own. Intellectual or service outputs generated are assumed to be ephemeral, consumed, gone, and hence implicitly not a portion of a nation's permanent wealth. Yet a nation's most valuable assets often lie (1) in the skills and attitudes of its trained people and (2) in its education, communications, transportation, health, financial, legal, and political systems—and not so much in its natural resources or accumulated base of physical assets. A simple comparison of the former USSR with Japan will make the point.

The same is true of corporations. There is little question that the "intangibles" of databases, personal know-how, technological understanding, communications networks, market knowledge, brand acceptance, distribution capabilities, organizational flexibility, and effective motivation are the true assets of most companies today and the primary sources of their future income streams. Yet, as with nations, the asset value of these intellectual and service infrastructures is nowhere to be seen on a corporation's balance sheets. And the value services contribute is often disguised (or treated only as an expense) by accounting conventions that allocate all benefits to product outputs. Increasingly, these accounting and economic measurement conventions are leading to poor managerial practices and to misguided national policies. Nationally, we continue to underinvest in the service infrastructures that give the nation its future intellect, productivity, and health. And at the corporate level, managers underinvest in the very things that generate value, creating opportunities for others, like the Japanese with their longer-term horizons, to purchase the real value of U.S. companies at bargain-basement prices.

These conventions, designed in the past, assume that capital—not talent or intellect—is the resource in short supply. Hence return on assets and its net companion, return on stockholders' equity or investment, have become the primary metrics of business success. These measures may have worked reasonably well when there was a severe shortage of goods, when repetitive mass-production depended largely on the investments one could muster, and when hired workers were simply a less costly substitute in production processes one could not automate well. But are they still valid when value-added derives primarily from intellectual or service inputs? When the scarce resources are the skills, knowledge bases, and service capacities of the enterprise? And when the value of these resources is expensed rather than capitalized?

APPRAISING INTELLECTUAL ASSETS

One of the few concrete measures that does tend to place a value on intellectual assets in Tobin's Q, the ratio (or difference) between a firm's market value and the replacement value of its physical assets. The multiple (or difference) is implicitly the extra value the market places on the intellectual and service value of the company, i.e., the amount knowledgeable buyers would presumably be willing to pay to reproduce its intangible assets, if they could be bought. In the normal calculation of Tobin's Q, the market is making certain assumptions—usually discounting assumptions—about how well the company's existing management will exploit these values. A more reliable evaluation may occur at the time an outside buyer chooses to purchase a whole firm rather than to build all its intellectual values from scratch.

Using Chapter 2's figures approximating Tobin's Q in the largest recent U.S. acquisitions, one can easily see how much of the market value of an enterprise is due to its intellectual and service capabilities. In most cases, market values are 250–500 percent of asset value (see Table 2–1). Tom Watson, Jr., was very realistic when he used to say, "All the value of this company is in its people. If you burned down all our plants, and we just kept our people and our information files, we would soon be as strong as ever. Take away our people, and we might never recover." Thinking about a company in this mode raises a host of new issues. It also suggests some new and more constructive ways to manage and measure value creation. Maybe the first is to regard and to manage (1) people and (2) knowledge systems as the critical assets of the enterprise. How can one approach this systematically?

IDENTIFY AND CATALOGUE

A good starting point is simply to identify and catalogue the firm's intellectual assets in their multiple forms. Most companies are aware of their patents, copyrights, and trademarks as assets and may even carry them that way in their capital accounts, but at cost rather than at market values. However, the majority of most companies' knowledge assets lie elsewhere in the minds of researchers, engineers, production workers, marketing people, functional specialists, and managers. Others are embedded in the myriad software packages, databases, and information systems that codify and store the company's knowledge. Still others reside in the personal relationships, commitments, and shared knowledge patterns that cement supplier or customer continuity. The basis for almost all lies in the company's service capabilities and relationships.

A company's loyal customer base, for example, is often its most valuable single asset. Its worth depends largely on how well it has treated (serviced) customers over the years. As Fred Reichhold, Bain & Company's service specialist, notes, "In a knowledge business, knowledge and information are the raw materials, and the assets are loyal customers and employees." To these assets we will add some others. Yet few companies have calculated the replacement value of these assets or segmented that value usefully. The few that have, like Sewell Cadillac of Dallas, Texas, find extraordinary customer retention values—i.e., $325,000 in average sales per individual customer for Sewell. Bankers estimate they make 85 percent greater profits from retained than from new customers.[2] Imagine what these values are for IBM's installed base of computer system users, or for American Express.

■ American Express (AmEx) is a company that implicitly recognizes this value. With its huge variety of services, $10.5 billion AmEx automatically collects massive amounts of data about its various customers. Its computers maintain and update weekly profiles on 450 attributes for each of 22 million cardholders. Then to make sure it is serving its customers properly, AmEx makes monthly surveys on forty-six customer matrices that it summarizes and tracks in a "customer satisfaction index," one of its most critical performance measures. AmEx can not only target "enhancements" for its own individual products more accurately, but can pinpoint its own $600 million of direct marketing and the advertising in each of its magazines ($150 million in sales) with greater precision than most of its competitors. Its various financial services—from banking to Shearson Lehman, to Investors Diversified Services—although not yet linked, promise to give AmEx invaluable further data on which to build totally new products for the future.[3]

Unfortunately, in most companies the significant asset value of retained—happy or unannoyed—customers is rarely specifically measured, hence appropriately considered, in investment and program budgeting decisions.

■ For example: the author has repeatedly encountered the following incident on one of the largest U.S. airlines. When onboard repairs are finished on a jetliner at an airport, the entire passenger contingent—several hundred strong—must typically sit and wait while the repair crew goes back to its base, "gets the paperwork" to be signed, returns for the pilot's signature, and finally leaves the aircraft. The measured time (sic) for this procedure is 15–20 minutes beyond the repair time itself. The internal cost savings of one repairman for twenty minutes on each repair may not justify a simple knowledge-based electronic verification procedure to replace this practice. But such calculations do not include the cost of 200–500 passengers each spending an unnecessary ¼ to ⅓ hour for every incident, getting quite annoyed, many missing connections, and some having to be provided overnight accommodations because of the added delays. Not only are these directly measurable costs to customers, but their perception of the company's service and reliability declines markedly. If considered seriously, these "relationship costs" would make the investment decision obvious.

Just systematically mapping the points at which high intellectual or relationship values exist, or can be captured, can lead directly to profitable ways to exploit them. Mapping did just this in focusing MBNA America on its profitable customer retention program.[4] It also enabled Intel to discover that by testing 10,000 units carefully it could obtain as much useful information for cost reduction as it could from the experience curve of producing a million. A similar analysis led Japan's consumer products giant, Kao Corporation, to perform its distribution in-house in order to obtain the information advantages it could capture from that system. Over time, this information significantly outweighed Kao's added margins, which may even have been negative, from more efficient distribution.[5]

FINDING A USEFUL METRIC

After cataloguing intellectual assets, one needs to find some meaningful metric for placing a value on them. The process begins by asking how much it would cost to replace the asset if it suddenly went away—i.e., what is the alternative cost of not having the asset? This by itself can lead to a helpful ordering of priorities. Plant and equipment can usually be replaced for a few million dollars or a few tens of millions. But the databases of a company like Citicorp, GE, Boeing, Sears, American Express, *Readers' Digest,* or Dun & Bradstreet are worth billions, if they are replaceable at all.

■ *Readers' Digest* is an interesting example. The *Digest's* worldwide circulation of 28 million is greater than that of *Time, Newsweek, U.S. News & World Report,* and *TV Guide* combined; and the *Digest's* readers are exceptionally loyal. Its renewal rate for subscriptions is over 70 percent. Because only 30 percent of its revenues—as opposed to an industry average of 50 percent—come from advertising, *Reader's Digest* is more recession-resistant than its competitors, booming upward in the 1990–91 recession. Yet the *Digest's* real value lies elsewhere. It has a mailing list of more than half the households in the United States, about 50 million strong. For each of these, the *Digest* has a "unified computer file," keeping track of all its relations with each customer. From its sales of videotapes, books, other specialty magazines, musical recordings, and other advertised specials, *Reader's Digest* can profile its customers in detail and target their changing tastes. Its database on customers, developed since 1969, is considered perhaps the best in its field. Its CEO, George Grune, says, "Our relationship with the reader is the key to the success of this entire company."[6]

Initially, just understanding the order of magnitude of such valuations and their relative rankings is worth more than any false precision in measurements. Early valuations will undoubtedly be experimental and *ad hoc.* But once a company establishes a reasonably satisfactory measure, it can reuse its technique every few years to see how well it is doing on a trend basis in growing its intellectual assets. As a starting overall metric, the company can, at a minimum, calculate whether its Q Ratio is growing or deteriorating relative to its direct competitors. One can sometimes use a product division's spin off or sale value as a surrogate. But much more detailed techniques and measures are needed for most groups at the functional or activity levels in more complex companies' operations.

■ Recognizing that intellect should be able to grow exponentially, some companies establish simple exponential performance growth metrics. In appraising its technical capabilities, for example, 3M insists that each division show that, in each five years, 70 percent of its sales come from new products derived from the company's technology bases and entrepreneurial skills. Japanese companies routinely use metrics of 10–15 percent productivity increases per year on established product lines. Similarly, American high-tech companies like Boeing and Intel have long planned both component performances and future costs to improve on even steeper (mathematically defined) slopes reflecting predictable experience curve effects. Japanese manufacturing companies routinely disdain Western "time and motion" methods of setting work standards in favor of these more dynamic "rate of improvement" measures which both set stringent targets and capture the exponential impact a team's intellectual inputs should have on innovation and productivity. This kind of progress metric further captures potentials that intellect embodied in components or systems can have on future products.

Such metrics can be pushed even farther by "dynamic benchmarking" against the progress and performance levels the best outsiders are achieving, to make sure the company keeps up with performance advances in both its current and its planned products and processes. Professional data-gathering groups and information consortia (like the Research Group) can provide useful outside checks on competitive capabilities and the slope of learning curves.

NOT ACCOUNTING MEASURES

With a few exceptions, standard accounting practices have not only been of little value in evaluating intellect but have often had a significant negative influence. Rather than regarding expenditures on intellectual or service developments as being investments in assets of enduring value on which one expects returns and then systematically quantifying these returns, accounting practices have classified them as "expenses" to be written off—and minimized if possible. In this vacuum, independent market-based appraisals offer the best available recourse. Just making periodic assessments of key groups' intellectual outputs, their potential sale value to an outsider, and any measurable trends in these values can offer a new perspective. Years ago, the author showed how this could be done for the outputs of industrial R&D.[7] Usually, no single metric will suffice; multiple measures are necessary. How does one proceed?

Conceptually, one lists the major outputs of the activity—say R&D—over a reasonable period. For R&D the "direct outputs" are technologies in different forms. Then a team estimates how much an outsider might pay to own each output (or group of outputs) at the time it was produced. For some outputs, like totally new products, cost-reducing techniques, or new processes, one can use standard cash flow techniques to assign a value. For others, like product improvements, one can estimate the loss of market penetration that would have occurred without them and calculate (within reason) the derived profits and experience curve savings these improvements actually allowed. For other outputs, like research papers, improved databases, or general knowledge, one calculates how much the company or an outsider would pay to own this result currently and then discounts it back to the time of generation.

Without claiming that R&D produces the resulting profits by itself—which it clearly does not—R&D does create these values as "opportunities to exploit." The process is much like evaluating a gold mine. Using the best available techniques, one estimates the likely cash flows one could achieve from exploitation and discounts these based on the probabilities and risks involved. Clearly the mine doesn't create the cash flows. The organization does. Yet the mine does have a value in itself. Like any other approach, one checks the calculated value against how much it would have cost to buy similar output (or output potentials) from an outside party at the time (see Figure 8–1).

Another interesting calculation is to determine what the company actually did with these potential values. One can calculate an "exploitation ratio," comparing the value of the "opportunities to exploit" that the activity created versus the value the company actually obtained from exploitation. This suggests how well the intellectual or service activity's outputs fitted the company's needs

FIGURE 8–1
Evaluating Intellectual Output: Research and Development as an Output System

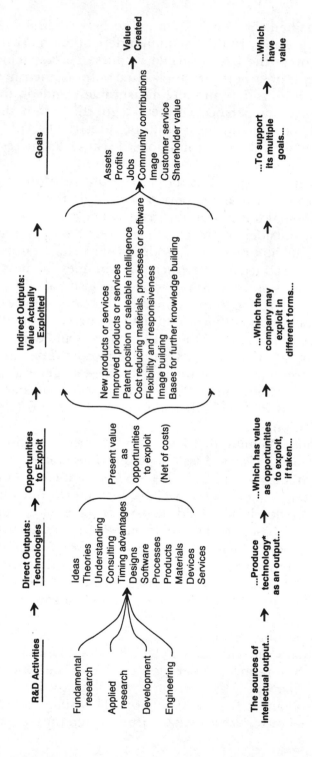

*Technology is knowledge about natural phenomena systematically applied to useful purposes.

and how effective individual divisions have been in exploiting the opportunities the activity (in this case R&D) produced. The patterns can be quite revealing for management and motivational purposes. Using similar principles, analogous techniques can be developed to calculate the output values—or costs avoided—that many other service activities generate.

How can one place a value on the whole research endeavor as an intellectual asset? There are perhaps several ways: (1) Calculate for what price the company would be willing to sell off the entire activity. (2) Estimate how much it would cost to rebuild from scratch the portions of the R&D unit the company would like to keep. (3) Assess how much it would have cost the company to buy from outside sources the "opportunities to exploit" R&D created. (4) Estimate the asset value of a continuing stream of "opportunities to exploit" having the value (net of costs) of those calculated using the approach of Figure 8–1. Each calculation gives a slightly different view of the value of the R&D group as an asset. Together they should bracket the true asset value rather well—just as using similar techniques would in placing a value on a gold mine.

However, most managements would quickly say, "But we're not interested in selling off the entire R&D activity, why do all that?" The answer is twofold. *First,* if in the process of making the "opportunities" calculation one breaks down R&D outputs to match up with their producing departments and using divisions, some very useful insights will emerge as to where R&D has been truly productive and where it has performed poorly. Managerial actions can make improvements. *Second,* operating and top managers have a more objective basis for their optimism—or pessimism—in trading off R&D expenditures against other investments. They begin to look at R&D as an intellectual asset instead of an accounting expense. As they do this for all aspects of their business, they have a better basis for managing the total enterprise for the long run.

PROCESS AS WELL AS OUTPUT MEASURES

One should not be misled into concluding that a high measured output for an activity necessarily means high efficiency. Direct costs of the activity and the backup investment to exploit it must of course be deducted in the cash flow analysis. Even then, one must look at other efficiency and quality criteria. For example, researchers may have gotten lucky on one big project and performed miserably on most others. They may have worked much more slowly and sloppily (with low efficiency), or have left wide gaps in their data (low quality) in ways that other professionals observing the process closely would find intolerable. Or they may have worked very skillfully and creatively on things the company chose not to exploit at all (poor management). Consequently, in addition to sophisticated *output* measures, one needs a set of internal measures to appraise the quality and productivity of the service producing *process* itself.

■ With this in mind, some leading companies have developed combined process and output models for their key service activities. Merck, for example, has made a model of its R&D processes. It uses the model to educate managers, board members, and financial analysts about the risks, time lags, and payoffs in different types of research. Motorola has modeled the payoffs from its employee training programs and concludes that some programs yield $33 for every dollar spent. Others produce far less. Oil companies have modeled their exploration processes and payoffs in exquisite detail; advertisers constantly model their market response rates relative to different media or to format shifts; and financial houses simulate the varying impact of different investment approaches.

As an example of the latter, American Express' IDS division has developed an "expert system" called INSIGHT to capture the expertise of its best account managers. By providing this system to its other managers and running continuous follow-up tests, IDS now claims its reliability of service has ballooned; its worst account managers perform better than its average managers did in the past, and its percentage of clients who leave has dropped by half.[8] Such modeling has dual benefits: it both measures the net benefit of better processes and helps capture these benefits for transfer to other elements of the organization.

■ To calibrate the efficiency of its service support activities, GE was the pioneer in developing internal and external techniques to identify the "best practices" available anywhere in industry and systematically to emulate, adapt, and implement them at GE when desirable. Internally, it uses another type of simulation—a series of "work out sessions" where teams work on their own to simplify tasks chosen by their bosses and to "take as much unnecessary work out of these jobs as possible." Then they seek out "best practices" on each element both internally and externally to overcome the not-invented-here syndrome and to spread good internal ideas quickly from one part of GE to another. The "best practices" technique does not seek to find and benchmark nonpareils in particular functions. Instead, it seeks out those management techniques, attitudes, and processes which seem to make both people and departments work better together in high-productivity companies.

Where GE in the past had focused on setting goals and keeping score, it now began concentrating on processes—how things got done—rather than what got done. This approach automatically captures much of the accumulated knowledge value in the processes it adopts. To emphasize process management even more, GE's "process mapping" brings employees, managers, suppliers, and customers together to map and improve every stage of a total process—and to set new standards for productivity. Instead of achieving individual worker or machine efficiency, the teams optimize entire systems, conserving both costs and investments in the ROI equation.[9]

MANAGING INTELLECT FOR HIGHEST OUTPUT VALUE

Measurements of processes and output are of course only artifacts or tools of the management culture. Their main contributions are in creating (1) an increased understanding about managing intellectual and service processes and (2) a mindset that improving the intellectual assets and their related service capabilities is highly valued. Their ultimate purpose is to persuade executives to pay attention to the sources of profitability, not its mere presence. What matters is managing as if intellectual output and intellectual assets really do count.

UNIQUE PROPERTIES OF KNOWLEDGE SYSTEMS

Although not pulled together in any definitive treatise to date, much is known about the generation and management of intellectual output. Knowledge systems have certain peculiar properties that can be exploited to advantage. A large portion, but not all, of an organization's knowledge resides in three human reservoirs: (1) the cognitive understandings, (2) the learned skills, and

(3) the deeply held beliefs of individuals. The first is apparent. However, one may know how to do something—play a piano or play football—but not have the skills to do it successfully in competition. Or one may have both the know-how to perform a task and the skills for success, but lack the self-belief, will, or motivation to succeed. We have all seen motivated but less well endowed groups outperform those with superior resources. Bringing the three together has been the success formula for most outstanding teachers, entrepreneurs, and coaches—whether in education, sports, the professions, or general business. Management of intellectual processes has less to do with capital planning and the deployment of fiscal and physical resources than with other forms of management. In fact, it probably most resembles successful coaching, i.e., selecting the right people, then helping them develop the knowledge, skills, and attitudes they need for a specific task, and finally placing them in team structures where they can use their capabilities to the fullest.

Another unique characteristic of knowledge is that it is one of the few assets that grows most—usually exponentially—when shared. As one shares knowledge with colleagues and other internal organizations, not only do these units gain information—linear growth—they usually feed back questions, amplifications, and modifications, which instantly add further value for the sender. As each receiving group learns and creates from its new knowledge base, the base itself grows, opening totally new exponential growth possibilities. Since learning feeds knowledge back to the base, the next step (even at the same percentage increase) will spring from a higher base and be a larger absolute increment. The process itself is exponential—a principle embedded in all experience curve or learning curve theories.

Exponential growth occurs in the value of each sharing group's knowledge base. As the groups share solutions with each other, the interactive potentials of their knowledge grow at an even steeper exponential. This concept has been formalized into what is called "network externalities"; the potential value of the network grows as a function of the interconnections one can make, with potential two-way interlinkages in communications defined by the exponential function $2^{(n-1)} - 1$. Planned knowledge sharing thus creates exponential value-added growth through "network benefits" up to the point where individuals encounter information overload.[10] This vastly exceeds the simple arithmetic growth one obtains by breaking a task into multiple discrete parts for parallel processing or the parallel development of non-interconnected teams.

EXPERIMENTAL LEARNING LOOPS VERSUS GREATER INVESTMENT

By concentrating on key elements of the learning process, companies can leverage intellect enormously. For example, semiconductors were long considered a classic example of the "experience curve effect" in industry. With each doubling of volume, there was a relatively predictable percentage drop in cost. The theory held that one could only approach mature yields and hence low costs after producing close to one million wafers. But Intel discovered that if it concentrated on the proper points in the knowledge process, it was possible to achieve such yields by processing only about 10,000 wafers. Sun Lin Chou, then leader of the DRAM technology development group at Intel, said:

> There are certain ways of learning that can be carried out at much lower volumes. . . . You don't learn quickly when you increase volume by brute force. You have to learn by examining wafers. Learning is based on the number of wafers looked at, analyzed, and the number of corrective actions taken. Even if you have processed 1,000 wafers, the technical learning probably only came from the 10 wafers you analyzed. Technical learning is time and engineering constrained, not volume constrained.[11]

By concentrating on wafer analysis and another key element in yield, defect density—the number of defects per square centimeter—Intel found it could push the traditional progress curve even faster. In an open loop production system, one can often see or even guess what sources in the surrounding environment might be causing many of the tiny defects in chips. Yet one might not be able to prove this analytically. Instead of doing an elaborate ROI or technical analysis, therefore, an Intel team now merely fixes *any* potential source of increased defect density it can perceive analytically or intuitively. Cycle times are shortened, and cost reduction and quality improvement curves are much steeper than under the old "systems analysis" approach.

To avoid other investments and to capture certain benefits that can only come from volume production, Intel taps another learning loop by going directly to the suppliers of equipment for the high volume DRAM producers. This equipment embodies much of the accumulated experience of all producers. By understanding, modifying, and further developing the best suppliers' equipment, Intel can capture most of the experience curve advantages of its larger rivals. By simultaneously focusing on its own design competency in lower volume, more complicated chips, Intel can produce higher value-added products at costs comparable to its high volume rivals. The combination of these several learning techniques has dramatically decreased Intel's front end investments and increased its ROIs.

Structuring such continuous and targeted learning can be one of managements' highest payoff activities. In the past, hierarchical structures and activity segmentation actively blocked learning processes. Each group, to protect its turf, usually built its own internal information bases and defended them against other divisions or groups, considered outsiders, if not "the enemy." Since knowledge grows most when shared, such structures truncated learning and intellectual growth. Now organizations—like Intel or GE's much publicized Bayamón (Puerto Rico) plant—highlight areas where the most learning can take place, systematically involve people from other activities at these key sites, and make sure they are rotated to or mixed with other skilled positions where they can share and use this knowledge. As their knowledge bases grow and they share them in response to new challenges, organizational learning grows exponentially. Rotation also helps overcome some of the most difficult communications and coordination problems, those which occur at the interfaces between departments. As a result, by carefully structuring this kind of "targeted perpetual learning system"—and installing the proper support systems and incentives—many companies find productivity quickly improves by factors of 30 to 90 percent. Chapters 11 and 12 will provide more details on needed approaches.

CHALLENGE AND SUSTENANCE

Another unique characteristic of intellectual processes is their capacity—indeed need—for continuous change. The alternative to such stimulation is boredom and mental atrophy. Nonintellectual or mechanical systems run best when least disturbed. Intellect grows most when it is challenged. The body of intellect can be maintained intact by repeated use or even by being recorded carefully. To blossom it needs the fertilizer of challenge. Consequently, an organization at the frontier of its intellectual field is more likely to stay at the frontier. It can attract and challenge more and better intellect than its competitors. By solving more advanced problems, it has more capacity to solve others. And so on. Intellectual dominance, sustained by challenge, can become a continuously growing competitive edge. Several leading companies' experiences will suggest how frontier challenges can be used to attract and hold the best people. These companies all convey a true "frontier vision" of their fields to participants. Their visions are effective because they are real, yet glitter, flash, and challenge. In this sense they tower above the pap of most Mission Statements one sees.

■ Thus we observe Genentech attracting and motivating the top microbiologists and geneticists in industry with its ringing entrepreneurial goals. "We expect to be the first company to commercialize this remarkable new [recombinant DNA] technology. With Genetech's technology, microorganisms may be engineered to produce protein to meet world food needs, or produce antibodies to fight viral infections. Any product produced by a living organism is within the company's reach." In its early years, Genentech's CEO, Bob Swanson, repeatedly affirmed Genentech's determination, "to build one of the finest scientific teams in this field in the world . . . to be a part of the scientific community with full responsibilities to its own scientists and science at large."[12] The vision conveyed a group of challenging purposes, meaningful to many stakeholders, which if achieved would bring abundant profits.

■ Intel's Gordon Moore and the late Bob Noyce used to reiterate, "We are in the business of revolutionizing society"; and their corporate goals, also constantly reiterated, said Intel was "To be, and to be recognized as, the technological leader in all the areas we pursue. To be, and to be recognized as, the leader in meeting our customers' needs for delivery, reliability, quality, and service." The statement continued, "[Intel will] seek out and retain the best people at all levels and provide them with challenging jobs, training, and opportunities for personal growth so that they may share in Intel's success." (For further details, see "Vignette One: Intel Corporation" at the end of this chapter.)

The term vision, like "culture," has been quite overworked in the last few years. Yet, if used right, a properly developed vision is one of the most powerful tools a manager can wield in professional or creative services. It is perhaps the core element in binding together and leading the highly dispersed components of today's most successful intelligent enterprises. An effective vision is neither a high-blown statement of philosophy, nor is it a bland "mission statement" of what the company purports to do. It certainly will not be found in the jargon of "maximizing profits" or "maximizing shareholder wealth," which appeal not a whit to those who have to do the maximizing. The vision's statements must appeal in an emotional way to those who will carry them out. They must express a continuing stretch or challenge, or they will be a yawn. Yet some elements must also be doable and measurable. "To be the world's best at (*insert the company's core competency here*)," and mean it, is a good starting point. Superlatives, like being "the best, the first, the most, or the best-known" compared to competitors can create a continuing challenge that is measurable and meaningful for years.

An effective vision will embrace (1) what we do for the world (our mission), (2) what we are best at (our core competency), (3) our basis of differentiation, and (4) the heart of our philosophy. The best attempt to encapsulate these elements in one or a few sentences that glitter and snap. DuPont's "creating better things for better living through chemistry"; MIPS' vision, "to make the MIPS architecture the most pervasive in the world by the mid-1990s"; or Matsushita's, "to provide reasonably priced products in sufficient quantities to achieve peace, prosperity, and happiness for all" are such beginning points. All need elaboration and reinforcement in supporting statements, actions, and slogans to become an internalized vision. As Matsushita's Kosaka-san said, "You must create a spirit all can share. . . . It is not a theory formulated after reading someone else's books, but something based on experience itself. Once the philosophy is clear, it talks to every individual, and all communications in the company can be based on it."[13] How effective are such visions? One study showed that investments in the twenty companies described by executives as "most visionary"—as opposed to the stock market's "average" company—would have outperformed the Wall Street norm by a factor of 50 over the last several decades.[14] Vision affects the pragmatic management of intellect in a variety of ways (see Figure

8–1). When the vision thoroughly embraces and creates an unalterable focus on the firm's core service competency and concept, it well may be the very heart of the management of intellect.

■ A number of companies have realized that the challenge to be best in their selected fields is imperative. Motorola, for example, states flatly that "to be second is to die." GE's Advanced Materials Division picks those specialized materials where it will be best and makes sure that it has overwhelming intellect assigned to them, staying ahead of all comers for decades. For the glass technologies it pursues, Corning Glass is determined "never to be second." All realize that once another party gets a lead due to more intellect, the gap will widen inexorably. The other party will be able to attract better people and thus have a greater knowledge base, enabling it to move ever faster down the intellectual experience curve. Once behind, competitors have to invest at *multiple* rates just to catch up with an exponential learning pace. And they also have to force marketing expenditures just to reach volume levels of production that even let them *see* the challenge of the next stages of development. Too few companies have recognized that, in intellect, the alternative to excellence is mediocrity, failure, and death. Staying at the top in intellectual capability means defining it, measuring it, and making an inexorable and visionary commitment to stay there. This has been the success formula for great enterprises for decades.

Yet organizational intellect is also ephemeral and organic. It can grow old, atrophy in spots, die, or even walk away. In addition to stimulation through vision, it needs preservation and nurturing. Hence the attempt by so many organizations to collect, codify, and capture as much of the organization's intellect as possible in databases, hardware, and software systems. Even in an accounting sense, these can convert intellect into measurable assets. As was noted in Chapter 5's section on the "voluntary" organization, these technology systems can become so powerful in themselves that they are key elements in attracting and keeping the world's best talents—by letting them work on the most advanced problems with the best available techniques.

■ Such systems both eliminate much of the routine from intellectual tasks and improve the quality of outcomes. Thus they leverage human intellect while leaving professionals in control of their specialist processes. Such leverages exist today primarily at three levels: (1) automation of data routines, (2) analytic or design support systems, and (3) diagnostic and "applied intelligence" software. The first includes the automatic data entry, data look-up, or accounting-reporting systems, which free professionals to do more interesting things. The second takes complex data and well-understood systems and checks them against agreed design rules to make sure all elements are properly included, related, and calculated. These include economic models, design modules for structures or aircraft, or systems for measuring process, weather, or environmental conditions. These systems measure and combine known data relationships to achieve faster, more accurate conclusions.

Applied intelligence systems embrace feedback loops that up-date their heuristics based on actual experience patterns and use their data to diagnose or predict with more reliability than human intellect alone would allow. Their outputs are usually probabilistic rather than definitive. Humans must usually intervene to take action as in medical diagnostic, tax or credit card fraud, resource drilling, or aircraft maintenance decisions. Sometimes the systems become so much better than their human masters that in certain situations—like stock market trades or scheduling maintenance—they are programmed to take action. In many cases, these systems capture and upgrade intelligence about key operations better than any human can and hence become a basis for competitive advantage. In time true "artificial intelligence" (AI) systems may perform more creative intellectual tasks. But true AI systems are rare today.

Technology systems that capture and update organizational learning can contribute a cornerstone for insurmountable competitive advantage. Yet these systems, while important, are only components or manifestations of managing intellect well. They are not the essence of it.

PROFESSIONAL INTELLECT

In the practical management of intellect, my colleague Henry Mintzberg has identified two special types of situations that re-quire quite different organizational and managerial approaches. One he calls the "professional," the other the "innovative" con-text. To these, our studies have added some others.

A "professional bureaucracy," as Mintzberg calls his first form, is characterized by very complex and intelligent work, which may be adapted or customized for each recipient but is composed of many more or less standardized components, requiring the *repeated use* of highly developed individual skills on relatively similar problems. Most of the work in actuarial units, dentistry, hospitals, opera companies, accounting firms, universities, law firms, construction units, aircraft operations, equipment maintenance, and engineering enterprises is of this character. Mintzberg says, "Such professional organizations rely for coordination on the standardization of skills achieved primarily through much formal training, carefully updated. They hire highly trained specialists—professionals—as the operating core of the enterprise and then give them considerable control over their own work. [The professionals] work relatively independently of their colleagues, but closely with the clients they serve—doctors treating their own patients and accountants maintaining personal contacts with the companies whose books they audit."[15]

DISCIPLINED, NOT CREATIVE

Most of the work in these organizations is not intended to be creative; it applies carefully learned and disciplined skills to a specific problem, which to the experienced professionals looks much like many others they have seen before. In essence, these professionals principally just (1) diagnose a client's problem and (2) apply a relatively standard set of tools for its solution. They rarely innovate totally new solutions. Yet their skills are developed in such depth that the value and productivity of the entire organization depends on their performance. Perfection, not creativity, is their goal.

As professionals they look for confirmation of their skills and reputations to their professions, outside their organizations and among their peers. If they break the rules of their profession, the profession will often discipline them. If they fail the customer, the customer seeks direct retribution. Thus the organization may need to exert considerably less direct control over professionals' actions, as individuals, than might be the case for employees in other settings. In fact, many professionals tend to actively resist internal administrative controls. They tend by nature to be perfectionists, not flighty mavericks. They regard administrators as their servants (or as the enemy) and have the power to enforce their will by ignoring the administrators or by threatening to leave.

Professionals, trained for years in their specialist skills and nurturing them through practice, often tend to regard themselves as an elite. The more expert they become, the more they have to function alone and take the full responsibility for what their units do—as researchers, surgeons, or lawyers do. Such people do not subordinate their egos well to another authority or to an organizational consensus. Instead, they tend to build fiefdoms where they are kings and to listen to outsiders only if they choose. Organizations forms tend to be voluntary partnerships, further symbolizing each individual's independence of spirit and thought. The best people in professional enterprises tend to be driven by problems challenging to themselves, and somewhat disdainful of all else. Others join this elite out of shared interests in problems, an initial desire to learn, and the hope some day to replace the top professional with their own expertise. Consequently, jealousies tend to abound, politics are high, and leading professionals look more toward outside peers than to internal colleagues for their reputations and stimulation.

SOMEWHAT CONTENTIOUS EGOISTS

Harnessing such well-trained egoists is a major challenge. A few towering intellects can create an entire institution. Most of the great laboratories, consulting firms, business schools, or even universities typically grew to prominence around the skills and personalities of only a few—two to five—key people. Selecting and supporting these few can be the entire strategy in some professions. Some, as McKinsey & Company did for so many years, hire only the very top talents and then carefully nurture and grow them. However, the probability of being able to guess which specific person and talent will emerge triumphant is so low that most firms use some kind of "shoot out" technique, consciously overstaffing at lower levels and letting individuals prove themselves in head-to-head competition on problems, with clients being the ultimate quality judges. For fairness, this argues for the flattest possible organization with extremely close personal evaluations of productivity and quality—practices ego-centered professionals often resent. Internal competition creates distrust, if not disdain, for peers and fuels a tendency to build internal empires around the information one can control and use to create a power block. Up to a point, internal competition can create high productivity and rewards. Unfortunately, if that competitiveness is not linked to customer evaluations—as it so often is not in hospitals, universities, corporate staff activities, or research groups—it quickly becomes destructive.

Because of their contentiousness, professional partnerships often find it hard to leverage their intellect by investing in systems technologies. Individual partners will invest in desktop technologies, which increase their own power or capability, but may hesitate to share knowledge or systems investments with colleagues.[16] In the professional environment, knowledge means power, independence, and higher incomes. The key to managing strategy in these situations is in selecting a "team" of people with the desired balance of knowledge fields and personality characteristics. Some may be introverted or contentious, some flashy and brilliant, some absolute gluttons for meticulous detail, and some gregarious and cooperative. The secret for most larger organizations is not to let any one type totally predominant, to stimulate information-sharing through joint incentives, and to motivate better personal performance by exposing individuals as much as possible to outside performance reviews by customers, peers, and head-to-head confrontations with competing groups. The vignettes on Arthur Andersen, Intel, and Bell Laboratories at the end of this chapter suggest some interesting and tested solutions to specific problems.

The management of professionals provides a prime situation for an "inverted" organization. Here true power does rest with the point person. The primary functions of administration are to provide support structures for the professionals, to negotiate jurisdictional disputes, and to create a learning and information infrastructure that causes the professionals to stay up to date. Occasionally professionals will subordinate their egos and opinions to the sheer authority of intellect—as the atomic bomb team at Los Alamos did for Oppenheimer.[17] More often, effective management in the professions means (1) "hands off" of specific operational matters, (2) continuous personal and team negotiations on strategy with only broad areas of consensus defined, and (3) a concerted effort to force the professionals to obtain and respond to feedback from both customers and their peer groups of professionals.

FLAT OR INVERTED ORGANIZATIONS

Effective organizational forms tend to be extremely flat, "spider's webs," or "inverted." Management tends to be more akin to collecting and herding prize cats than to directing an army or raising sheep for the market. One mainly selects, nurtures, and cajoles. Strategy and decision processes tend to be egalitarian, egocentric, and highly political. In governance meetings, every individual tends to be bright and articulate and want to be heard. Success criteria are often quite subjective. As a consequence, management at the strategy level seems to involve getting political power blocks organized before meetings, working coalitions to the limit, and essentially managing political processes. Enterprise-wide decisions are usually made on a committee basis. The keys to corporate power therefore become controlling appointments to committees and the agenda of committees. Beyond this, each individual works largely on the basis of his or her referent power. This is the type of organization to which the "garbage can" model of strategic decision-making[18]—"throw anything in until it tips over"—occasionally even applies. A high degree of individual discretion works well when professionals are competent, conscientious, and disciplined externally. It can be disastrous when they are not.

Nevertheless, quality and efficiency must be maintained. To the extent that the routines of the professions can be captured in software and monitored in detailed reports, as they are in hospitals, accounting, software, or architectural firms, some safeguards exist. Information and real-time "physical control" or "work-monitoring" technologies can clearly help enforce these, as they do in many medical, flight, or design operations. But personal performance evaluations in most professions also require the use of extensive internal judgments, along with the strongest possible corroborative evidence from customers and peers, to make them work. There are often no absolute standards for productivity or quality in professional organizations. Hence close personal observation, trust, and a sense that the processes of evaluation are as fair as possible are the keys to making internal evaluations work.

INTERDEPENDENT PROFESSIONALISM

One of the most complex problems in managing professionals is to get them to share and thus leverage their knowledge capabilities across the entire organization. This is true of research, academic, staff, and consulting groups alike. Multinational firms long ago realized that they had to force technology exchanges by putting research labs next to operations, aligning R&D around specific end-use-directed missions, purposely forcing cross-national projects, and so on.[19] But even these techniques were of limited use if incentives were not restructured severely. Consulting and professional service groups have found that new electronic "networking" or "bulletin board" techniques, like AA&Co.'s, can be extraordinarily useful as intellectual leveraging devices—but only when strongly supported by other internal systems.

Unlike personal information-sharing systems, "bulletin board" users don't have to know who the experts are or how to find them. Instead of interrogating only three or four people for help, bulletin boards extend the network to hundreds of thousands with greater leveraging potentials. The big problem is to get professionals to take the time to enter their solutions, to check their bulletin boards frequently, and to respond constructively to inquiries. When they do, multiple benefits occur. Answers are faster than telephone tag or personal searches. Responders are more likely to document answers and have an equity in them. The question answerer usually learns as much as the interrogator. Learning increases exponentially. Sharing information helps build a common culture; those who benefited from answers begin to go out of their way to pay back the system. Others discover both an interesting new problem and a potential solution, and then they immediately see other applications. And the exponential learning cycle explodes again.

As this process grows, people can move beyond mere dialogues with one's professional colleagues to what Bob Elmore of AA&Co. called "metalogues," the capacity "to pull together people worldwide from many different disciplines to attack a problem simultaneously with many different techniques and at different levels of perspective and resolution." Solutions quickly move beyond those achievable from the "independent professionalism" so cherished in the past to those allowed by "interdependent professionalism." Instead of just having a small team serving the client, a professional firm can bring to bear the full force of a "virtual organization" hundreds of times larger. The benefits for both client and producer can be multiples of those provided by older independent professional processes. But few enterprises are structured properly to realize the full potential gains. To achieve them, structures and performance measures must move (1) from an individual (or independent unit) to a group (or cross-unit) basis, (2) from an organization-centered to a process-oriented focus, and (3) from an internal cost-revenue orientation to metrics that measure and reward performance based on customer benefits.

■ Robert Elmore, Managing Director of Business Systems Consulting at Arthur Andersen (AA&Co.), says:

> Our Group Talk system was installed about four years ago and there is no question among our practitioners that it gives us competitive advantage and has made a direct contribution to our sales growth. Our business strategy says that we will leverage the intellectual capital of our people, the intellectual capital of our firm, and the intellectual capital of the business world at large. In order to do that, we made a decision to have a computer in every single professional's hands, and they are obliged to sign on to the bulletin board a minimum of once a week. It allows you to ask questions and get answers to questions from peers all around the world. For each of the six hundred people directly on our network, they probably have another ten they relate to closely, so we can essentially network to 6,000 minds.
>
> The system forces people to be more precise in the questions they ask and in the responses they present. One of the things that Group Talk does is to allow us to build a new culture. What happens also is a new form of training. People learn by interacting. We call it just-in-time knowledge information transfer. You give them a framework for learning, a language to learn in. Each person becomes a teacher, and the teacher learns more than the students by articulating questions and responses carefully and clearly. Then people learn indirectly "through osmosis" by just reading the give and take of questions and answers on the bulletin board. They have access to thousands of conversations about advanced questions in offices all over the world.
>
> The catch-22 of this thing is to get people to use the system regularly. We have incentives for this, but in the initial stages, I would guess that we have less than 250 following the policy of regular use. We are going after the brand new employees and getting them trained in the habit of use. You no longer can think about just the technology. You have to think about the process that goes along with it, the attitudes, values, processes, and peo-

ple involvement you can use to get a better answer. Most of the investment in our type of company is not in the software, but in the training.

Although no respondent in our sample claimed yet to be satisfied with its measurement and reward systems for such networks, several were in the process of implementing more customer-oriented solutions. The best seemed to follow certain patterns. Individuals' intellectual contributions were evaluated on the quality of the new solutions they had originated for the electronic bulletin board, the number of their responses to inquiries, and their direct performance on company teams. After each major team project there was an internal evaluation of each member's professional and organizational contributions. Some firms then checked this evaluation with their clients' perceptions of performance. Many evaluated each individual and group against MBO objectives on a variety of longer-term skill and customer development criteria. Overall, customer perceptions were then further checked by external surveys and compared to internal metrics like lost accounts, repeat business, share of market, new client acquisitions, percentage of bids accepted, new product sales to clients, and so on. The combination evaluated performance in depth against all four critical dimensions: personal, professional, organizational, and customer. The next chapter will offer many more details and examples about how individual firms attack this complex problem.

MANAGING QUALITY IN PROFESSIONAL ORGANIZATIONS

There is always some mix of creativity and rules-based action in professional services. Otherwise such firms would quickly be automated out of existence. How does one manage quality and productivity in these circumstances? Automating as many repetitive details as possible—e.g., accounting balances, spell checks, boiler plate clauses, testing routines—of course helps avoid simple errors. More complex quality checks are enforced by proactively managing the culture and exposing results to outside professional reviews (as they are in research, education, and publishing). When outsider review is impossible, most high-performance professional organizations establish a "gatekeeper" process, where the most esteemed internal professionals review service products before release, and have mixed internal–external boards to review cases *post hoc* where problems seem to exist. The former is the presumed role of senior partners or officers in accounting, tax, legal, and lending institutions. The latter falls to peer review or professional regulatory groups. And the system usually works well when conscientiously implemented. *The New York Times* presents an interesting example of managing for quality in a highly professional organization.

■ The heart of *The New York Times* is its news department. Its 460 professional reporters and photographers make up the largest field staff of any single newspaper. *The Times* wants its reporters to be creative in acquiring and writing stories, but faultlessly accurate in presenting facts. As an institution, it wants to respond until the last possible moment to late or fast-breaking news, yet it needs to maintain a depth of coverage and style that are the distinguishing features of *The Times*. Quality control in these circumstances is difficult conceptually and in execution.

Through electronics, *The Times* has linked its editorial offices directly to its printing facilities and to its reporters in the field, so that editors can check stories with field sources even as they go to press. Ultimate quality control, however, is exercised through the constantly reinforced value system of the company. As the photographs of its sixty-one Pulitzer Prize-winning reporters along the corridors to the executive dining room constantly remind, *The Times* seeks the best reporting talent in the world and as "a reporters' newspaper" relies on them heavily. Most of the rules of *The Times* are unwritten and inherited, not only concerning what is a fair story, but how a reporter can use or not use an anonymous quote, what language is permissible, and so on. Although *The New York Times Book of Style* documents as many of these as possible, it can be updated only every five years or so, and the actual style of writing and editing has to be personal and fluid. The standards for responsible and effective presentation of the news must evolve in a controlled fashion case by case, day by day, section by section.

The keys to quality control are (1) the desires of the reporters as professionals to maintain their reputations in their field, and (2) a daily "front page meeting" that reviews all the day's stories and decides what will appear on the front page and how. At these meetings the heads of each editorial group and the managing editors pose queries about each story, constantly re-inforcing *The Times'* rules about verification, objectivity, style, ta-boo words, news coverage, and values priorities. These editors are the personal gatekeepers of news quality as it continuously evolves on a negotiated basis among the professionals. A pam-phlet, "Winners and Sinners," circulated internally every few weeks, points out "for every eye to see" any breakdowns that inadvertently pass into the system and celebrates instances of su-perior quality, thereby reinforcing its definition. Thus quality standards are both defined and enforced internally by culture and by peer pressures, and reinforced daily by *The Times'* unique set of educated, affluent, and influential readers, who either buy the paper or do not.[20]

Such structures help in the management of professionals. But much more than in other areas, management must be personal. Effective bosses understand the detail and get into it. They have to develop deep intuitions because numerical measures are weak. They spend inordinate amounts of time on personnel selection, evaluation, and coaxing. They use the professionals' own sense of pride to discipline them, and keep pushing the demands higher. "You can do better than this" and "This is not very professional" are stinging rebukes. Constantly reinforcing the culture—"This is why we are here"—being willing to critique, to listen, to coach, and occasionally to cheerlead seem to be the core management techniques. Sweetness and light combined with thunder and light-ning are required.

Professionals rise to the top as they are tested, and they usually respond to a test they think is fair. They constantly need to be pressed by new talent being rotated in and by exposure to exter-nal intellect. The one thing they grouse about more than being challenged is an atmosphere or a management that fails to do so or to reward high performance appropriately. One of the greatest laboratory directors I ever met summarized it well: "You know what built this organization? This nose! You have to know the chemistry, the people, and the problem in depth. Then you can recognize success when you see it. You've got to try to feed the egos of those who do good careful work and ignore all the verbal flack these guys can create. Force them to face the problem and their peers, and they'll be as good and motivated as they can possibly be. Very simple really."

CONCLUSIONS

Whether in professional, creative, or—as we will show shortly—mass services, the management of intellect lies at the heart of value in services. Unfortunately, methods of measuring and evaluating the output of intellectual systems—and of companies as intellectual asset builders—have been slow in developing. This is especially true for the professional groups that are major contributors of value in most companies. There is an extremely limited literature on the management of professional intellect. This is largely due to the high degree of uniqueness and egoism that accompanies most professional activity. Yet even here, some useful constructs have emerged. These tend to be quite different from other management concepts. Some have been summarized here; others will appear in Chapters 10 through 12.

The professions start with high-level intellectual skills internalized through prolonged training, practice, and certifications imposed by the various rules-setting bodies of the profession. The best enterprises hone these through further training and specialization to near perfection. Virtually all of the value-added in a profession comes from deep professional knowledge, reliability, and precision delivered with unswerving dedication. As professionals' expertise, specialization, and competency grow, they begin to see themselves as an elite whose value lies in their very knowledge specialization. They tend to protect their information sources and to disdain all those outside their knowledge circle. The result tends to be an atomized series of autocracies where the professional is internally a lord over his small fiefdom, yet externally must keep the goodwill of his barons (specialist peers) and to a less extent his people (customers).

Egos grow, and hierarchical submission is difficult. Organizations tend to operate as partnerships of equals, politically clustered around specialties. Strategies tend to be negotiated and fluid. And management, to the extent that it exists, tends to be based on charisma, referent authority, and—to a lesser extent—allocation of support by administrative infrastructures. The most successful professional firms manage primarily through choosing the right people, nurturing their individual skills, locking them to the firm by incentives, and providing leverage for their skills through internal technology systems and external networks they could not obtain elsewhere. Management depends largely on designing technology and incentive systems that appeal to the professionals' egos, yet discipline their actions toward productivity and customer needs. The most successful professional organizations reinforce these measures by subjecting performance to internal and external scrutiny by peers and by establishing as much direct contact with and direct performance measurement by customers as is possible.

A key element in managing both professional and creative intellect is designing appropriate technology systems. In the professions, technology is needed more for control and to lower costs. In creative organizations, it is more often used to generate options and to interact with customers. Nevertheless, in both cases technology leverages the value of individuals and creates strong exit barriers for their leaving the organization. The major value-producing capability of both types of organizations is in the trained intellect and skills of individual employees. They and their customers—along with the codified knowledge that binds them—are the true assets of the firm. Both are leveraged and enhanced to the greatest extent by concentrating management on the value systems, technology systems, working atmosphere, and motivation systems that surround them. Later chapters will develop these themes in further depth for creative and mass service organizations.

VIGNETTES:
Managing Professional and Creative Intellect

Vignette One: Intel Corporation*

Intel, the most consistent leader in semiconductor innovation, provides an interesting example of many features in managing the creative intelligent enterprise. As co-founder and Chairman Gordon Moore said, "If you look at our semiconductors and melt them down for silicon, that's a tiny fraction of cost. The rest is intellect and mistakes." Intel focused its strategy on linking frontier product innovation to reliable, high-yield production. To manage this intellectual linkage, it had to create many new organizational forms and management techniques.

For success it had to attract and hold both the wild-eyed, bushy-haired young geniuses that came directly from Ph.D. programs as well as the straightlaced, crewcut, experienced leaders of manufacturing—and get these two radically different types to work closely together in development. For this, it used small "skunkworks" teams with conscious "vertical mixing," making sure that both young geniuses and experienced manufacturers worked with and for each other on *ad hoc* design teams. Marketing people were really engineers who worked inside customer premises to understand customer needs in intimate detail, yet they participated on *ad hoc* design teams to fulfill these defined needs inside Intel. All teams were trained in a communications technique called "constructive confrontation," designed to focus the team's full intellect on problem-solving rather than the social amenities and politics that compromise most committee activities.

All trappings of authority were removed to the extent possible. Everyone, including co-founders Robert Noyce and Gordon

* Personal Interviews and "Intel Corporation" (case), in H. Mintzberg and J. Quinn, *The Strategy Process*, 2d ed. (Englewood Cliffs, NJ: Prentice Hall, 1991).

272

Moore, worked in "open space" offices with no doors and with only chest-high walls. There were no reserved parking spaces. Engineers on a project could spend $250,000 for equipment with no signature, provided the project budget allowed it. While allowing design teams access to its powerful centralized systems, Intel simultaneously kept the secret innards of the most advanced chip design software system available anywhere. At the top, Intel had a three-headed executive office: Chairman Moore, as the company's cerebral long-range thinker; the gregarious and technically superb Noyce as the team's Mr. Outside; and the highly organized, people-oriented Andy Grove driving internal operations. Any of the three was likely to plop down at a lunch table with the most junior members of Intel's staff. And one of them always led off the company's extensive training programs on "The Intel Culture."

The company was decentralized into very small operating units. Noyce was a great believer in small-size production units to give each person a maximum sense of responsibility and to eliminate the time delays and errors inherent in indirect communications. To accomplish this and to increase quality and reliability, Intel used what became known as its "McIntel" approach to production: debugging production in a small unit, and then cloning that unit—as McDonald's hamburgers did—in complete, discrete units to expand production as needed. Virtually all staff functions—purchasing policy, operating procedures, employee compensation, etc.—were handled by "councils" of line managers. There were usually several dozen councils—ninety were once counted—operating at one time. All people participated as equals on these councils, regardless of age or title. The idea, said Grove, "is to remove authority from an artificial place at the top and to place it where the most knowledgeable people are. I can't pretend to know the shape of the next generation of silicon or computer technology any more. People like me need information from those closest to the technology. The technology is moving too fast for hierarchical barriers."

Like all other groups and individuals in Intel, the councils were required to set performance objectives and be measured against them. Performance measurement pervaded everything. Said Noyce, "We are seeking high achievers. And high achievers love to be measured, because otherwise they can't prove to themselves that they are achieving. Measuring them says you care about them." Intel had MBO everywhere. Each person had multiple objectives. All employees wrote down what they were going to do, got their multiple bosses' agreement, and reviewed how well they performed with both their bosses *and* their peer groups. A key to the system was "one-on-one" meetings between each person and his or her bosses, where the "subordinate" determined the agenda. These were required monthly for everyone but might be weekly for newcomers.

Intel was leery of formal organization charts. It had a basic "product group" structure—Components, Microcomputers, and Systems—with planning across all units by a Strategic Business Segment. Within these, however, adhocracy prevailed. Teams constantly formed and re-formed around special problems. Using variants of this system to manage its intellectual resources, Intel has led its industry in major innovations for two decades.

Vignette Two: AT&T-Bell Laboratories*

Bell Laboratories has been one of the most outstanding intellectually based service groups in the world. Despite its fame, however, the management causes of its success are often misunderstood. Prior to the breakup of the Bell System, the philosophies, policies, and practices of Bell Labs had been relatively constant for several decades. Without attempting to reflect their full complexity and dynamics, some of the most important of these will be briefly described here.

RESEARCH DEPARTMENT

Bell Labs' Research Department—less than one-tenth of the total Labs' budget—sought further understanding of natural phenomena. The objective of Research was to develop a scientific base for new communications technologies 10–20 years before their ultimate need as system devices. Because the company had defined its activity as that of producing communications services, its knowledge base had to cover all scientific areas that might contribute to a better understanding of human communications and any means for one machine to communicate with another.

The Research Department was to be a "window between the

---

* "AT&T Bell Laboratories" (case), in Mintzberg and Quinn, *The Strategy Process*.

AT&T-Bell System and the world." Scientists from all over the world were welcomed on visits to the Labs, and in return Research Department personnel were welcomed in scientific circles elsewhere. The department's aim was "to be a major participant at the center of the world's knowledge stream." It kept up with communication technology created elsewhere and was expected to make a "fair share of the fundamental contributions to the world's communications knowledge." The Research Department felt that it must make its knowledge freely available to other groups if it hoped to be informed of what others were doing. One of the main functions of Research was "to be able to appreciate technology as soon as it became available." This ensured that its parent corporations could exploit such knowledge as soon and as intelligently as possible. And no outside group would be able to keep Bell System's operating corporations from using important new technologies.

The Research group was not held to any return on investment standard. Instead the parent corporation assumed that if Research produced enough really new knowledge of interest to communications, it would probably pay for itself over a period of time. A few devices resulting from fundamental research had probably more than justified the entire Laboratories' activities for hundreds of years. These included (1) the photovoltaic effect, (2) the transistor, (3) the MASER–LASER, (4) the multiphase carrier system for transmission, and (5) fiber optics for communications. But Research had produced thousands of other useful principles of greater or lesser value as well.

RESEARCH PLANNING

The heart of research planning at Bell was "to recruit top-flight scientists and let them think up something to do." Management's task was not to select problems but to find areas where knowledge would expand most rapidly. Highly qualified people were hired to work in each such area. These individuals then selected their own problems. Management tried (1) to stimulate and encourage their imaginations, (2) to provide them with the material and personnel backing they needed, and (3) to create an environment in which the individual scientist could be most creative.

The Research Department's organization was flexible. Section heads had to ensure that there were no duplications or gaps in inquiries made in their knowledge fields. But the organization was never used to confine the imaginations of individual researchers. Researchers could pursue their problems into any knowledge area, even though that area might be the primary responsibility of another group. If research developed in certain directions, section heads might find they did not have "their people" under their control. Members of one section might work directly with members of other sections, whose section heads could become more familiar with their work than their own section heads. The scientists would then look to the former for consultation and guidance.

Mitchell Marcus, one of the world's leading "speech recognition" scientists, said of his first acquaintance with Bell Laboratories:

> When I came for a visit, I was just amazed by the people and the attitude. . . . There was and is a community of people who talk to each other depending only upon what their interests are and not limited by their fields. At a place like MIT, for example, psychologists work with psychologists, linguists work with linguists, and computer people work with computer people. They don't get close to each other unless they are writing an interdisciplinary grant proposal.

Bela Julenz, world expert on optical information, amplified further:

> The tradition at Bell Laboratories has been to help each other. We are employed here not to teach, but rather to consult. There is an artificial emphasis here on cramped space. When I was a visiting professor in Zurich, my office was bigger than this whole corridor. Here the idea is that distances are so constructed that you can, if you have an idea, rush over to someone who is an expert on, say, stochastic processes or invented [some exotic] electronic device and consult him. It's so nearby that it takes you less time to go over and see an expert than to suppress the idea [as you would in a university setting].*

Over a period of time scientists slowly redirected their own researches. They tended to move toward those problems which were most challenging. Section heads said that it would be impossible to "direct" fundamental research from above. They pointed out that their scientists knew as much about their chosen fields as

---

* J. Bernstein, *Three Degrees Above Zero: Bell Labs in the Information Age* (New York: Charles Scribner's Sons, 1984).

anyone in the world. It would therefore be brash for a supervisor to tell them which areas to look into or how to investigate them. Managers were supposed to be able to appreciate research when they saw it, but not to direct research in detail.

However, scientists were not allowed simply to wander unchecked. They were expected to be "successful" in handling the problems they chose. Success might be defined as obtaining complete, partial, or indisputably negative answers to major problems or subproblems. Scientists were informally encouraged to look into those aspects of their problems most applicable to the communications business, but research managers tried to use as few of the pressures of authority as possible. They simply tried to discuss problems with researchers "as one scientist to another." The department's philosophy was that results were determined not by how large a research effort was but by how smart each of its scientists were.

If scientists' results seemed to research managers not to warrant backing their activities further, they were encouraged in new directions, stimulated to go into other phases of the Laboratories' activities, or motivated to transfer to another company or a university. The individual's performance was compared against a composite standard of how "a good researcher" would have performed the same task. This standard existed only in the minds of the researcher's supervisors and peers, as checked by the professional journals to which results were submitted.

In addition, each individual was compared with all other scientists in the department annually. The scientists' performance decile was determined and displayed against their wage decile groupings on an "age-wage" chart. Each individual's salary was reviewed in relation to the wage decile that would correspond to his or her performance decile. As a result of this constant performance evaluation—and the fact that some scientists voluntarily moved out of the department either to follow one of their inventions into development or to accept positions more attractive to them personally—only about one in ten of its highly selected scientific group remained in Research permanently.

SOURCES OF INFORMATION

Information on technological needs for the communications field flowed to Research from many sources. One source was the set of unsolved problems important to Operating and Development Department managers. Both formal channels (memoranda, technical-economic studies, program evaluations, activity and technical progress reports) and informal channels (luncheons, seminars, and the nonroutine get-togethers) were used by research managers to assess the fundamental knowledge needed by operating groups. In addition, Systems Engineering, the long-range technological planning section of Bell, tried to foresee the Corporation's technological needs 10–20 years ahead and reported those needs to Research managers. Systems Engineering also watched Research output and tried to see how it could be applied to future development problems. Research managers, all top-flight scientists themselves, kept an active watch on the literature in their fields and attempted to ensure that all pertinent knowledge areas were adequately staffed. Seminars held at the Laboratories by the world's leading scientists also helped calibrate the program.

Occasionally Western Electric or a Bell System operating division would come to the Research Department for an explanation of some unusual phenomenon or to have specific fundamental technological problems solved. A special aspect was the Engineering Complaint System. If an operating company reported a particular technical operating problem through this system, the Bell Laboratories system *had to specify* within about thirty days either the problem's solution or how the Laboratories would attempt to solve the problem. Routine follow-up occurred until the problem was solved. The degree to which Development and operating engineering groups asked Research to consult was regarded as a measure of the latter's success. Periodic formal "seminars" were held to inform operating technical groups of research progress on problems of interest to them and to exchange views with these groups. Research personnel also reported their activities in companywide reports, in the Bell Labs' own technical journal, and in formal scientific publications at professional meetings or in refereed professional journals.

SYSTEMS ENGINEERING

The Systems Engineering Department had a special role in technical planning. It acted as a liaison department between Bell Laboratories and the rest of the AT&T, Western Electric, and the Bell System complex. Its specific responsibility was long-range technological planning. It discharged this responsibility by obtaining from operating divisions information on their present and future technological needs. To these were added the technical-economic systems problems that Systems engineers foresaw themselves. Systems Engineering tried to think in terms of systemwide approaches rather than in terms of solutions to local problems.

Desired solutions were expressed as "black boxes," which defined the specifications for needed communications gear. How these boxes could be constructed was not a problem for Systems Engineering. What the box must do was its province. Systems Engineering was not expected to develop raw data on markets itself. It had to request help from other business research groups in the AT&T-Bell system. After recognizing a need, Systems Engineering wrote up an objective specification telling Research and Development what the problem was, what the input and output characteristics were for devices needed to solve it, and sometimes what approaches to the problem looked promising. Systems Engineering estimated the cost, demand, labor savings, dollar savings, or improved service benefits the devices might create. If these specifications were approved by top laboratory and corporate management, they were sent to Development to produce prototype devices, which were subjected to extensive tests for reliability and systems compatibility before they were accepted for use in the Bell System. Several parallel programs were almost always started for important new technological systems.

Development might in turn look to Research for solutions to basic scientific problems before it could complete its task. Systems Engineering tried to look at least twenty years ahead at all times. Its plans were flexible, but it constantly had to think ahead to the communication systems the next generation would need. Facilities installed today but useless in the future because of technological changes could cost the parent corporation billions of dollars in replacement losses. It was System Engineering's mission to avoid such waste and to help ensure that the Bell System's operating divisions had the proper equipment available to provide the world's best telephone service.

As a result of its combined forecasts, Systems Engineering prepared a booklet of projects—"cases"—with assigned priorities. These proposed projects, and those in process in Development, were reviewed periodically by corporate top management. No work could begin or continue without approval of its "case" writeup and budget by the parent corporations.

SETTING OBJECTIVES AND GOALS

All work in either the Research or the Development Department was carried out under "cases." In Research, cases were originated by the scientist and supervisor who were going to perform and oversee the work. The broad objectives of the research, hypotheses to be tested, syntheses or tests to be made, avenues of investigation, etc., might be described in the case writeup. The more basic the research, the more general the writeup. For some frontier projects, no specific applications might be apparent. Some cases estimated the applications of the research's results without specific economic data. Others might include a forecast of the economic benefits that might be forthcoming if the project was successful. The latter types of projects were generally in the more applied phases of research. Estimated costs were included with each new case. But this was not an inflexible control limit and might even be expressed as a range of possible costs.

Once inaugurated, cases were formally reviewed annually by Bell Laboratories management, by Western Electric, and by AT&T. For this review the case description included progress, if any, made in the preceding year; a description of the project objective; and a forecast of activities and costs for the forthcoming year. A summation of the forecast costs of research cases for the forthcoming year equaled the requested budget for the Research Division for that year.

In the early fall, advanced copies of cases were sent to AT&T and to Western Electric for review and comments. Plans were revised on the basis of the resulting exchange of views. A final set of cases and summary budget information then went to the Research Committee for final approval. Representatives of the Laboratories, Western Electric, and AT&T sat on this committee. Specific cases then were approved by Western Electric and AT&T, funds were allocated by the parent corporations for the forthcoming year's projects, and a revised cumulative budget was issued for each case.

No attempt was made by the parent corporations to dictate fields of inquiry for the Laboratories staff. Corporate officers annually reviewed expenditures for and general fields of basic inquiry, not for the purpose of suggesting new fields but to ensure a balance between fundamental and more applied research expenditures.

EVALUATION OF THE RESEARCH PROGRAM'S PROFITABILITY

It was the feeling of many in the AT&T-Bell Labs executive group that it would be impossible to price out the cost of a given benefit from a research program. As one executive said, "The continuity of a major development defies identification of all its costs or benefits within any reasonable time span. Developments coming to fruition in 1987 might depend upon the 1910 solution of fundamental mathematical parameters. In turn, a device introduced in 1987 might be improved by further research until the 2005 model bore little resemblance to its 1987 operating counterpart. From conception of a principle to an ultimate operating design is a continuum of joint costs and benefits."

Periodically AT&T had been forced by various rate-setting groups to justify the charges it made to a regional operating company for Bell Laboratories work. In those cases the corporation had been able to go back over an extensive period of time, list some of the advances the Laboratories had created in that period, estimate the value of these advances to the particular operating company, and prove such an overwhelming margin of contribution that the "Bell Laboratories service charges on telephone calls had never been disallowed." It was possible that the development of a single major technology, like fiber optics, could have justified the Laboratories' existence in perpetuity. Managers felt that over the years the Laboratories had paid its way to the American people with a substantial margin to spare. And they felt that further research efforts should continue to pay large dividends.

Nevertheless, in evaluating the effectiveness of its overall research program, AT&T management did consider the following criteria:

1. ***Knowledge output:*** Did the Laboratories produce its "fair share" of important discoveries? "Fair share" was defined over a long period of time by management judgment.
2. ***Competitive performance:*** Did the American telephone system more adequately serve the population than its foreign domestic counterparts?

3. *Customer satisfaction:* Were the operating companies buying and satisfied with Western Electric equipment? Operating companies could purchase equipment from any source.
4. *Defense position:* Was the patent trading position improving? This was a subjective evaluation.
5. *Administrative performance:* Were the operating divisions and top management personnel satisfied with the technical and administrative efforts of Bell Laboratories?
6. *Financial performance:* Had there been a satisfactory margin of contribution from the Laboratories over the years? Other than the specific studies for rate-setting bodies, no formal quantification of this criterion was attempted. The total value of the contributions was assessed by management judgment.
7. *Quality-price performance:* Was better service being provided to the American consumer at a comparatively lower cost? Had the quality of U.S. communications service improved more than the cost of the service and at a rate faster (or more timely) than in other countries? This evaluation was again a matter of executive judgment.

THE NEW AT&T

In a series of historic court decisions and out-of-court agreements, the former Bell Laboratories complex was broken up in 1983. At midnight, December 31, 1983, the Bell System's twenty-two local operating companies—providing telephone and communications services to individual regions of the United States—were grouped into seven regional holding companies quoted separately on the Stock Exchange and managed exclusively by their own officers and boards, and supported by a unit, called BellCore, broken off from Bell Laboratories. AT&T retained the long distance, other R&D (most of Bell Laboratories), manufacturing (dominantly Western Electric), and other businesses not assigned to the divested units. The "New AT&T" was freed from many former regulatory constraints and was allowed to compete in world markets on a scale not permitted in the past. Its innovation systems began to change accordingly.

Vignette Three: Sony Corporation*

Sony Corporation began in the rubble and chaos of Japan at the end of World War II. Its first quarters were a small corner room of a burned-out department store in Tokyo's Ginza district. Masaru Ibuka, through his Japan Precision Instrument Company, had supplied vacuum tube volt meters and other instruments to the now defunct war effort. Mr. Ibuka felt an obligation to provide continued work for his people. "We realized we could not compete against companies in existence and against products in which they specialized. We started with the basic concept that we had to do something that no other company had done before." From these inauspicious beginnings sprang one of the world's most innovative companies, with 1991 worldwide sales of $26 billion.

In May 1946 the company was formally incorporated as Tokyo Telecommunications Engineering Company (TTK), capitalized at 198,000 yen—$500 to $600 in exchange value. Its first permanent facilities were some shacks in the Shinagawa district that were so dilapidated that executives had to use umbrellas during rainstorms. TTK tried innumerable products, including an electric rice cooker, an electrically heated cushion, and a resonating sound generator for telegraph systems. Ibuka insisted on such rigorous design and quality standards that TTK—through clever use of a carefully designed supplier network—was soon performing all of Japan Broadcasting Network's (NHK's) revisions, converting its equipment to modern standards.

BE PATIENT, AND TRY EVERYTHING

One product TTK considered seriously was a wire recorder, first introduced by the military in World War II. Then one day, as he was visiting the office of NHK, Mr. Ibuka was shown a tape recorder from the United States, and history was made. Tape re-

* "Sony Corporation" (case), H. Mintzberg and J. Quinn, *The Strategy Process, op. cit.*, 1991. Most quotes are from personal interviews. A few early historical quotes are from speeches by A. Morita, "International Marketing of Sony Corporation," Tokyo, July 14, 1969; "Decision Making in Japanese Industry." Manila, September 30, 1975; and "What Is the Difference Between Japanese Management and the American?" Chicago, February 17, 1972. A special acknowledgement goes to Nick Lyons for his excellent book, *The Sony Vision*, which vividly describes Sony's history through 1975.

corders were then unheard of in Japan—there wasn't even a word for them. Ibuka rapidly purchased rights to available patents, but there was little published information about either magnetic tapes or recorders. In Japan there was no plastic available to produce tape and no way to acquire any plastic through Japan's stringent import regulations. The TTK team tried cellophane; it stretched. They tried paper—Ibuka made tapes in his kitchen from rice paper and a paste of boiled rice—but its edges caught and broke. Finally Mr. Morita, who had joined the company by then, got a cousin in a paper manufacturing company to prepare a batch of specially calendered paper with a slick surface. TTK had to compensate for the less controllable paper base by designing extra quality into the circuitry, recording head, feed systems, and amplifiers in the recorder. It was a great struggle. The accounting manager constantly warned that they were spending too much; they could bankrupt the company. Morita and Ibuka kept saying, "Be a little more patient and we will make a fortune." Finally, after many months, they created not just a new concept in tapes but a new recorder, a new testing technology, and their own complete tape coding machine.

In late 1949 TTK made its first unit, the G-type recorder, weighing more than 100 pounds and selling for $400. But neither Ibuka nor Morita had marketing experience. After many months of effort the first unit sold to an oden shop, a kind of Japanese pub where people came to eat, sing, and talk noisily. Technically the expensive cumbersome device performed well, but no one quite knew what to do with it. Ibuka's response was to take all his top engineers to an inn and work night and day to reduce the recorder's cost by 50 percent and improve its size, weight, and portability. The result was a concept for a suitcase-enclosed recorder at a reasonable price, and less than half the G-type's weight. Its first large market was NHK's English-language programs for use in schools, a most unexpected source of sales.

A "POCKETABLE RADIO": MOTIVATE THEM TO THEIR BEST ABILITIES

In 1952 Mr. Ibuka went to the United States to explore possible markets for his tape recorder. While he was there, a U.S. friend told him that Western Electric was ready to license its transistor patent for the first time. Ibuka investigated, but when he heard the price was $25,000, he left the United States knowing the price was too much. As he worried on the long trip home, he became convinced that the transistor would revolutionize electronics, though no one then realized how. As he pondered what to do, another concern occurred to him. He had hired a number of young physicists. "Would tape recorders be challenge enough for them, motivate them to use their best abilities, or let them grow to their full potentials?" Ibuka was convinced they would not.

By the time Mr. Ibuka reached Tokyo, his questions had crystallized into a strategy. A short time later he announced, "We're going to use the transistor to make radios small enough so that each individual can carry them for his own use, but with a receiving ability that will enable civilization to reach areas that have no electric power." At that time "portable radios" weighed 10–20 pounds, were briefcase size, and had batteries that lasted only a few hours. Ibuka spoke of a "pocketable transistor radio." But no one had applied transistors to radios—or to much of anything else. The thought of a quality radio the size of a cigarette pack seemed almost beyond belief. Nevertheless, Mr. Ibuka continued to reiterate his challenging goal.

Then came a shock. Texas Instruments announced the world's first transistorized radio, produced for Regency Co. In early 1955 TTK's team pulled out all stops, moving with what was available. In August it put the first transistor radio on display. It was about 4″ × 8″ × 1½″. Still Ibuka wanted a "pocketable radio." Despite the skepticism of marketing experts who thought the product would be too small, squeaky and unreliable, Ibuka pushed this goal as a "figure of merit."

Component suppliers of TTK (shortly thereafter named Sony) refused to modify their standard product lines, which were largely copied from world designs at that time. They were too doubtful of the product's success to invest. Ibuka singlehandedly persuaded them to go ahead by offering Sony's technical support and production guidance. It was a momentous change for Japan. Japanese manufacturers had to become truly independent of foreign technology for perhaps the first time. In March 1957 the "pocketable" Type 63 radio was introduced, using almost exclusively Japanese knowhow. Since the Type 63 was still slightly larger than a shirt pocket, Sony made special shirts into which they would fit. More than a million Type 63s were soon sold.

"DO SOMETHING CREATIVE" IN BOTH PRODUCTS AND ORGANIZATIONS

Sony's personnel grew more than tenfold in the 1950s and four times in the 1960s. Many of its personnel policies derived from its original goal to "establish an ideal factory—free, dynamic, and pleasant." To Ibuka this meant "to have fixed production and budgetary requirements but within these limits to give Sony employees the freedom to do what they want. . . . This is the way we draw on their deepest creative potentials."

Mr. Ibuka chose people for their creativeness and gave them full responsibility. For example, he put Mr. Shigeru Kobayashi in control of Sony's Atsugi plant after its brief—and only—strike in 1961. Ibuka told Kobayashi, who knew nothing about semiconductor technology, "You are free to do there whatever you like. Try to do something truly creative." Kobayashi soon revolutionized the plant's work measurement techniques; eliminated cafeteria lines by allowing people to deposit their meal coupons, unmonitored, into collection boxes; shutdown the forbidding dormitories used by most Japanese companies and built small prefabricated homes for Sony's employees; and removed all time clocks and recreated essential trust by allowing workers to set their own time standards.

Further, he developed a series of vertical and horizontal interconnecting teams or "cells" in the plant, where workers could more easily develop a team spirit and help each other. Each cell would respond to input from all other cells above, below, or on its sides. Each cell would determine what methods to follow and evaluate its own output. Management's job was to assist the cells, to help them solve problems, to set overall goals, and to praise superior performances, while the cells were to control specific tasks at the workplace and group levels. The specifics of Kobayashi's "cell system" are different in each plant today, but the spirit and values it conveys continue.

GIVE THEM AUTHORITY, ROTATE THEM FREQUENTLY, AND "DO THE JOB RIGHT"

Mr. Morita recently said, "The best way to train a person is to give him authority. . . . We tell our young people: don't be afraid to make a mistake, but don't make the same mistake twice. If you think it is good for the company, do it. If something is wrong, I am the man who should be accused. As CEO it's my job to take on the critics from the outside. For example, this year our profits are down; I tell my management, don't you worry about that, just do your job right."

Unlike other Japanese companies, where seniority determines responsibility, young Sony employees are loaded with work and responsibility. But there is a complex "godfather system" in which a high-ranking executive watches over and specifically trains younger talent. A new executive interacts almost daily with his corporate mentor and receives sophisticated insights and a corporate perspective. Mr. Morita expressed the overall philosophy this way: "Sony motivates executives not with special compensation systems but by giving them joy in achievement, challenge, pride, and a sense of recognition."

In most areas, all employees—whether law graduates or finance specialists—must spend several months on the production line learning to appreciate the company's products, practices, and culture. All engineers and scientists hired still must work in sales for several weeks or months. Promising people are shifted every two to three years to new areas, in order to expand their knowledge and to identify their abilities for promotion. Typically workers learn several processes and are switched among tasks to keep up their interest. Production lines may be purposely segmented so they can be restructured rapidly if product mixes change. Rewards flow not to individuals, but to groups.

A PRIORITY ON INNOVATION: "A PRODUCT OF OUR OWN"

As its pocketable radio business boomed, Sony turned to all-transistorized television. At first Sony's system could drive only small picture tubes, 5" to 8" across, but not the larger tubes then popular. When Ibuka proposed to introduce a "mini-TV," the market experts again said, "It will never sell. RCA tried it and failed. The market wants big screens." Undeterred, Ibuka introduced an 8" set in Japan (May 1960) and in the United States (June 1961). The road to the marketplace was complex and difficult, but Ibuka's "tummy television" sets soon became eminently successful.

By 1964 color television had begun to take over the U.S. market. After some diverse experimentation, virtually every color manufacturer operated under RCA's "shadow mask" system, using a triangle of three electron guns and a grid of tiny color "dots" to create color. But Ibuka said, "I could see no fun in merely copying their excellent system." He said, "We must produce a product of our own. There is nothing more pitiable than a man who can't or doesn't dream. Dreams give direction and purpose to life, without which life would be mere drudgery." A long and chaotic period of development ensued in which numerous novel approaches were tested. But Mr. Ibuka never wavered from his goal of finding a totally new design for color TV tubes.

Then toward the end of 1966, a young engineer, Mr. Miyaoka, made a mistake while experimenting. Using a single gun and three cathodes, he had produced a blurred picture. Intuitively, Ibuka recognized the promise of this approach and said, "This is it. This is the system to go with." Ibuka became the project manager himself. His team often worked all night, taking a few hours off to rest on the sofa. For months they had problems with electronic acceleration and control. Finally on October 16, 1967, the new "Trinitron" system really worked for the first time. It was a totally unique concept—using phosphorous stripes, a one-gun, three-beam system, and a vertical stripe aperture grille in a market dominated worldwide by the shadow mask system.

SETTING CHALLENGING GOALS: FIGURES OF MERIT

Again, Mr. Ibuka set a challenging goal. He wanted the product in the marketplace in six months. Although it seemed impossible at the time, by limiting the screen size to 12"—because of fears that the Trinitron's glass bulb might fail in larger sizes—teams, working until they lost track of night and day, got the Trinitron to market in a 12" size. The Trinitron earned the first Emmy in the United States ever given to a product innovation. Although personally named for the prize, Ibuka saw to it that his key engineers shared in it. Sony could not catch up with world demand for the fabulously successful Trinitron until the late 1970s.

The first practical video tape recorder (VTR), the Quadruplex, was introduced by Ampex Corporation (of the United States) in 1956. Japan's national television network bought a Quadruplex and encouraged electronic manufacturers' engineers to become familiar with it. Mr. Ibuka took a team to see the "Quad," which cost about $60,000 and was a complex machine filling several closet-size equipment racks. In 1958, three and a half months after Mr. Ibuka first saw the Ampex machine, a team under Dr. Nobutoshi Kihara and Mr. K. Iwama completed an operating prototype using similar principles. When asked how Sony approached the radical innovations leading to its successful VTR series, Dr. Kihara noted, "Mr. Ibuka would often come in with the 'seed or hint' of an idea and ask me 'to try it out.'"

For example, shortly after Dr. Kihara helped build the first VTR prototype (which would have to be priced at about 20 million yen, or $55,000), Ibuka said, "We want to make commercial video recorders. Can you develop one that will sell for 2 million yen [$5,500]?" After Kihara did that, Ibuka said, "Now can we make a color recorder for the home at 200,000 yen [$550]?" Dr. Kihara later noted, "I was not sure I could meet this challenge." Nevertheless, Sony's first commercial machine (in 1963), although lacking Ampex's fidelity, was one-twentieth of its size and sold for less than one-fourth of its $65,000 price. By 1965 Sony had the compact CV-2000 for $600, operating reel-to-reel in black and white to high commercial standards. Its U-Matic machine, the first video cassette recorder, became quite successful in commercial color markets in 1972 at $1,100.

But Sony's ultimate target was the home market; its product was to be the legendary Betamax. In achieving this development, Mr. Ibuka frequently set figures of merit as challenging targets for the development team. Ampex had invented a four-head machine. Sony invented the one-head machine. Mr. Ibuka said, "We developed our own system. I specifically ordered Sony engineers *not* to develop a broadcasting machine. Many engineers wanted to imitate the Ampex machine and make a good business in the broadcast field. I strongly ordered that we would make a $550 home machine."

Mr. Ibuka continued, "We decided that the video tape recorder must be a cassette type. Our experience in audio said that open reel types were not good in home market. We succeeded with the U-Matic, which was the first video cassette recorder in the world. We decided on the U-Matic [U format] standard, Japan Victor and Matsushita agreed on it. We supplied our technology to both companies. Shortly after, we were able to come up with the beta form of recording which is a helical system using all the space on the tape. . . . We asked Matsushita to join us in that standard. But they had a license to operate with our original patent. So they denied us."

MULTIPLE APPROACHES

In describing Sony's approach to innovation, Dr. Kihara said that in the VTR development "my group started ten different test options or approaches. Within these we developed two or three alternatives for each subsystem. . . . Much of the development process was trial and error. We did not have formal written plans. . . . For example, we developed a loading system with one reel and a leader, not two reels. . . . We developed single heads, double heads, the skip system, and the azimuth system for reading and writing on the tapes. And so on. By taking the best of each option we ultimately developed the Betamax." Dr. Kihara contended: "There are only a few people directly involved in a new technology who have adequate information or knowledge about that technology. With new products, one must create a new market. Not many people know how these new markets will develop, what a product can do, how well it will function, how well it could be used by customers." Said Dr. Kihara: "We have never been told by Morita or Ibuka 'this product's sales will be this big or must make this much money.' "

Dr. Kihara continued, "Most companies make profit the first priority. Sony's primary mission is to produce something new, unique, and innovative for the enhancement of people's lives. Technical people report right to the top of the organization. There is no formal technical committee, but many joint discussions. . . . If an idea is merely under development, I don't report it. After I obtain a working model, then I report it to Morita and Ibuka. . . . In the early development stages there are typically only five or six people involved on a project team; for example, in the Mavica camera, there were seven to eight. We work together until we have made a prototype model. After we get the go-ahead, the project may be expanded to perhaps thirty people."

DIRECT CONTACT AT THE TOP

At Sony, people from other areas join the development team directly. They are trained on the spot by Research and Development people. Those most suited for production will go on with the project into production. This practice leaves a vacuum in Development, which can be filled by new people who infuse the department with fresh blood and ideas. Mr. Morita frequently telephoned or brought ideas from around the world to the R&D

department on how to apply physics in new ways. Mr. Ibuka used to visit many places in Sony randomly. He would often drop in at the laboratory to see things, touch things. One researcher said, "Recently Mr.Ibuka came to the laboratory and touched his tongue to a new tape compound, to taste it, to see what it was. He leaves people very excited." Dr. Kikuchi, then Director of Research, said:

> We as management must define the problems, but only with sufficient specificity to leave many directions open for technical work. . . . The goal must be clear and not change easily. We let the technical leaders choose the approaches. Periodically, I give a "crystal award" for highly evaluated work. Even if a team has lost a competition within Sony, we will still give them a crystal award if the quality of their work is especially good. . . . We also may give engineers a certain percentage of a new product's first year's sales if their ideas had particular merit. The amount of money is significant, but not huge.

THE SONY SPIRIT

From the beginning, Sony was driven by some carefully crafted statements of purpose and policies that became known internally as "the Sony Spirit." The Sony Spirit itself was often referred to in interviews. People would describe an incident or practice as demonstrating "Sony Spirit." This seemed to be a set of unwritten rules that permeated the organization. However, the original statements of philosophy that drove the corporation have remained relatively unchanged over the years. These have included the "Purposes of Incorporation" and the "Management Policies," which drove the organization.

Purposes of Incorporation

- The establishment of an ideal factory—free, dynamic, and pleasant—where technical personnel of sincere motivation can exercise their technological skills to the highest levels.
- Dynamic activities in technology and production for the reconstruction of Japan and the elevation of the nation's culture.
- Prompt application of the highly advanced technology developed during the war in various sectors to the life of the general public.

- Making rapidly into commercial products the superior research results of universities and research institutes, which are worth applying to the daily lives of the public.

Management Policies

- We shall eliminate any untoward profit-seeking, shall constantly emphasize activities of real substance, and shall not seek expansion of size for the sake of size.
- Rather, we shall seek a compact size of operation through which the path of technology and business activities can advance in areas that large enterprises, because of their size, cannot enter.
- We shall be as selective as possible in our products and will even welcome technological difficulties. We shall focus on highly sophisticated technical products that have great usefulness in society, regardless of the quantity involved. Moreover, we shall avoid the formal demarcation between electricity and mechanics, and shall create our own unique products coordinating the two fields with a determination that other companies cannot overtake.
- Utilizing to the utmost the unique features of our firm, which shall be known and trusted among acquaintances in the business and technical worlds, we shall open up through mutual cooperation our production and sales channels and our acquisition of supplies to an extent equal to those of large business organizations.
- We shall guide and foster subcontracting factories in directions that will help them become independent operations and shall strive to expand and strengthen the pattern of mutual help with such factories.
- Personnel shall be carefully selected, and the firm shall be comprised of as small a number as feasible. We shall avoid mere formal position levels and shall place our main emphasis on ability, performance, and personal character, so that each individual can show the best in ability and skill.

CHAPTER 9
Managing the Innovative Organization

Another, quite different, set of patterns pertains to managing intellect in a continuously innovative context. Innovation is the first reduction to practice of an idea in a culture. A professional bureaucracy tends to drive toward a low-risk norm although individual events may sometimes involve higher risks. By contrast, high risk is inherent in the very nature of the innovative process. And processes of innovation tend to be unique and chaotic, not orderly or easily planned. To quote Mintzberg again:

> To innovate means to break away from established patterns. Thus the innovative organization cannot rely on any form of standardization for coordination. It must avoid all the trappings of bureaucratic structure: sharp divisions of labor, extensive unit differentiation, highly formalized behavior, or an emphasis on planning and control systems. Above all, it must remain flexible. . . . Sophisticated innovation requires a very different configuration, one that is able to fuse experts drawn from different disciplines into smoothly functioning ad hoc teams. . . . These became the original adhocracies of our society.[1]

Innovative adhocracies, as intellectual entities, seek unique solutions directly on behalf of their clients. Creative advertising agencies, research groups, consultancies, and real estate syndicators are typical of this breed. Units usually operate under contracts or specifications, assemble a specialized team matched to a particular problem, and disband the team when that problem is solved. For the time these units are together, administrative and operating work tends to blend. Lines between organization groups, managers and workers, and different disciplines blur. The task and the technology provide the essential disciplines of control. The goal of creating a unique and desired problem solution dominates. As Ray Gilmartin, CEO of Becton Dickinson, says, "Forget structures invented by the guys at the top. You've got to let the task form the organizations."[2] If the team's goal is not achieved, the whole team, not just an individual, fails. Hence innovative teams tend to operate as open systems having strong liaisons with outsiders who can also help solve the problem. Such connections greatly leverage the resources of the innovative team through the types of "network externalities" described earlier.

The innovative environment is always dynamic, opportunistic, and unpredictable—calling for a very flexible, responsive, decentralized organization structure. Yet problems also tend to be very complex, calling for high specialization and hence centralization of skills. Since adhocracies are the only organization form that can deliver both simultaneously, they are most extensively used for innovation. All the "most innovative" organizations in my 1976–80 worldwide study of innovation in large companies—including European, American, and Japanese firms—used some form of "skunkworks" adhocracy. Most also used internal competitive teams to improve the timing, motivation, probability of success, and information levels in the innovation process. All worked with relatively small teams in very flat organizations and with extensive external networking to improve productivity. The series of articles and cases on "innovation and managed chaos" (presenting the results of these studies) explains the reasons why these practices work and offers many practical examples from real companies.[3] Among these, Intel Corporation—described in the vignettes preceding this chapter—provides an especially rich example of how cluster and *ad hoc* configurations can work together for maximum creativity and productivity.

TYPES OF INNOVATIVE ORGANIZATIONS

In these studies the specific form of organization and the management techniques used to stimulate innovation varied widely according to each company's strategy. We encountered some twenty different basic innovation strategies. Contrary to conventional wisdom, not all sought to be first into the marketplace or to respond to each customer's whims in a customized fashion. A few examples will make the point. For convenience these are also diagrammed in Figure 9–1.

■ *Large system technology producers* like AT&T-Bell Labs, Boeing, or the "oil majors" design large-scale systems that may cost billions of dollars and must last reliably for decades. They do extensive long-term formal marketing and technology forecasting of system needs, define these carefully as performance specifications at customer and system interface levels, and allow two or three simultaneous projects on each system to compete for best performance at the prototype level before choosing one for implementation. Then they test potential new solutions for substantial periods before making systemwide commitments. They plan for long-term incremental improvements even as a new system is being invented. They usually have strong basic research programs to understand developing scientific and technological possibilities in their fields and to prevent others from shutting them off from a key technology. Systems are slowly scaled up to full-size test runs before release. These companies' systems are so costly that they must be right when installed. Often they sacrifice speed of entry for long-term low cost, performance reliability, and avoidance of major errors at the time the system is installed (see "Vignette: AT&T-Bell Labs" preceding this chapter).

■ *Basic research companies* like Hoffman-LaRoche or Merck also make tradeoffs between the timing of their products' entry and their defensibility in the marketplace and safety-efficacy in use. These companies take their risks at the research stage, supporting large science laboratories with better facilities, higher pay, and more freedom than is found in most universities. They leverage their internal spending through research grants, clinical studies, and research consortia in many universities throughout the world. They select product entries carefully. Before they invest the $25–$150 million needed for drug clearance, they want to be sure they will have a patent-defensible, safe, and effective drug in the marketplace with as much understanding as is possible about the science of its curative capabilities, side effects, and metabolism in the human body. Their organizations are designed to be on the cutting edge of science, but to be very conservative in terms of test-

FIGURE 9–1
Innovation Structures

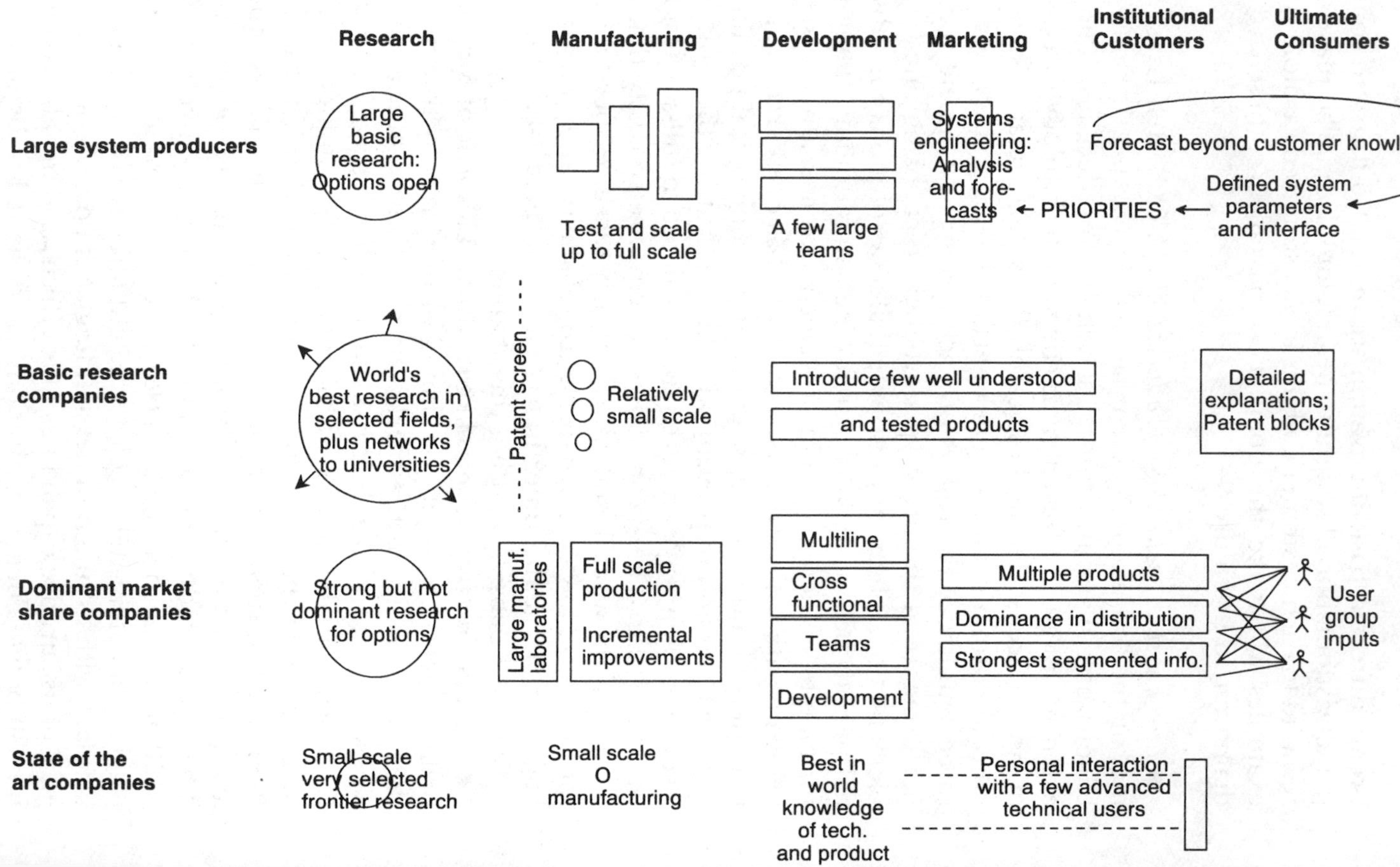

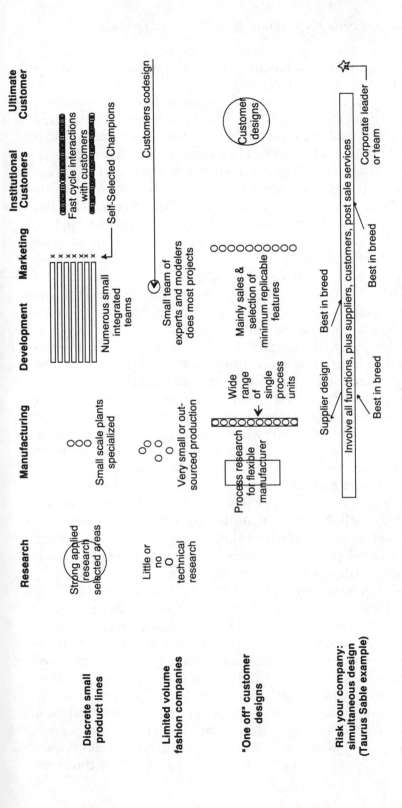

ing, quality control, and reliability. A few successful drugs build a company. One error could destroy it.

■ *Dominant market share-oriented* companies like Matsushita and IBM often are not the first to introduce radical new technologies. They do not particularly want to disturb their successful product lines any sooner than necessary. They support large basic research laboratories to keep all technological options open and to obtain early warning signals about new technologies. But they do not rely on these laboratories to drive products to market. As market demands appear, they try to establish very precise price–performance windows and form competitive project teams to come up with the best available "state of the market" solutions. To decrease market risks, they have their industries' largest distribution networks, which provide them with more detailed market information than their competitors can possibly have. To enter the market with highest potential impact, they utilize full-scale product "shootouts" as close to the time of market entry as possible, develop extreme depth in production technologies to keep costs low and quality high from the outset, and try to dominate the distribution of any products they do release. They depend on their market power, incremental product improvements, and phased releases of new products essentially to overwhelm "state of the art" producers. They often sacrifice market timing to achieve lower long-term costs, greater reliability, and decreased market risks.

■ *State of the art technologies* like those of Cray Research, Genentech, Hughes Electronics, or Kyocera have often been developed in freestanding technical units, not directly connected to formal marketing units. Heads of these projects often know more about the technologies than anyone in the world, including potential customers. So long as demand in the industry to which they sell is driven solely by technical performance criteria, the lab head can essentially define the characteristics of the next generation of products. Timing and technical performance, not subjective taste, give intellectual outputs their value. In these cases, pure "technology skunkworks"—small interdisciplinary technical teams operating alone—can exist almost independently of other functions. This is the way many classic inventors have operated in their private laboratories, and it can work in larger enterprises when a strong primary market for sheer technical performance exists.

■ *Discrete freestanding product lines*, by contrast, are developed in companies like 3M, Sony, or Raychem using a very different approach. They form units that look and act like entrepreneurial startups. Each company has a strong research unit with dominance in specific limited classes of technology. Each entrepreneurial unit is a small team led by a self-nominated champion, usually in low-cost facilities. They allow many different proposals to come forward and test them as early as possible in the marketplace. They have control systems to spot significant losses on any single entry quickly. They are more willing to take risks at the market level, knowing that market research studies for unique small-scale products can cost more than losses in the marketplace. Such studies will also miss some big winners and are rarely as effective as actively engaging in sale of the product and modifying it interactively with the customers' help.

■ *Limited volume or fashion companies* operate differently again. Single designers or small teams will sketch up concepts and make small-scale layups or models. These are presented to actual buyers for their reactions. Based on these reactions, new sketches and models are tested until the subjective tastes of the designer and buyer blend together. Even then, production may proceed with further direct feedbacks from the customer and designer, modifying the product until it reaches completion. Designer clothing, military weapons, buildings, ships, movies, theatrical productions, and commissioned art are all examples. An intermediate mode involves interactive design and test of sketches and models followed by a commitment to limited line production volumes—as Steuben Glass, Edward Marshall Boehm, and Franklin Mint do. Special depth in genuine artistic talent, in some selected materials or fabrication technologies, and in a specialized methodology for interpreting consumer and expert panel responses are usually the keys to success for this strategy.

■ *"One-off" job shops* are an extreme form of creative strategy. Here the customer provides most of the continuous creativity. But today's job shop is not just a low-tech tail wagged by a large or sophisticated customer lion. The job shop can maximize its own and customers' value by (1) breaking its product-producing potentials down into the smallest possible replicable units, (2) designing its processes for maximum flexibility in handling these units, (3) providing the most user-friendly customer interface to allow customers to create their own designs using these units, and (4) managing a worldwide network to coordinate the selection and fabrication of the best quality-cost components to fit each customer's need. The American Standard, Motorola pager, Toyota and Buick self-design, ASICs, software, and financial services systems (already described), are just a few examples of approaches that greatly leverage the intelligence of smart buyers, producers, and machines while allowing unique customized solutions for customers.

There are myriad other continuous innovation strategies. These vary from those of the individual inventor, through those of raw materials–dominated enterprises, through process-based strategies, to mission-based strategies like those of the armed services. The point is, each of these represents a unique challenge for leveraging creative intellect in maximizing value-added for both the producer and customer. And each requires a unique organizational configuration and supporting control and incentive systems to make it work properly. To suggest that any one system will fit all needs is dangerous nonsense.

COMMON CHARACTERISTICS OF INNOVATION

Nevertheless, there are some common characteristics of innovation processes that need to be considered in the design and implementation of any continuous innovation strategy. There is now a strong research-based literature about innovation and innovation processes. Interestingly, the most successful continuous innovators have intuitively or consciously reflected these findings in their strategies. One may in fact be the cause of the other. The "most innovative" companies included in our 1976–80 studies tended to embrace certain common characteristics—also later verified by others—that closely matched the way in which innovation, knowledge, and technology tend to develop. And these characteristics were, in turn, those which various forms of adhocracies supported well. Innovation tends to be:
  • *Need-oriented.* Seven of ten major successful innovations on average are driven by a recognizable market need, rather than a new concept, technique, or technology seeking a need.[4] Customers with a genuine need tend to be more tolerant of the uncertainties inherent in being lead customers for innovations. Further, over half of all innovations in many industries are made by customers leading or adding value to a producer's innovation.[5] Inventors rarely estimate customers' reactions well; hence the high

payoff from integrating innovative teams directly with customers and from interacting as quickly and as often as possible with them during design and early use cycles.

- *Probabilistic.* No one can predict whether a particular solution will work, how well it will work if successful, whether customers will accept it if it works, or how customers will use it once they have it. The first use of major innovations is often in unexpected markets, and market research is often wildly wrong. Hence the need for multiple parallel development approaches and continuous, fast, empirical, and flexible response systems connected directly to the marketplace. In low-probability systems, networking is especially needed to increase the probability of finding a workable answer at all. A capacity to attract and contact best-in-world expertise is also an essential in improving probabilities of success. These people tend to concentrate intensely on their specialties but need the direct stimulus of real problems to make them creative. Small committed, open, *ad hoc* teams provide the best environment for all these features.

- *Complex.* Few important innovations today are carried through entirely by single individuals or within single disciplines. In each discipline, probabilities and value-added improve if the individuals have close to best-in-world capabilities. If the best-in-world people can't do it, who can? Yet, many such contributors are required to generate and integrate the detailed expertise needed for a significant enough advance to convince customers to take introduction risks or to change familiar patterns. Still, everyone's expertise is rarely required for the full innovation cycle. Hence the need to bring together groups of experts for the intensive short-term interactions and the close communications adhocracies allow.

- *Time-consuming.* Components, subsystems, systems, and physical disciplines interact in such unpredictable ways—and with such asynchronous timing—that each potential interaction must be checked carefully, experimentally, and repeatedly. Time schedules are rarely met precisely. If they are met, there may be a necessary tradeoff in quality. A corollary to Murphy's Law says that if you anticipate it, you will design for it. So the unexpected is what always happens. Given this predictable unpredictability and likelihood of delay, the progress rate on an innovation is often best measured by the number of successful and relevant experiments one can make per unit of time. Hence the strong need to shorten cycle times and to increase interaction rates with customers and other technical experts. This calls for multiple small teams of experts with different talents trying different approaches and interacting with each other and with users in as much of an unstructured "skunkworks" environment as possible.

• *Spurts, delays, resistance, setbacks.* All major studies of innovation, particularly technological innovation, show that innovation rates are rarely linear.[6] Innovation—whether in art, theater, technology, science, or sports—occurs in spurts, with setbacks and unforeseeable delays interspersed with random interactions that lead to progress. Unexpected costs always occur, and overruns are common. Ambiguity is high, as are active antagonism and resistance to change. Innovation is disruptive, and those who are disrupted tend to resist the innovation. Hence the need to enable and actively support the *ad hoc*, boundaryless organizations, "bootlegging," coalition behavior, and wide-ranging external networking that (1) facilitate innovative problem-solving, (2) lower measured costs, and (3) allow innovators to work in unplanned spurts and to bypass resisters if necessary.

• *Intuition and uncodifiable knowledge.* Because spurts move so rapidly at times, and because the sought-after result itself by definition has never been achieved before, it is almost impossible to rely on codified knowledge.[7] Much of the information used in an innovation process must inevitably come from personal knowledge and the intuitive insights of individuals, which go beyond carefully documented past sources. Discovery and invention themselves are largely nonrational processes where the subconscious suddenly associates one matrix of ideas with another which it has never intersected before. This is the "Eureka" phenomenon that is often the essence of discovery or invention.[8] Successful innovation systems therefore consciously frustrate innovators with the intensity of the need (close customer interactions), then release them into informal or unstructured circumstances (adhocracies) where the subconscious mind and the stimulus of high interaction rates with others can take over.

• *Fanatics or champions.* Numerous studies also note that dedicated fanatics or innovation champions are needed to overcome the frustrations, ambiguities, time delays, and resistances inherent in the process.[9] Because bureaucratic layers discourage independence, champions emerge best in organizations that stay flat and largely voluntary. As the best studies note, true champions cannot be appointed; they must be psychologically committed to the innovative concept itself and must emerge for personal reasons, i.e., they identified the need, they created the invention, or they have a high need for personal recognition. Designating champions is counterproductive in any event. Given the high expertise other contributors need to have, champions must lead largely through their own charisma or referent authority, not delegated authority. Again the psychology and structure of adhocracies supports the behavior and practice demanded by innovation systems.

All the characteristics of the innovation process listed above are well-documented. It is because the characteristics of "adhocracies" match this process so well that this organization form and its associated systems dominate the management of intellect in innovative service organizations. Adhocracies have no special intrinsic worth. They are not justifiable just because they somehow suit the life-style or tenor of the times. They make solid sense because (1) they fit the basic nature of the innovative process and (2) innovation is a central strategy for many knowledge-based service organizations. When other characteristics dominate, solutions other than adhocracy may be more felicitous.

DIFFERENT STRUCTURES AND INCENTIVES

As Figure 9–1 and its accompanying text indicate, innovative adhocracies can differ enormously. Each type will call for different team sizes, skill mixes, management styles, incentives, planning horizons, innovation approaches, pricing strategies, supporting policies, and reward systems. Many of these are keyed to the normal design cycle and product life cycle of the innovation. Figure 9–2 suggests how different industries (on average) tend to fit these characteristics. Within a given industry, companies may vary widely according to their particular strategies. Nevertheless, by comparing their situations with industries generally having similar cycles—or having cycles they are trying to emulate—executives can see how their organizations, leadership styles, support policies, and incentives may need to vary to fit specific situations. Too many companies try to adopt a new organization form—especially those intended to shorten cycle times in innovation—without adjusting all the necessary supporting structures needed for the task. Not surprisingly, most fail. What are some of the common characteristics of the different cycles?

FIGURE 9–2
Typical Time Horizons by Industry

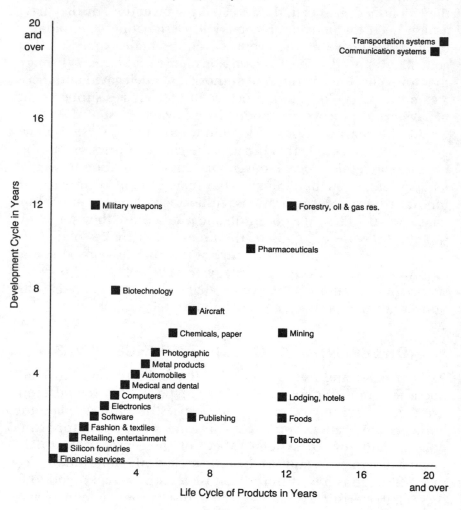

Source: Adapted by the author from a concept first introduced by Professor W. H. Davidson of the University of Southern California at a seminar at Boca Raton, Florida, spring 1986.

• *Instantaneous response to one-year cycles,* like fashions, toys, or financial services, usually involve individual or small team structures, based on the creativity of a few specialists or artists. In these situations participants may tolerate very ego-centered or authoritarian styles, with few articulated policies or plans of any sort.

Energy is focused almost exclusively on the current deal, product, or line. Organizations typically form around the creative genius on the basis of highly personalized relationships. High risks are common, and skim pricing tends to dominate. Since teams (or companies) may dissolve once the sales "season" is gone, short-term profit sharing or cash bonuses are entirely appropriate.

• *Two-to-four-year cycle* companies, like auto, computer, and machine tool firms, tend to use somewhat larger teams with more specialists and supporting infrastructures. Since many different skills are necessary for success and people must work together for extended periods, more participative styles are common. Although champions provide leadership, both teamwork and deeply specialized skills are prized. To maintain continuity, more documentation and articulated rules are needed. Planning horizons extend out three years or more and include much more formal milestones and PERT-type tracking. Innovators often "design through" the current generation of products to provide an effective platform for future incremental innovations at low cost. Incentives focus on meeting milestones and on options with three-year and longer vesting periods.

• *Five-to-seven-year cycles*, like major construction projects, tend to involve a series of more specialized teams handling different phases of the project, with even more formalized plans and permanent bureaucracies needed to maintain continuity. A small team of champions and a sheltering high-level "protector" are usually necessary. Since investments may be large, teams often involve management specialists (as well as technical specialists) assigned to the project for substantial periods. To maintain institutional memory, programs require careful documentation and systematic review. Planning horizons extend at least five years, with highlights beyond. Common stocks with reversion rights become common incentives, and pricing moves more toward the penetration and defensive spectrum to spread innovation costs over more units.

• *Ten-to-fifteen-year-cycles,* like those for pharmaceuticals or telecom infrastructures, approach the bureaucratic realm. Again large phased teams, with a mixture of managers and specialists, are common. Much of the innovation may occur within specialized research, construction, regulatory clearance, and other bureaucracies, designed to handle limited, low-risk, highly specialized phases of the problem. Quite formal program planning, system management, and evaluation procedures are needed to maintain focus within cross-functional activities. Joint ventures or cost sharing are often used to lower risks and front-end investments. Internal incentives tend to be salary reviews supplemented by a few "special recognition" awards. Pricing depends largely on industry practice and the protection one can receive on intellectual property.

• *Happy Valley companies,* like branded foods or household product firms, tend to build up strong brand franchises, supported by products and processes that are incrementally improved over many years. Innovation groups concentrate on making innumerable small changes, interactively tested directly in the marketplace. Highly specialized groups in research, production, and marketing constantly fine-tune technologies, processes, and market positioning. Often the consumer is not even aware of specific changes. Stable bureaucracies protect their functional expertise but participate on crossfunctional teams. Product managers tend to coordinate cross-functional matters. Since ordinary workers or salespeople may originate many innovations, suggestion plans can pay high dividends. Salary reviews, supplemented by occasional special suggestion or invention awards, provide most of the incentive structure.

• *Death Valley* venturers rarely want to be there. Companies are usually headed by frontier technologists who expect their technologies to last longer or to come to fruition sooner. Some involve advanced technologies (like information or biotechnologies) that are advancing so fast that, despite long innovation cycles, they are quickly supplanted in the marketplace. Given the uncertainties and long development cycles, innovators tend to be genuine fanatics on their subjects or alternately to be high-tech researchers supported by government funding. Organizations, rewards, staffing, pricing, and systems are obviously quite different depending on which funding or innovation source is involved.

Each of the above is a scenario of a rather typical class of innovation system. Details will vary a bit with the strategy of each enterprise within each class. Nevertheless, the "product development–product life cycle" framework suggests the widely differing organizations and supporting control-reward systems which may suit particular types of innovation situations. Management systems for successful innovation do not all fit neatly into the small, mobile *ad hoc* team model often suggested as a panacea for all firms. But enough do to make it a useful target and reference point for organizational design of many systems with different strategic purposes.

CREATIVITY WITH PROFESSIONAL PRECISION

Because it is more glamorous, the "innovative organization" has received much more attention than has the "professional bureaucracy." But both deserve a high position in the pantheon of managing intellect. One rarely wants a surgeon, savings banker, telephone operator, overnight package deliverer, stockbroker, airline pilot, opera singer, fireman, accountant, or safety regulator to be terribly experimental. Instead, in these roles one normally seeks deep professional competency, perfection, and complete reliability in the tasks undertaken. For every successful innovative organization in most industries, five or six truly competent professional organizations can thrive. It is reliability and the "quality of perfection" we seek in most of our services (banks, airlines, post offices, hospitals, communications, transportation, accounting, distribution, and education systems) and not creativity. Sometimes, however, both creativity and professional accuracy must be combined in the same process. Architecture, news reporting, medical research, and software development are typical examples where one wants both high accuracy and personal creativity. The systems programming activity of Andersen Consulting Division of Arthur Andersen and Company (AA&Co.) provides an interesting view of some issues and approaches for integrating strong discipline with creativity in the same organization.

■ Through Andersen Consulting, AA&Co. has emerged as one of the world's premier systems software providers. Usually it must provide both a unique solution for each customer's problem and deliver a thoroughly tested, fault-free product. It therefore combines a highly decentralized process for writing each section of the code with a rigorous centralized system to coordinate and control the whole system.

At the center of its process have been two programs called METHOD/1 and DESIGN/1. METHOD/1 is a carefully designed, step-by-step procedure for modularizing and controlling all the steps needed to design a major systems program. At the highest level are roughly ten "work units," each broken into approximately five "jobs." Below this are a similar number of "tasks" for each job and several "steps" for each task. Each component is numbered in hierarchical form and defines the exact elements the programmer needs to go through at that stage of the process. METHOD/1 has estimated times and costs built in for each step the programmer goes through. The project manager can explicitly override, substitute, or eliminate individual tasks or their time estimates as necessary for the specific project. As yet, METHOD/1 has not been set up as an "applied intelligence" tool, learning from the experiences it supervises.

Supplementing this program is another program, DESIGN/1, which is a very elaborate computer-aided software engineering (CASE) tool. METHOD/1 and DESIGN/1 are each compiled programs of 20–30 diskettes in length, taking the place of a wall full of systems programming manuals Andersen formerly used to control programming. Only a special team has access to the innards of these programs. DESIGN/1 keeps track of all programming details as they develop and disciplines the programmer to define each element of the program carefully. Among other things, it governs relationships among all steps in the flow chart to avoid losing data, entering infinite loops, using illegal data, and so on. Most importantly, (1) it is structured to fit the METHOD/1 system so that each step in a work plan will be executed by those using DESIGN/1, and (2) it allows customers to enter "pseudo" data or code so the customer can periodically test the "look and feel" of screen displays and data entry formats for reasonableness and appearance during development.

For quality control, a system designer establishes the overall project's flow chart and defines each of the interfaces between the program's modules. To attract and motivate good people, individual programmers are allowed to work alone on each small section of the code and must completely test all the metrics within their assigned section. To ensure compatibility, each programmer has been trained in exactly the same training program—centralized in one of a few (2–3) locations worldwide. A separate group does a systems or functional test for each type of business problem the code is to handle. Through DESIGN/1, this can be displayed for the customer. Through METHOD/1, the project manager keeps track of progress on the entire project, checks that all steps are performed, estimates next stage needs, assigns programmers for these, and then updates progress and cost records for the system. METHOD/1 provides a number of internal checks to avoid overassignments of personnel, to verify cost and sequence controls, and so on. Although quality control ultimately comes down to the personal creativity and skills of the programmers, the technology system disciplines quality to a higher level than individuals could possibly achieve alone. Management's primary job is to oversee the individual selection, training, and motivation of programmers—and the constant upgrading of the technology system and the relationship of programmers to it. Managers evaluate each programmer on an elaborate grid for each project they perform. And there are personal feedback sessions at no longer than three-month intervals.

ESTABLISHING "FIGURES OF MERIT"

These kinds of professional-creative combinations are relatively common in managing high-technology innovation systems, where creativity and deep competency in the technology must be combined with absolutely rigorous adherence to the constraints imposed by science, impinging technologies, or system interfacing requirements. To obtain both the information and motivation benefits of *ad hoc* teams, yet to ensure compliance with system constraints, an increasing number of professional-innovative groups use system checks like METHOD/1 and targeted "figures of merit" as powerful disciplining devices. For the latter, goals of the project are defined as numerically as possible in performance terms: "If these goals are met, we are sure to be successful." These are then exploded backward into "performance windows"—desired performance goals and specific interfacing restraints—for each subsystem. Each major system and subsystem has specific "figures of merit" attached: "If we hit these, we win."

This requires benchmarking of present and future competitive capabilities in each system and subsystem. Given these "figures of merit" and a management technology—like IMKA (described in Chapter 11), Method 1 or 2, or "best in class" tracking techniques—independent teams can be turned loose in highly dispersed units to meet the goals. This works especially well when the culture of the company has been designed to support innovation, with all the "support infrastructures" suggested in the preceding sections. There are many classic "figures of merit" that have driven successful innovation systems, from Ford's eighteen benchmarked "best in class" features for each Taurus-Sable sub-system, to Mr. Ibuka's (Sony Corp.) intuitive benchmarks for VTR developments, to AT&T-Bell Labs' "black box specifications," Pilkington Brothers' insistence that float glass "obsolete all other flat glass systems," to Intel's use of Moore's Law[10] (see "Vignettes: Managing Professional and Creative Intellect"). Far from being incompatible with the loose *ad hoc* cultures necessary for innova-tion, specific figures of merit enable such systems to operate. They provide the cohesive targets needed to focus and stimulate inno-vation. Virtually all of the "most innovative companies" we stud-ied used a variant of this technique. Because the application of this concept can usefully take on such diverse forms, the Vignettes immediately preceding this chapter provide some more complete descriptions of this very successful practice.

CONCLUSIONS

In contrast to professional groups, creative organizations tend to break all the traditional structural rules of organizations. These knowledge-based groups tend to demand high individual exper-tise in a number of specialized disciplines, where all are depen-dent on the others and no one can rule supreme. Innovative organizations tend to be *ad hoc*, fluid, cross-disciplinary, and co-operative. There are many different types of adhocracies from which to choose for a specific innovative purpose. Tasks tend to define relationships more than formal authority or control sys-tems do. Processes tend to be chaotic rather than orderly as in the professions, more cooperative than political, and more subject to challenge, vision, and interaction with users than in the profes-sions.

One should expect the randomness, chaos, and disorderliness that are inherent in the innovation process. Those who accept the process for what it is and try to manage in the chaos are likely to be far more successful that those who try to pretend it can be made orderly if only one can introduce more structure into the process. This does not mean simply "turning good people loose to innovate." Adhocracies fit the innovative process well, but they do not create innovation if merely left alone. Of great importance is the *hoc*—the goals—to which *ad*hocracies *ad*here.

Great innovative organizations—like other great service orga-nizations—are driven by great visions, which attract superb people and motivate them to contribute in desired directions. But to be effective, these visions need to be anchored to concrete realities. This is the function of clearly defining the firm's core competencies—what it intends to be best in world at doing—and then establishing customer-based and competitive metrics that make sure everyone understands what these goals are in concrete terms. Systematically defined "figures of merit" then can convert these into challenges that bring real cohesion and strategic focus to the innovation process.

The final step is to capture as much of the organization's accumulated system and managerial knowledge as possible in its information technologies (IT) and databases. Well developed IT systems help eliminate errors, leverage intellect, capture experience curve effects, and attract and hold key people in creative enterprises. In some, they become a basic component of the company's core competency. When carefully developed visions and targets are combined with very flat *ad hoc* organizations and technological systems specifically adapted to the company's particular strategic concept, managers can achieve the best of both the creative and the professional worlds. They can obtain the flexibility, drive, and creativeness that make adhocracies match the innovative and continuous learning processes so well. Yet they also achieve the cohesion, focus, and challenge that are essential in stimulating specialist intellect efficiently toward desired goals. In the next chapter we shall see how similar concepts—carefully modified—can create high payoffs in mass service situations.

PART 4
Managing the Intelligent Enterprise

CHAPTER 10

Managing Intellect in Mass Services: A Customer Based Quality Focus

Most service organizations and service tasks do not fit neatly into the category of either "professional" or "creative" services. This is true even within such examplars as *The New York Times*, Intel, Bell Labs, Arthur Andersen, or Sony. But it is especially true for "mass services" companies. These include chain stores, airlines, brokerage houses, package delivery services, fast food chains, banks, insurance companies, hotels and motels, large wholesalers, railroads, and telecom companies, all of which deliver fairly standardized services to large numbers of people. All these enterprises utilize very sophisticated professional and creative people in certain tasks. However, many crucial tasks involve a good deal of knowledge-based routine, without demanding great creativity or the training, expertise, and dedication of a true professional.

Many mass service tasks do, however, require some creativity in solving customer problems interspersed with long periods of routine. Some jobs, like those of bank tellers or insurance brokers, call for constant clerical precision, along with the periodic application of highly trained skills. Some, like those of airline flight attendants or travel agents, require much routine constantly punctuated with personal interactions demanding positive social skills and attitudes.

With the exception of editing and some interview examples, this and the following chapter were written before the January 7–8, 1992, organizational meetings of the National Research Council's "Committee to Study the Impact of Information Technology on the Performance of Service Activities," of which the author is Chairman. Views presented here are solely those of the author.

315

There are service jobs that are mostly routine production tasks, like those of window washers, hamburger flippers, or baggage handlers. But most mass service tasks are some combination of knowledge-based routine coupled with a need to interact positively with outside parties, usually customers, at varying intervals.

Are there any common challenges, techniques, or useful management approaches applicable to these very different regimes? Perhaps a few. In mass services, the dominating challenge is to obtain high productivity from both capital and workers, yet to achieve the levels of responsiveness, personalization, and "enthusiasm-courtesy-competency" customers want at the point of contact. To accomplish this, most successful mass service enterprises have been built around a strategically designed blend of (1) *proactively creating an effective culture and value system* for the enterprise, (2) *carefully designing and managing the company's technology systems* to support the company's particular service concept, and (3) *installing the proper organization, training, and incentive structures* to implement and reinforce these two systems.

MANAGING VALUES AND TECHNOLOGY

Although many strategic analyses focus dominantly on measurable economic factors, our studies showed that managing values and attitudes—and particularly employee perceptions at the customer contact level—was among the most leverageable, lowest-cost, and most pragmatic tasks that managers could undertake.[1] When managers strongly inculcated meaningful corporate values at all operating levels, morale was palpably higher, service levels improved, creativity and productivity went up, time horizons often lengthened, increased delegation was possible, personal conflicts decreased, and control system costs dropped radically—all with very high profit impacts.

One of the most thorough studies of service management has noted: "Too many service workers are overmanaged and underled. [Our studies indicate that] people in service work need a vision in which they can believe, an achievement culture that challenges them to be the best they can be, a sense of team that nurtures and supports them, and role models that show them the way. This is the stuff of leadership. [Too often] the goal of profit takes precedence over the goal of providing a service good enough that people will pay a profit to have it." These studies say clearly that the entire organization must believe in a service vision, that superior service is a winning strategy, and that profits will follow from it. The studies also emphasize that service leaders tend to be "zealots" about "doing it right the first time," engaging in "a full court press all the time," and "building a climate of team work and personal integrity."[2]

VALUES MANAGEMENT IS PRAGMATISM . . .

These things at first sound like motherhood—or is it fatherhood? But virtually all the successful service companies of the 1980s—from Wal-Mart to Microsoft—have found these to be the keys to profits. Strongly held and inculcated values tend to generate, at a minimum, the pragmatic benefits outlined in Table 10–1, "Pragmatic Impacts of Values Management." These are practical results that should be meaningful to even the most hard-nosed manager. By themselves, they are impressive enough. But they create even greater benefits for owners and managers.

In an excellent study, Kotter and Heskett demonstrate conclusively the significant positive impact that corporate culture has on competitive performance. They found that: "firms with cultures that strongly emphasized all the key management constituencies (customers, shareholders, and employees) and leadership from managers at all levels outperformed firms that did not have these traits by a huge margin. Over an eleven year period, the former increased revenues by an average of 682 percent versus 166 percent for the latter, expanded their workforces by 282 percent versus 36 percent, grew their stock prices by 901 percent versus 74 percent, and improved their net incomes by 756 percent versus 1 percent."[3]

In service companies, there is a special reason why increases in shareholder value accompany a strong emphasis on culture and human values. Ultimately, when shareholders purchase a service-based company's stock (or acquirers seek to buy into the company), they will pay more for an enterprise whose performance and integrity they can rely on. They are to a large extent buying the continuity that inculcated values ensure. Conversely, when executives approach their organizations as mere money-making tools, which can be sold (like cattle) at will, they completely undermine the crucial sense of self-worth and organizational purpose that creates service quality—and in the not-too-long run the very financial values they may personally be seeking to achieve.

TABLE 10–1
Pragmatic Impacts of Values Management

- Consistent values will attract the kind of people who genuinely want to work for the company, and mutually held values create the trust necessary for flexibility and effectiveness.
- Trust, created by common values, allows efficient delegation. People will work independently toward commonly held goals.
- People work harder to fulfill values they believe in, thus enhancing personal motivation and enterprise productivity.
- People who share common values will help each other, generating teamwork and adding value through shared solutions.
- Creative people can work efficiently on their own toward commonly held goals and can share the long time horizons needed for innovative success.
- Common values create group identity, improve morale, and eliminate needs for more detailed controls.
- High-morale organizations will band together, work intensively for short spurts to solve critical problems, and protect group secrets.
- People at distant points in the organization can be trusted to use their intuition to solve unique problems in ways consistent with organization purposes.
- Value-activated people will consciously seek new opportunities to fulfill these values and will not waste time on those that do not.
- Commonly held values tend to minimize squabbles, decrease internal frictions, and reduce time needed to manage them.

. . . WHEN COMBINED WITH TECHNOLOGY

It also turns out that a dual orientation toward technology *and* managing values is crucial in service-based companies. Together in our sample the two yielded some of the greatest successes in modern business history. When one was ignored, disasters could happen.

■ Many are familiar with the explosive growth Donald Burr created with his charismatic leadership ability and the loose "cluster organization" he instituted at People Express. At first, the company's shared vision was fully communicated and internalized in all areas of the organization. This and other associated personnel practices led to a highly committed, efficient, and responsive company with the lowest unit labor costs and the highest employee productivity in the industry. However, People Express failed in large part because of Mr. Burr's disdain, if not active dislike, for technology.

Despite the pleading of some of his key people, People Express was not connected to the major automated reservation systems, key operations were not computerized, and flight services became ever more confused and difficult for passengers. Finally, other airlines with more sophisticated information about flight patterns and rate structures were able to chip away at People Express' niche without severe cost to themselves. Over time, it became ever more difficult to implement the company's vision, especially as People Express attempted to expand operations without a sufficient computer infrastructure. Finally, morale began to lag and fail because of the frustrations of operating in confusion, costs flew out of control, and customers abandoned the airline.

By contrast, Wal-Mart stores, the last decade's fastest-growing and most profitable major retail chain, offers an excellent example of how the combination can be implemented well.

■ Wal-Mart focuses its advanced technologies and all its efficiency efforts on serving its customers better and lowering prices, not just on cost-cutting or margin generating *per se*. Unrecognized by many, Wal-Mart has perhaps the best technology-based communications system in its field, including satellite and interactive video links to many stores. With its detailed stock management systems, it can delegate and control to the counter level. This allows its personnel to run a "store within a store" for better personal motivation and more focus on the customer. To drive its customer-oriented value system, Wal-Mart executives spend 2–5 days a week personally talking to customers and employees in the field, and then return for a Friday–Saturday "idea session" at headquarters to exchange ideas on how to improve operations.

Wal-Mart often employs people (who might otherwise be temporarily displaced) as "people greeters" to increase customer satisfaction, and it keeps more checkout lines open for faster service than its competitors. Both are made possible by its technology-induced productivity—about $250 per square foot versus $150 for its competitors.[4] This is Wal-Mart's "productivity loop," letting it make more profits, with which to provide more service to make more profits. One of Wal-Mart's unique services is its extensive "Buy American" plan, which helps Wal-Mart's dominantly blue-collar customers through $3.8 billion of U.S. purchases, providing an estimated 100,000 U.S. jobs. All practices support the company's constantly reinforced theme that "serving the customer right is what makes profits."[5]

■ Randy Fields, president of Mrs. Fields' Cookies, said:

The goal of our technology is to replace people in all the things people do that machines can do as well. . . . We try to capture all the mechanical, numerical, and nonhuman functions of operations in our electronic systems. Then we can free our management and front-line people to work on the things they do best, sensing what the machines cannot do and fixing them. Being a software guy, I tend to concentrate on the electronics side, leveraging our special knowledge as much as possible through expert systems. Debbi [Fields] has been absolutely extraordinary in creating a culture in which people want to excel and perform all those unique things only people can do.

The purpose of the technology at Mrs. Fields' is to simulate the capabilities of a few extremely knowledgeable people at the center through expert systems, then to push this out to the field so that the quality of field decisions gets better and better without having to put more highly trained people into the field. So powerful is the combination of its technology system and Mrs. Fields' culture development program that it is often said: "People who could probably only be shift leaders at McDonald's can be full-fledged unit managers at Mrs. Fields', and are developed to be so."[6]

A CONSTANT AND FOCUSED REINFORCEMENT

Just as in Wal-Mart and Mrs. Fields' Cookies, inculcating desired values in any organization requries constant and focused management. It all starts with the selection of the right people. Too few companies approach the rigor of the best.

■ Toronto-based Four Seasons Hotels puts candidates through four or five interviews to find those with the personality and values it is seeking—once interviewing 14,000 candidates for only 350 slots. Home Depot, a $5 billion home improvement and hardware chain growing at 25 percent a year, tries to recruit former carpenters and electricians for salesmen, knowing they will understand the product line better and will be able to help solve customer problems. Stocking 30,000 items, Home Depot trains its people to understand every item in their sales area and in the two adjacent aisles. It then constantly retrains and upgrades its people through programs, using its own internal television system and supplier demonstrations of new products.[7]

In values-activated companies, all managers and new employees are typically put through a course explaining and cheerleading the company's values. If these courses are to work, the very top management team must actively participate, as Debbi Fields (Mrs. Fields'), Bob Noyce and Gordon Moore (Intel), Akio Morita (Sony), and Fred Smith and Jim Barksdale (Federal Express) in our studies did. One of these key people always tried to appear on the first day of important in-house executive and training courses to personify and emphasize corporate values. Value themes were iterated and reiterated in all the company's brochures, public presentations, meetings, slogans, and myths. Quality-oriented companies also may give new employees a "big brother or sister" (Four Seasons) or "godfather" (Sony) to help them understand and grow in the culture. Most importantly, values are continuously reinforced and not subverted by executive actions.

■ For example, Mr. Morita and Mr. Ibuka constantly proved their commitment to innovation and high principles in their handling of people. Key to inculcating these values in the organization were their unflagging support of innovation, active participation in the innovation process, sacrifices to encourage the intellectual growth of their engineers, inspirational visits to technical laboratories, and willingness to take complete blame for losses and downturns at Sony—while maintaining full employment for their workers. Messrs. Morita and Ibuka and Dr. Kihara became the subject of many Sony myths, which in turn became the core of the "Sony Spirit." For example, when Mr. Ibuka was offered the first-ever product Emmy for his Trinitron "Tummy

Television," he refused to accept it alone. It was given to the design team. Similarly, at Honda Motor Company, Mr. Honda often worked in the pits with his designers, picked up trash, and wiped out washrooms on his plant visits to reinforce values concerning innovation and the attention to details that produce quality.

Many believe some of these executives' dramatic eccentricities were purposely intended to create or reinforce values-producing myths. Symbols, constantly used, are a much more efficient way of communicating complex values than words. Consistent management actions and reinforcement by incentive and reward systems are the ultimate routes to making selected values the driving forces of a culture.

Two of the least glamorous services—maintenance and hairdressing—show dramatically how managing the combination of technology, values, and incentives can create huge premiums in unexpected places. The benefits of leveraging service technologies and treating employees as if the corporation is truly a "voluntary" organization are not limited to just professional or creative personnel.

■ ServiceMaster—from its sixteen years' experience and a database of more than 17 million equipment units—can lower its clients' costs immediately by utilizing detailed models of exactly how each unit should perform, when preventive maintenance pays, and when replacement should take place. But when Service-Master comes in to manage hospital or other equipment maintenance services, it typically finds maintenance people in a survival mode, with their equipment deteriorating daily and no training or career paths to break out of seemingly dead-end jobs.

ServiceMaster's first actions are to get the system cleaned up and operating right, give the people needed training, and make them feel more in control of their lives and operations. Morale immediately goes up. Then it introduces maintenance personnel to a career development program, shows them how they can move on to an associate's degree in plant engineering, become group or facilities managers for ServiceMaster, or even head a Service-Master unit. As Senior Vice President Craig Frier said, "Our technologies enable them to run things right. But we can't do anything or reach any of our goals for the facility until we can get rank-and-file maintenance, housekeeping, or dietary employees to understand and believe in themselves, their futures, and their worth."

■ Visible Changes, in the fragmented hairdressing industry, constantly achieved 3.5 times the sales per employee of its competitors, twice the average sales per customer, and almost four times the industry's average product sales in its outlets. Starting with hairdressers—who generally have no loyalty to their employers and see their profession as a low-paying dead-end—Visible Changes tries to give its personnel a sense of proprietorship, without stock equity. Employees make their own decisions and always must earn their rewards.

Nothing comes as a "benefit." People earn their health insurance from their sale of hair care products. They have to earn the right to go to advanced hairstyling programs. But as a reward, hairdressers—when customers especially request them—receive a 35 percent commission and a right to raise service fees by up to 40 percent. Bonuses, based on performance ratings, can add another 10 percent; and profit sharing 15 percent more. A computer-based system helps measure and reward each individual's performance down to the finest detail to maintain needed cost controls, point out where performance can be improved, and create equity among individuals. The typical employee earns three times the industry's average wage.[8]

Values management sometimes sounds very mushy and not very "hard-headed" to tough-minded executives. But the market value of most service companies is very dependent on each management's particular style and leadership qualities, the culture that management creates, and the way key people respond to its initiatives. No financial analysis of the "breakup" or "takeover" value of a service company means much without a realistic assessment of whether a new management could—and would—continue to build similar value through its people. To enhance a firm's value in the financial marketplace, as well as its attractiveness to employees, managers often try to capture as much of the firm's uniqueness as possible in their operating systems and technologies. But these never quite reproduce that last, most important, ephemeral, and highly leverageable element in services: the internalized skills and attitudes of the key operating and management people who actually produce service quality and productivity.

QUALITY IN SERVICES

Assuming that service-oriented managers accept the paramountcy of values and technology in performance, toward what goals should they try to harness these forces? Most authorities suggest "service quality and productivity" and not "the bottom line" as the most powerful and directly useful goals.[9] If the first two are right, the third will come. An overemphasis on profits, rather than on those things that achieve profits, with rare exceptions forces an internal and short-term orientation that is actively destructive to service delivery. As the CEO of a multibillion-dollar international service enterprise said, "Maximizing profits, shareholder wealth, or ROI are abstractions so far removed from most people's daily work (and so beyond their control) that as motivators, they are almost meaningless to operating personnel—other than beancounters." By contrast, studies repeatedly show that producing a service that is worthwhile, producing it efficiently and effectively, and making customers feel good about the service can create the motivation and identity that breed financial success.[10]

Mistakenly, in attempting to stress profits, too many companies try to reduce cost and output measures to internal engineering metrics like length of lines, order service times, numbers of complaints, or follow-up service costs. If they survey customers at all, they get a highly subjective reading on customer feelings. Bain & Company suggests starting with a more customer-oriented metric: Do customers stay with the company? Bain has found that boosting customer retention by 2 percent often has the same effect on profits as cutting costs by 10 percent. The customer exit interview alone can prove a powerful profit lever.[11] Many companies have found that by interviewing customers who are closing out accounts, they can both retain the customer and correct the real problems that made them want to leave. With some studies showing that long-term customers provide 85–90 percent more profits than short-term ones, concentrating on customer satisfaction metrics can produce high returns.

In more than a hundred interviews with leading service companies, we found that—contrary to our expectations—most had well-developed techniques for surveying customers about their perceptions of the company's service quality. But only about one-third of these had converted these surveys into metrics used for performance measures for customer contact groups. Of these only 10–15 percent (3–5 percent of the total sample) used the survey rankings directly as performance measures for individual compensation. Instead they used surrogate engineering metrics like telephone response times, order fill times, shipping error rates, and so on. Many more, however, said they were trying to move to more direct customer-based incentives at the present time. Details will appear in later sections.

WHAT IS QUALITY IN SERVICES?

Despite such disappointing observations, a focus on quality and productivity from the *customer's viewpoint* is still the critical one for service success. Fortunately, since these two key factors, when developed with a true customer focus, tend to be strongly reinforcing in services, more companies seem to be moving to exploit their synergy. The flip side, however, is that both are terribly difficult to measure using the standard tools developed for manufacturing industries. The problem is in identifying and measuring outputs. Exactly what units of output does a waiter, broker, travel agent, retailer, educator, banker, doctor, or consultant produce? As Walter Wriston of Citicorp once said, "The number or dollar value of loans a bank officer makes doesn't mean much; it's how good the loans are that counts."

Unfortunately, one often cannot know at the time the service is produced whether its quality is high or low. Actual results may not be known for some time, and responsibility for the outcome may be even more difficult to determine then. Was the doctor, the broker, the patient, or the customer responsible for the final outcome? Quality is so intertwined with what is produced in services—and the way the customer uses what is produced is so important—that we literally do not know what has been created until we know the quality of ultimate outcomes. And this often depends to a great extent on outside factors. With bad breaks, one can experience disastrous results as the outcome of a well-performed surgical procedure (a weak blood vessel elsewhere breaks), of professional travel arrangements (an airplane crashes), or of sound investment advice (there is a war-induced stock market crash). On the other hand a bit of good luck can turn bad service performance into a spectacular outcome. One could meet the love of a lifetime at an otherwise obnoxious hotel or could convert a mediocre educator's random comment into a fortune. Or, for reasons completely beyond any competent service producer's control, the exact opposite could happen. Service providers often must watch in horror as their recommendations are ignored or are incompetently implemented.

These are some of the essential dilemmas of service measurement and management. Outcomes frequently cannot be measured at the time the service is delivered. Actual outcomes depend very much on customers' attitudes, actions, and perceptions. And all the internal management in the world may not assure desired consequences. Yet both perceived efficiency and quality depend on actual results. All managers can do is to improve the percentage of time they deliver what they intend to deliver. With care, they can get this as close as possible to what the customer expects, needs, and will use. And they can ensure that the target service is delivered with internal efficiency and in ways the customer is likely to regard as creating value. There are certain critical dimensions in managing service quality this way.

MANAGING EXPECTED QUALITY

All the major studies of quality in services agree that service quality is so subjective that it can be measured only in terms of what customers want or define as quality. (To the author, a quality rock-concert is an oxymoron, while this doesn't seem to be so for many others.) Within this personal definition, the perceived quality of a service is determined by the ratio—or differential—between the quality customers expect and what they actually receive. People expect different service in McDonald's from that in the Four Seasons restaurant. They expect different things of an outback emergency room versus the emergency room at the Mayo Clinic. And people judge the quality of an enterprise's output largely against the standard of what they expect from the producer. Not surprisingly, therefore, *"reliability" or "predictability" constantly shows up as perhaps the one most cherished element of performance* in most service quality studies.[12] But the nature and the degree of reliability customers demand can vary widely among companies or industries, depending on what they have come to expect. Contrast the different expectations one has for an ophthalmic product salesman (eyeglasses) versus a used car salesman, or when buying the same product (a watch) from a jeweler versus buying it in a discount house.

This introduces a surprising caution in service quality management. Executives need to ensure that their marketing programs—in their attempts to hype up customer interest—do not create expectations their delivery systems cannot fulfill. When promotions, ads, pricing, point-of-purchase, or other marketing policies lead customers to expect especially prompt, friendly, or competent service, they are angered—not satisfied as they might otherwise be—when they encounter only average service. By contrast, they are thrilled to receive even minimal service in a "cut-price joint." On the one hand, Delta Airlines constantly ranks high in satisfaction studies because it delivers on its friendly, homely hospitality even though its on-time arrival record is often among the industry's lowest. On the other, Southwest Airlines gets consistently high marks—despite its spartan planes and almond-snack menus—by delivering against its image of low fares and frequent flights.[13] Senior executives need to target and carefully manage both sides of the perceived quality interface: expected quality and delivered quality (see Figure 10–1).

Any good marketing text will lay out how the choice of media, message, promotional style and methodology, pricing presentations, brand names carried, and facilities appearance (location, frontage, signage, lighting, counter displays, layouts, and so on) help create customer expectations. There is no need to detail them here, except to underline how destructive these techniques can be if they engender images of service levels the company does not later produce. When one buys a cruise ticket envisioning beautiful people dancing, dining, swimming, and careening to tourist sites and encounters only geriatrics being helped (however kindly) through a different kind of vacation, the whole value to the customer will be destroyed—unless that customer is geriatric. Conversely, the most excitingly executed cruise concept will be worthless if its marketing does not attract its target customer group. For service quality, image and reality must reasonably match.

FIGURE 10–1
Customer Perceived Quality

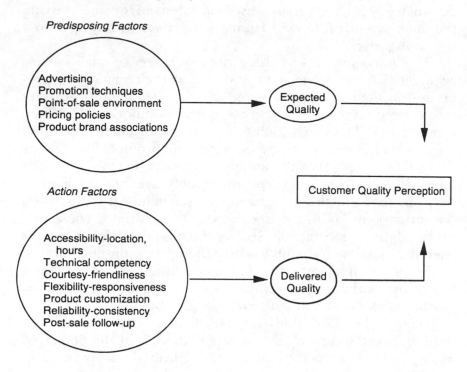

SOURCE: Modified from V. Zeithaml, A. Parasuraman, and L. Berry, *Delivering Quality Service* (New York: Free Press, 1990).

MANAGING DELIVERED QUALITY

Delivered quality in services is a function of other—mostly internally determined—action factors like those indicated in Figure 10–1. Again, other texts will list and define the relevant factors and their components in a richness of detail that is not appropriate here. The most important issues from a strategic viewpoint are (1) treating service factors as the most important elements in creating value-added, differentiation, and maintainable barriers that prevent competitors from stealing one's customers, (2) matching delivered quality to expected quality, (3) measuring and rewarding quality performance in terms of customer-oriented—not internally driven—criteria, and (4) exploiting the powerful positive relationships between delivered service quality and lower costs. Two examples will make the relevant points:

■ Recognizing that other manufacturers could probably build a car of equal technical quality, Nissan based its Infiniti luxury car's strategy on the fact that superior dealer service could distinguish it in the customer's mind from other brands. It puts all Infiniti dealer employees through an intensive six-day training camp in Scottsdale, Arizona, the longest such training period for any car line. Dealer personnel, from receptionists to owners, are taught in detail (1) to treat customers as "okyakusama," honored guests, and (2) to know and experience all possible comparative advantages of the Infiniti versus other brands. Trainees actually drive all competing brands and Infiniti over test tracks for most of three and a half days. All this indoctrination is later backed by annual awards of up to $100,000 based on customer satisfaction scores for dealers.[14]

■ A few years ago Xerox followed a conscious strategy of shipping a copier from its plant to a customer faster than its competitors. But, through careful interviews, Xerox found its customers really cared more about knowing exactly when the copier would arrive, having it installed and working on schedule, and being billed accurately. Xerox could not comply until it realigned its entire order processing, tracking, and billing procedures. When it did, customer satisfaction ratings quickly improved from 70 to 90 percent. When it used a similar process to coordinate the physical flow of its copiers and parts, Xerox cut inventories by $200 million as well.[15]

For years economics and management texts—from Adam Smith, Frederick Taylor, and Fayol to Samuelson, Fiegenbaum, and Taguchi—have focused on making goods more efficiently and making them as *technically* perfect as possible to meet customer needs within cost constraints. This process is approaching an asymptote. Technical quality—holding carefully defined physical specifications and producing a defined product function reliably—is fast becoming a common expectation for all products, a *sine qua non*, a nondifferentiable commodity. The main focus of management's strategic thinking therefore must be on what *services* should be embodied in their products (be they physical or service products) and how other intangible services could enhance their products' value. Managers need to determine precisely where in the service-value chain their company should focus and how to develop needed service elements with uniqueness and in winning depth. An increasing number of companies use customer surveys that break customers' service perceptions down into multiple variables and track their shifting views about each. For example:

■ American Express' $6.8 billion Travel and Related Services (TRS) group takes sample measurements of client satisfaction monthly on such matters as timeliness, accuracy, and problem resolution on all its transaction types. It tracks some forty-six measurements—defined as important by client research—broken down into six main categories. AmEx asks its clients to weight the importance of each issue. From these it creates a weighted "customer satisfaction index" that summarizes the key metrics and aggregates the number of "dissatisfying incidents" recorded in interviews and in customer complaints. AmEx uses these as direct measures of its quality performance. These metrics are tied into a TQM approach throughout the division for improving overall effectiveness (efficiency and quality) of operations. AmEx's CEO, James Robinson III, backs this focus with his strongest possible personal commitment, repeatedly stressing that "quality is the only patent protection we've got," supporting AmEx's Quality University in Phoenix, making repeated speeches on the subject of quality, and making slogans like "Promise only what you can deliver, and deliver more than you promise" a part of the AmEx culture. He emphasizes to everyone who will listen: "If we are the low-cost, high-quality producer, market share will follow."[16]

■ MBNA, the country's fourth-largest bank credit card issuer, measures seventy points of quality performance each day and posts its ratings for fourteen of the most important ones for all to see. These include a number of easily measured internal variables, such as whether telephones are answered within two rings, whether requests for credit line increases are processed in one hour, whether the computer is operating twenty-four hours a day, and so on. All employees, from floor sweepers to top executives, are on a bonus program related to those fourteen points and can receive bonuses as much as 20 percent above their salaries by meeting established quality goals.

To ensure delivered quality, as in the several cases above (Xerox, Nissan, AmEx, MBNA), each service element to be emphasized needs a "service design"[17]—a specific plan that sets forth how that element of service will be produced, interlinked, delivered, and measured in customer terms. Unfortunately, this caveat is more often modified or ignored than followed in practice.

■ Typically, the CFO of a major insurance company said:

We have done a fair amount of direct customer research on what our customers want, and then we have tried to tailor our major program investments to that. But one can often get different interpretations about what comes out of focus groups or questionnaires. Therefore, it's a combination of the science of customer research and a lot of judgment and intuition as to what gets converted into internal responses. Generally, the customer is not involved in the design of the system itself: [participation] happens more on an *ad hoc* than a formal basis. After installation we sometimes do check to see how customers are responding to the system. But that is sporadic. . . . And to date we have rarely converted these metrics into performance or reward measures for our operating groups or individuals.

For strategic advantage the company must not only determine what most customers want but how its service will be *different from and better than* any other direct or functional competitor's. Since *direct output measures* for benchmarking in services are so difficult to come by—or to get others to share for strategic reasons[18]— many more benefits usually accrue from investigating, understanding, improving on, and *positioning against the service processes* of best-in-world sources. To assist in this analysis, a number of companies have joined groups which agree to contribute benchmark data about their internal processes to an independent consultant, an industry group, or a statistical survey company, which then compiles and distributes the data on an anonymous basis to each of the members.

Sometimes the payoff can be extremely high: for example, introducing new products up to 2.5 times faster, lowering inventories (in distribution firms) by orders of magnitude, and achieving error rates that are 0.1 to 0.5 percent of previous levels.[19] More often, the direct changes are less dramatic but can start a series of actions that influence the whole company's culture.

■ The Senior Vice President of another major insurance company said:

> One area where we did benchmarking was in pensions. This is a highly competitive market dealing on thin margins. The differentiators are quality, response times, and cost of service. The key question was, could we really deliver the service competitively in today's environment? How could we compare favorably with the Fidelities, Vanguards, and other big names there? We did "best practices" work with all of these; we looked at about twenty different companies. We also did a lot of subjective comparisons based on what we thought they were doing. We went out and talked to all of them. But we don't have objective internal measures to compare with them yet. . . .

> Benchmarking was an absolute culture break for us. The individual who was charged with driving re-engineering across the company, a very bright guy, was basically convinced [at the outset that] our company was the best at everything we did. When he started talking to our competitors, both insurance and noninsurance, he came back and said, "Not only are we not the best, but in some places we may not even be up with the worst." He saw some incredibly dumb things that we do. This basically drove the Office of the Chairman to one of its strategies, saying, "We want to be one of the three best in breed," and giving each strategic unit a time frame in which to accomplish this.

For successful transfer to and implementation of new processes in the company, however, it takes more than careful external analyses. It takes extremely detailed planning, i.e., the type of step-by-step process implementation or rigorous "service blueprinting" called for by Shostack or the detailed "process mapping" approaches recommended by Rummler,[20] where each element in the service delivery process is laid out in minute detail to make sure all elements are captured, improved, taught, executed, monitored, and updated. Many of our respondents noted the strong tendency to underestimate the time, cost, and management attention needed to transfer and implement new service systems.

MANAGING PROCESS QUALITY

In many cases the *process* through which a service is delivered can dominate all other factors in perceived quality. Production and consumption of services frequently are simultaneous processes occurring largely at the point of customer contact. The customer often participates actively and interactively in the production process, giving orders, answering questions, evaluating alternatives, helping to design the service (from haircuts to pension purchases), or operating service equipment (ATMs, gas pumps, or cellular telephones) personally. In these interactions, the customer becomes a part of the team producing the service. And if the process is not a benign, efficient, friendly, and productive one, the customer will become thoroughly alienated. Perceived quality and the outcome's value for both buyer and seller will quickly become negative.

Not only do most companies not include real customers in designing these processes, but Bain & Co. has estimated that 70 percent of all major service providers have no systematic means for measuring perceived service quality later. The results are tragically predictable. At a minimum, Bain suggests concentrating on the metric of customer defections, a strong clue to customers' feelings about the company. It recommends setting up a target of "zero defections" of customers and establishing measures to track progress against this. Most companies would find higher payoffs by using this measure in combination with (1) a series of constantly surveyed, customer-based metrics that calibrate the quality customers really expect versus the quality they are receiving, and (2) driving these metrics to make them training and incentive targets for all employees, as AmEx (previously described) and McKesson do:

■ McKesson has defined forty-two "customer satisfactors" that it surveys externally and measures internally on a routine basis. It has a seven-page questionnaire that goes to more than a thousand customers every year, with quarterly updates on a smaller set of factors considered to be the most important. It is now trying to link these to its compensation-incentive systems. At the strategic level McKesson also has five strategic "themes" that it emphasizes for competitiveness. These include customer-supplier satisfaction, people development, market positioning, relative net delivered cost, and innovation. For all these factors, McKesson uses internal and external metrics to track its own and competitors' positions as perceived by customers.

CUSTOMER BASED QUALITY METRICS

In our survey of advanced users of information technology, we found a number of other companies that were developing direct customer-based metrics on service quality. To the extent possible, they were implementing these as in-line measures whenever possible. Many posted daily or weekly quality metrics for parameters they could measure directly. Many more used customer surveys to calibrate their overall quality performance.

■ Mr. Richard Liebhaber, Chief Strategy and Technology Officer of MCI, said:

> There are basically two reflections or images of quality that our customers see. . . . Obviously one key grouping contains all the metrics in the network that pertain to how the call sounds. Underlying that are all the reliability measures on signal variability, strength, connection delays, downtime, and so on. Our data show that the AT&T network has failed four times in the last two years in major ways. Ours hasn't. I view reliability as an artifact, as I view service provisioning features—you must have it, otherwise you can't do business. I couldn't sell automobiles if I only put three tires on them. . . . We not only run tests on our network, we run extensive tests on the Sprint network and the AT&T network. Quarterly I get an analysis of our network and theirs. We compare all the engineering metrics. There is a database that goes back sixty years maintained by BellCore that says if your decibel loss is 2DB at this level, then it is bothersome for certain users. Variability has to be controlled and measured, and of course digitization has made all that a lot easier. This is sampled in-line, continuously. Computers make the calls. Computers measure the metrics.
>
> The second important metric to the customer is the invoice. If I give you an invoice with telephone calls on it that are ninety days old, or is inaccurate, that is not quality. You will not see a telephone call on your MCI invoice that is forty-five days old, unless it is international. If we don't invoice all our traffic this month, someone explains to me why.
>
> We do in-depth customer surveys about twice a year, and we do get feedback at a lower level of detail (ten-question questionnaires) monthly. Every customer above about $30,000 in billings a month is surveyed once a year, either informally or in depth. The in-depth interviews are done by an outside company. We do our own statistical analyses of surveys from samples of residential customers, and we do focus groups to get a "feel" for how those customers are responding. We also measure loss rates,

geographically, by customer service center. In Business Communications, we measure them by branch office at all 132 locations. We measure loss rates by customer segment. We also do extensive internal employee satisfaction surveys every eighteen months, because I think employees' attitudes are an important factor in customer service.

■ In another example of in-line quality control, Mr. Martin Stein, Vice Chairman of Bank of America, stated:

In 1991, Bank of America won the Society for Information Management Award for our branch automation system, which is called COIN—Customer On-line Information Network. COIN cost over $250 million and took four years to implement. The goal of COIN was twofold: First, to make our transactions faster and easier for customers, and to be more cost effective. Our second objective was to help understand the entire relationship we have with a customer, so we can use this information in marketing and in servicing them. COIN gives a teller a complete summary of a customer's accounts. For example, a customer can go up to a window, swipe an ATM card through a terminal, and then key in the PIN number. The teller then knows what types of relationships this customer has with Bank of America. This gives a teller a lot more authority to service a customer and to minimize calls for approvals to the branch manager or others.

COIN facilitates the whole transaction. For example, rather than go through the time-consuming process of filling out several government forms by hand for a transaction over $10,000, COIN prints all of them automatically. That saves us money and allows customers to do their business quickly and efficiently at Bank of America. Can I tell you that's the reason why our retail business is robust? No. But I think it's part of our success. Our chairman, Dick Rosenberg, felt that COIN and the improved service it provides was an important way to differentiate ourselves from our competition, and to add more value to what people normally consider a commodity service.

To make sure we are providing the best service possible, we do customer-based metrics. That's when we survey customers and measure how they actually rate our service. We do it several ways. One method is to do a lot of testing with customers and groups to determine what appeals to them. Another is to use the customer relationship data that we have and do a lot of analyses on customer preferences and utilization trends. We also look at what automation can do to facilitate that.

From a pure productivity standpoint, we have input for a stochastic model. We have some rules that are set by the branches as to what are appropriate waiting times in line, what is acceptable, and what service rates should be. Through COIN, we are able to capture arrival rates of customers at teller stations and the amount of time they spend there.

We also measure service by quantitative goals outlined in agreements with our business partners. For example, if our business parter said we have X number of days to turn around a real estate loan, we are measured against that goal. These goals are reviewed periodically to ensure we are delivering the service our business partners want. We have yet to convert these into incentives for our operating people, but we believe they are good guidelines and are improving our operations overall.

Other leading edge companies develop customer-based quality metrics on a less automated basis. For example:

■ Mr. Melvin Ollestad, Senior Vice President of CIGNA, noted:

We do auditing which consists of randomly selecting claims that are reviewed at the benefit analyst, unit, regional office, and national levels. We get a sense over time of the accuracy levels. We audit for financial accuracy, payment accuracy, and coding accuracy. We try to get it down to a perfect claim which is what our goal is—a claim that has absolutely nothing wrong with it. Secondly, we track at the defects level, which is a more direct indicator of what our customers notice. People send us stuff back. There are errors, refund reversals, incomplete claims, and so on. We count these kinds of "defects" and try to implement changes that will reduce the numbers. The third thing we do is survey our customers on an ongoing basis, and with major periodic checkpoints. We sample people who have called in with questions or claims. We check on how fast, how courteously, and how completely we answered them.

A periodic customer survey is also done by an outside firm. They will contact a sample of customer companies of various sizes who have different carriers and different kinds of benefits.

They will go through an analysis at various levels to get a handle on what the customer's expectations are and a ranking of how well we're meeting the expectations relative to how the other guys are doing. We do it again every 12–18 months to find out whether we are on the right track. We also have an ongoing set of basic audits and surveys that go out from our claims offices. They're done a little differently from office to office. They're developed for local information. We try to get a few common questions we can roll up on a national basis, but what is most helpful is the direct feedback that comes to the people who are actually processing the claims.

■ Mr. Jon d'Alessio, then Staff Vice President and Chief Information Officer of McKesson, said:

At the data center we track and do a fair amount of publicizing of the number of orders and the accuracy of how many get through the first time correctly. That has been very successful. One of the things we push and market to our external customers is the reliability of our whole system. We've been able to get some very nice service levels in terms of when we receive an order and whether customers receive it the next day. We have worked hard on that and are trying to eliminate all unneeded exchange points and all the classical things along that line. We post results weekly. We have been successful at it, and our system's reliability is being marketed by the drug company. At the data center, the guy who runs it pushes the slogan "Quality costs less." And for 5–6 years now he basically has a track record to show that it works, that we have improved our quality and cut our costs. If we don't have errors, we don't have to rework or fix things, and we have fewer people working on those activities.

Although most of our respondents reported some form of structured quality measurement system, few had tied the surveys directly to individual employees' or groups' performance ratings or compensation systems. Most still used some variant of the Hay point system or simple salary surveys to set wages, although a very few, like Visible Changes, had gone to very direct incentives for selected types of performance. This is a major area for further study and development in service-based companies. The frequent complaints about U.S. service quality, although not always deserved, are unlikely to go away until more firms develop systematic means of both measuring quality from the customer's viewpoint and locking these into company performance measurements and compensation systems.

CONCLUSIONS

One of the most complex problems in managing knowledge-based and service systems is measuring the output of such activities, particularly the quality dimension. Although many leading companies are measuring quality as perceived by customers, no company we interviewed had yet been able to convert those measures directly into financial payoff metrics. Barring this conversion, service companies are likely to continue to push cost-cutting investments over quality-enhancing ones—the same error that U.S. auto and consumer products companies made.

Many studies indicate that most service companies rely largely on their management's intuition about what customers want. And this intuition is often wrong. Utilizing customer-based engineering metrics and customer surveys for quality measurement is a long step beyond where these companies are today. By contrast, leading edge companies are generally using such techniques. A key to productivity improvement for virtually all companies will be blending these quality metrics with other productivity performance measurements into customer-based incentive systems for all employees. The next chapter will suggest how some companies are approaching this complex issue.

CHAPTER 11

Managing for Service Productivity

In recent years there has been a cacophony of articles deploring the lack of productivity improvement in services. On close inspection, one finds that problems in output definitions, data collection methodologies, and quality measurements account for a large portion of the slow growth in services productivity so often reported.[1] But the Bureau of Labor Statistics' productivity data, calculated under new methodologies, in fact show productivity in numerous service industries growing faster than that in some major manufacturing industries over long periods of time. And U.S. service productivity compares well to that of almost all other industrialized countries, including Japan. The final chapter will present these data and a summary of the macro economic issues surrounding service productivity.

While these data present some much-needed encouragement at the national level, improving service productivity at the enterprise level is still a central concern for most managers. Productivity is defined as the level of output an enterprise achieves per unit of input. In services, *inputs* can usually be measured with precisions comparable to those in manufacturing. Defining reasonable *output* measures is often a problem. In a few service industries, there are some readily quantifiable measures of output, for example, ton miles or passenger miles produced in transportation, packages handled in overnight delivery, kilowatt hours or cubic feet of gas delivered from utilities, tons of effluents processed by environmental enterprises, or telephone calls or packets transmitted by telecoms. But in many services, the qualitative nature of outputs makes precise numerical definitions difficult, if not impossible. For example, in what units does one dimension the output of accounting, legal, consulting, financial advisory, surgical, psychiatric, dental, software design, counseling, advertising, promotional, entertainment, fire, police, emergency, long-term care, or similar service enterprises?

Even in more measurable services, output figures have little relevance unless they are accompanied by meaningful quality measures. In banking, the value of loans or the number of loans handled is virtually useless without information about the quality of those loans. How many tons of waste a company handles means little without knowing the thoroughness, permanency, and risks of its disposal techniques. In comparing two health care institutions, the number and cost of procedures performed is not very informative unless one knows their difficulty and success rates. And even success rates must be qualified by the amount of discomfort or later care costs that patients must incur.

OUTPUT VERSUS QUALITY MEASUREMENTS

Although there are other problems, the most pervasive issues companies encounter in managing service productivity lie in (1) measuring service quality and (2) determining its economic value. This is true whether in comparing two services simultaneously or in comparing a service output at one time versus an output at a later date. Service quality is usually an intangible whose real value exists only in the mind of a customer. How much more value is it to a customer to receive a bank statement within forty-eight hours rather than a week later or to have twenty-four-hour access to an ATM? How much is a cleaner, neater, more professional letter or bit of copy worth? How much is it worth for a customer to have a shorter wait, a quicker credit clearance, or a smiling, more relaxed clerk in an automated checkout line? What impact on sales or profits do faster response times, more complete data, better analytical bases, or higher-powered computing capabilities generate in financial services?

Fortunately, at the firm level in services—as in manufacturing, where Feigenbaum, Deming, Crosby, and others have meticulously established the fact—quality, productivity, and low cost are intimately correlated. Especially important is the reliability dimension in perceived service quality. Buzzell and Gale's analysis of PIMS data graphically demonstrates the strong positive relationship between service quality and profitability (see Figure 11–1).

Earlier sections have indicated how important reliability is to perceived quality. Other studies also indicate that a high percentage of service costs are related to correcting errors within the service producer's system. Just giving customers what they have been promised, accurately, the first time through, cuts both the producer's and the customer's costs enormously. Like Xerox, in customer interviews Pillsbury Co. found that these factors were clearly the payoff elements for its huge retailer customers; Pillsbury's product quality and price were fine, and no longer as important to its customers (at the margin) as delivery and postdelivery services. In the late 1980s, when it focused on these customer satisfaction elements, its sales and profits immediately improved, as did its ratings for customer satisfaction. In the semi conductor industry, reliable delivery services offer the customer extensive premiums that cannot be matched by price. Late deliv-

FIGURE 11–1
Relative Quality Boosts Rates of Return

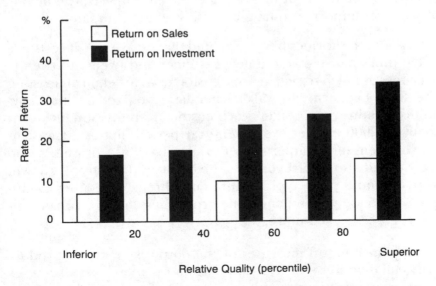

Source: *The PIMS Principles: Linking Strategy to Performance,* by Robert D. Buzzell and Bradley T. Gale. Copyright © 1987 by The Free Press, a Division of Macmillan, Inc. Reprinted with permission of the publisher.

ery of a low-cost semiconductor will shut down a customer's whole auto, computer, or appliance line, costing it more than the price of the entire semiconductor order. If quality control services fail, a faulty semiconductor memory—not discovered in time—could cause even more disastrous losses for a computer producer or its customer. Similar quality costs occur in other industries:

■ In the early 1980s a Merrill Lynch task force estimated that the firm's annual direct cost of errors in service handling was $210 million, including the cost of staffing those departments dedicated primarily to correcting service problems.[2] In its sample of financial service firms, TARP (Technical Assistance Research Programs, Inc.) found that poor customer service and ineffective communications caused up to one-third of the sample companies' total workload.[3]

RELIABILITY AND GOODWILL
AS INTELLECTUAL ASSETS

In addition to these internal costs, however, service failures will cost infinitely more in terms of customer goodwill. And the value of goodwill, in terms of marketing costs and impacts, can be one of the most important intangible assets of any company.

■ Various authorities have estimated that on average it costs five to ten times more to land a new customer and twenty to twenty-five times as much to regain a lost customer as to retain an existing one. Stew Leonard, Norwalk's legendary food retailer in a low-unit-cost industry, considers each customer an investment worth about $50,000 in sales over a ten-year period, not as a transient who happens into a supermarket to spend $100.[4] Customers who are satisfied also offer Leonard's the best free advertising known, word of mouth. They typically influence three to five others, helping to increase volume and scale economies, and to spread unit overhead costs even more.

Any meaningful measures of the output side of the productivity equation in services must focus on *customers'* cost structures and their perceptions of utility. Proper definition and measurement of productivity in service-based strategies, therefore, usually requires several important readjustments in thinking. First is a shift in focus from *individual product profitability* to the *total profit potential* in a customer's relationship with the service provider. Second is a reorientation from *short-term transaction* measures to *long-term customer outcomes* measures. Next is a shift from *internal engineering* or cost-performance criteria (and the measured "technical quality" of service production) to *external performance* measures based on customer perceptions. Finally, one needs to move *from structurally oriented* and *toward process-oriented* indicators of how well tasks are performed.[5] One cannot merely count outputs of widgets and compare them with their factor costs. One must essentially measure satisfaction in the customer's mind, where output value is really created. And like other knowledge processes, the proper metric for this will tend to reflect cumulative, rather than linear or transactional factors.

Service Based Productivity Focus Shifts

From	*Toward*
"Product"-based profitability	Total profitability from the customer relationship
Short-term "transactions"	Long-term customer outcomes
Internal cost-performance criteria	External customer perceptions
Measured "technical quality"	Perceived customer utility
Structurally oriented indicators	Process-oriented indicators

Unfortunately, most traditional management techniques and measures of productivity have been just the opposite: product-based, short-run, noncumulative, internally focused, technically dominated, and structurally oriented (i.e., around profit centers, sales volumes, transaction costs, inventory turnovers, facility utilization rates, and so on). Although useful as "secondary criteria" of productivity, traditional measures do not get at the core issue in service productivity: What *values do customers perceive* the firm as producing versus the *resources they must use* to obtain their desired outcomes? Unless the secondary criteria relate directly to this ratio, they are essentially irrelevant.

CHANGING TO CUSTOMER BASED METRICS

Macro measures, derived from internal data sources or even the perceptions of internal contact-point people, can be quite misleading. Zeithaml, Parasuraman, and Berry's studies note many glaring examples of (1) intuitive misunderstanding of customer preferences or (2) misplacing of priorities on internal measures of quality and productivity.

■ For example: privacy or confidentiality during transactions was considered a critical performance criterion in every banking or brokerage focus group in one study; but this was never even mentioned by the financial service company executives interviewed on the other side of the same study. The authors noted a strong tendency for executives to rationalize customer expectations or complaints (and even to discount measured outcomes) into problem definitions or solutions they could deal with. Executives rationalized customers' complaints about turnaround times into being acceptable because they merely represented "fluctuating demands," "lack of trained personnel available," "flukes" caused by vacation scheduling, or other measurable or explainable causes—not as quality–productivity issues to be faced directly and resolved on a long-term basis.[6]

■ Mr. Edward Hanway, President of CIGNA Worldwide, reported:

> In developing our quality metrics, we undertook a significant number of customer and broker interviews, some of which told us things we didn't know before—like people don't really care how fast we settle a claim, as long as there is somebody on the other end of the phone when they call up who can tell them exactly where their claim is in the process. That was much more important to them than how fast they got the check. Heretofore, we would have always said, "If we can improve from two weeks to four days, we will have done a great job." Unfortunately, the customer really didn't value that as highly as we thought they did.

Broadly based samples indicate that—unlike our respondents—most service companies sadly lack, or seriously underutilize, customer-oriented performance measures, trend tracking, and performance-reward systems based on objective customer evaluations of their service. As a result decision systems tend to reenforce the kind of short-term, cost-cutting, underinvesting, and customer alienating solutions that brought whole sectors of U.S. manufacturing to their knees.[7]

Developing a proper customer focus starts at the very top of the organization. Too often intense time pressures and intermediate organization levels screen executives from the bruising daily contacts with customers they need to drive internal systems aggressively toward satisfying customers. Top executives especially need direct, independent, customer-based perceptions and measures of (1) what outputs the company is actually creating for its customers and (2) the relative value the customer places on each element of that output. Some companies' top managements, like those of Wal-Mart, Marks & Spencer, or SAS go to great extremes to achieve this through personal contacts in the field. Others have found more specifically structured techniques to be helpful.

■ Procter & Gamble's senior VPs try to spend three hours a week answering the company's 800 number, responding directly to customer complaints and questions and reviewing the recorded patterns of these complaints.[8] British Airways in its turnaround set up customer complaint booths in Heathrow Airport for passengers to air grievances on videotapes so managers could receive their full impact.[9] And MCI's top two operating managers daily reviewed a "flight plan" summarizing the on-line measurements of quality from their network and weekly summaries of complaints (by category) from all parts of the system.[10]

Productivity in services means delivering at lowest cost the greatest value mix in what the customer wants and will pay for. Its proper measurement and management begin with systems linked directly to customer responses.

A CHANGE IN MINDSET

For most companies, the biggest challenge may not be to find adequate measurement techniques but to change the collective mindset from dealing with easy countables to managing and measuring what is important. In larger, more sophisticated service situations a complete array (or portfolio) of methodologies already exists for measuring a customer group's desired service mix. One's choice can vary from careful analyses of customer complaints or customer analogs in other industries; through use of customer panels, key client studies, in-depth psychological interviews, or transaction segmentation studies; to seamless interactive joint relationships with individual customers, or even continuous comprehensive consumer-expectation and service-rating studies like those Nielsen provides.[11] Each has its different costs and differing levels of benefits. Any good market research text will describe their merits.

The important point is not the use of a particular technique but getting managements: (1) to develop clear customer-based, multiple-dimensional measures of expectations, and (2) to use these to drive internal productivity toward a selected strategic vision through appropriately structured organizations, performance measures, and reward systems. Figure 11–2 diagrams this flow.

The diagram is conceptually simple, philosophically important, but seemingly difficult to implement. The most difficult problems are: (1) defining and measuring the factors customers consider most important and the trade-offs among them, (2) relating customer-based metrics to profitability and (3) finding measures that workers find realistic and acceptable for compensation purposes. Various respondents defined the current state of affairs.

■ Mr. Melvin Ollestad, Senior Vice President of CIGNA, said,

In some of the claims areas, we have variable compensation that is based on a piecework kind of process. Now, every four months peoples' salaries are reevaluated on their productivity in terms of "claim unit measures" that involve some customer sampling. We use "accurate claim units" processed by the individual. Now we're reevaluating all of that in light of our implementation of teams in these offices. We will have a new compensation system that will reward a combination of individual and team results, using quality and output metrics. At the higher levels, there are bonuses related to these, although we can't relate them directly

FIGURE 11–2
Customer Driven Productivity

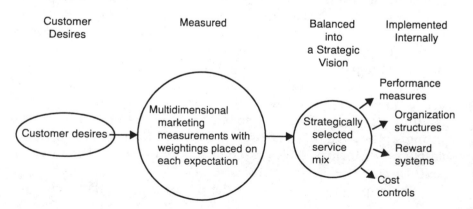

to profits. We are finding this approach quite successful in our environment, and we intend to have more variable compensation deeper in our ranks.

■ The Operations Vice President of one of the country's largest wholesalers noted,

We have introduced a number of projects that have a fair amount of external customer metrics in terms of turnaround time on processing, error rates, waiting times for response, and so on. Our external metrics aren't perfect, but we do have internal metrics as well. . . . Although we have not been able to convert these into dollar measures of value to the customer, we do have a strong focus on what we call persistency. That means the extent to which our customers stay. And most of our business units have metrics around whether their customers are staying or voting with their feet. But we have never been able to actually quantify benefits in dollar terms.

■ Mr. Richard Bere, President of Kroger, observed,

We have customer advisory committees in many of our stores, to ask what they like about the store, what they don't like about the store, what we need to change, and so forth. Out of that you may get some general ideas, but it is the store people who ultimately must say this is what we need and order the materials, displays, and systems.

In short, respondents in our survey of leading edge companies generally tried to obtain direct readings of customer responses to their offerings. They stated they found these useful in tailoring the overall strategy of the enterprise or outlet, but they rarely had tied them directly to personnel performance and reward systems. When that is done, major problems occur in keeping metrics and practices up with the constant dynamics of the marketplace.

CONTINUOUS EXPERIMENTATION AND UPDATING

Since customers' attitudes and preferences constantly change, measuring their desires and updating internal patterns to conform to them needs to be continuous. In small service settings, individual proprietors through constant personal contacts may be able personally to sense and change dynamically with customer preferences. With professional or institutional customers, one can often use "dedicated personnel" on customer premises to get continuous direct readings on their needs. By making these personnel the leaders of customer-directed cross-functional teams, one can achieve strong internal goal alignments if pay systems are dominated by customer-based metrics.

Mass services require more elaborate methods of updating. The most successful fast food and retail chains—in addition to using the usual opinion sampling, industry data, and stock sampling services available—daily aggregate and segment the detailed readouts from their EPOS systems. They also carefully utilize selected outlets to test a constant stream of new products and concepts in the most accurate possible way, by seeing how and whether real customers buy them. They measure experimental results and trends until patterns develop. As successful sales or concept responses are achieved, they broaden testing to better understand, fine-tune, and target markets before a system rollout. After full introduction, constant EPOS feedback and other detailed checks of customer preferences follow the product or concept through its life cycle and continuously reposition it, often using self-updating "applied intelligence" models.

Meanwhile the system starts all over again sampling new concepts to replace maturing successful ones. As in any other innovative system, what will actually work is largely unknown until the customer actually begins to buy—and changes continuously thereafter. Companies that lock in on a single customer buying pattern and delivery format, no matter how carefully conceived and implemented, soon find—as Fotomat did when consumers abandoned their strip malls—that their customers' buying patterns can change quickly and disastrously.

■ Wal-Mart's late Sam Walton defined the key as follows: "Be an agent for customers. Find out what they want, and sell it to them for the lowest possible price. Ninety-nine percent of the best ideas we ever had came from our customers and employees."[12] He knew that what would actually work was unpredictable. Observers described Walton's philosophy as: "Rely on the customer. Try lots of stuff. Adopt what works, and drop what doesn't."[13]

Service-driven strategies (1) let the *customer* determine what the right mix and balance of products, features, and presentation forms is; (2) try to understand, define, and measure that mix in depth; (3) keep up with it hourly or daily as necessary; (4) provide it as fast and inexpensively as possible; and (5) surround it with the degree of personalization appropriate to the strategy chosen. Then—within a clearly defined and finely tuned strategic niche—flexibility, interaction, responsiveness, and incremental change often become the strategy itself.

MASS-CUSTOMIZATION

In some businesses managers go even further, arguing that services are too intangible to be planned, measured, or standardized in any meaningful way. They maintain that true service is the process of customizing outputs to each individual customer's particular needs and style. They see maximizing value during that interface, and not cost reduction, as the real path to productivity. But even in highly customized services, like making bridal dresses or writing wills, many discrete elements can be standardized or routinized without customers being aware of anything counterproductive. Thousands of unique adaptations can spring off a few selected fabrics, colors, styles, laces, or beading varieties (for bridal gowns) or from a few dozen carefully screened phrases (in the law). A certain amount of standardization may even make the service appear more flexible and responsive, since it can be delivered more quickly, in greater variety, at lower cost, with fewer errors, and with greater attention to those unique details that really do make a difference. With care the entire process can be "mass-customized" to give the customer the maximum benefit of mass production economies and maximum customization.

This is the essential reason for concentrating on the "minimum replicable unit" of service production, suggested in an earlier chapter. The key to productivity in many services lies in driving knowledge about producing systems to this maximum depth of detail, standardizing as many replicable details as possible, and then getting employees to combine these "minimum replicable units" as flexibly as possible with customer inputs at the point of contact. Effective control of both cost and quality usually rests on the definition and automation of these repeatable units. One needs to know precisely the amount of time and other inputs required for each unit of maintenance work (ServiceMaster), food preparation (McDonald's), programming (AA&Co.), document search (law firms), telephone response (Fidelity), package pickup

(UPS), teller service (banking), and so on. These units are the keys to effective scheduling, work assignment, performance monitoring, inventory adjustment, customer service levels, and so on. When they are properly set, lowest cost, highest customer value, quickest response times, and maximum flexibility merge. The organization can achieve its greatest potential productivity levels, while minimizing the uncertainties and risks inherent in most fast-response customer interactions.[14]

SERVICE ACTIVITY MEASURES

At the service activity level, a number of other useful measures begin to emerge. *First*, one can apply value-added measures. How much is the product worth before and after the activity takes place? If one bought (or sold) it in the marketplace at both points, what would the incremental value be? How does this value-added compare with the activity's costs? *Second*, how does the cost of the service internally compare to purchasing the same service elsewhere? From other divisions internally? From specialists externally? This is a simple benchmarking exercise. *Finally*, one can compare the activity's costs and time consumption with how much they *should* have been. This means identifying the best possible *processes* for doing the job, then comparing one's own processes to this. This is the essence of the "best of breed" analyses. When attacked with vigor, each of these approaches can yield useful information about a service's productivity. Those few companies which have done so rigorously have found high payoffs.

■ Mr. Ollestad of CIGNA said,

> We can do extensive internal benchmarking. Because we have about twenty-eight offices now, we can rank the offices against each other. When there are teams within the office or unit, they can benchmark within the office as well. We have also done quite a bit of internal "best-in-breed" or "best process" types of benchmarking. At times it's gotten a bit on the weird side, because some groups got overly competitive. Positively used, there is a lot of power in it. If you can establish an environment where the people who are actually doing the benchmarking are the ones who are interested (that is, they want to do it versus being forced by someone else), it works a lot better. I was in Cincinnati recently and found one of the teams there doing a series of benchmarking projects. One particular team had taken on the

productivity of the claims process and how much time they were spending actually processing claims versus doing other things. They had kept careful track of their time—for each individual on the team—and were alarmed to find out that (1) they didn't spend as much time as they thought they should in actually processing claims and (2) certain members of the team did substantially better at certain things than others. They essentially had set themselves up to do internal person-by-person benchmarking for best results.

We've also done external benchmarking periodically. In the last one I participated in, about three years ago, we joined a group that had a consulting organization put together a report for us. We all sort of blindly dumped in a bunch of information they requested and got results back, not knowing which company was which. But you know who you are in the group. All these things let us calibrate the activity much better.

In a classic of service technology benchmarking, Mr. Richard Liebhaber, Chief Strategy and Technology Officer of MCI, said:

When we started in this business we wanted to get the most cost-effective technology. There were only three manufacturers of telephony equipment in the U.S. at that time (AT&T, IT&T, and GTE). None of the three would sell off-the-shelf technology to outsiders in the U.S., so we had to go offshore. There we could compare performance easily because we found a very competitive technology supplier business. They were digitizing, and they were doing things that weren't being done here because the U.S. had basically monopoly technology businesses. MCI was the first to install single mode fiber extensively, the first to install high-speed single mode fiber. We bought it from Fujitsu. There wasn't any commercially available in the United States. [This became the core of MCI's infrastructure.] In April 1992, we were the first major carrier to deploy Corning's "dispersion shifted" optical fiber which transmits signals almost twice as far as standard single mode fiber.

Looking at the price performance of the technology of computer systems and switches and looking at where the control of the function was, we said, "The hardware isn't where we want to focus." We want to control the software, because the software is how we can customize the technology. Secondly, we are not going to build based on telephone computers. We're going to build based on general purpose computers, because on a price-performance basis, they are nine to eleven times more efficient than telephone machinery. DEC makes more computers in a week than Northern Telecom manufactures in a year for telephone switching machinery. Since the price-performance of the technology is based on volume metrics and not just on function or capability, it would be crazy to build things around telephone rather than computer machinery. Since it is all digitized, what is the difference?

Now we do about 60 percent of our software development work internally. About 40 percent is done under contract, although we manage our contractors in detail. Our view is that the least important part of developing the software is actually *writing* the code. We do not do an RFP for a billing system. We do all the specification, process rating, operational procedures, and system testing inside our company. We contract out the actual writing of the code, the detailed testing of the code, or other things that we can parametrically box in. We design the system. We control the process and let others do what they do best.

RE-ENGINEERING FOR PRODUCTIVITY

Both within and among activity levels, companies have found very high payoffs from using standard industrial engineering approaches to re-engineer their service processes. Analytically, and with the cooperation of those who must perform the tasks, a team first maps the entire process. Next it defines the basic outputs desired from that process and determines appropriate metrics for each. Then the team systematically attempts to eliminate, combine, or simplify first whole systems, then subsystems, then tasks. Many have found process re-engineering, rather than automation, to be the key to obtaining enormous worker productivity gains—and to avoiding unnecessary equipment investments. As Paul Strassmann notes, the productivity problem in services is often more an issue of how managers choose to attack an issue than whether technologies or systems exist that could produce higher productivity levels.[15]

■ Mr. Raymond Caron, CIO, CIGNA companies, noted:

We have a large claims organization at CIGNA with a staff of about 7,000. They believed that the solution to improving their productivity was developing a more sophisticated technology system. After a year and a half of effort, the system was still three years away from delivery and would have cost over $50 million. At that point, we worked with claims management and started to reengineer the claims process. One of the things we found was that there was a whole series of changes that could be made that had nothing to do with technology. We eliminated unnecessary tasks, reorganized offices according to teams, in the process of shifting from traditional "control management" to a leadership type of management, and team leader management.

The metrics the office had used were generating the wrong results. They were interested in how much mail was handled per hour, instead of doing claims correctly to begin with. We changed the metrics. We changed the tasks. We changed the management structure. We changed the teams. We introduced a lot of training which we found had been weak. And we had some remarkable results, without a new technology system. If we had gone on and built that "galactic application" they requested, I think it would have made things worse for about a decade. So we pulled the plug on it and abandoned the idea of a "silver bullet" technology to solve a workflow problem.

. . . We now have two kinds of re-engineering at CIGNA. We have functional re-engineering and what we have termed strategic re-engineering. In a functional re-engineering setting, we work with a claims department, an underwriting department, or a marketing department, looking at the processes within the function.

The more powerful and more difficult approach is strategic re-engineering. Our company is functionally organized. The problem with that kind of organization is that we don't have an easy time taking a customer driven process and analyzing it across functional lines. The strategic re-engineering activity says we're going to look at a business from the customer's viewpoint, slice it across our very strong functions. It takes a lot of effort to do that because of organizational biases. But we find it has the potential to yield the most results. It clears things up very quickly in terms of what adds value, what does not add value, what gets in the way of meeting customer needs, and what the cost is of providing products and services. We try whenever possible to include in the effort customers, distributors and all of the organizations within the business that are involved with the value chain, as well as the suppliers.

MEASURES VERSUS GESTALT TECHNIQUES

Utilizing re-engineering and other well-known work measurement principles, one can easily manage productivity in certain service activities. Hard, numerical, engineering-based productivity measures directly related to customer desires can be used for repetitive physical service elements—mail sorting, warehousing, materials handling, fast food preparation, data center operations, financial transaction processing, baggage handling, package delivery, routine maintenance, and so on. Here, with properly aligned incentives, productivity can approach industrial norms. Repeatedly, our respondents said they could target cost reductions in these areas, re-engineer their processes, automate them when desirable, and achieve desired paybacks through either process changes or automation. Similarly, distribution companies can target and measure returns on the lowered inventory or space expenditures that accrue from just-in-time inventory management.

However, as one moves beyond these kinds of "production" savings, productivity measures become much more difficult. For example, few would deny that improved design, prototyping, supply coordination, materials planning, transportation, distribution, and market feedback technologies have made it possible to introduce new products faster and at lower costs than ever before. But it is almost impossible to place a dollar value on the improvements because competitors are also doing similar things. Paradoxically, in some fields with fast volume growth—like electronics devices—these service technologies have so changed capabilities that they have essentially destroyed the traditional methods of achieving and measuring productivity. Such strategies offer scant opportunities to exploit generic low-cost, production scale, or experience curve strategies. They have forced a new survival strategy: "Make it quickly while there is a market, because tomorrow it will be obsolete." Thinking about productivity in terms of how much unit production costs have dropped is not too helpful in these circumstances. The whole purpose of the strategy is to maintain price and margins by adding features. Unless one measures productivity in terms of functionalities produced per unit cost, as is done in computers, formal productivity measures have little meaning. Consequently some insurance and financial service companies have developed careful measures of the different complexities of various policy terms, claims, procedures, inquiry answering phenomena, etc., and use these as weightings in finely tuned metrics for individual productivity.

But it is in the more subjective intellectual areas of service production that productivity troubles truly abound, particularly in less repetitive office or knowledge worker situations. Word processing, spreadsheet, and desktop publishing systems clearly increase the quality, speed, and ease of document preparation. And faxes, WANS, and LANS can eliminate innumerable handling steps and save days in document movement. But these technologies have lowered transaction costs so much that in most companies the increased numbers of documents prepared, revised, and transmitted overwhelm unit cost savings. While admitting the quality and timing benefits that may result, none of the executives we have interviewed to date said that they could measure the increased value of outputs or quantify significant reductions in the workforce from such general office installations. The only exceptions were when technologies were installed for specific purposes—and processes were completely re-engineered—such as improving an order processing or transaction handling system.

THE GESTALT APPROACH: SIMULATING A MARKET

Some of the most difficult problems in managing service productivity occur when there are large numbers of possibilities internally for trading off quality or value-added (for the customer) against cost savings (for the company). When in these circumstances there are also numerous complications in directly measuring what the customer wants on the output side of the equation, managers often abandon the traditional "cost control system approach" of (1) determining precisely measurable goals in advance, (2) measuring actual performance in these terms, (3) comparing actual and target, and (4) taking action to correct the difference. Instead, they move to more of a "gestalt" basis— operating and evaluating the overall service unit as if it were an independent customer-driven business. When measurability problems, interaction complexities among producers and customers, or mix changes become sufficiently high, it may pay to drop the pseudo-accuracy of engineering metrics and create a simulated marketplace that includes all these subtleties in its interactions. But certain conditions must usually exist for success.

Gestalt approaches work best when all internal groups are free to buy the service internally or externally as they choose. Within the group itself, all performance measures need to be customer-oriented and the organization made as flat as possible, enabling each individual's performance to be measured as directly as possible in customer terms. The extent to which an individual contributes on projects, is specially sought out by customers, and is chosen by colleagues to be on project teams become critical *individual* performance measurements. All other measures focus on *unit or team* performance. Restrained only by proprietary considerations, each unit is free to sell its services internally or externally. Thus productivity is measured directly by how well and how often the unit serves its customers. This can work especially well for corporate or divisional staff activities. Layoffs and group profit incentives control staffing levels. All other measures focus on customer service criteria.

■ Mr. Herbert Hofmann, President and CEO of Loews Corp.'s Bulova Group, noted:

> This approach works very well as long as you severely constrain the head count of the service providing unit *and* have profit measures on their internal customers. Some of the most bloated overheads and misused MIS investments occur when you don't. You want both sides to have to allocate their limited resources. In MIS, for example, the limited resource is really qualified and business-oriented systems analysts who understand the client's problem well enough to give business-oriented, not sophisticated software, solutions.

Gestalt techniques all approach productivity development primarily as a motivational and enabling—not a measurement and control—process. For years, private consulting and professional groups, driven by external competition, have operated on this basis. This only moves a proven technique into an internal setting. The new organizational forms described in Chapters 4 and 5 all facilitate this approach by making performance more visible and customer-linked. Repeatedly, in interviews, we were told that in small, flat, network, cluster, or self-directed team structures, "performance measures will take care of themselves . . . you don't need them . . . the customer and the organization will handle all of that themselves."

■ An example from BellSouth will make the point vividly. Said Dennis K. Allen, Assistant Vice President, Employee Relations:

> We have about fifty self-managed teams operating in a customer-driven mode. A good example is our service technicians who have been equipped with a hand-held computer that (1) enables them to receive customer call data, (2) fills out maintenance reports, and (3) enters their reports and field data directly into a database. While handling a higher volume and much more complex set of problems, our number of service technicians has remained flat for the last five years.
>
> There have been both field coordination efficiencies and enormous goodwill created, because the field person no longer has to wait for instructions before moving to the next job. The field terminal has virtually eliminated the dispatcher's job title; those people were generally merged into higher-level analytical duties. [In many of our self-directed teams] we have gone from individual goal-setting and evaluations to collective team goal-setting and evaluations with much better results. How are people evaluated? Usually by members of the team and maybe by a resource person who is their coach. It's amazing how unimportant that becomes when people are focused on other things. Their own goals drive the appraisal.

COMBINING GESTALTS AND MEASURES

Despite the attractiveness of the pure market-gestalt approach for some service situations, most will benefit by combining it with the kinds of minimum replicable unit, best of breed, performance benchmarking, and customer-based metrics outlined above. In this approach, the whole activity set is still regarded as a marketable service to be sold as much as possible to internal and external customers on an arm's-length basis. Simultaneously, however, to avoid inefficiencies and "internal customer biases," the total activity and that of each of its elements are periodically checked (both on a process and a value/cost basis) against the best groups performing similar activities, both internally and externally. When it is possible, such benchmarking lets the corporation and the activity manager reach better strategic decisions as to whether to continue, consolidate, eliminate, or outsource the whole activity or any of its component parts. "Best in world" performance, rather than mere adequacy, becomes the productivity driver.

■ Mr. Randall Miller, partner of Deloitte & Touche, describes their process as follows:

> The first thing we do is an assessment plan: What are the issues the service unit needs to address? What are competitors doing? What are the new things going on that we should look at? This strategic assessment is a particularly valuable part of the process. The analysis usually gives a broad perspective on what's going on and provides some incentives to do a few new things people otherwise might not think about. We don't have 20 to 30 companies in the comparative study, usually 6 to 10 that are really focused on some key areas of interest. We try to quantify a number of things, including spending levels, head counts in different areas, how they are currently applying resources and technologies, how old different applications are, and what specific areas of functionality they might be working on.
>
> The benchmark company doesn't have to be a direct competitor, but someone who has similar characteristics and, ideally, is a leader technologically. We try to develop from this a kind of "bubble chart," which plots the effectiveness of each company's technology versus its level of investment, usually represented as a percentage of sales. Everyone on the plot is anonymous to the others, but of course knows which bubble is theirs. Companies participate because they know they'll be kept anonymous and they get the survey results themselves. This helps people to set realistic yet challenging targets for their own internal service functions. It is also a very effective tool to enhance general management's understanding of the potential role of technology in its business.

For a total approach to service productivity, many of the most successful companies in our survey combined all three mechanisms: (1) using minimum replicable unit measurements to guide and enhance all the repeatable elements of service performance, (2) developing process and output benchmarks for overall calibration and motivation of each activity in the system, and (3) establishing as many market-oriented structures and incentives as possible to encourage motivation and flexibility. For example:

■ One of the world's largest brokerage houses uses a variety of these techniques to manage its data centers. It uses an elaborate set of metrics established with customer inputs to measure the centers' cost and levels of service to customers. The centers subscribe to all the standard data center information sources for benchmarking data on unit costs of operations and periodically participate in special surveys of such costs. Customer performances against established criteria are summarized and published weekly and monthly. In addition, the centers have monthly meetings with customers and groups developing new applications to review these standards and performance against them. In some areas, the firm has formal written service level agreements. In others, the centers agree to broad service criteria with their customers, periodically review and calibrate these directly with the users, and then recalibrate both performance and criteria as necessary.

MEASURING AND MANAGING CAPITAL PRODUCTIVITY

A special problem exists in measuring and managing capital productivity—especially investments in information technology (IT). Service technologies (particularly IT) have been advancing so fast that it has often been impossible for a company to fully recover its investments in new technologies before it is necessary to make the next generation of investments. Simultaneously, the great output potentials of the technologies and the fact that functional capacity is added in large discrete units has generally assured the existence of significant system overcapacity. Since IT systems also have high fixed costs, this leads to dropping margins, because there are usually relatively low barriers to installing the technologies and high costs to established companies if they do not install. Problems in achieving productivity growth have been compounded by the fact that, in their early stages, new technologies also call for an extensive learning period, which delays anticipated payoffs at the very time competition is compressing margins. Perversely, the knowledge technologies used in service activities have, in addition, demanded somewhat higher-priced knowledge workers to replace less skilled clerical or blue-collar workers. All these factors—and some plain bad management—have often decimated measured returns on IT investments at both the firm and macro levels.

■ Mr. John Loewenberg, Chief Executive Officer, Aetna Information Technology of Aetna Life & Casualty, said:

We recently took a protracted view covering about a fifteen-year time period to see whether real productivity had improved when you looked at expense-to-revenue ratios. It's a beautiful graph that basically says productivity hasn't improved one iota. Yet you know you would never have been able to increase your handling of health care claims from 250,000 per week to 1.3 million a day without it. Everyone acknowledges this and the fact that the business is very profitable. But when you look at the relative ratios, you can't prove a productivity increase.

DOES TECHNOLOGY PAY OFF?
THE ALTERNATIVE COST APPROACH

Nevertheless, service companies have continued to invest heavily in new technologies, particularly IT. As explained by our respondents, the main reason is straightforward. None of the productivity metrics outsiders use take into account what the alternative costs would have been—what would have happened to individual companies—if they had *not* made their technology investments. In most cases, it is so obvious to managements that they could not operate today without their substantial infrastructure systems that they haven't even tried to evaluate them *post hoc*. This is true of almost all back office automation in financial services, EPOS systems in distribution, reservation systems in travel services, communications infrastructures in all companies, medical care automation, packet handling systems in communications, automatic flight control systems for aircraft, and so on.

■ Bob Elmore, Partner and Managing Director of Arthur Andersen's Business Systems Consulting Group, said:

It is often not necessary to take a detailed look at paybacks on many strategic investments. Strategic use of information should be dealing with a 100-to-1 return or at least 10-to-1, and the paybacks should be obvious. If the potentials are anything less, it probably isn't a strategic investment, and cost studies may be required to justify incremental benefits. For example, our electronic bulletin board was installed about four years ago, and there is no question among our practitioners that it gives us a competitive advantage and that it has made a large direct contribution to sales growth. We expect our line of business to triple in size in the next few years. We couldn't even think about being that large if we did not have electronic conferencing in place. That type of investment is like having a pencil. It's not something we need to bother doing an ROI calculation about. It's a necessity to leverage our intellectual capital across the entire division.

■ Roger Ballou, President of American Express's Travel Services Group (USA), noted the pragmatic problems of making detailed calculations of paybacks on infrastructure investments, even when one wishes to do so:

A good example of such an infrastructure investment would be our automated authorization system. To determine the benefit of that system, I'd have to recreate mathematically what would exist if we didn't have it and only had our old personal telephone authorization system. For that you'd have to guess how a twenty-year-old system would operate in today's world. That would be a highly theoretical exercise.

For those who doubt that the "survival argument" for infrastructure investments is valid, the fate of the midsize financial service firms, airlines, and hospitals that failed to develop adequate technology infrastructures is instructive. They disappeared as independent entities.

MANAGING TECHNOLOGY INVESTMENTS

However, the survival argument alone is not sufficient to justify the large sums major companies must invest in service technologies (particularly IT) today. Recognizing that productivity or return measures contain so many problems and uncertainties, how can one most sensibly approach investments in service technologies for increased productivity? Our survey of leading practitioners demonstrated a rather consistent pattern of breaking investments into several categories, using quantitative measures when they were appropriate and strategic judgments when they were not.

■ Mr. Thomas Sawyer, Manager of MIS Planning, of Dayton-Hudson's Department Store Division described that company's approach to IT projects as follows:

We divide our projects into three groupings. For each we build a business case, but that varies by type. First are a set of required projects for which there are not options; you have to meet a government regulation or a reporting requirement set by the financial community, for example. For these there is no financial or other justification system; you just execute them the best way you can. In many other cases we can estimate cost savings and ROI pretty accurately, just as we would for any other labor-saving investment. Then there are projects that affect strategic capabilities; these are the ones that are tough and really growing rapidly. They will change our overall position in the market-place. These we take out of the divisions' long-range plans, handle them separately, and look at their total corporate impact.

One example was a project that would use much more extensive UPC identification of merchandise, selling the merchandise through "signing" instead of putting it through our standard marking process. If we could do this over a number of items, it would be very profitable; but it would mean significant changes in the way we present price to our customer. If it worked, the overall cost could be spread over millions of units, and benefits would be huge; but if it didn't, we could lose sales on all those units. It was very difficult, if not impossible, to judge the exact effect this one program might have against the background of everything else that was going on in merchandising. Only the customer will ever really know how well it worked. The ultimate management judgments on this, therefore, had to be very subjective—and would be well nigh impossible to identify specifically on any income statements.

Many companies have implemented major technology pro-grams—like those illustrated above and throughout this book—which are rigorously evaluated using both numbers and intuition, and clearly do enhance productivity. In contrast to these, there have been some companies and industries in which rigorous evaluation has not been the norm. Giesler and Rubenstein, for example, found that 90 percent of the banks in their study had no rigorous system for preproject review and postproject audit of their IT investments. In many cases these companies had moved rapidly just to keep up, and had limited technical sophistication at the top.[16] In our studies, however, *among the more advanced users* of IT across a full spectrum of service industries, we found a wide variety of careful pre- and post-investment evaluation practices, along with a high degree of technical sophistication (although sometimes recently introduced) at the top. Most of these compa-nies tended to separate out different types of investments and system problems and—with good reasons—did detailed cost-benefit analyses on some items, not others. Most used a three- or four-level classification system, which included at least the following: cost-saving or new product investments, infrastructure or required investments, and strategic investments.

COST-REDUCING AND NEW PRODUCT INVESTMENTS

Cost-reducing or new product investments were handled in much the same fashion as in manufacturing industries. When asked how they evaluated their payoffs from service investments, most respondents quickly cited some major programs in which they had eliminated entire components of an operation or layers of hierarchy. All stated something like, "When we use technology to replace people in existing tasks, we can make all the standard calculations and expect them to be met if we automate our processes properly." Typical examples were the elimination of routine accounting tasks, a data center, back office tasks, steps in order processing, reports prepared, or communication steps in producing a particular (service or product) output. Executives also reported: "When we use technologies in support of a specific new product entry, we can predict and track IT payoffs as well as we can for any other technologies. When we use the technologies to ensure accuracy or consistency in service presentations, we can also foresee and measure operational—but not always financial—outcomes in a pretty predictable fashion."

The problem is that in most services, the first wave of such changes—what Ted Levitt called "the industrialization of services"—has pretty well passed through.[17] Technology has long since taken over many of the routines in handling fast foods, telephone calls, accounting records, securities transactions, banking and credit operations, secretarial work, hotel management, government record keeping, airline or railroad operations, inventory or distribution system management, and so on. Most managers we interviewed could easily illustrate that these early investments had been dramatically profitable in reducing unit costs. There will, of course, be more savings as these applications grow and defuse for many years.

■ But, as Herbert Hofmann, President and CEO of Bulova Group, Loews Corp., said:

> We generally are past the point of big production systems where you can cut X number of jobs, and the return on investment is

the labor saved. We know these investments paid off. We couldn't
be competitive without them. But we're at least a generation past
this and into decision-support type projects. It's often very difficult to put a dollar number on these projects. What is it worth to
make your advertising more effective, based on better information? We know that promotional dollars put into a certain geographical or demographic area will help you competitively. You
can quantify it. But how much is a crystal ball? It's impossible to
justify any [particular] quantification if anyone really wants to argue it in detail. What we do is make sure the user division can
specify a genuine benefit and understands the costs. We can't always put an ROI number on the benefit. But we can insist that
both the Division and MIS understand the benefit sought, and
that the Division ranks the investment in its strategic plans. By
constraining total MIS funds and personnel and by carefully
staffing MIS with people who have business acumen, we can get
a pretty good match between MIS investments and each business'
strategic needs. . . . Still, without having hard numbers on all of
them, I'd say there were very few projects that didn't pay back in
three years.

Even in areas like cost reduction and new product introduc-
tions, where results are more quantifiable, it is difficult to separate
out the contributions of IT versus other elements of investment
or operational activity. Like any other investment, IT is just a
portion of an enabling system. Like a milling machine or a
grinder, IT merely enables a company to produce a good or service. Actual production requires many other support, training,
organizational, systems, or even materials inputs. In principle,
one should therefore measure total system effects, then analyze
IT's contribution on a factor cost basis. But, as in other investments, the complications of doing so are such that no respondents
said they had used "multifactor productivity analysis" on a rigorous basis in evaluating IT investments, either before or after the
project's introduction. For similar reasons, they had performed
no overall evaluations of total returns on IT investments *per se*
across the company.

THE INFRASTRUCTURE LEVEL

A second wave of technology has made it possible for executives
to manage the much expanded scales and product scopes that

their earlier technologies allowed. It has also enabled companies to deal with the much higher levels of regulatory and financial reporting now required for all companies. Most managers tend to classify this second wave of investments as "infrastructure investments" necessary for competitive service levels or even survival. Although individual companies' definitions varied, most considered their core telephone, fiber optics, satellite interconnection, record keeping, and transaction processing systems necessary to carry on business to be in this category. What is defined as infrastructure will vary over time, as customers come to expect more basic facilities from their service providers. In evaluating these investments, standard (ROI or PV) financial evaluations were often inappropriate or useless.

■ Most of our respondents provided their own paraphrase of the following:

> We can't really put realistic numbers on these investments' returns, unless it is the cost of losing the whole business. We simply could not operate in the complexity of today's market without a competitive information technology infrastructure. It would be like trying to be in the carpentry business without a hammer. Once we decide what we want the infrastructure to do, of course, we use all the intelligence we can to buy the least-cost, most advanced, and most flexible systems for the purpose. Easy to say, difficult to do right. We keep searching, benchmarking, and adapting incrementally—trying to keep one step ahead in performance terms. But the benefits of these investments are spread over so many outputs that they are impossible to measure realistically.

Most respondents noted that they tried to justify each infrastructure project individually, but that it was often impossible to calculate specific ROIs.

■ For example, in the hotel business having simple intercom connections to housekeeping units allows coordination of room cleanup schedules, provision of special services like ironing boards or ice, pickup of room service trays, accommodation of customers who want a delayed check-out or early check-in, and so on. Putting specific dollar values on these individual benefits would require more subjective judgments than just deciding that "in that aggregate, the customer will be better served and some costs will be saved for a relatively low investment."

Similarly, few calculations are necessary to determine that a modern broker needs a PC, the right software, and the communication links to connect into Wall Street and research analysts' data banks. While the "first movers" of the technology may have to make some order-of-magnitude calculations to justify their infrastructure investments, everyone else is forced to follow the basic pattern, once established. It is at a later level—concerning which "bells, whistles, and further services" to add—that the real dilemmas in judging investments and payoffs occur.

OFFICE AUTOMATION: THE PRODUCTIVITY DILEMMA

This is particularly true once one enters the realm of automating office activities and interconnecting knowledge workers through data networks so they can be better informed. None of our respondents said they could justify their extensive office automation explicitly in dollar terms. They generally felt "a better job was being done," but no reliable metrics had been developed to say to what extent greater output and improved results justified their cost. Many CEOs and CFOs were skeptical on this point.

■ The Senior VP and Chief Technology Officer of one of the largest investment houses stated it this way:

> The premise is always that if information were instantly available, there would be a competitive edge to the firm based on [a particular] technology investment. Before you embark on a project, you cost it out and try to gauge the return. But sometimes you suddenly realize as you go forward that you are dramatically increasing the cost of the product or process by managing it in real time. . . . At first the user usually thinks: "my software maintenance, networking charges, and support charges will be less than if I do it in a data center in a comparable way."
>
> However, we're now beginning to discover that our operating units are having to build the same kind of industrial strength worthiness into their local bureaucracies that they took for granted in the data centers. These are new costs they hadn't anticipated, and they are very high. . . . In my thirty-three years in data processing, no one has yet showed me that decentralizing anything has a lower cost attached to it. . . . The biggest chal-

lenge over the next few years is how to implement the new workstation technology, sequencing its installation, finding the right applications, maintaining risk control, creating appropriate backups, and providing sufficient access to data and protection for intellectual property. I submit that any firm that does this properly, three years from now, may be gaining competitive advantage, but its cost structure might not be lower.

■ Mr. James Stewart, CFO of CIGNA Corp. said:

I don't particularly view the IT area as capital. I tend to view various projects in the context of our business strategies, what we intend to accomplish, how we compare with competition, and how we can best serve the customer. IT is only one of the means we use to execute strategy. For example: we are busily trying to get this company onto a standard PC platform where everyone has common equipment, common software, and where we will have a better ability to communicate with each other. To do that we need to spend $4 million or so reconfiguring the wiring in one building. What is the benefit of better communications in a particular location? . . . This is a nagging question. I can measure the costs to rewire that building easily. But what are the benefits? I think the PC technology has the potential for a significant enabling effect. But we can't quantify it. Sometimes all I see is increasing expenditures for what I occasionally perceive as toys in the business world, which may not add up to measurable output or profit results. Better discipline in the effectiveness of PC technology is one of our major challenges.

The major exception, where desktop automation genuinely seemed to boost productivity, was when it was installed to improve a specific function like product or process design, inventory control, distribution logistics, order processing, or customer service. If adequate process engineering was done (preinstallation) and new performance metrics and incentives were installed, the results of such process automation could be spectacular. For example:

■ CIGNA Corp. has automated its interfaces for its pension plan customers through both voice and database systems. Both customers outside the company and CIGNA's own contact people have PCs hooked into CIGNA's networks. In addition to allowing fewer people to handle many more customers and more complex customer issues, the PC-based system gives faster, more accurate, and more detailed responses than the old voice-based system could. Similarly, Time-Warner Corp.'s weekly magazine stories are produced on PCs, complete with graphics and layout. These go to the editor's PC, then to another PC that formats the magazine and scans the pictures for it, then directly to the printing floor for production, increasing the flexibility and productivity of these professional processes enormously. As Time's Chief Financial Officer, Joseph Ripp, said, "We can demonstrate very significant payoffs on that kind of office automation. In other areas, it's much harder to prove."

STRATEGIC TECHNOLOGY INVESTMENTS

It is at the strategic level, however, that most companies now anticipate their greatest payoffs from using new technologies. Yet this is where calculating returns is most difficult. Strategic investments are those that either (1) change the firm's basic position in a marketplace or (2) ensure its very viability. In either case, so much else is likely to be happening simultaneously that it is difficult to make precise calculations of the specific causes of changes or their impacts. Usually a major portion of potential benefits will accrue to customers and not to the investing company. The investor then has to ask how much of that gain it can capture through improved market share or customer loyalty. Even then, fast-moving competitors can often catch up fairly rapidly.

■ As the Chief Financial Officer of a major distribution group said:

> You can't get a sustainable lead through technology alone. What we have found is that customers tend to join you and stay with you not so much because of the measurables, but because they become comfortable with the fact that you are reliable, your prices are reasonable, you try to do a good job consistently for them, and your people operate in a mode they like. We can't put a number on these things. Sometimes you can strategically create a whole new business that you can measure. More often you have to use broad judgments of benefits versus cost. For every strategic project we insist that both elements—cost and benefit—be specified as much as possible. Then we rank all projects—albeit subjectively at times—across all divisions and invest on a

priority basis. Then we do a follow-up five months after installation and three years after installation to check with *customers*
how they perceive the changes and what benefits they may be
able to specify. Beyond that, we monitor our market share and
relative profitability like a hawk. It is the best we can do for now.
Not entirely satisfactory, but it keeps the emphasis on the right
things.

In general, at the strategic level, there were two distinct possibilities. If the investment created a totally new business, benefits
could usually be quantitatively measured and justified, subject to
the factor contribution limitations cited earlier. On the other
hand, if the investment merely improved the quality of outcomes,
few metrics—other than management judgment—seemed appropriate.

■ As the CEO of one company said:

We know for instance that ABC Company is a $20 million ac-
count, and if we set up EDI (electronic data interchange), we'll
have an inside track. The account's margin contribution might
be $10 million. We don't know whether we would have lost the
account without EDI, whether they would have cut back purchases without it, or whether the competition would or would
not have installed the EDI. Would ABC have kept us if we hadn't
put in EDI? We don't know the answer to these questions. But
we do understand that it's a $20 million account that wants bet-
ter service, and we're in the service business. Still, if it were a
$200,000 account the answer might be no, unless we could see
another hundred accounts out there. But even then it's not re-
ducible to specific dollar and probability terms.

■ The senior vice president of one of the major brokerage
houses said:

In this industry the capacity to do CMAs had a tremendous
payoff, but Merrill Lynch took a huge risk at the time. The big
question was how quickly could or would the competition duplicate the service and how would that affect Merrill Lynch's
position? With our data base one of the areas where we think we
can have a high payoff today is the potential to understand—
quickly, rapidly, and very carefully—the demographic mix of
our clients. We have multiple millions of clients and accounts,

and we're always looking for ways to satisfy current clients' requirements better and to identify new opportunities for those
clients and for new ones. Some of this would indicate moving to
large, relational database systems with significant degrees of
massive parallel processing. But we're not quite sure what new
opportunities this could eventually yield. . . .

In some areas of this business, there are very large swings in
profitability. You can make tons of money if you hit it right; or
if you're not set up properly, you can lose tons. That's dependent literally on your ability to do a very complex series of analytical processes faster than your competitors. All of you may be
attempting to close a certain type of transaction, and whoever
gets there first with the right information will get the business.
We're talking about small, individual, very highly customized
transactions done very quickly and nimbly for a large base of
people. You're adding up a lot of relatively small profits into
something that's very large. But what does having a subsecond
response time compared to a competitor's two-second response
time really mean? Can you truly measure the impact? And if we
did get ahead, how long would it take our competition to react?
Might we even erode profitability by providing certain information more rapidly to our client base? These are big question
marks, and there are no reliable numbers available for these
decisions.

INCREMENTAL VERSUS MEGA PROJECTS

In part because of such difficulties in evaluation, many of our
respondents said they had broken away from "galactic" or "mega
projects" crossing multiple divisions as being too long-term, too
difficult to implement, and uneconomic. Instead, they try to break
large-scale projects down into smaller, more discrete units, each
of which can be justified individually but can also be linked into a
larger-scale system. Otherwise such projects require so many different participants and the accommodation of so many divergent
long- and short-term requirements that they become unmanage-
able. Desired end results are often so compromised by political
bargaining during the project that they are never achieved. Timing goals are not met because of complexity. When combined with
the high front end expenditures for such projects, accurate
present value calculations would show such projects to be uneco-
nomical in both prospect and retrospect.

In using the incremental approach, broad system integration goals and interface standards are, of course, established at the outset. Then, by breaking programs down into definable smaller projects, each with a finite timing and payoff, both risks and total investments can be decreased. Initial feedback from early projects can be used to guide those later in the sequence. Project management is simplified and more focused. There is less political reaction to the project as successes ease concerns. And individual segments of the project—and the project as a whole—can often be developed in a single division, debugged there, and rolled out across other divisions with minimum disruptions.

"Mega projects," by contrast, generally turned out to be major sources of corporate inefficiency. First, they cost more in time and investment terms. Second, by the time they were implemented, competitors could also come out with similar systems—but often with much lower costs because of cheaper technologies developed during program delays. Third, because of delays, large programs also ran a much higher risk of not being matched to customer needs by the time they were implemented. Given all these factors, respondents said that even for strategic projects, they had moved to more discrete, incremental development patterns.

CONCLUSIONS

In services, even more than in manufacturing, quality and productivity are intimately interrelated. Perhaps the most critical issues in managing mass services lie in optimizing these two factors relative to customer needs. Unfortunately, both are extremely difficult to measure, whether at the corporate or the macro economic level. Conventional cost accounting and macro economic measurement techniques are of little use in this process.

However, if companies focus all their management systems and performance metrics intensively on customers' needs and perceptions—and if they break down their technology investments into proper categories and evaluate them as carefully as possible against internal and external benchmarks—they can come very close to optimizing both service quality and productivity. All this requires a major shift in management mindset as well as significant changes in internal control and reward systems. Chapters 10 and 11 have set forth a cohesive structure for attacking this problem, have defined many of the more important parameters involved, and have outlined the specific approaches many of the most successful service companies use to drive their productivity and quality programs.

The service quality–productivity issue is very complex. And each strategy and type of service may call for a quite different balance among specific techniques. Nevertheless, several consistent suggestions about how to improve service productivity and quality emerge from our interviews: (1) interactively design all systems with user (and if possible ultimate customer) inputs, (2) focus all metrics on customer needs, (3) model each service unit to be as much of a freestanding, customer-driven operation as possible, (4) re-engineer all service activities and processes before automating them, (5) benchmark all activities wherever possible against internal "best performers" and external best-in-world processes or capabilities, (6) manage all repeatable elements at the smallest replicable level, (7) design organizations specifically adapted to meet the dominant strategic concepts the units or their divisions need to stress, (8) plan for high levels of training, coaching, and follow-up (these factors are at least as important to success as hardware and computer software investments), (9) break major changes down into a series of finite pieces, each of which can show progress and payoffs, and (10) redesign all performance measurement, incentive, and reward systems—using customer-based metrics—to support the intended structures and goals of any new organizations created.

As basic as these may seem, it is surprising how many companies fail to manage service productivity and quality systems thoroughly on all accounts. Yet these have been (and will continue to be) the real sources of payoffs from service-based strategies. To develop this structure most effectively requires extremely careful management of the enterprise's value system, technology system, and the supporting organizational, control, and reward systems that implement strategy. Easier said than done. But these are the keys to service management and the management of the new organization forms described earlier. These two chapters have set forth some initial approaches to these crucial problems. Chapter 12 will amplify these, extend them to managing outside entities, and suggest how careful managers make the transition to the more knowledge-based, disaggregated structures now best described as "intelligent enterprises."

CHAPTER 12
Managing the "Intelligent Enterprise"

All the trends, new capabilities, and radical organization forms analyzed in earlier chapters are converging to create a new enterprise, best described as: a highly disaggregated, knowledge and service based enterprise concentrated around a core of set knowledge or service skills. This is what we refer to more succinctly as the "intelligent enterprise," a firm that primarily manages and coordinates information and intellect to meet customer needs.

Instead of being vertically integrated and focused around "products," these companies strategically excel in a few core knowledge-based service activities critical to their customers. Internally they surround these with whatever other activities are necessary to defend that core. Then they use advanced information, management, and intelligent systems to coordinate the many other diverse—and often physically dispersed—centers of excellence needed to fulfill selected customer needs. A number of these centers tend to be outside suppliers and partners. The combination of effects is leading to a redefinition of the very nature of corporations and their management functions.

Earlier chapters have discussed many of the most critical organizational, structural, and economic aspects of this phenomenon. But there are some remaining management issues. The most important are:

- What happens to the structure and skills of top management in these new knowledge-based service organizations? What are the consequences of de-layering and disaggregation for middle managers?

- How does one manage more extensive outsourcing for greatest efficiency, effectiveness, and safety? What special approaches are needed for strategic partnerships?
- How can a management most effectively make the transition from more traditional and centralized organizational forms to these more disaggregated knowledge-based structures?
- What are the most likely effects of knowledge and service-based strategies on the nation's competitiveness, employment patterns, and future growth potentials? How can a company best position itself to take advantage of a service-based future?

Perhaps the most striking impacts of knowledge and service-based strategies and of "intelligent enterprises" are the way they (1) simplify and flatten the internal organization, (2) enhance both the company's productivity and its responsiveness to customers, and (3) decrease investments and increase strategic flexibility. These are rewarding strategic goals toward which management efforts can usually be directed in any enterprise. How can these new knowledge and service-based entities be brought about? And what are the specific impacts on management likely to be? Many practical examples and guidelines now exist.

THINNER, HIGHER-QUALITY MANAGEMENT STRUCTURES

As has been noted, companies have long attempted to decentralize and outsource selected activities. It is not the fact, but the diversity, nature, scale, effectiveness, and worldwide scope of these practices that have changed. To date no respondent has said that flattening organizations or disaggregation was the primary target of its service technology investments. Yet such investments and a much enhanced capacity to manage outsourcing are the principal enablers of the changes we are observing. What are the main internal effects and implications?

First, top management, headquarters, and internal overhead groups can be much smaller. Headquarters in multibillion dollar firms are shrinking toward a few dozen to a hundred or so people.

■ Apple and Compaq, with two of the flattest organizations in the computer industry—and significant outsourcing strategies—

led the other ten of the top twelve computer companies in 1991 by factors of 2 or 3 to 1 in terms of revenue per employee ($451,000 for Apple and $317,000 for Compaq versus the $148,000 average of the next ten companies).[1] SCI with $1.2 billion in sales had only 130 managers for its 7,000 employees. IBM, as it began to disaggregate, found a way to move 20,000 people from its staff to line (mostly sales) operations in 1989–90,[2] and more later. Philips dropped its staff activities from 30 percent of personnel costs to 13 percent between 1986 and 1988. Nonintegrated Nucor, the seventh-largest American steel company, operating with an extremely flat organization, recently reported only seventeen people in its corporate office, while $7 billion Burlington Industries counted seventy-seven, and giant ASEA Brown Bovari had 150.[3]

In these new structures the relatively few who remain at top levels tend to need different skills from those that led to success in the past. At the very top, creating and driving a consistent vision of the company's or group's purpose is the primary skill that provides the glue for all its highly disaggregated units. Second is the capacity to create the trust, sense of shared values, and consistent viewpoint that stimulates people in dispersed activities and locations to self-activate around the vision. The old stereotype—the self-centered, hard-nosed, political climbing executive—doesn't fit these roles well. Leadership and coordination, rather than order-giving, seem to predominate, while functional skills and training become more valuable than functional specialization.

To support these needs, companies operating in more disaggregated modes carefully rotate executives through various divisions and functions, as well as placing them on multifunctional teams to solve specific problems. Many use extensive MBO systems everywhere, as Intel and HP do. They often develop elaborate software systems (1) to track employees as they crisscross the organization and (2) to record and update the goals and performance measures these people have agreed to. For example:

■ Apple's new Spider System will combine a PC network and video conferencing with much more detailed databases to monitor each person's skills, availability, and current task loads. With these, project managers can engage in remote, but direct, interviews with individuals when selecting or coordinating teams. Cypress Semiconductor has a computer system that records each employee's current MBO goals and commitments, so top management can monitor current progress, sense potential imbalances, and offer help when necessary.[4] New multimedia workstation technologies will further support this kind of disaggregated, self-directed organization of tasks.

HEIGHTENED MANAGERIAL EXPERTISE

Far from becoming devoid of expertise, the top level perhaps needs even more intellectual capacity to manage such systems. Without a supporting bureaucracy of specialists, how can this be maintained? For years, many of the most effective staff heads—and many CEOs—have operated with "only a desk and a secretary" and have disdained managing bureaucracies. By actively networking with the best outside experts, they obtain more stimulation and insights than any insider group could possibly offer, unless that group is really the core competency of the organization. In other situations:

■ Top planners profitably network with the very best external economists, futurists, sociologists, analysts, and strategists, whom they never could afford to engage full time. To break out of the entrapments of bureaucracy, U.S. and Japanese auto companies are beginning to use a network of small advanced design groups in California to configure their most experimental models. Many of the world's most productive research units long ago found that a few talented "gatekeepers"—exchanging information with dozens of outside sources—generate a huge percentage of their implemented ideas.[5]

Similarly, under proper circumstances skilled corporate legal, personnel, accounting, finance, advertising, or public relations heads can significantly leverage their expertise externally and destroy bureaucracies internally by extensive networking and selective outsourcing. When this is done, the remaining few top staff people must be—and can continue to be—more skilled than ever before. By learning from and coordinating independent outsiders, they can stay at the top of their professions, continuously interacting with the very best talent in the world, not just the best in the next office.

MIDDLE MANAGEMENT IMPACTS

We have focused on top managers first. But virtually all respondents who have engaged in managing these new disaggregated organizations—and their concomitant outside coalitions—noted that problems typically lie not at the top or the bottom of the organization, but in middle management. Just as Gorbachev could change the top level of the USSR and establish grassroots support for change quickly—but not move the middle layers of his bureaucracy—Western midlevel managers resist radical changes endlessly. Jan Carlzon found it easy to change the top and motivate point people at SAS, but devilishly difficult to move the huge midlevel bureaucracies that past practices had built up. Few middle-managers want to change from the style and skills they have so painstakingly learned. Their old predictable progress ladder is suddenly gone. And they wonder: How can one go up, when the organization is flat and there is no up?

But those questions are easy to answer, if middle managers are willing to act in ways that genuinely increase their value. How staff networking can increase value without bureaucracies has just been outlined. Similarly, line managers, by outsourcing parts, subassemblies, or services that were traditionally produced internally, can also become much more, rather than less, valuable (as Ford's Team Taurus became) if they are willing to interact with and learn from best-in-world suppliers and other functional groups on an extended basis. The new techniques they learn can make them more proficient line managers, better able to evaluate—and help—both internal and external producers who are not performing up to standard.

Internal operations people, teamed not just with departmental colleagues skilled only in doing things the old way, find that other functional operating people and outside executives are more likely than internal colleagues to ask the basic question: "Why in the heck are you doing it that way, not this?" While many companies and middle managers worry that they will lose their skills and value-adding potentials if they outsource and participate on teams with "less knowledgeable people," perhaps they should worry more about what will happen to their capabilities if they don't! Still, most have to be coaxed, cajoled, or threatened into the new mode.

Because midlevel transitions are so difficult and career-threatening, most top managers find they have to proactively manage change in an incremental mode. The first step is to teach present and future middle managers cross-functional skills as naturally and painlessly as possible, by putting them on integrated teams. Simultaneously, successful change managers install special rewards for those undertaking formal training in new skill areas. Next they make successful lateral moves highly visible and create new "skills" or "team-oriented" titles to replace hierarchical ones. "Apprentice, junior, intermediate, senior, or master" technicians, engineers, scientists, accountants, or secretaries provide the usual functional or discipline titles. To these one can add "specialist, associate, deputy, team leader, or chief" as team titles.

By mixing these together, executives can create endless possible psychological potentials for apparent promotions. Special customer-driven team, task, and divisional awards can supplement individual wage levels and other awards, and so on. Such problems are soluble, once the company's top management commits to a more flexible format. In fact, as American Express and Bell South found out, once such formats are proved experimentally, many volunteer to come on board and actively begin to force top managements to make needed changes.

"IF I'M NOT IN CONTROL, IT'S OUT OF CONTROL"

The most interesting challenges appear in getting middle managers to reconceptualize their jobs. The old managerial concept of "if I'm not in control, it's out of control" has to give way to genuine delegation and rewards for "coaching" and "coordination." But middle managers tend to give up power reluctantly. Some companies, like Becton-Dickinson, found they simply had to overload the existing organization until middle managers were forced to delegate. Others found that they had to automate a few complete operating departments out of existence before middle managers would willingly redeploy. Others have broken program goals down into targets for so many task teams that there is no option for middle managers but to be flexible and cooperate. Most try to inculcate new behavior experimentally on a few tasks, then promote, make heroes and coaches of those who succeed, and give others time to readjust. Genuine roadblockers are, of course, eventually removed.

Fortunately, however, when goals are clear, customer-oriented, measured, and rewarded, both the psychic and material rewards of the cooperation quickly become apparent. As Xerox CEO, Paul Allaire, says, "You can't get people to focus just on 'the bottom line.' You have to give them an objective like 'satisfy the customer' that everyone can relate to [and then measure results in customer terms]. It's the only way to break down barriers and get people from different functions working together."[6] The kinds of "gestalt," group-based, customer-oriented productivity and quality systems suggested in the last two chapters—supported by micro measures of repeated performance where possible—provide the infrastructure for this approach.

But middle managers also need new skills and attitudes to deal effectively with much more complex outside relationships. Cross-functional teams generally find they can accomplish their tasks better if they include members from supplier or customer groups to help them sense or solve new needs. Virtually all of the respondents in our survey of leading IT companies said they included *internal users* in their system designs. Over half said they also included *outside customers* when the project dealt directly with customer—not simply accounting, personnel, or other strictly internal—matters. One astute observer, Tom Peters, makes the point with his own colorful prescription:

- Want a 50 percent reduction in product development time? Put the engineers, designers, manufacturers, marketing, and finance people together in one team space.
- Want a 60 percent reduction? Move that space two miles from headquarters, renting an old, unused restaurant.
- Want a 70 percent reduction? Make sure that the old warehouse or restaurant you rent is next door to a pub, to induce after-work, casual interchange.
- Want about an 80 percent reduction? Put full-time customer and vendor people on the team in the isolated location.[7]

The aggregate of such influences is what GE's CEO, Jack Welch, refers to as the "boundaryless organization," with expanded team-oriented behavior both internally and externally to embrace suppliers, customers, and outside partnerships. The goal is not only faster but higher-quality results, much better matched to customers' true needs.

MANAGING OUTSOURCING—PARTNERSHIPS

How well do such systems really work when they include outsiders? Outsourcing of a complete or partial activity often creates great opportunities, but these may also present new types of risks, as outlined earlier. Risks may be further amplified if strategic alliances are used. How do successful managements deal with the risks and dilemmas of more extensive outsourcing and partnering?

Most large companies have already developed very sophisticated techniques for handling traditional outsourcing of parts, subassemblies, supplies, equipment, construction, or standard services. The main managerial adjustments required are those needed to cope with the increased scale, diversity, and service-oriented nature of these activities. These center on (1) a much more professional and highly trained purchasing and contract management cadre (as compared with the low-rated purchasing groups of the past) and (2) a greatly enhanced logistics-information system (to track and evaluate vendors, coordinate transportation activities, and manage financial and materials movements throughout the process and into customers' hands). There is a full MRP and EDI literature on the manufacturing aspects of the latter.

Now similar concepts are rapidly being extended to the management of knowledge and service based activities. For example, a number of companies are establishing direct computer connections between their service suppliers and the top managers controlling that function, as Apple has done with various of its consulting and PR groups. To manage these functions effectively, contracting and logistics functions need to be elevated to corporate strategic levels, as does the development of the knowledge-based systems that can capture and analyze detailed data about the company's own internal processes and those of vendors. Although some companies' systems handle a few elements of knowledge capture about supplier systems and processes today, they tend to be narrowly focused, slow, and expensive. More efficient systems for knowledge-based management are in design and early implementation stages. For example:

■ A consortium headed by DEC, Ford, Texas Instruments, U.S. West, Carnegie Group, and AlCorp is developing a next generation software tool, allowing the capture and management of many different aspects of knowledge as a corporate asset. The system, called IMKA for Initiative for Managing Knowledge Assets, is to store, access, represent, and transfer information on selected critical applications, like vendor capabilities, on an enterprisewide basis. Built around the proven knowledge-based systems of DEC and TI, IMKA uses many of the features found in object-oriented programs that allow the collection and comparison of knowledge from a variety of different end nodes—inside and outside the company.

Based on ROCK (Representation of Corporate Knowledge) software, IMKA is being designed to handle hundreds of thousands to millions of representations. A first application at Ford is to lay out and track the electronics architecture in a car. IMKA can maintain the design rules of each vendor and component supplier and check these against the design parameters of each part and subassembly to make sure systems are properly coordinated and design specs can be met by the various plants making a particular set of circuits. Each plant, all over the world, has different design rules. IMKA can check each subsystem's circuit performance, manufacturing, design, interconnection, weight, cost, or power requirement parameters, among others, for 100,000 objects against the capabilities of all possible supplier plants in milliseconds. In time, the system should also capture process variations, fallout rates, and other production dynamics to ensure that parts are produced in optimum locations at lowest cost and to spec. Although elements of these capacities exist in many other systems today, IMKA will facilitate a much wider range of data capture and much faster, more flexible analytical capabilities. In theory, it can capture and manipulate data about any set of knowledge-based "objects" one wishes to track.

PARTNERSHIPS AND ALLIANCES

Such systems will support much more extensive and controlled outsourcing in knowledge-based and service areas. The most complex and interesting new relationships, however, occur when outsourcing extends beyond mere coordinated purchasing into the many new forms of partnerships, strategic alliances, and joint ventures that companies use to leverage their own core competencies. Again, there is a lively literature[8] detailing the problems and approaches specific companies have confronted in developing partnering relationships. It is not possible to summarize or duplicate those endeavors here. But it is worthwhile to emphasize two important points that experience and the literature clearly demonstrate. (1) Partnerships, when properly developed, can be very productive and financially lucrative. (2) Such partnerships are not easy to manage properly; yet when they are, they can provide exceptional leverage for a company's capital and intellectual resources. Dow-Corning, Fuji-Xerox, and Toyota-GM's NUMMI provide a few, among many, cases in point.

Many of the most successful partnerships involve a "dominant" partner or evolve into separate jointly owned companies over time. Many mutate into forms unexpected when they were begun, and about 70 percent do not last more than five years. Nevertheless, recognizing they cannot be "best in world" in all the areas related to their businesses, more and more companies are attempting to leverage their core competencies by linking with others who have complementary expertise. Partners need not be large, nor do sizable partners always force majority or 50–50 ownership onto their lesser brethren. For example:

■ IBM's Business Partner Program was put in place to provide a common umbrella under which to coordinate more than 1,500 independent downstream entities supporting IBM's products. It has Authorized Applications Specialist, Cooperative Software Supplier, and Authorized Remarketer programs to support and utilize companies who have specific technology or expertise of significant interest to IBM. Partnering companies include Index Technology, Bachman Information, American Management Systems, On Line Software, Easel Corp., OpenConnect Systems, Barrister Systems, MSA, and Knowledgeware, among others. By providing financial and market information support to these companies, IBM got involved in areas it considered strategic to its own future, helped ensure the success of the new marketplaces it wanted to develop, and increased its own potential hardware and support-service sales to these sectors. The partners received needed capital, increased credibility, and some co-development, joint marketing, and technological consulting support. In some cases they received preferred vendor and guaranteed purchase agreements. Yet IBM consciously tried to avoid interference in their internal management, looking to the Business Partners to be fast, responsive, and generally independent vehicles for reaching emerging or specialized markets.

Other very large—as well as very small— companies are finding that they must form partnerships to access the expertise and resources to be competitive in the future. A few large-scale examples will make the point:

■ Hitachi, Sony, and Motorola have joined forces to develop new multimedia work stations and home entertainment systems capable of combining interactive or passive voice, data, computer, communications, video, text, graphics, CD ROM, and teleconferencing capabilities. This will doubtless lead to other competitive consortia to exploit this next startling generation of information and entertainment technologies. In a series of related moves, Sony has entered alliances with Microsoft to develop software for its Bookman CD-ROM-XA player (6″ × 7″ × 2″ in size) that will display on a screen a new kind of digital-media electronic bookreader in very compact form. Microsoft, the world's largest supplier of software for personal computers, owns part of a book publisher and is expanding its efforts to create software titles for education and entertainment.

■ On an even larger scale, telecommunications companies are finding that they cannot provide the global support service their multinational customers demand without entering partnership arrangements. Pacific Telesis and Mannesmann AG will build and operate a digital cellular system in competition with Germany's Deutsche Bundespost. BellSouth, Motorola, and two Argentinian companies combined to build the first privately owned cellular network in South America. Along with France Telecom and Grupo Corso (a Mexican diversified company), Southwestern Bell joined Mexico's Telmex in a $12 billion venture to increase that country's number of telephone lines by 12 percent annually. Grupo Corso will manage administration, labor, and regulatory matters, and Southwestern Bell will maintain lines and develop a supporting cellular system.

A number of major companies, including National Car Rental, Kodak, Cummins Engine, Matson Navigation, and Enron, have decided to outsource their data processing systems. Since these arrangements cannot easily be reversed, they amount to a major partnership. Companies that have carefully benchmarked such operations find they not only save operating costs but can redirect the capital they were investing in their internal systems into other activities closer to their core competencies.

All of the above have the characteristics of genuine long-term alliances linking one company's core competencies with different ones from another company. Unfortunately, as Hout and others have pointed out, many West European and American companies have used alliances to solve short-term problems, particularly finance. The usual result is that the foreign "partner" often becomes the owner and takes over the technology or core competency the Western company once had. A major proposed alliance illustrates this threat clearly.

■ Cash-strapped McDonnell Douglas in late 1991 announced negotiations for an alliance with Taiwan Aerospace and other Southeast Asian companies to develop an MD-12 long-range jumbo jet to compete with Boeing's 747-400. The main contribution of the Asian consortium partners would be a big piece of the $4 billion investment needed to develop the MD-12 and the deep pockets of their host countries as co-sponsors and potential customers. If the deal comes off, the transfer of technology is likely to be permanent, while the capital transfer will be repaid in time.

KEY FACTORS FOR PARTNERING SUCCESS

Despite the threats they pose, such large international partnering arrangements are likely to be increasingly common in high-tech areas—as they have been for years in large-scale natural resources, real estate, architectural, major construction, and international finance projects. We have studied a number of alliances comprising major service activities like research and development, product or process design, software development, data processing, strategic transportation, or distribution relationships. Although the particulars varied among different partners and individual programs, some useful guidelines did emerge. Since this topic could take volumes in itself—yet is central to managing disaggregated knowledge-based companies—we shall simply present some useful highlights of issues and management approaches as they relate to the main arguments here.

Reduced transportation costs. Many references suggest that the big problem with partnering arrangements is increased transaction costs. We found that partnering relations are generally needed for just the opposite reason; the timing, costs, or complications of either internal production or straightforward purchasing are too great. In short, *if partnerships are well designed, they should reduce transaction costs,* and this should be a major focal point in arrangements. A careful analysis and listing of costs to be avoided by the partnership will create a proper focus, especially if used later as a control tool and reminder. With this in mind, many companies go through a several-stage process analyzing the following questions in sequence:

1. Should we produce the good or service internally? If we do, are we willing to make the backup investments necessary to be "best in world" at it? Is it critical to defending our core competency? If not,
2. Can we license technology or buy know-how that will let us be best in world on a continuing basis? If not,
3. Can we buy the item as an off-the-shelf product or service from a best-in-world supplier? Is this a viable long-term option as volume and complexity grow? If not,
4. Can we do a joint development project with a knowledgeable supplier that gives us the desired capability to be best in world at this activity? If not,
5. Can we enter a long-term development and purchase agreement that gives us a secure source of supply and a proprietary interest in knowledge or other property of vital interest to the supplier? If not,
6. Can we acquire a best-in-world supplier to advantage? If not,
7. Can we set up a joint venture or partnership that avoids the shortcomings we see in each of the above? If so, list the goals sought and the transaction costs to be avoided. Set up specific program controls to realize desired benefits.

For partnering relationships to be as "seamless" as possible— i.e., to minimize transaction costs—requires much proactive management. Most participants in alliances agree on the three things that will reduce these costs most: (1) an overriding goal congruence, (2) strong mutual trust, and (3) an integrated information system that allows continuous real-time monitoring of all key variables. Without these, most partnerships prove disastrous. These and several other critical parameters are developed briefly below.

Goal congruence and strategic compatibility. Humans work together best when they share the same goals. At the program level in most ventures, this should not be too hard to verify. Preprogram analyses can investigate and document in detail potential areas of joint gain and potential conflict. Implementation plans can build defined mutual gains into all incentive structures. Program policies can set clear limits for each partner where conflicts are likely to occur, and mechanisms can be established to resolve anticipated conflicts. Unfortunately, such analyses must go well beyond the program level. Major conflicts tend to occur over time when one of the parents begins to see the project as vital to its achieving an unanticipated or newly desired future posture, or even as affecting its viability in its industry. Often we saw individual divisions of two companies effectively collaborating until one parent company—or another division of one company—decided the project matched or opened a new strategic position it wished to pursue. Prepartnering analyses, therefore, needed to investigate potential goal conflicts all the way through interdivisional to corporate strategic levels. Some companies have Corporate Alliance Coordinators for this purpose. To make sure things work out equally in any partnering arrangement, analysts need to pay at least as much attention to how the intangibles of strategy, culture, style, and potential commitment will affect the partnership as they do to the technologies, output specifications, and financials involved. Unfortunately most don't.

Mutual trust. The critical element such intangibles make possible—mutual trust—is much ballyhooed yet often slighted in planning and implementation. Trust usually takes time, personalization, and consistency, not features provided by companies with rapidly rotating executives, short-term-oriented policies, deal-oriented analysts, and highly diverse divisional cultures. Some of the most enduring partnerships start small and grow very slowly around mutual interests and compatible cultures. The surprising thing in our studies was how many of these continued with no formal documents, other than on specific price-quantity issues and some broad philosophical statements of mutual interest. In successful ventures, trust was consciously nurtured through three rules: reliability, cooperativeness, and openness. "We always deliver what we say," was rule #1. Rule #2 was the attitude: "We can work it out." Rules 1 and 2 had to be carefully reinforced through responsive personal interactions at the three levels specified in the next paragraph. Rule #3 was to provide enough information so the partner could always check on the status of the program and rely on the data received. Without trust engendered by these mechanisms, the smallest misunderstandings, which always occur, can quickly become large issues rather than a pattern of small successes that help reinforce trust itself.

Three-level connections. Repeatedly we found that effective partnerships and alliances depended upon supportive interactions at three levels: (1) operating people who were thoroughly competent and expected to share the information necessary to get the job done, (2) dedicated project heads from both parties whose careers depended on success, and who were selected for both their technical and their cooperative skills, and (3) very top-level (Presidential or CEO) supporters on both sides who worked well together and had sufficient power to break any priority bottlenecks that might develop. If any one of these was missing, troubles were sure to develop.

Protected core competencies. For each party the logical reason for an alliance is to obtain some essential competencies that it lacks or cannot build in a reasonable time-cost frame. For an alliance to endure, each party must continue to dominate its own core competency to such an extent that the other party cannot effectively bypass it to the marketplace. If in the process of achieving the program's goals, either party will have to surrender key elements of its special competencies to the other, that party is likely to be eliminated over time. This, unfortunately, has happened repeatedly when U.S. companies "shared" their technologies with Japanese partners. One wonders what will happen now that the sharing is often moving in the opposite direction.

Managing scale differences. When one party to an alliance is sufficiently large relative to the other, *success* for the venture, oddly enough, can become a serious threat to the smaller. The larger partner can insist on rapid growth the smaller cannot finance or manage. When a small project—at first politically ignored within a larger partner—grows to sufficient size, other parties in the large enterprise may see it as a threat in resource allocations and attempt to kill it. They may, on the other hand, try to capture it as an opportunity. In either event, the continuity of the project's management partnership is threatened. Conversely, a large partner can with little loss to itself destroy a small partner, especially in a new venture, by simply delaying its decisions or payments for only a short while. Without great skill and care a small partner may have difficulty in getting the priority attention and most talented resources it needs from a much larger associate. Thinking through and specifying resource needs, key people's commitments, bottleneck-breaking mechanisms, and means of adjusting priorities are crucial—but may not be sufficient—when size differences are enormous.

Organization and decision structures. Ventures tend to work best when partners have comparable organizational and decision structures. A small division of a large product–decentralized company, able to make fast decisions, will be thwarted if it has to work with a similar-size partner that is functionally organized. The latter will often have to get all functional groups to sign off on project decisions or go to the corporate CEO for internal conflict resolutions, forcing the smaller division to go above its operating head and involve its corporate CEO if real problems develop. Debilitating frustrations also develop when one group uses consensus processes and the other does not. U.S. companies, ready to go with a project, have often found delays in Japanese decision processes so long that they have disbanded their venture teams, assuming a lack of Japanese interest in the project, or they have put their own planning on "hold" during this cycle, only to find the Japanese partners have been making steady advances and suddenly appear with complete consensus and a detailed project plan to support it. Then the Japanese partner may feel its Western counterparts are unplanned, disorganized, or uncaring.

Congruent decision and incentive rules. If partners do not install comparable decision and incentive systems for the project, major problems can develop. If one partner is driving for market share and the other is seeking ROI, intractable conflicts will occur over pricing strategies, marketing policies, and incremental investment programs. Similarly, if one partner has access to low-cost capital, it may want to invest heavily when the other cannot or should not. These problems are compounded when the project managers in each company have incentive compensation plans that are quite different. Fully understood and shared goals can quickly be subverted by decision rules or incentives that are noncongruent. Co-designing these support systems usually helps, but hidden decision rules can subvert even the best-laid formal systems. Again, real understanding of organization and decision systems takes significant time and commitment.

Systems compatibility. Many problems can be avoided if systems for project accounting, databases, and information handling are made mutually transparent. Open systems help both in direct project coordination and in inculcating trust. Large outsourcers (like Ford, GM, or Toyota) can insist that routine suppliers adapt to their systems. When two firms of equal size partner, compromises to each party's system—or a separately and jointly maintained system—may be costly but essential. Clearly defined and coordinated real-time EDI systems avoid many of the problems partners otherwise encounter, but integrated knowledge-based systems are a long step better. Successful alliance builders have found that they must spend at least as much time in their negotiations on establishing management processes that ensure organizational and infrastructure compatibilities as they do on technical specifications, financial arrangements, and other "commerical" agreements.

Strategic tracking. Alliances tend to last only so long as there is mutual dependency. In addition to keeping its own core competency protected and at "best in world" status, each company needs to track its partner's changing strategic posture in depth. Over time, one partner may develop a sufficiently strong across-the-board skill base to decide to go it alone. The partner may engage in new outside alliances for other purposes (like the rapidly changing alliances of Sony today) that give it alternative access to needed strengths. Its overall strategic balances may shift so that the shared venture, once peripheral, becomes vital to its future, in which case it will attempt to take over the project, even at high cost. Or, conversely, a project, once important, may become so irrelevant that the partner will not give it the talent and resource priorities it needs for success. Given the rapidly changing product lines and coalition arrangements of major partners today, alliances require continuous strategic monitoring. Some companies find it useful to formally model all the information they have about their partners so they can (1) negotiate prices and needed changes more realistically and (2) anticipate the partner's moves in time to avoid disasters. By developing thorough strategic tracking models they frequently assemble more detailed information about the partner than the latter's own negotiating team or top executives have at their fingertips. This offers immense advantages during later bargaining sessions adjusting transfer prices and technical or sales relationships.

Corporate alliance coordinators. Because of coordination complexities, many corporations have found that they need a special office at the top management level to provide extra analytical depth or expertise for negotiating, monitoring, and advising line managers concerning alliances. Highly diverse companies can easily find their divisions negotiating alliances with conflicting partners or being suddenly squeezed out when an important large partner incrementally ends up with a conflicting set of stronger alliances. Such offices—or the specialized professional outside suppliers who can offer such services—are less important for more narrowly focused companies. These offices, of course, are not a substitute for the full array of other carefully designed line interactions already suggested for analyzing or coordinating partnership arrangements. Table 12–1 summarizes these and some other common management issues which tend to need emphasis and coordination in partnering relationships.

ONGOING MANAGEMENT ISSUES

Despite careful negotiations and development of compatible relationship structures like those outlined above, problems with alliances are inevitable. But so are problems with sister divisions, internal service suppliers, or contractors for routine parts and subassemblies. The management problem is to make sure the *marginal* transaction costs of dealing with external partners do not exceed the *marginal* benefits their skills and resources can bring. One cannot hope to avoid all the potential problems in Table 12–1, but a number of studies indicate that the preventive measures outlined previously and some well-considered actions during implementation can decrease transaction costs and reduce potential conflicts substantially. A brief outline of some critical actions follows.

Jointly developed goals and plans. Many companies have found that openly sharing their overall goals for the project with partners, and then jointly developing explicit goals for the project team's management, can eliminate much confusion and ill feeling. Each side needs to see clearly where the opposite party's interests lie and where joint interests coincide or may diverge. Developing a detailed joint plan to support broad program goals can generate many specific and needed insights. Successful alliance builders say such plans—a key element in developing early trust among the parties—should be in more detail than internal plans normally are. The planning process enables more information to be shared. No one commits to what they can't deliver. And the plans provide much needed benchmarks for each party to self-coordinate and to

TABLE 12–1
Common Issues in Alliances

- Establishing clear win–win goals for all partners, and agreed limits to actions
- Understanding how the project fits each partner's total strategy
- Assessing the impacts of partner's culture on decision processes and priorities
- Understanding each partner's value chain, how it profits, where geographically
- Anticipating partner's or customers' moves into related markets
- Partners' lacking true joint commitment; having an intention to take over full alliance
- Obtaining multiple approvals when projects cut across business or functional units
- Multiple contact points creating confusion in information and perception
- Technology or scale shifts in midstream causing conflicts
- Monitoring external environment changes that may require relationship adjustments
- Creating and maintaining compatible information systems, continuously updated, with understood protocols
- Gaps: each partner thinking the other is doing it
- Speed: one partner needing faster responses than the other
- Achieving organization-incentives compatibility
- Project managers not being able to get approval of all key players in *both* partners
- Projects depending on champions for a very long time, 3–7 years
- Political attacks: other divisions resenting outsiders sharing "their" resources
- Personnel in the venture losing their corporate careers, becoming "the enemy"
- Less able people being assigned to manage "outside" ventures
- Corporate cultures remaining dominated by old product lines, internal power relations
- Other divisions and managers delaying decisions or vetoing them *post hoc*
- Parent divisions playing down venture successes, overemphasizing their own contributions

monitor the other. The biggest operational problems in alliances are in maintaining similar priorities among the parties. Jointly developed plans are one of the most effective mechanisms to facilitate this goal.

Avoiding niche collisions. Detailed plans help divide tasks clearly, reinforcing the intended roles and relationships of the partners. Prior to finalizing such plans, each party needs to analyze carefully where each partner might intrude into the sacred territory of the other—geographical, demographic, customer, technology, or componentry niches of strategic importance—and block these off by *corporatewide* agreements for a finite period. Without these, if the alliance develops successfully, either the venture's management or the divisions of one partner will see opportunities to move into realms that create strategic "niche collisions" or direct competitive conflicts—for example, one partner's selling jointly developed technology as componentry to downstream competitors of the other party. In addition to formal arrangements to avoid these problems, carefully defined "Chinese Walls," like those Coca Cola erects to keep the critical formula for its syrup mix from its bottlers, strongly supported by internal training and policies, may be needed to protect vital know-how—especially that of core competencies.

Structuring the team. Managing alliances successfully seems to require a unique combination of technical know-how and savoir faire. In choosing a team, "predisposition counts more than position" is the creative guideline used by one especially successful venturer. To obtain maximum benefits, the management team needs to contain technical experts who can provide or gain the most possible information quickly in any exchange, yet can create the confidence and goodwill that all joint activities require. It also usually needs people who are natural team players or team builders on both sides. Early and extensive contacts are needed to test and establish the exact climate, ground rules, and personal chemistry needed for cooperation. But long-term, mutually supporting, and flexible attitudes are all that make alliances work when push comes to shove, as it eventually will.

Clear communication links. Because each party needs to be brought up the experience curve relative to the other, early communications tend to be intense and confusing. Having clear contact points at the technical-operating, project manager, and top management levels—especially in early stages—can avoid major conflicts in information and impressions conveyed. Often, confusion comes as much from misunderstanding about whom to contact or ignorance of the partner's internal processes and decision rules as it does from the complexity of the information to be transferred. Purposely committing extra people to understand the partner's processes—and consciously allowing time slacks to deal with confusion—generally pays high dividends in early stages. Commonly understood information systems, terms, and procedures are *sine qua non* in decreasing later transaction costs.

***Understanding cultures*.** Culture differences constitute the other major cluster of forces increasing transaction costs. Unless specific arrangements are made in advance, creative companies (like Genentech or Microsoft), operating in adhocracies, generally find their programs slowed by the bureaucracies of their more conservative partners. Entrepreneurial startup companies lose crucial time and experimental advantages when they hook up with large development partners, while their partners find the upstart "too wild, erratic, and unplanned" to provide "credible" data for their systems. Both are slowed down. Cultural conflicts are especially acute with foreign partners. But every culture (not just those in foreign countries) has its different language, style, internal politics, and hidden decision rules, which, until understood, exact a high price. For most large continuing partnerships, companies find that they need, like Nike, to have full-time monitors, fluent in the native language, living in their partners' premises and actively participating in specific operating decisions. Because customers or suppliers living on the other's premises contribute much innovation and interactive problem-solving while there, both parties usually benefit.

***A structured learning process*.** Companies enter alliances because the partner can do certain things better than they can. From the beginning, therefore, it is helpful to codify and to transfer knowledge gained from the partner to those who can best use it. Before and after each negotiating session there should be a cataloguing of "what do we know now" and "what do we still need to know" about the partner. Periodically, representatives of all units on the alliance team need to be brought together to share results from the process and to design further steps to gain more knowledge. The partner that does this best will gain most from the alliance, will have an advantage in all negotiations, and will maintain the greatest flexibility if things go sour. If possible, the process should be extended beyond the alliance team to improve the overall company's processes and knowledge bases. If it can be accomplished, this practice both leverages benefits and helps to sell the remaining organization on the value of the alliance—very helpful in internal politics.

A division, not an enemy. Those who serve in an alliance need special support and protection. Too often internal groups treat the venture not as a benefactor but as a competitor seeking their resources and people. Executives who participate in the venture are suddenly no longer included in internal decisions or receiving the exposure they need for advancement inside the company. When the project ends, there is often no natural internal succession spot available for them. Any failures of the venture receive high publicity. Its successes are claimed by internal groups. And so on. The top management liaison person or team guiding the venture must be high enough in the organization—and directly enough involved in the venture—to protect and nurture its people and to give the whole group the kind of long-term support a division would receive. Successes need special internal publicity and extra incentives or bonuses to reward participants for the added risk and pain they undertake. If not, all later alliances will get third-rate people and little support, and will surely fail.

Flexibility within strategic control. Like any other division, an alliance is unlikely to stick strictly to its plan. Environments are too unknowable. If every change has to be cleared by the full decision apparatus of both parties, the venture will quickly die. Within approved goals and a few clear approval limits, therefore, most such ventures need a permitted flexibility of action at least as wide as that of a comparable internal division. Again, this demands a credible high-level alliance leader, much trust, and a superb monitoring system. It also usually calls for some understood "walk away" limits, which define for each partner what actions will automatically terminate the relationship. What a venture does not need are the full (double) bureaucratic controls of both partners and their staffs.

None of the above pretends that managing outsourcing or alliances is easy. However, there is an accumulating body of experience that suggests that the added power and flexibility that partners bring can easily outweigh their added transaction costs, if any. One must remember that most such arrangements start because (1) analyses indicate that internal sources are not best in world and have little hope of getting there in time, (2) standard purchasing or sourcing techniques will not work well, (3) the partner's skills and capital capabilities will more than offset transaction costs, or (4) executives will have to spend too much time managing unresponsive internal groups or contracted suppliers (causing excessive transaction costs) to make other options viable. New technologies make alliances more attractive today than a few years ago, both because more specialized outside partners can now perform many value-adding tasks better than the company itself and because new technologies make it easier to monitor, coordinate, or manage in ways that avoid major disasters. But these capabilities must be managed aggressively for success.

MANAGING TRANSITIONS TO THE INTELLIGENT ENTERPRISE

Is there anything inherently too dangerous about moving to the more disaggregated forms of a knowledge and service-based "intelligent enterprise"? No more so than moving to any other strongly niched strategy, and a good deal less for most companies than moving toward more highly integrated or bureaucratized forms. The nature of outsourcing, the needs for it, and the capacity to control relationships have changed dramatically. As long as multiple external suppliers exist and managers plan properly, *the enterprise can protect itself when outsourcing.* Internally, if the company adopts an appropriate organizational structure for its particular strategy and backs this up with well-designed micro measurement, benchmarking, information, and incentive systems, *more disaggregated organization forms may present considerably less risk than staying with traditional hierarchical forms.* The key to risk control when moving in either direction is usually "managed incrementalism."

A startup can, of course, initiate any form it likes. To move an ongoing company all at once to a radical new form—unless the enterprise is already in crisis—is inviting disaster. Even companies like IBM or GE, now dedicated to radical change, will find that many of their units operate best in something like their traditional mode. And companies significantly increasing their outsourcing, like Ford and GM, will doubtless maintain many excellent internal suppliers. With some rare crisis exceptions, an incremental process, rather than a quick changeover, will facilitate successful change. But this does not mean that the change process need be slow, random, or haphazard.

MANAGED INCREMENTALISM

Managers generally proceed incrementally for good reasons. Using incrementalism for major changes in larger organizations decreases risks and helps managers cope with the varying time frames needed (1) to generate needed information, (2) to overcome entrenched political positions, (3) to obtain genuine understanding and organizational commitment, and (4) to redeploy resources intelligently behind any major strategy change.[9] This is especially true for the types of basic resource redeployments and organizational changes suggested here. Few managers would want suddenly to junk all the structures that have brought their company's past successes. Nor would they instantly know how to manage effectively in the new format if they did. How then does one proceed with managed incrementalism? No single paradigm will fit all situations, but several steps seem central in managing major change processes proactively.[10]

BUILDING INITIAL AWARENESS

How does one get started? Rarely do signals for major strategic changes arrive with ringing clarity or with full-blown solutions in hand. More rarely still do they come from the company's internal formal horizon-scanning, planning, or reporting systems. The bottom-up nature of most planning systems tends to extrapolate mild modifications of present patterns into the future. A notable exception is Royal Dutch Shell's well-publicized scenario planning system, which is designed to get managers to think about the consequences of jarring changes. In most healthy companies, top management's initial sensing of the need for change tends to be very intuitive. Most things tend to be working pretty well. Change managers say their first perceptions are usually "something you just feel uneasy about," "inconsistencies,"[11] or "anomalies" between some group's posture or performance and some general perception of what the future environment is likely to call for. To make sure they are exposed to these concerns early enough and to avoid internal information screens, effective change managers consciously develop multiple, credible internal and external sources to provide more jarring and objective views about their company and its surrounding environments.[12] Some of these methodologies have been suggested in previous sections.

In these early stages, change managers seem consciously to generate and consider a wide array of alternatives without getting irrevocably wedded to any.[13] They don't know yet what the right solution is or what will actually work in their situation. While tapping the collective wit of the organization, they simultaneously try to build awareness and concern about new issues. They assemble objective data to argue against preconceived ideas or past practices. Yet they want to avoid seriously threatening power centers that might kill important changes aborning—before potential supporters can understand what is at stake and what the opportunities and options for them really are.

■ As one executive said:

> [Typically] you roll an issue around in your mind and with a few friends until enough people think there is a conclusion that makes some sense for the company. Then you go out and sort of post the idea more broadly without being too wedded to its details. You then start hearing the arguments pro and con, and some very good refinements usually emerge. Then you pull the idea in and commit some resources to study it so it can be put forward more formally. You may use "stimuli occurrences," experiments, or "crises" to launch pieces of the idea . . . but they lead toward your ultimate aim. You know where you want to get. You'd like to get there in 6 months. But it may take 3 years . . . and when you get there, it may not look much like your original idea.[14]

At this stage, processes are likely to involve small discussion groups, studying, challenging, questioning, listening, talking to creative people outside ordinary decision channels, generating options, but generally avoiding irreversible commitments.[15] Top executives may have a good feeling for the general directions they want to emerge but only offer broad visionary statements as guides, preferring to let others actively shape specific solutions and become committed to them.

BUILDING CREDIBILITY: CHANGING SYMBOLS

Knowing they cannot communicate directly with the thousands who must carry out a change, many executives undertake to change a few highly visible symbols. For example, restructuring their own executive teams first, changing their attendance patterns at top management meetings, obliterating some outmoded procedures and committees, or beginning more open consultations in informal attire with lower-level employees. Without such moves, people may interpret even forceful verbiage as mere rhetoric and may delay their commitment to new thrusts. Managers will often create discussion forums in which no decisions are intended, and will consciously allow some slack time for organizations to work through threatening issues. They put in the time and resources to generate an improved information base that lets managers unfamiliar with new options compare them more objectively with past practices. Mere familiarity makes solutions that fit an executive's past experience appear less risky or less costly than new alternatives that may be much more attractive when viewed objectively. Guiding executives often start small experiments to test ideas safely and to create an internal experience base. They do not want to exacerbate uncertainty—and its handmaiden, hostility—by pushing new solutions too fast from the top.[16]

Change managers usually don't terminate this "diagnostic phase"[17] until they feel sure there are enough key people on board to make a solution work. Then they may begin to extend the credibility and information base for the new concept through some larger experiments, e.g., trying experimental teams on a few important problems or outsourcing a few major functions as test vehicles. As these experiments succeed, their successes are conveyed as a new set of myths. And the grapevine will amplify them in the retelling.[18] Errors are killed as quietly as possible, unless they too can contribute to a "what not to do" set of myths, in which case they may be consolidated and categorized for training purposes.

TACTICAL SHIFTS AND PARTIAL SOLUTIONS

Early solutions tend to be partial, tentative, and experimental. They may be handled as mere tactical adjustments within the firm's existing strategy. As such they may encounter little opposition. At this stage, top executives themselves may not know how far they want to go or what optimum formats will be. They will often undertake parallel experiments, using different methodologies. None of these will risk the firm's or the activity's total viability. These early steps can still lead to a number of possible success scenarios. Each experiment needs to be monitored, and a conscious attempt made to evaluate its outcome. Some companies create independent monitoring teams or use outsiders to try to capture the organizational learning that takes place.

As these experiments proceed, successes are reinforced. Failures are culled. And the resulting pattern becomes a central element in the new strategy. Some broad goals—"a move to a much more flexible organization style" or "staying only in positions where we are number one or number two"—help create focus. But no overall strategy may yet be announced.[19] Whole departments or divisions may be stimulated to restructure themselves and become benchmarks for others. Successful coaches for self-directed teams will be moved around to coach others. Successful team heads get the bigger tasks. Incentives that work get reused. Failures are shelved. Even then, as Jack Welsh said of his many experiments in trying to reinvigorate GE, "There are no failures in this kind of system, just bright ideas that didn't work." The healthy part of an organization's ongoing posture is maintained, while shifting momentum at the margin toward new needs.[20] The heads of successful experimental groups become champions, not just "buying into" the idea but actively championing it as their ticket to success. The result is that the new strategy is half-implemented before it is formally announced.

TOLERATING CHAOS

As companies experiment with these new organization modes, a fairly standard cycle of confusion and progress seems to ensue. The first step is pretty straightforward. People are at first bewildered and somewhat uneasy as they learn new skills. But with adequate training, coaching, and support planning this cycle can be relatively short. The second stage tends to be euphoria and high enthusiasm. People suddenly feel empowered. They can do their jobs better; they feel appreciated, often for the first time; and there is a genuine excitement in meeting new people and dealing with them and with new problems in new ways. Working together on exciting new goals seems to overcome all problems.

Then comes a crunch. In self-directed teams, things tend toward chaos internally. External customers often feel the job is being performed extraordinarily well as compared to the past. But internally, people begin to be frustrated by new system limits that may lie well beyond the boundaries of the task as they originally perceived it. People jockey for power and position in the new system. New jealousies develop, and new rules must be invented by the group. Managers often want to intervene and introduce more structure to eliminate the chaos. Often this can be totally counterproductive. If decentralization is the goal, the individuals or the team must work out solutions, not to turn to an all-knowing management to solve their problems. Coaching, advising, and patience—while allowing the chaos to frustrate people until they solve their own problems—usually shortens the period of chaos more than direct intervention will. The American Express example cited later provides an illustration. Most managers, very uncomfortable with all this, unconsciously recentralize operations by intervening.

If managers get through this stage, genuine decentralization occurs. New leaders form in the disaggregated groups, and effective new patterns of interaction—often designed by the employees and their customers—tend to emerge. At this stage, the concept begins to be viable.

BROADENING SUPPORT

Up to this point, projects may be kept small, *ad hoc*, and not integrated into a formal program or strategy. However, at some point executives may want to broaden political support for their experiments and blend them into a few formal strategic thrusts that require wider support. Committees, task forces, and retreats are favorite mechanisms for this purpose. By selecting these groups' membership, leaders, timing, and agenda, the guiding executive can predict and manage a desired outcome, yet nudge others toward a participative consensus.[21] More cautious executives will want to maintain complete control over these as "advisory processes" subject to their personal influence and control.

Others regard these consultations as an essential portion of genuinely decentralizing decisions and giving more people a commitment to disaggregated structures. Reports of these groups are crucial in explaining and giving credibility to new options. The supporting processes of generating strategic analyses, preparing careful cost-benefit assessments, validating potentials through experiments, and hearing the reports of enthusiastic champions tend to allay the fears of the timid, build information bases, and broaden consensus.[22] In addition to facilitating smoother implementation, many executives report that interactive consensus-building substantially improves the quality and consistency of decisions. As important as getting the concept right, they say, is the positive and innovative assistance participants will give in working out solutions when things go wrong, as they always do in any major change.

CRYSTALLIZING FOCUS: IMPLANTING THE VISION

Crystallizing focus at critical points is vital. Sometimes executives will express a few specific goals at an early stage to generate action or cohesion in a crisis situation. More often they keep early goals broad, challenging, and appealing to attract support and to avoid unnecessarily threatening individuals or power centers that could be disruptive. Despite adhering to the rhetoric of specific goal-setting, most change leaders are careful not to state many new goals in concrete terms until they are sure they can be achieved, or until they have carefully built consensus among key players. To do otherwise could decrease their own credibility, preempt interesting options, inadvertently centralize the organization, or provide a common focus for an otherwise fragmented opposition.[23]

When to crystallize an emerging viewpoint or when to maintain open options is one of the true arts of management. The crystallization often comes in phases: "We must be best-in-world at whatever we do internally"; followed by, "We will benchmark every overhead activity in the division"; followed by, "We need a flatter, more responsive organization"; followed by, "There will be no more than two layers between the contact person and top management"; followed by, "Our remaining internal overheads must be less than 25 percent of total cost"; and so on. Often in strategic changes of the magnitudes suggested, crystallization comes later rather than earlier, and appears in formally written strategies only when the process is well into implementation stages.[24] Strategy implementation and formulation in fact tend to be simultaneous events. Early formal announcements of intention could threaten so many that the options themselves would be subverted before they ever had a chance.[25] Yet it is vital to move as rapidly as information and internal system constraints will permit.

FOCUS ON PEOPLE AND PROCESS

Successful transitions toward any of these new organization forms or concepts will focus more on people and the processes of change than on formal structures of organization or control systems.[26] Moving boxes on organization charts typically won't help much. In intelligence-driven organizations, the quality of people and their psychological responses must be the central focus; getting the right people to respond favorably to change is more of a process issue than a structural issue.[27] Since, like all others, intelligent people tend to resist change but welcome success, the process problem is to decrease the threats of the former while intensifying and implanting positive perceptions about the probability and benefits of the latter.

Our interviews showed that most companies did not start off with a goal of introducing any particular new mode of organization. Instead, they arrived at the organization form as a specific response to a defined problem. In virtually all cases, the presence of service technologies enabled radical organization changes, but only one respondent to date has reported this as a specific overarching goal of introducing the technology. Nor did such changes come about because people with PCs on their desks voluntarily figured out how to do things differently. Many respondents noted that it took extensive training, coaching, and backup support systems to implement these radical new organizations. Few were imposed from above, except those caused by consolidation of facilities or introduction of a totally new information structure (like ECONOMOST or SABRE)—or those associated with the startup of a new enterprise. Instead, in the most successful changes there was almost always interactive development, involving actual knowledge workers and point people in the process. Introduction was usually performed first locally on an experimentation basis, followed by a regional trial, and finally a systemwide rollout with heavier sponsorship from above.

DIFFERENT ROUTES FOR DIFFERENT RESULTS

Self-directed teams or cluster organizations tended to come most often as specific solutions to situations requiring multifunctional responses to a repeated set of problems, usually at the customer or supplier interface level. Typical examples were handling customer inquiries, deploying expert teams to solve customer problems, or developing new solutions to defined R&D issues. Infinitely flat organizations tended to evolve incrementally, as managers of large systems gained confidence in a new system's capability to handle problems on an error-free basis. The development of systems for aircraft control, national brokerage networks, fast food chains, or more localized power in banking and retailing outlets were typical examples. These generally involved large initial systems developments, implemented first locally, then regionally, then systemwide.

"Spider's webs" tended to involve a visionary systems investment with rather specific information-enhancing goals (like those of DARPANET, ECONOMOST, or AANET) to provide infrastructure. This was typically followed by a learning cycle of use, followed by policies targeted toward encouraging specific strategic uses, and ultimately requiring a series of new incentives to mold activity patterns in desired directions. What did not seem to work was placing a blizzard of PCs on all desk tops and leaving their new owners to work out uses—or, alternately, deciding at the top that the company needed to be more "team," "cluster," "people," or "technology" oriented and then looking for ways to do it.

AN INTEGRATING VIGNETTE: IMPLEMENTING AN INTELLIGENT ENTERPRISE

Perhaps the best way to show how all these change concepts fit together is to present a somewhat longer-than-usual example: American Express Travel Related Services Company, Inc.'s (TRS') move to utilize self-directed teams for a new charge card. While not suggesting that each element is directly transferable to all organizations, it provides a rich body of insight on many of the most important change issues cited above. Internal quotations are from Wendy Brown and Geri Rowe, chosen as co-leaders of the Executive Corporate Card team, called Project Renaissance,[28] in its development phase.

THE STARTUP

From a market perspective, there was clear evidence that a group of existing customers truly wanted a new business card. Once the project team defined its customers as business owners and senior executives (and identified what their unique needs were), the TRS

Office of the Presidents agreed to position the product on "service delivery"—i.e., selling premium service delivered by a unit of highly trained "executive assistants." Given the defined need and its accompanying strategy, it was clear that the project team had to restructure operations completely in order to deliver a new set of travel, information, and financial services—flawlessly the first time and everytime—through a single point of contact. To accomplish this the project team had both to develop a whole new way of delivering service—and to identify and motivate people who would present it in a very different fashion.

The customer wanted a single point of contact. The only way for American Express to deliver this was for each servicing representative to be able to handle any issue completely and immediately from beginning to end. This represented a significant change from the existing functional approach to servicing. For example, resolving a disputed charge would have ordinarily required at least three people in three different organizations handling it. If exceptions to policy were called for, it also involved up to three levels of management. The Executive Card Team proposed to speed resolution times and to increase customer focus by collapsing these responses into a single "executive assistant" job description. For starters, the group immediately took out two layers from the traditional organization. In addition, it moved people who had been performing a single function into a cross-functional unit handling responsibilities that had been lodged in four different departments previously. Oddly enough, this meant having one coach for every eight people at first—as opposed to an earlier span of one to eighteen. However, Brown and Rowe noted, "Once people have become completely functional in their new roles, the spans will increase. The concept of span of control doesn't really mean much in this type of activity any more. Our contact people will make more decisions on their own, and team leaders' and facilitators' responsibilities will rotate within the teams. One group we know of (where we did some benchmarking) had 150 people per manager."

RE-ENGINEERING AND BENCHMARKING

The Executive Corporate Card development team began by building on TRS' Total Quality Management (TQM) approach, called Amexcellence, a continuous improvement process designated not only to serve the customer better but also to offer definite financial benefits from productivity improvements in the organization. The first step of this cross-functional project team was to consolidate learning from some "best practices," customer needs research, and external benchmarking exercises.

Best practices pilot groups and external benchmarking are frequently used to test and evaluate changes in work processes, which can then be rolled out to the larger servicing organizations. Much of the actual R&D process at American Express (generating, testing and evaluating ideas) happens within the everyday operations groups. Servicing representatives are also encouraged to make recommendations for changes that can increase employee satisfaction, customer satisfaction, or profitability—and can be readily implemented as solutions.

The project team thought both Cardmembers and TRS would benefit the most if work flow redesign (using the best practices technique) were combined with the potentials of a team-based organization. The official in-house description of the Executive Corporate Card approach to servicing stated: "The team members who comprised the Executive Service Desk are highly trained across all servicing functions, 'own' the process of creating customer satisfaction, and follow each inquiry from beginning to end." Using teams, service delivery was improved by:

- Finding service-oriented people to hire by identifying those who in their current jobs had found ways around traditional policies and procedures to serve the customer, by interviewing them over the phone, and by making hiring decisions through team consensus.
- Implementing single phone number servicing, which ensures the highest quality and consistency of each and every contact and leverages the resources of American Express' global network;
- Re-engineering the work flow process and realigning decision-making authority to encourage pro-active servicing, immediate resolution, follow-up initiative and ownership of customer satisfaction—ensuring management of relationships not just transactions.
- Re-designing the floor plan layout into team 'pods' to facilitate communication, learning, and cooperation.
- Revising management-business reporting to focus on quality not quantity of output;

- Instituting a reward and recognition program based on Card-member and peer feedback.

Once all work flows had been re-engineered, the team focused on redesigning the organizational and management decision support structures. In addition to de-layering the organization to reduce the number of levels required to make key decisions, the project team also redefined leadership roles. Initially, the servicing organization had two "business leaders," one responsible for communicating the business vision (establishing cultural, quality, and interpersonal expectations) and another responsible for managing the information about the business (overseeing data gathering, analysis, and reporting). There were several team coaches, each of whom oversaw a team of 8–12 service representatives who handled customers. These "servicing teams" began as a cross-section of functional specialists who, over time, would each learn to handle all functions (account set-ups, general inquiries, account changes, and credit management) themselves. A separate team of consultants providing training, quality assurance, call traffic management and financial reporting expertise—with the expectation that over time these support functions would be assimilated into the servicing teams.

The "single point of customer contact" and team-based organizational structure both increased the amount and complexity of information required by each front-line servicing representative. To provide technical support for these newly empowered representatives in their conversations with a Cardmember, the look up, updating, and help features of the mainframe customer database system were made considerably more user-friendly through an improved "front-end" interface. The team developed a working prototype which consolidated the most frequently accessed mainframe data elements and functions on a single screen, bypassing the ten to fifteen screens earlier required to retrieve the same information. The involvement of front-line service representatives during the prototype stage not only provided valuable feedback to the central systems design team, but also reinforced how much participation and change were expected from the representatives. In its fully functional form, the technology will eliminate much of the training time previously needed. It will also allow each customer representative to get any relevant information quickly and to obtain answers from the system as necessary, while carrying on a conversation with the customer. This simplified information access and processing system helps the representative focus on the customer's questions and make sure the inquiry is handled right the first time.

VISION AND COACHING

The Executive Corporate Card strategy for re-engineering the service delivery process and organization was part of a broader corporate vision to improve employee and customer satisfaction while reducing costs through increased teamwork. Since it was at the leading edge of this culture change, the Executive Corporate Card team required a significant degree of senior management commitment to protect and endorse its plans. As Brown and Rowe said, "What this really took to get going was vision and trust. The vision foresaw that better service meant working a new way. A few top people were willing to invest real trust, try things on a small scale, and hope they worked. They are unique individuals, willing to take that kind of risk. Once they had cleared the broad strategy they said, 'Go make it happen on this project.' We kept them informed in the early stages to make sure they were comfortable with the concept and with progress. We tried to keep very open communications." Their support for re-engineering began with the project team's approach to developing the product and has continued since product launch.

During the development phase, when the project team realized it didn't know enough about the specific activities needed to accomplish its goals, it put together a TRS-wide "task force" of about eighty people who either had the needed knowledge or would be critical in implementing the product across the company. The team leaders tried hard to get them inspired, excited, and committed to the vision. The task force ultimately became a credibility and communication vehicle for implementation throughout the rest of the organization. Even though this was a completely new product, it needed the full support of other elements of the operation. Two top VPs within TRS supported the project constantly by making positive comments in private and speeches at meetings, essentially reaffirming, "This is an important project." When necessary they made exceptions to break roadblocks. Many of their actions were very symbolic. The team leaders noted, "If that trust and support hadn't been clear, we never could have gotten this project to the marketplace in record time or with the same high degree of quality."

MANAGING THE TEAM PROCESS

Once the Executive Corporate Card was launched, the project team transitioned into ongoing product management roles. During the development phase, the project team had to learn first-hand how to develop ownership and to tap specialized expertise by using informal teams like the task force. In the launch phase of the project, implementing and evolving a more formal "team organization" led to further challenges and learning.

The most important lesson was that the team had to go through all the classic stages of team building. There was the initial cycle of jubilation and elation, the "Oh my goodness, they are really letting me do this and I love it! I am so excited!" stage. Then the group went into the "chaos" stage. This was the most difficult stage to handle throughout. Management's first reaction was that it could get through this phase quickly. The attitude was: "We know what we are doing, we'll just manage through it." The business leaders said:

> Everyone understood that chaos was an important stage to go through. But thinking that you can "manage" that stage, we learned is a total fallacy. If you think that way, it can actually inhibit the process and the important learning that the team gets through chaos (in terms of understanding capabilities, building trust, and developing decision-making and interpersonal skills). We have finally come out of the chaos phase and are getting into phase 3, "the leader centered phase." You think when you enter the "leader centered phase" that people will begin to focus back on you as leaders. They don't necessarily do that. What happened to us was that individual people within the teams (at different levels) were gaining much more confidence and much more advocacy, and they were becoming much more adamant about what they wanted and expected. They also now knew what to ask for. During both the "chaos" and "leader centered" phases, the teams often rejected our guidance, not unlike the way in which adolescents reject their parents' advice and are heavily influenced by one or more special or powerful peers. This can be very disconcerting indeed.

During the initial "euphoria" phase, team members seemed to think the whole process was exceptional; everyone was very excited. But that ultimately created some challenges in dealing with the rest of the organization, especially during the chaos phase. Because the Executive Corporate Card team was explicitly changing the way American Express had done things for years, the rest of the organization felt threatened and unappreciated. At first, other organizations often saw the Executive Corporate Card teams as "elites." Some thought they were being given preferential treatment. Many did not understand what was happening, and some resented it. Then, as the teams outwardly seemed to fall apart during the chaos stage, there was a tendency for the rest of the organization to say, "I told you so!" A number of people looked at what was going on in the teams and thought, "It's out of control." Opponents tended to listen to anything people said that was negative. The team employees themselves sometimes became very disillusioned. It was hard to keep the supporting systems up with the teams' expectations. Because it was difficult to define roles well, it was also hard to get needed changes in the compensation system. The team leaders said:

> We learned that during this phase everyone sees the typical signs of chaos and wants to control it. There is a strong tendency to step in and start managing the chaos because people think they are losing control. If that happens, you lose the entire effect you were seeking. You need to train the team itself in problem-solving and then bring them the problems. Problem-solving training and feedback-training are the keys. If you can train people to handle and deliver feedback in a productive manner so that everyone can raise complaints and not feel defensive about dealing with them, you can make real progress. You need to give team members support and perspective during the chaos stage and the tools and training to bring themselves out of it, not run the process yourself.
>
> If you try to intervene too directly in the chaos phase, you will be rejected out-of-hand by the teams. People may feel betrayed. Even if you try to help them with simple technical things (like structuring a planning process), they may jump all over you because you didn't consult them on the process. They will respond, "I don't agree with those goals, I wasn't included." And so on. You need to let the teams work through this wild era. No matter how

much you think it through, you are probably not going to handle decisions during the chaos phase right the first time, so you have to build a very fluid process that is simply very open and coaches the teams to not only raise issues, but also *own* the solutions.

RESULTS OF THE PROCESS (KEY LEARNINGS)

Evaluating the performance of the new processes and new organizations against Amex's employee satisfaction, customer satisfaction, and profitability goals has been difficult. More traditional productivity measures turned out to have little relevance to the new work flows and work unit definitions. In fact, the extent of change—in both process and product terms—has necessitated a corresponding redesign of measurement systems, and therefore made it difficult to benchmark progress.

Several traditional measurements were eliminated as performance indicators because they were internally focused, not customer focused. Average call handling time (AHT) was an example. Since a customer wanted resolution of issues at the first point of contact, the Executive Corporate Card teams realized that they needed to spend more time handling the call initially. When they did, they eliminated much more in backend costs for analysis, correspondence, and phone calls by other functional units. Although AHT is important to track for staff planning purposes, the teams felt strongly that this indictor did not measure the effectiveness or efficiency of their incoming call handling.

The big question the project team is now trying to answer is, "What is the return on investment for team-based organizations?" Information technology (phone systems, databases, reporting systems) have lagged behind the team's needs, making it difficult to collect the data needed to calibrate costs and benefits in order to calculate gains. Compounded by the rapid growth of the customer base (as much as 25% in a given month) and the constant tweaking of work flows and job functions, a simple answer to the question, "Is this better than a traditional functional organization?" remains an open discussion. As the team leaders said,

That may be our single greatest current challenge in evaluating the success of this new approach. At a macro level, we can measure profitability and service levels, but we don't have other products or organizations to compare them to. We know the key variables we need to improve—profitability, employee satisfaction, and customer satisfaction—and we are developing measures, goals, and action plans for each of these. [But we don't have a base line of what costs and benefits would have been under another system].

On customer satisfaction, we measure performance based on three different kinds of surveys to determine overall satisfaction, key dissatisfiers, timeliness, accuracy, and professionalism for critical transactions. We have very complex scales that adjust for both the frequency and the importance of different events. Using these measurements, and several behavioral indicators, we can assess the "overall health" of our Cardmember franchise. Being a new and small group, we don't have the resources to conduct a full battery of customer surveys yet. However, our initial transaction-based indicators suggest that customers perceive a positive difference in service quality, but that our consistency from month to month is still a problem.

We also periodically survey our employees on their satisfaction with their jobs and with the process. During the "chaos phase," our team members were dissatisfied on many dimensions. However, when asked whether they believed teams were the right way to organize, the answer was a resounding yes! Ever since we started re-engineering, how we do business has been based much more on feedback from employees. It's been a challenge to keep up with their new and ever increasing expectations for change.

One of the toughest things for us to change was the traditional compensation system. People felt that their tasks had been expanded very significantly and they *had* been. But it took us a long time to get a new pay scale negotiated that the Human Resources people felt comfortable with. We are still dealing with relatively traditional compensation schemes and review systems tied primarily to individual, not team, rewards. We think we are measuring the right things in the business, but we haven't figured out yet (1) how you really hold a group of people jointly accountable for the measures and (2) to what extent you should compensate them for team versus individual performance.

As it ended up, the product met its profitability objectives for its first year of operation by being highly responsive and flexible to change. When the team decided to scale back its growth objectives significantly to ensure profits with the new servicing approach and organization, it had to cut costs and revise investment plans to offset a lower revenue stream. The flattened management hierarchy facilitated quick decisions, the cross-functional organization forced net-benefit tradeoffs, and the team met its commitments on profitability and customer service while lowering costs significantly. Senior management, in turn, gave team leaders the freedom and encouragement to make their own decisions and to learn from their mistakes, without burdening them with additional analysis and reporting requirements. Ultimately, the team eliminated three of seven layers of management. The key was for point people to be empowered and able to make tradeoff decisions only managers had been allowed to make previously.

Customers were clearly more satisfied dealing with a single person with the power and authority to resolve their questions. One of the new issues raised by this organizational design was how to ensure that the right business decisions were being made by individuals. In essence, each team was now making decisions on how the company would spend and collect its money. To do so judiciously, team members needed to understand how their individual decisions affected the company's profits. The team leaders had to get the group to comprehend in depth how to balance the tradeoffs needed to meet the company's three basic goals: customer satisfaction, employee satisfaction, and profitability. For example, adding to staffing levels would improve employee satisfaction and customer satisfaction but hurt profitability in the short run. Conversely, tightening receivables management would diminish customer satisfaction but help profitability. And so on. In each case how much each factor will contribute to optimizing system benefits is a judgment call. As the teams leaders said:

> We understood that the whole process involved a number of tradeoffs among our three goals. We needed to do extensive profitability training with our teams so they could understand this to a greater degree. We had to make the whole thing as comprehensible and realistic for everyone as possible. Instead of having one group pushing for greater service to the customer and another group trying to minimize risk exposure, our team members themselves need to worry about and decide, "Do I let this party spend? Will they or won't they pay us? What will be the

effect on Card sales, volume, satisfaction, and profitability if I turn down this request?" Information is critical in this decision-making process. We have a new technology that provides a way to access and analyze large amounts of information quickly and consistently, during the conversation with the Cardmember, not after it. Every Cardmember contact requires a judgment call. Our challenge is to make certain that these calls are consistent and logical across our base overall, and over time with each individual Cardmember.

THE PEOPLE ARE CRITICAL

They continued:

> Perhaps the most interesting thing we've learned is that the kind of people you have involved in a project like this is your single most critical success factor. You can have all the technology in the world, but to go through a cultural change and implement a move to this kind of radically different organization while starting up a brand-new product is almost solely predicated on your ability to find the right people to lead the change initiative and then to participate in the new process on an ongoing basis.
>
> One of our current problems is that we seem to be having a very high number of people applying for promotional opportunities outside our team. They have picked up so many new skills that they are qualified for a broad range of jobs—although we have been able to reclassify jobs for a lot of people and, in essence, give them internal promotions. But now that the support for and the success of team-based organizations like ours has been clearly established, everyone wants people who have been successful with teaming to help them implement change.
>
> We are very happy about this. The people who joined in the project saw it as a growth opportunity; they scrambled to participate in it despite the risk of failure. There were clearly other people who said, "It's a great idea, but I'm going to make sure it's successful before I hitch myself to that wagon." Fortunately, there were enough people who felt it had to happen; it was the right thing to do."
>
> The only thing that made the new organization work, ultimately, was that the strategic commitment to the project—to change not only the product, but the organization to meet customer needs—transcended all of the narrower conflicts the

project engendered, both during development and after launch. How quickly this team-based organizational approach spreads throughout the company will depend on how much we can learn about how to develop future team leaders as they coach new teams through a similar evolution. In addition, we will need to change more of our companywide measurement, control, and incentive systems to support this approach.

SUMMARY AND CONCLUSIONS

Other chapters have attempted to deal with the issues surrounding services in the economy, the opportunities and problems a core competency approach poses, how to manage each of the radical new organizational forms, the issues at the interface of services and manufacturing, and the new techniques needed to promote service and quality in knowledge-based service enterprises. This chapter has tried to respond to some of the most common (as yet unanswered) general management questions about the paradigm of the more disaggregated, knowledge and service based type of enterprise this book presents. What happens to management skills? What happens to promotion and incentive opportunities? How does one manage such extensive outsourcing? How can you really make strategic partnering work? How do we make transitions to this type of enterprise without excessive risk? These have been common questions in presentations to audiences in the United States and abroad.

Without attempting to write a book on each question, which they might well deserve, we have tried to offer some useful overall guidelines and structures—and some more detailed references to lead managers onward if they wish to pursue any subject further. To do otherwise would detract from the balance of subject emphasis we have sought in the rest of the book. The main purpose of the book is to present an integrated new emerging paradigm suggesting how 1990s corporations can be managed for greater strategic effectiveness. It is not to offer detailed instruction on how to manage outsourcing, partnering, change management, or promotion and reward systems. These are important issues, and we have tried to offer some strategic insights about them, but they are not the essential arguments of this book.

CHAPTER 13
A New Economic and Management Paradigm

Services and their knowledge-based technologies are leading all modern economies into a new cycle of change. Every advanced country already enjoys an economy dominated by services (see Table 13–1). Services and the management of intellect will be the keys to future economic success for nations—as well as for all businesses regardless of whether they are in the "manufacturing" or the "services" industries.[1] It is about time we changed not just our management but also our economic and political paradigms to reflect this fact.

THE COMPETITIVENESS DEBATE

This is particularly true about the debate on "national competitiveness." Despite the tendency to deride services and even to blame them in part for the country's "decline" in competitiveness, nothing could be farther from the truth. Not only is the U.S. services sector among the world's most efficient—significantly more so than Japan's—it has provided three to four times the new jobs for the nation that the goods sector has, an almost equal multiple of its value-added, and virtually all the economy's growth in value over the last several decades.

In addition, the effectiveness of U.S. service industries and U.S. manufacturing is mutually intertwined. As we have demonstrated, effective services actually create new markets for manufactured goods, lower costs for manufacturers, and are central in

415

TABLE 13–1
Industrial and Services Activities in the Largest Ten OECD Countries[a]
(definitions standardized for OECD differ somewhat from U.S. definition)

Country	Value-added in Industry[b] as % of GDP		Value-Added in Services as % of GDP		Employment % Services
	1968	1988	1968	1988	1988
United States	37%	29%	61%	69%	70.2%
Japan	44	41	48	57	58.0
Federal Republic of Germany	48	40	48	58	56.2
France	39	29	54	67	62.9
United Kingdom	38	32	59	67	68.0
Canada	34	31	62	66	69.8
Australia	38	33	53	63	67.8
Sweden	38	30	57	67	66.7
Belgium	40	31	55	67	69.3
Austria	45	37	48	60	54.5

[a] For which comparative data are available.
[b] Industry figures include mining, manufacturing, and public utilities, but exclude construction and agriculture, hence industry and services do not sum to 100%.
SOURCES: *OECD in Figures: Statistics on the Member Countries,* Supplement to the *OECD Observer,* No. 164, June–July 1990, p. 10, 11, 28, 29; *Economic Outlook Historical Statistics 1960–1988,* OECD, Tables 5.2 and 5.4, pp. 62 and 63.

increasing the value-added for almost all manufacturers. Manufacturers and service companies are locked together in many ways—as partners, suppliers, customers, and innovators for each other. The secret to success for both is to creatively leverage the interaction possibilities.

Unfortunately, to date there has been a tendency to focus policy discussions about competitiveness almost exclusively on manufacturing. Yet if the economy is to grow strongly over the next several decades and provide real gains in per capita income and wealth, services will have to be the main driver. Services productivity will, in large measure, determine the nation's capacity to create jobs, provide high real wages, and generate a higher real standard of living. This is even more true if one considers the service activities included in manufacturing and the external sources for those services that are emerging everywhere.

Despite the concerns about services productivity and quality cited here and elsewhere, the United States has been quite innovative and productive in the services sector as compared to its major trading partners (see Table 13–2). Both OECD statistics and data developed by the Japan Productivity Center say the United States leads Japan in service productivity by a sizable margin.

To date, U.S. services productivity has been driven to a great extent by the country's general affluence, huge market sizes, large geographical scale, and great spirit of entrepreneurship. However, our earlier publications—and those of Roach and Strassmann outlined in the next section—have suggested that some major problems may be developing in the U.S. services sector. Current U.S. rates of services investment are not as high as those in other countries (notably Japan). As measured by macro economic techniques, U.S. services investments do not seem to be paying off as they should be; the productivity of other nations' service activities is growing more rapidly than that of the United States. And U.S. service quality has been a constant complaint. As in manufacturing, service company managers seem more mesmerized by share prices, current ROI, and economies of scale than in building and maintaining the strong customer franchise that is the cause of these measurable returns. These are precisely the same problems that drove selected areas of U.S. manufacturing into decline—and they can devastate services just as easily.[2] Only this time there will be no other rising sector to save the economy as services were able to do during the decline in manufacturing jobs.

With 77 percent of all jobs at stake in the services sector alone—and above 90 percent of the nation employed in all service activities, including those within manufacturing concerns—it is crucial to the nation's employment and standard of living that services be effectively managed. Not only do today's jobs and profits depend on services, so do those of the future. The best available estimates of how important they are in the aggregate are included in Tables 13–3 and 13–4. Whether or not they will be good jobs depends on whether the services sector can achieve high levels of productivity from its human and capital resources.

TABLE 13–2
Relative Levels of Labor Productivity, Eleven OECD Countries and Korea, 1988 (*man-year basis, Japan = 100*)

	Japan	U.S.	West Germany	France	U.K.	Italy	Belgium	Sweden	Spain	Canada	Australia	Korea[a]
Agriculture, forestry & fishery	100.0	338.4	163.4	223.0	254.8	176.2	313.6	186.9	128.5	226.0	240.5	66.3
Mining & quarrying[b]	100.0	204.8	34.7	66.2	—	—	35.1	40.4	—	177.1	219.8	20.3
Manufacturing[c,d]	100.0	124.2	84.6	94.9	123.6	118.3	120.2	66.2	95.9	104.4	81.2	47.7
Electricity, gas & water	100.0	59.0	59.1	59.3	86.5	—	90.0	62.8	66.8	68.0	40.1	123.4
Construction	100.0	102.6	107.7	120.2	113.3	95.5	147.5	100.5	123.2	169.8	116.5	82.9
Wholesale & retail trade[e]	100.0	179.9	120.7	166.7	113.7	168.1	207.8	106.4	156.1	120.7	111.9	48.3
Transportation, storage & communication	100.0	154.5	119.6	134.8	144.9	126.1	140.4	82.3	113.4	141.5	111.4	75.8
Finance, insurance, real estate & business services[f]	100.0	95.4	85.6	118.9	112.5	—	137.7[g]	78.5	128.7	92.7	78.4	64.6
Community, social & personal services[h]	100.0	87.3	118.2	91.1	65.4	104.8	88.7	60.5	99.0	84.7	69.3	35.1

[a] 1987.
[b] This sector of U.K., Italy, and Spain are included in Manufacturing.
[c] Mining and quarrying of U.K., Italy, and Spain are included in Manufacturing.
[d] Electricity, gas, and water of Italy is also included in Manufacturing.
[e] This sector includes Hotels and restaurants, exc. Japan, Belgium, Australia, which are included in Community, social & personal services.
[f] This sector of Italy is included in Community, social & personal services.
[g] Original GDP data for Belgium of this sector do not include a part of imputed bank service charges. In this table, they are estimated and added by JPC Secretariat for the purpose of consistent comparability to the other countries.
[h] Government Services and Other Producer's products are included in this sector for all countries.

SOURCE: *Worldwide Comparison of Labor Productivity* (Tokyo: Japan Productivity Center, Productivity Laboratory, 1991), pp. 108–17.

TABLE 13–3
Employment by Major Industry Division Projected to 2005 (*numbers in thousands*)

Industry	1975	1990	2005			Change, 1975–90	Change, 1990–2005		
			Low	Moderate	High		Low	Moderate	High
Nonfarm wage and salary[a]	76,680	109,319	122,775	132,647	139,531	32,639	13,456	23,328	30,212
Goods-producing	22,600	24,958	22,877	25,242	26,362	2,358	-2,081	284	1,404
Mining	752	711	598	668	690	-41	-113	-43	-22
Construction	3,525	5,136	5,552	6,059	6,484	1,611	416	923	1,348
Manufacturing	18,323	19,111	16,727	18,514	19,189	788	-2,384	-597	78
Durable manufacturing	10,662	11,115	9,467	10,517	10,915	453	-1,648	-599	-200
Nondurable manufacturing	7,661	7,995	7,260	7,998	8,274	334	-735	3	279
Service-producing	54,080	84,363	99,898	107,405	113,168	30,283	15,535	23,042	28,805
Transp., comm., utilities	4,542	5,826	6,203	6,689	7,019	1,284	377	863	1,193
Wholesale trade	4,430	6,205	6,669	7,210	7,585	1,775	464	1,005	1,380
Retail trade	12,630	19,683	23,306	24,804	25,856	7,053	3,623	5,121	6,173
Fin., ins., and real estate	4,165	6,739	7,599	8,129	8,525	2,574	860	1,390	1,786
Services[a]	13,627	27,588	36,223	39,058	41,109	13,961	8,634	11,470	13,521
Government	14,686	18,322	19,899	21,515	23,074	3,636	1,577	3,193	4,752
Agriculture[b]	3,459	3,276	2,969	3,080	3,181	-183	-307	-196	-95
Private households	1,362	1,014	648	700	736	-348	-366	-314	-278
Nonagricultural self-employed and unpaid family workers[c]	6,165	8,961	10,415	10,763	11,095	2,796	1,454	1,802	2,134
Total[d]	87,666	122,570	136,807	147,190	154,543	34,904	14,237	24,620	31,973

[a] Excludes SIC 074,5,8 (agricultural services) and 99 (nonclassifiable establishments) and is therefore not exactly comparable with data published in *Employment and Earnings*.

[b] Excludes government wage and salary workers, and includes private sector SIC 08,09 (forestry and fisheries).

[c] Excludes SIC 08,09 (forestry and fisheries).

[d] Wage and salary data are from the BLS Current Employment Statistics (payroll) survey, which counts jobs, whereas self-employed, unpaid family worker, agricultural, and private household data are from the Current Population Survey (household survey), which counts workers.

SOURCE: M. Carey and J. Franklin, "Industry Output and Job Growth Continues Slow into Next Century," *Monthly Labor Review*, November 1991, Table 1, p. 46.

TABLE 13–4
Employment by Major Occupational Group, 1990 and Projected 2005
(*moderate alternative projection*)

Occupation	1990	2005	Percent Change 1975–90	1990–2005
Total, all occupations	122,573	147,191	37.4	20.1
Exec., admin., managerial	12,451	15,866	83.1	27.4
Professional specialty	15,800	20,907	59.9	32.3
Technicians and related support	4,204	5,754	75.7	36.9
Marketing and sales	14,088	17,489	55.1	24.1
Admin. support occupations, including clerical	21,951	24,835	33.9	13.1
Service occupations	19,204	24,806	36.1	29.2
Agricultural, forestry, fishing, and related occupations	3,506	3,665	−9.8	4.5
Precision production, craft, repair	14,124	15,909	28.9	12.6
Operators, fabricators, laborers	17,245	17,961	6.7	4.2

NOTE: The 1990 and 2005 employment data and the projected change 1990–2005 are derived from the industry-occupation employment matrixes for each year. The data on 1975–90 percent change were derived from the Current Population Survey (CPS), because a comparable industry-occupation matrix for 1975 is not available.

SOURCE: G. Silvestri and J. Lukasiewicz, "Occupational Employment Projections," *Monthly Labor Review*, November 1991, Table 1, p. 65.

THE SERVICES PRODUCTIVITY CONTROVERSY

There is much concern about the apparent lack of productivity growth in U.S. service industries, despite massive recent investments in technology infrastructures, especially in information technologies. Stephen Roach, Principal and Chief Economist of Morgan Stanley, has repeatedly documented the services productivity problem as measured by national databases.[3] He points out that investments in information technology (dominantly by the services sector) have grown to exceed those for industrial equipment (see Figures 13–1 and 13–2). Yet paradoxically, services productivity and white collar productivity—as measured—have not grown significantly. Dr. Roach says:

> Until recently, [U.S.] services have been sheltered from competition and have had little incentive to drive out inefficiency. Shielded by regulation and not confronted by foreign competitors, service companies have allowed their white collar payrolls to become bloated, their information technology investments to outstrip paybacks, and their productivity to stagnate. . . . There is a painful irony at work: job creation, the very attribute proponents point to as proof that the services sector can propel the U.S. back to economic preeminence, is in fact a symptom of the sector's chronic neglect of economic efficiency.[4]

Roach's concerns have real validity and he documents the macro case well.

PROBLEMS AT THE INDUSTRY LEVEL

Paul Strassmann, in his book *The Business Value of Computers*,[5] has also expressed deep concerns about the productivity of services investments, particularly in IT, at the industry and company level. In an extensive survey of how industries and individual concerns

FIGURE 13–1
Information Technology Capital per White-Collar Worker

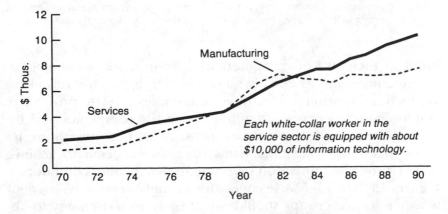

SOURCE: S. Roach, "Technology Focus," *U.S. Investment Research*, Morgan Stanley, November 22, 1991. Used with permission.

FIGURE 13–2
Investment in Technology Outpaces White-Collar Productivity

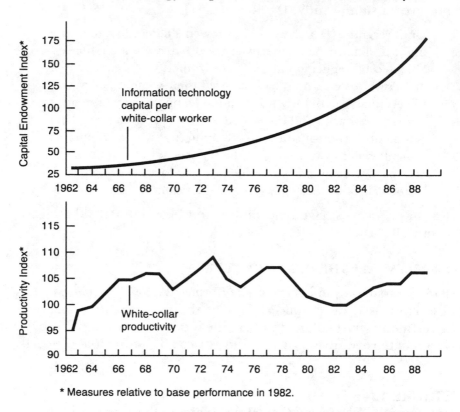

* Measures relative to base performance in 1982.

SOURCE: S. Roach, "Service Under Siege: The Restructuring Imperative," *Harvard Business Review*, September–October 1991, p. 85. Reprinted by permission of *Harvard Business Review*. Copyright © 1991 by President and Fellows of Harvard College; all rights reserved.

fared in their use of computers and information technologies, Strassmann found essentially no correlation between levels of investment in information technology and sales growth, profits per employee, or returns to shareholders in the companies and industries he studied. Citing many measurement complications, he notes that some individual firms nevertheless seem to achieve quite reasonable returns on investments, while others do not (see Figures 13–3 to 13–5). He concludes strongly that the issue is not whether service groups should invest more in technology to obtain productivity, but how they should manage investments for greater productivity. This has been a primary focus in this book.

FIGURE 13–3
Relationships Between Profitability and Information Technology Spending Appear to Be Random

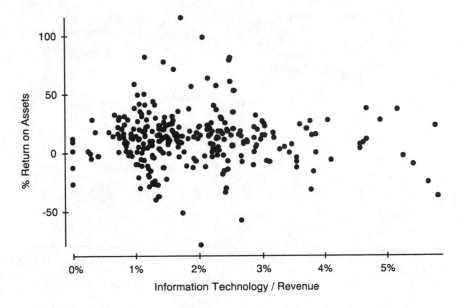

SOURCE: P. Strassmann, *The Business Use of Computers* (New Canaan, CT: Information Economics Press, 1990), p. xviii. Reproduced with permission.

Strassmann, a former VP and Chief Information Officer at Xerox Corp., summarizes as follows: "A computer is only worth what it can fetch at an auction. It has value only if surrounded by appropriate policy, strategy, methods for measuring results, project controls, talented and committed people, sound organization relationships, and well designed information systems. . . . The productivity of management is the decisive element that makes the difference in whether a computer hurts or helps." We concur. Strassman then provides a formidable seventeen-page "Policy Checklist" describing just what policies he believes will make such management productive. While very comprehensive and thoughtful, these need to be sifted carefully and tailored to meet the firm's own specific strategy, as we have suggested here.

Neither of these two productivity critics is pleased by his discoveries. In fact, both have published widely to focus more of management's attention on the disturbing implications. But they

FIGURE 13–4
**Ten-Year Shareholder Return Versus I.T. Cost per Employee
at 14 Banks**

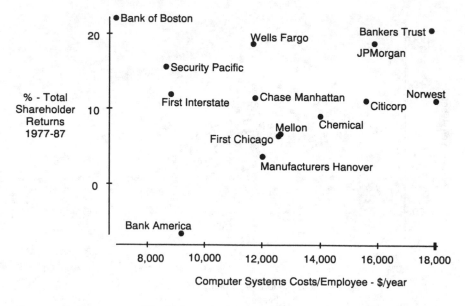

SOURCE: P. Strassmann, *The Business Use of Computers* (New Canaan, CT: Information Economics Press, 1990), p. 36, Figure 3.4. Reproduced with permission.

have to some extent been trapped by the limitations of available data and measurement techniques for evaluating service productivity. Both would agree that the best way to measure the output side of the services productivity equation is in terms of what value the service produces for its customers as well as its producers. With this in mind, both have used market measures of sales volume, profit, and investment returns to the extent possible. But both would also admit that macro measures cannot always capture the quality gains and—more importantly—the "opportunity costs" of demise that technology investments may avoid. Executives evaluating company performance face the same problem, as was outlined in Chapter 11. How does one reflect in internal productivity measures the fact that the entire institution—bank, hospital, or airline—could not *exist* without its technology investments? Or that X percent of its clients might have been bankrupt, dead, or totally incapacitated if it had not made these investments? As in measuring services quality, a whole new set of metrics is necessary.

FIGURE 13-5
Profit per Employee Versus I.T. Expense per Employee

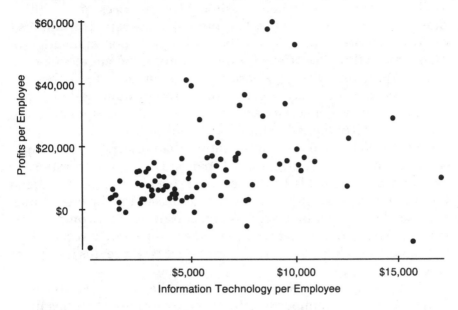

SOURCE: P. Strassmann, *The Business Use of Computers* (New Canaan, CT: Information Economics Press, 1990), p. 52, Figure 3.16. Reproduced with permission.

SERIOUS PROBLEMS IN MACRO MEASUREMENTS

Given the problems of measuring productivity at the company level, it is not surprising that there are major complications in interpreting productivity at the industry and macro economic levels—and even more problems in making international comparisons. Any macro figures must be used with great caution. Without resorting to elaborate and overly expensive sampling and measurement techniques, it is very difficult to find metrics that truly measure the value of outputs in some service industries. Although in a few fields reasonably useful output measures exist (like ton miles in transportation or kilowatt hours for public utilities), in most service industries outputs are very difficult to define.

Government-collected data attempt to introduce a deflator that adjusts outputs measured by prices to represent output volumes more fairly. For a variety of reasons, even adjusted prices are not always good output measures. For example, life-enabling medical care or safety services may normally cost little more than a hotel room or a good restaurant meal—or they may not be available at any price when needed. Many services' prices (like those for many professionals: accountants, lawyers, consultants, or social services workers) are based on cost, not value-added. Many others (brokers, travel agents, architects and engineers, real estate agents, or sales reps) are based on standardized fees or commissions, which may or may not represent value-added. And the outputs of major service sectors (police, fire, emergency, government, environmental, educational, and public health services) are measured by their cost inputs rather than prices. Finally, many services long were price-regulated, particularly in the transportation and utilities fields. As these have been deregulated, their lower current prices create a downward bias in measuring output gains as determined by prices. When substitutes and competitive pricing exist, properly deflated prices may represent a reasonable surrogate for value, but there are many areas where this is not the case.

The way in which national data have been defined and collected has led to a number of other potentially important negative biases in measured service productivity.[6] Chief among these is the fact that, although quality and productivity are integrally interrelated, improvements in service quality are rarely reflected in macro economic measures.

■ For example, today's health care systems can cure more diseases, more quickly, and with greater reliability than ever before. Pain control, rehabilitation, and survival potentials have improved enormously for many deadly ailments (for example, various cancers, diabetes, and heart disease) and many other lesser diseases. Vast numbers of other diseases which were debilitating to fatal a few decades ago (polio, measles, smallpox, scarlet fever) can now be prevented or controlled completely. Law firms can do much more thorough background analyses, scientific researchers can search databases in greater depth, and educators can have more data at their fingertips for classes than ever before. Through new telecommunications technologies, homes enjoy entire entertainment centers, instant connections to worldwide communications networks, and access to disaster prevention systems that did not exist a few years ago. The dispatching and responses of fire, police, and emergency units is much faster, safer, and more accurate than ever before. Financial services can be provided instantly and accurately, worldwide, with less difficulty than ever before. And so on.

None of the above quality improvements shows up directly in the macro measures. Consequently there is a downward bias in productivity measures when comparing these industries' outputs either with those of other industries or with their own outputs in the past.

WHAT DO MACRO MEASURES REALLY MEAN?

Because the outputs of so many services—including police and fire departments, pollution control, government and social services, museums and libraries, and even certain aspects of banking and health care—are measured in terms of their costs, one could hardly expect to find measured productivity improvements in these important sectors. With almost one-third of U.S. GNP in government and other public services whose outputs are mostly measured by their costs, one wonders whether highly aggregated measures have much meaning. In many other service areas, as earlier chapters have noted, competition is so fierce that cost savings must be passed on to either customers or suppliers. Lacking direct measures for physical outputs in the realms of private health, accounting, legal, financial, consulting, and other professional services, national databases measure their output in dollar sales terms. Even though these firms perform much more complex tasks faster than ever before, because of competition they must pass savings through to their customers. Improved productivity in these and other services, therefore, often shows up—if it can be captured by the databases at all—as an improvement in their customers' or suppliers' (often manufacturers') performance. For example:

■ As wholesalers like McKesson or SuperValu improved their service capabilities for customers, they actually lost percentage gross margins. McKesson's wholesaling margins have dropped from about 7 percent to 3 percent over the last fifteen years, making another 4 percentage points available for its retailers' and producers' margins. As David Malmberg of McKesson said:

> You pass savings on in two different ways. One is through lowering prices, and the other is by providing a higher level of

service. In our industry it's happened both ways. In order to be competitive you have to provide the higher service. For example, all the price stickers and price files are maintained by the drug wholesaler now. What used to be an extremely time-consuming expensive thing for the retailer is now done by the technology, but it doesn't show up in our margins; and our competitors have to match the service. In essence we've upped the investment ante for everyone.

Many of the automated tasks that used to be the core of professional practices (like audit checks in public accounting or preparing bubble charts for portfolio analyses in consulting or financial services firms) have now become almost loss leaders. Much of their value is passed through in order to sell clients other services. In addition, from a macro economic viewpoint there is much parallel (duplicative) investment among companies. In a period of "revolution" or "transition," as IT is now, multiple companies will try a new technology and only a few will succeed. Thus investment goes up while returns do not. There are also lags until workers learn the new system and confusion costs as systems are debugged. Workers may barely reach full capabilities with one system before the next replaces it. And as work moves from clerical to knowledge worker levels, hourly wages for the tasks may rise, further confounding payoff measures.

IT also often permits not just doing things better (efficiency) in the old way, but doing new things that provide greater benefits for outside parties (effectiveness). Because of competitive factors these may not always be capturable in increased ROI, sales, margins, or macro statistics. In particular, the intangibles of better responsiveness, longer hours of availability, convenience, or timing may not show up in macro measures. Nevertheless, they may increase the value to customers enormously or decrease their costs—also not captured in the macro data—of transit, waiting, home storage, or communications with vendors.

Although there are also marked inadequacies in the product sector's productivity measurements (especially in the measurement of quality improvements), it is much easier to measure decreases in the inputs needed to produce a single car, television set, ton of steel or grain, or square foot of housing construction. Executives in the service sector, and many macro economists, are seeking better ways to measure services productivity—and to explain to investors the seeming problems in payoffs from technology investments, especially those in information technology (IT). Intensive efforts are under way to improve services productivity measures at both levels. The National Research Council's "Committee to Study the Impact of Information Technology on the Performance of Service Activities" will issue a full report in the fall of 1992, offering a much improved sense of the utility, limitations, and future needs of macro data in U.S. services and some guidance concerning the way leading edge service companies approach the productivity problem.[7]

WHAT ARE THE PROSPECTS FOR WAGES?

Macro economic measures of services productivity do have some serious shortcomings. But they also pose some key questions. Is productivity in services great enough to provide a high standard of living? Can productivity increase fast enough for that standard of living to grow rapidly in real terms? The Japanese have answered both questions positively. They are paying a 30 percent average premium for service labor at the same age-experience level as for people in manufacturing. And their high service investments are currently increasing productivity in the service industries at over 5 percent a year. Our PIMS data analyses of value-added per person, as well as our company interviews, suggest similar potentials exist in the United States.

Both our data and the Japanese experience suggest that when technology systems are well designed and implemented, value-added per person can be high enough in services to support wages comparable to those in manufacturing industries, unless wages in the latter are arbitrarily established by labor monopolies or trade barriers. In fact, average wages in individual service sectors and service occupations—like transportation, professional services, investment banking, medical practice, communications, or entertainment—have been comparable to or higher than those in many manufacturing sectors for prolonged periods (see Table 13–5).

A preeminently service economy can produce wealth at rates as high as any manufacturing-oriented one, provided it manages its services with care. This does not imply a dichotomy or a conflict between services and a productive manufacturing sector. As has been noted, these same services provide such important markets and infrastructure supports for manufacturing that they are essential to the health of manufacturing and the vital jobs and ex-

TABLE 13–5
Average Hourly Earnings in Private Nonagricultural Jobs
(*production or nonsupervisory workers*)

Industry	1982	Mid-1987	June 1991	Compound Average Annual Growth Rate, 1982–91
Total Private Sector	$ 7.68	8.94[a]	10.37[a]	3.39%
Mining	10.77	12.44	14.30	3.20
Construction	11.63	12.61	13.98	2.07
Manufacturing total	8.50	9.87	11.19	3.10
Transportation & public utilities	10.32	11.91	13.23	2.80
Wholesale trade	8.09	9.57	11.23	3.71
Retail trade	5.48	6.08	7.01	2.77
Finance, insurance, & real estate	6.78	8.68	10.50	4.98
Services (other)	6.92	8.35	10.29	4.51

[a] Seasonally adjusted.

SOURCES: Bureau of Labor Statistics, Establishment Data Base: Average Hours and Earnings of Production or Nonsupervisory Workers on Private Nonagricultural Payrolls by Major Industry (November 1983) and "Current Labor Statistics," *Monthly Labor Review*, November 1991, Table 15.

ports that sector brings with it. The sectors are symbiotic, not antagonistic, in furthering the nation's trade. For decades, even as manufacturing trade balances have slipped, services have provided positive net trade balances and support for U.S. manufacturers in world trade (see Table 7–1).

GOVERNMENT POLICY ISSUES

Recognizing these important facts, and others introduced in earlier chapters as context, what are the central policy initiatives needed at the national level to support the effective use of technology in services? In most instances, market forces are quite sufficient for reasonable allocations in the services sector. Government intervention is justified only in situations where market imperfections or externalities make it unlikely that private initiatives can meet the challenge. Fortunately, the basic macro economic and tax policies to support a strong services sector are quite compatible with those desirable for a healthy manufacturing sector. This is not surprising when one understands the substitutability and interrelatedness of the two sectors.

CAPITAL COST POLICIES.   As in manufacturing, radical innovations in services tend to take many years. Federal Express' COSMOS II tracking system took eight years, Citicorp's development of automated teller machines spanned more than ten years, and the cellular mobile telephone waited eleven years from AT&T's public filing to market implementation. Similarly, it took decades to develop and deploy fiber optics communication networks. The time frames for major technology developments and implementation in services appear to be relatively comparable to those in manufacturing. Hence major technological changes in both are very sensitive to high capital costs or tax laws that bias decisions toward short-term investments.

Primary among the stimulants that would help both sectors are policies that would lower capital costs by stimulating national capital formation and investments in technology and producing assets.[8] Because of the high capital-intensiveness in large-scale services, the effects should be as helpful in services as they are in manufacturing. Decreasing taxes on earned interest or the double taxation of dividends would, of course, assist in such a reemphasis, as would increasing the relative percentage of government tax revenues from consumption as opposed to taxes based on income production.

The electronic integration of world capital markets has made a policy of arbitrarily low capital costs much more difficult for any country to maintain, even for Japan. Nevertheless, selectively lowering capital costs for longer-term investments (through a capital gains benefit that had at least a three-year vesting period) is—as most of the other leading nations in OECD have proved—a viable strategy, especially if combined with less inflationary fiscal policies. As many have noted, the most important such policy shift would be decreasing the federal government's deficits to lower pressures on available capital resources as well as to ameliorate investors' uncertainties and inflationary expectations. Although the economic benefits and political costs of these measures have been debated extensively, the substantial leverage of the benefits for and from the services sector has rarely been considered.

INFRASTRUCTURE INVESTMENTS.   In addition, increased and better-managed government investments in both hard and soft services infrastructures (research, education, communications, data collection, transportation, waste disposal, and health care systems) could improve the competitiveness of U.S. services and goods producers as much as many private investments could. Recent studies suggest high economic benefits from increased public investment in such infrastructures.[9] Historically, government-supported service infrastructure investments—starting with mail, road, canal, and water transportation systems, and expanding later into higher education, basic research, electric power distribution, and health care systems—have been major components in building both U.S. productivity and human capital bases for a higher per capita income. Just as the Rural Electrification Administration built huge markets for appliances and other goods by supporting electrical infrastructures, other large markets could be opened by supplementing private investments in high-bandwidth rural communications infrastructures. Unfortunately, however, real public sector investments and public capital stock per government worker have been allowed to drop steadily during the 1970s and 1980s. Focusing government budgetary discussions toward public sector investments which also create employment and away from income transfer and income supports is clearly needed.

REGULATORY ISSUES.   Because of the extensive cross-industry competition noted in earlier chapters, it has become ever less effective to regulate companies or industries on an industry or institutional basis (i.e., regulating banks or airlines as individual industries). Although more efficient market structures allow competition to replace certain regulatory requirements, new forms of intervention may be desirable to overcome new market imperfections. Nonregulation—as the S&L, banking, and insurance industry crises indicate—can be very costly and is clearly not an answer. Increasingly, however, regulation is likely to be more equitable at a transactional level (i.e., establishing similar disclosure, safety, or insurance requirements for a particular class of transaction), regardless of which institution actually handles it, or at the functional level (i.e., establishing similar health, maintenance, environmental, safety, or electronics interface standards across all industries that might compete). Regulation (such as the Glass–Steagall Act) at the single industry or institutional level merely encourages disintermediation, i.e., bypassing of the overregulated institution. It also promotes inefficiencies by eliminating potential competitors and their alternative products. As John Kendrick and others have often said, it is imperative that regulations be goal-oriented, rather than means-specifying, and that the goals be constantly coordinated and reevaluated in a systematic manner across agencies.

In industries providing such services as software, music and video recording, and databases, the protection of intellectual property (both domestically and across national borders) is crucial. Information achieves its maximum value in a society when it can be shared. Clearly understood and enforceable intellectual property rules encourage sharing of knowledge through more complete disclosure (including the patent or copyright itself), thereby allowing others to build more effectively on the protected concept. Currently, the patent law lacks clear or reliable rules for defining infringement versus legitimate copying of software. Consequently, important software is often available only in uncopyable form, and computer companies expend considerable effort to prevent others from cloning and selling software they spent years and tens of millions of dollars to create. Lack of protection militates against innovation and wastes the valuable resources of innovators who must seek tricks to keep others from stealing and exploiting their efforts. Clearly, international coordination is badly needed.

TRADE POLICIES. Finally, trade policies should increasingly reflect the importance of service industries and activities. It is estimated that there is more than $700 billion in international services trade, which is virtually all outside GATT. Because so much of the services sector in most nations is government-owned or government-managed, it will take years for a general agreement such as GATT to substantially ameliorate each country's unique constraints on services trade. Specific bilateral or limited multilateral negotiations seem the most likely road to progress in the near future, especially with the less-than-hoped-for results from the Uruguay Round of discussions. Open access for foreigners to the huge U.S. services market should be used as a powerful bargaining chip in obtaining more open access for U.S. companies wishing to trade manufactures or services in other nations.

The threat of tariff barriers is rarely effective in services trade, but selectively being able to deny acquisitions of U.S. companies by foreign enterprises whose countries do not offer reciprocal access may be helpful in leveling the playing field with major competitors. Services trade and merchandise trade are inseparable in many instances. For example, Japanese service exports in transportation, finance, and downstream services derive naturally from Japan's large merchandise export activities. Leverage can be brought against countries with strong product trade balances (like Japan) to allow U.S. manufacturing companies to operate under equivalent rules, including provision of U.S. services and entry of U.S. service companies in support of product sales in those countries. To do otherwise is to allow competitor nations to exploit their advantages in manufacturing, while denying the U.S. the right to benefit from its relative strength in services.

PUBLIC EDUCATION AND WAGES

It is increasingly apparent that education and human skills development are the foundations of value-added in many industries and that provisions for lifelong education are critical for individuals to obtain and upgrade the skills called for in today's rapidly restructuring economy. Job-specific training by companies is often the most appropriate way of training for economic adjustments. However, there are many situations in which the benefits an employer can capture are significantly less than the social benefits of enhancing a skill base. In those cases, public support of training and education is crucial. This is especially true for individuals with less formal education. Sadly, these individuals are also the least likely to derive benefit from on-the-job training provided by employers. They should be the primary target for public training and retraining initiatives. Public incentives for on-the-job retraining could also yield high gains for the country—as many studies of past programs indicate they do. But government support for all such endeavors has dropped substantially in real terms over the last decade.

Many other studies have also suggested that for the government to try to define and target specific skills for development in public education institutions is very inefficient, if not counterproductive. These studies indicate that general levels of education and literacy, rather than targeted skills, provide the greatest long-term flexibility and growth opportunities for individuals and the society. They also show substantial payoffs for both individuals and the nation from higher levels of education. Improving the quality of the U.S. public education system, therefore, is probably the outstanding policy area where federal and state governments could make most contributions to the future development of the services sector.

One important consideration contributing to a more productive treatment of the educational issue, however, would be a more sophisticated discussion of service wages in public policy debates. Comparing average wages in manufacturing (especially past manufacturing wages) versus those of the services sector is particularly misguided. Because great variations exist among specific job categories and industries, a more relevant focal point would be on the wage levels and opportunities in particular service industries or occupations versus those in individual manufacturing categories (see Tables 13–3 through 13–5).

Even then, certain important adjustments should be made. Today, services—not blue-collar jobs—provide the most available entry point for new, secondary, or part-time workers, as well as for high school students, females, and retirees entering or reentering the workforce. When analyzing wages in services, one should adjust for these entry conditions, the greater convenience and better working conditions, the lower experience requirements, and the more flexible hours offered by many service jobs. Such jobs are essential for multiple-earner families and for developing the attitudes, skills, and disciplines needed for more permanent job holding.

Disparaging services wages in policy conversations seems singularly unproductive. Services have undoubtedly absorbed displacements from manufacturing into local jobs. The economy has benefited if the wage levels in growing service areas—and the value-added that is presumably necessary to support them—are higher than those that the displaced workers would have had to accept to keep their companies from going overseas. In many cases, the workers spurned the job conditions and the wages that would have been necessary for competitiveness. As service company outputs become more substitutable for manufacturing tasks in the manner noted earlier—notably in design, materials handling, quality assurance, maintenance, accounting, marketing, research, sales, and other support tasks—wages should progressively equilibrate between the two sectors. New data indicate they have steadily begun to do so in the past few years. The real question is whether they will equilibrate among countries as well. This will depend on how much each country can innovate, increase productivity, and invest to leverage its human and intellectual resources.

AN ENDLESS HORIZON

Policies like those outlined above are essential if the country hopes to exploit the full potentials services offer for the future. The capacity of services to create value is limited only by the capacity of human imaginations to think up more important things to do with their time as intermediate customers or as final customers—and the imaginations of others to think up better ways to serve their customers' health, financial, communications, transportation, entertainment, security, distribution, storage, lodging, gastronomic, education, design, information, comfort, cultural, environmental, public service, and specialized knowledge needs. Although this book has tried to show how to perform some of these services more effectively, it has also attempted to suggest some of the endless technological opportunities and challenges that these activities present for the generation of future jobs and wealth production.

Looking to the future, one can easily see myriad new strategic investments that could revolutionize the way major service industries will develop. Uncertainties and delayed paybacks may make many of these hard to justify now or in the near future for an individual firm or on a macro economic basis. And they may make new service investments look relatively unproductive during this decade. Whether new service innovations go ahead will be determined largely by the faith, persuasiveness, and energies of a few entrepreneurs and visionaries. As in many past innovations, uncertainties are high and aggregate paybacks in the short run may well be negative. In the long run, however, individual companies and countries are likely to benefit dramatically as entrepreneurs bring certain new service opportunities into being. For example:

■ The health care industry will be revolutionized in immeasurable ways by new drugs and biotechnology. In addition, new knowledge-intensive technology systems for continuously monitoring and adjusting body chemistry and organ function will allow much greater individual freedom for patients. Micro surgery techniques will make many more massive surgery procedures—with their pain and incapacitation—obsolete. The capacity to map the human genome and to see the interaction of microbiological entities at the cellular level will speed research and make currently unknown cures routine, perhaps leading to more people suffering more difficult diseases in later lie. All will restructure health care systems in unimagined ways, many of which cannot be captured by macro economic measures.

Scanning tunneling microscopes (STMs) will revolutionize processes in chemistry, materials, and surfaces—leading to unforeseeable new products and their associated byproduct problems. High-definition video technologies, digital audio technologies, and virtual reality systems will stimulate another revolution in home entertainment, creating whole new industries and demolishing many that exist today. And integrated communications, imaging, and printing technologies will steadily redefine, then destroy, the boundaries among today's communications, entertainment, news, photography, and advertising industries. The desirability of many companies' elaborate investments in fixed facilities, along with their real estate value, may well disappear as more workers provide their own facilities—either at home or in decentralized nodes elsewhere. And so on, *ad infinitum.*

WHAT IS THE ECONOMIC PAYOFF?

Almost all of these will require strategic service investments for someone, creating rapid cycles of very uncertain investments for some and destroying for others the payoffs from earlier investments in related fields. In a sense, these earlier investments may never achieve acceptable paybacks. Yet without them, customers would have been less satisfied in the interim, and successful innovators would have lacked the resources to go on to the new innovations. Investments in these new industries may not pay off in the aggregate for decades—as has often been the case of specific DRAMs—because of low probability of success ratios, high investments, and severe competition. Nevertheless, through such competition, individual companies will thrive in each cycle, and customers will prosper. The only meaningful way to look at the macro productivity of technology investments in these kinds of rapidly developing, very competitive service systems is whether customers feel better served by the systems and will pay some vendors for them—and whether some producer is willing to put up the capital and energy to create the system itself.

To ask whether home videos are more productive per labor hour than movie houses, or whether micro surgery takes fewer capital and human inputs than scalpel surgery, seems to beg the point. One is not selling hours or machines, but the perceived value customers place on a given output and whether individual enterprises—or all a nation's institutions in the aggregate—are delivering that output at lowest reasonable cost. Perversely, as in manufacturing, better technology will probably lower costs and hence prices for all producers and make it harder for anyone to make a profit. But staying with old systems and technologies would be even worse; there would be no new jobs and improved customer benefits at all. One needs to remember the long, hard development cycle of airlines, where the hours of life lost in aircraft accidents through the early 1920s exceeded the hours saved by commerical passenger travel. Productivity would have had to be judged as miserable in this case, yet in retrospect the groundwork for multiple industries was being laid—which now might justify even those heavy costs.

Service productivity potentials generally will not be determined by hardware systems or the capacity to lay off workers, but by software and the capabilities of human imagination to conceive creative ways service technologies can be used in new strategic applications. The keys to future service productivity lie in (1) seeking out and effectively delivering new and greater values for customers, rather than in further routinizing internal operations, and (2) reorganizing the entire relationship between customers and the company's internal structures and work practices. Both require new strategic applications of service technologies—exactly where forecasting or measuring results is most difficult. How many at the outset would have predicted the mammoth successes of CNN, Microsoft, Home Video, 7-Eleven, *USA Today*, UNIX, MCI, Jiffy Lube, Mrs. Fields' Cookies, or Federal Express? Conversely, who would have predicted the decline of most general audience magazines, many major airlines, the U.S. education system, most center-city department stores, Drexel Burnham, S&Ls, or many savings banks?

Far from being the peripheral outputs of a society, services are the essence of that output. These are the truly endless horizons of a modern society. Services are not to be feared but embraced, nurtured, and managed as the economic engine of future progress. It is time we changed our attitudes and misconceptions about service-based economies and businesses and developed new paradigms for thinking about the economy, business strategy, and management in an integrated way.

A NEW PARADIGM

Here, we have attempted to develop a new strategic paradigm that restructures and links the way managers and policymakers should think about knowledge-based activities and services in both the service and the product sectors. We have tried to link the macro economic, business strategy, organizational, and technological implications of the massive changes services and their technologies are creating.

Clearly, the leverageable base of most companies' core competencies is in service activities. These in turn usually rest on some special knowledge-based or intellectual skills. Increasingly, therefore, developing and managing human intellect and skills—more than managing and deploying physical and capital assets—will be the dominant concerns of managers in successful companies. With this must come a management shift from short-term, product-oriented, inwardly focused strategies toward longer-term, people-centered, service-oriented, knowledge-based, and customer-focused strategies. New metrics are needed at the operations, corporate, and national levels to evaluate and manage these kinds of systems. No one yet has a complete fix on precisely what these new metrics are or what their associated management systems will be. What is needed today is a willingness on the part of managers to (1) recognize the huge opportunities services and their technologies have created, (2) begin to think about them in new, more constructive ways internally, (3) design their strategies around their core knowledge and service skills, (4) focus on the human and process factors that create these core competencies, and (5) begin systematically to implement the kinds of new attitudes, organizations, and control-incentive programs these call for.

This book has tried to provide a useful framework for thinking about these problems at the national, corporate, and operations levels. As our research team develops more data, we shall support these recommendations in greater detail, moving from the preponderantly strategic overview of this book toward the refinements of the "intelligent enterprise" no one has yet thoroughly mastered. We have tried to present a well-researched beginning point for changes we expect to emerge over the next few years and decades. We hope it offers some new insights for researchers and policy makers who must meet the awesome challenges facing our society at the macro economic, industry, and enterprise levels.

NOTES

Chapter 1. Services Restructure the Economy

1. Bureau of Economic Analysis, "The National Income and Product Accounts of the United States," Series in *Survey of Current Business*, July 1990 and October 1991.
2. Manufacturing employment in 1974 was 20.1 million, in 1989, 19.5 million. Bureau of Economic Analysis, "Business Statistics 1961–88," *A Supplement to the Survey of Current Business*, December 1989, and *Survey of Current Business*, July 1990.
3. Bureau of Economic Analysis, "U.S. International Transactions," series in *Survey of Current Business*, various years and quarters.
4. For a summary, see J. B. Quinn and B. Guile (eds.), *Technology in Services: Policies for Growth, Trade, and Employment*, National Academy of Engineering (Washington, DC: National Academy Press, 1988).
5. R. Kutscher and J. Mark, "The Services Sector: Some Common Perceptions Reviewed," *Monthly Labor Review*, April 1983.
6. A. Smith, *The Wealth of Nations* (Oxford: Clarendon Press, 1976), is a good current edition.
7. K. Marx, *Capital*, trans. Eden Paul and Cedar Paul (New York: Dutton, 1972), is an excellent translation.
8. Profit Impact of Market Strategy (PIMS) data are collected from cooperating companies on a voluntary basis by the Strategic Planning Institute of Cambridge, Massachusetts. Data were analyzed under royalty arrangements with PIMS.
9. S. Roach, "Services Under Siege: The Restructuring Imperative," *Harvard Business Review*, September–October 1991.
10. Kutscher and Mark, "Services Sector."
11. J. Mark, "Problems Encountered in Measuring Single and Multi-factor Productivity," *Monthly Labor Review*, December 1986; M. Baily and R. Gordon, "The Productivity Slowdown, Measurement Issues, and the Explosion of Computer Power," Brookings Papers on Economic Activity, no. 2, 1988; and E. Brynjolfsson and B.

Bimber, "Information Technology and the Productivity Paradox," Working Paper, Brookings Institution, February 1991.

12. J. Kendrick, "Service Sector Productivity," *Business Economics*, April 1987.

13. J. Mark, "Measuring Productivity in the Service Industries: The BLS Experience," in Quinn and Guile, *Technology in Services*.

14. J. Kendrick, "Productivity in Services," in Quinn and Guile, *Technology in Services*.

15. B. Bluestone and B. Harrison, *The Great American Jobs Machine* (Washington, DC: Joint Economic Committee, U.S. Congress, 1986); M. Dertouzos *et al.*, *Made in America: Regaining the Productive Edge* (Cambridge, MA: MIT Press, 1989); and S. Cohen and J. Zysman, "Why Manufacturing Matters: The Myth of the Post-Industrial Economy," *California Management Review*, Spring 1987.

16. R. Gonenc, "Changing Economics of International Trade in Services," in Quinn and Guile, *Technology in Services*.

17. T. Peters, "Fashions. Projects. Markets. Tries . . . and Carnivals!" TPG Communications, 1991. Thomas Peters will develop the thesis further in his new book, *Liberation Management: Necessary Disorganization for the Nanasecond Nineties,* to be published October 1992.

18. P. Keen, *Competing in Time: Using Telecommunications for Competitive Advantage* (Cambridge, MA: Ballinger, 1988).

19. Booz, Allen, Hamilton, *Outlook*, Fall 1982; M. Porter, *Competitive Advantage* (New York Free Press, 1985).

20. J. Goldhar and D. Burnham, "Concept of the Manufacturing System . . ." in *U.S. Leadership in Manufacturing*, National Academy of Engineering Symposium, Washington DC, 1983, were the first to develop this concept.

21. J. Naisbitt, *Megatrends* (New York: Warner Books, 1982).

22. G. Moore, "The Services Industries and the Business Cycle," *Business Economics*, April 1987.

23. R. Chand, "Employment During Recessions: The Boost from Services," *Canadian Business Review*, Summer 1986.

Chapter 2. Focusing Strategy on Core Intellectual and Service Competencies

1. M. Dertouzos *et al.*, *Made in America: Regaining the Productive Edge* (Cambridge, MA: MIT Press, 1989); R. Hayes and W. Abernathy, "Managing Our Way to Economic Decline," *Harvard Business Review*, July–August 1980; S. Cohen and J. Zysman, "Why Manufacturing Matters: The Myth of the Post-Industrial Economy," *California Management Review*, Spring 1987; L. Mishel, "Manufacturing Numbers: How Inaccurate Statistics Conceal U.S. Industrial Decline," Economic Policy Institute, 1988.

2. These examples and the charts included in this chapter were the core examples and exhibits included in the *Sloan Management Review* and *Harvard Business Review* manuscripts as submitted to those publications in 1988 and 1989. The first draft was submitted to *Harvard Business Review* in September 1988.

3. Office of U.S. Trade Representative, *U.S. National Study on Trade in Services* (Washington, DC, 1983); T. Vollmann, "The Effect of Zero Inventories on Cost . . ." in *Cost Accounting for the 1990s: The Challenge of Technological Change* (Montvale, NJ: National Association of Accountants, 1986).

4. E. Clemons and W. McFarlan, "Telecom: Hook Up or Lose Out," *Harvard Business Review*, July–August 1986.

5. J. B. Quinn, J. Baruch, and P. Paquette, "Exploiting the Manufacturing–Services Interface," *Sloan Management Review*," Summer 1988.

6. "The Best Companies," *The Economist*, September 7, 1991.

7. See "Ford: Team Taurus" (case), in H. Mintzberg and J. Quinn, *The Strategy Process*, 2d ed. (Englewood Cliffs, NJ: Prentice Hall, 1991).

8. A. Morita and S. Ishihara, *The Japan That Can Say "NO": The New U.S.–Japan Relations Card* (Kobunsha Kappa-Holmes, 1989); R. Reich, "Who Is Us?" *Harvard Business Review*, January–February 1990.

9. Office of U.S. Trade Representative, *U.S. National Study*; Vollmann, "Effect of Zero Inventories."

10. A. Rappaport and S. Halevi, "The Computerless Computer Company," *Harvard Business Review*, July–August 1991.

11. W. Davidson, "Apple Computer, Inc.," Case UVA-BP219, University of Virginia, 1984.

12. M. Moritz, *The Little Kingdom: The Private Story of Apple Computer* (New York: William Morrow, 1984), details these relationships.

13. J. Fierman, "How Gallo Crushes the Competition," *Fortune*, September 1986.

14. "E & J Gallo Winery" (case), in Mintzberg and Quinn, *Strategy Process*.

15. M. Donaghu and R. Barff, "Nike Just Did It: International Subcontracting and Flexibility in Athletic Footwear Production," *Regional Studies*, December 1990.

16. *Annual Report*, SCI Inc., 1990.

17. T. Peters, "Get Innovative or Get Dead," *California Management Review*, Fall 1990.

18. C. Handy, *The Age of Unreason* (Boston, MA: Harvard Business School Press, 1990), p. 53.

19. "The Incredible Shrinking Company," *The Economist*, December 15, 1991.

20. P. Drucker, "Sell the Mailroom," *Wall Street Journal*, July 25, 1989.

21. C. Prahalad and G. Hamel, "The Core Competence of the Corporation," *Harvard Business Review*, May–June 1990.

22. R. Pascale, "Perspectives on Strategy: The Real Story Behind Honda's Success," *California Management Review*, Spring 1984; "Honda Motor Co." (case) in Mintzberg and Quinn, *Strategy Process*.

23. T. Sakiya, *Honda Motor: The Men, The Management, The Machines* (Tokyo: Kodansha International, Ltd., 1982).

24. "Honda Motor Company" (case), in Mintzberg and Quinn, *Strategy Process*.

Chapter 3. Leveraging Knowledge and Service Based Strategies Through Outsourcing

1. See "Control Data Corp." and "Honda Motor Company" (cases), H. Mintzberg and J. Quinn, *The Strategy Process* (Englewood Cliffs, NJ: Prentice Hall, 1988 and 1991, respectively).

2. See T. Peters and R. Waterman, *In Search of Excellence* (New York: Harper & Row, 1982); J. Quinn, "Managing Innovation: Controlled Chaos," *Harvard Business Review*, May–June 1985.

3. Keen, P., *Competing in Time: Using Telecommunications for Competitive Advantage* (Cambridge, MA: Ballinger, 1988); G. Stalk and T. Hout, *Competing Against Time: How Timebased Competition Is Reshaping Global Markets* (New York: Free Press, 1990).

4. R. Reich, "Who Is Us?" *Harvard Business Review*, January–February 1990.

5. E. Von Hipple, *The Sources of Innovations* (New York: Oxford University Press, 1988).

6. "The Ins and Outs of Outing," *The Economist*, August 31, 1991.

7. M. Blaxill and T. Hout, "The Fallacy of the Overhead Quick Fix," *Harvard Business Review*, July–August 1991.

8. *Wall Street Journal*, January 16, 1992.

9. T. Steiner and D. Teixeira, *Technology in Banking* (Homewood, IL: Dow Jones–Irwin, 1990), provides further details.

10. *Yankee Watch*, prepared by the Yankee Group, 200 Portland Street, Boston, MA 02114.

11. "Telecommunications: Special Survey," *The Economist*, October 5, 1991, p. 25.

12. "Paying the Freight," *Distribution*, June 1988.

13. "Big Blue Apple," *The Economist*, October 5, 1991.

14. "Polaroid Corporation" (case), in Mintzberg and Quinn, *Strategy Process*, 2d ed.

15. D. Kirkpatrick, "Why Not Farm Out Your Computing?" *Fortune*, September 23, 1990.

Chapter 4. Revolutionizing Organizational Strategies

1. A. Chandler, *Strategy and Structure: Chapters in the History of the Industrial Enterprise* (Cambridge, MA: MIT Press, 1962).
2. C. Walker and R. Guest, *The Man on the Assembly Line* (Cambridge, MA: Harvard University Press, 1952).
3. Jan Carlzon develops this theme in his book about the dramatic turnaround at SAS Airlines. J. Carlzon, *Moments of Truth* (Cambridge, MA: Ballinger, 1987).
4. M. Porter, "Generic Competitive Strategies," in Michael Porter, *Competitive Advantage* (New York: Free Press, 1985).
5. This was the secret to McKesson's, SuperValu's, and Toys "R" Us's success.
6. C. Keith and A. Grody, "Electronic Automation of the New York Stock Exchange," in *Managing Innovation: Case Studies from the Services Industries* (Washington, DC: National Academy Press, 1988).
7. T. Levitt, "Industrialization of Service," *Harvard Business Review*, September–October 1976.
8. V. Zeithaml, A. Parasuraman, and L. Berry, *Delivering Quality Service* (New York: Free Press, 1990).
9. "Lots of Respect, Little Love," *The Economist*, July 27, 1991.
10. T. Peters, "Get Innovative or Get Dead," *California Management Review*; Fall 1990; D. Q. Mills, *Rebirth of the Corporation* (New York: J. Wiley & Sons, 1991).
11. P. Drucker, "The Coming of the New Organization," *Harvard Business Review*, January–February 1988.
12. "Federal Express Corporation" (case), in H. Mintzberg and J. Quinn, *The Strategy Process*, 2d ed. (Englewood Cliffs, NJ: Prentice Hall, 1991).
13. J. Bright, *Automation and Management* (Boston, MA: Division of Research, Graduate School of Business Administration, Harvard University, 1958).
14. C. Handy, *The Age of Unreason* (Boston: Harvard Business School Press, 1990).
15. Mills, *Rebirth of the Corporation*.
16. Speech by Walter Brown of Marshall Field, "Field's Computers Enriched Customer Service," at 1987 National Retail Marketing Association meeting in New York.
17. S. Davis and W. Davidson, *2020 Vision* (New York: Simon & Schuster, 1991).

18. R. Miles and C. Snow, "Organizations: New Concepts for New Forms," *California Management Review*, Spring 1986.
19. Derived by Victor E. McGee, Amos Tuck School, Dartmouth College, quoted in J. B. Quinn, "Managing Innovation: Controlled Chaos," *Harvard Business Review*, May–June 1985.
20. H. Mintzberg and A. McHugh, "Strategy Formulation in an Adhocracy," *Administrative Science Quarterly*, June 1985.
21. R. Eccles and D. Crane, "Managing Through Networks in Investment Banking," *California Management Review*, April 1988.
22. Handy, *Age of Unreason*.
23. "Corporate Little Helpers," *Australian Business*, August 7, 1991.
24. "NovaCare, Inc." (case), © 1992, James Brian Quinn.
25. P. Keen, *Competing in Time: Using Telecommunications for Competitive Advantage* (Cambridge, MA: Ballinger, 1988).
26. T. Steiner and D. Teixeira, *Technology in Banking* (Homewood, IL: Dow Jones–Irwin, 1990).

Chapter 5. Service Based Disaggregation with Strategic Focus

1. T. Peters, "Get Innovative or Get Dead," *California Management Review*, Fall 1990.
2. J.B. Quinn, "Managing Innovation: Controlled Chaos," *Harvard Business Review*, May–June 1985.
3. C. Handy, *The Age of Unreason* (Boston: Harvard Business School Press, 1990).
4. D. Q. Mills, *Rebirth of the Corporation* (New York: J. Wiley & Sons, 1991), p. 15.
5. Ralph J. Sarich, interviewed by the author, September 1991.
6. J. Newport, "American Express: Service that Sells," *Fortune*, November 20, 1989.
7. S. Roach, "Services Under Siege: The Restructuring Imperative," *Harvard Business Review*, September–October 1991.
8. T. Stuart, "GE Keeps Those Ideas Coming," *Fortune*, August 12, 1991.
9. "The New York Times Company" (case), in H. Mintzberg and J. Quinn, *The Strategy Process*, 2d. ed. (Englewood Cliffs, NJ: Prentice Hall, 1991).
10. S. Zuboff, *The Age of the Smart Machine* (New York: Basic Books, 1988).
11. L. Berry, lecture at Executive Focus, Inc., Executive Roundtable, Palm Beach, Florida, April 1991.
12. V. Zeithaml, A. Parasuraman, and L. Berry, *Delivering Quality Service* (New York: Free Press, 1990).
13. P. Keen, *Competing in Time: Using Telecommunications for Competitive Advantage* (Cambridge, MA: Ballinger, 1988).

14. *Ibid.*
15. *Ibid.*

Chapter 6. Exploiting the Manufacturing–Services Interface

1. M. Dertouzos *et al.*, *Made in America: Regaining the Productive Edge* (Cambridge, MA: MIT Press, 1989).
2. J. B. Quinn, J. Baruch, and P. C. Paquette, "Technology in Services," *Scientific American*, December 1987.
3. T. Levitt, *The Marketing Mode* (New York: McGraw-Hill, 1969).
4. "Zayre Corporation" (case), in H. Mintzberg and J. Quinn, *The Strategy Process* (Englewood Cliffs, NJ: Prentice Hall, 1988).
5. Office of U.S. Trade Representative, U.S. National Study on Trade in Services, Washington, D.C. 1983; S. Roach, "Technology in the Services Sector," in *Technology in Services* (Washington, DC: National Academy Press, 1988).
6. S. Roach, "Technology Focus," Morgan Stanley, July 31, 1991.
7. A. Rappaport and S. Halevi, "The Computerless Computer Company," *Harvard Business Review*, July–August 1991.
8. "Federal Express Company" (case), in Mintzberg and Quinn, *Strategy Process*, 2d ed.
9. W. Beeby, "Manufacturing Information Flow," in *U.S. Leadership in Manufacturing* (Washington, DC: National Academy of Engineering, 1983), p. 86.
10. P. Keen, *Competing in Time: Using Telecommunications for Competitive Advantage* (Cambridge, MA: Ballinger, 1988); G. Stalk and T. Hout, *Competing Against Time: How Timebased Competition Is Reshaping Global Markets* (New York: Free Press, 1990), have developed these themes thoroughly.
11. T. Stewart, "GE Keeps Those Ideas Coming," *Fortune*, August 12, 1991.
12. "Levi's Net Strategy Pays Big Dividends," *Network World*, September 4, 1989.
13. "Spec 2000 Weds Airline Procurement Systems with Automatic Technology," *Air Transport World*, January 1987.
14. R. McKenna, "Marketing in an Age of Diversity," *Harvard Business Review*, September–October 1988.
15. T. Peters, "Fashions. Projects. Markets. Tries . . . and Carnivals!," TPG Communications, 1991.
16. Keen, *Competing in Time*.
17. Rappaport and Halevi, "Computerless Computer Company."
18. C. Loomis, "Can John Akers Save IBM?" *Fortune*, July 15, 1991.
19. "The Pillsbury Company" and "General Mills, Inc." (cases), in Mintzberg and Quinn, *Strategy Process*, 2d ed.

20. "CLS Explores New Logistics Frontiers," *Distribution*, September 1987.

21. P. Nulty, "The New Look of Photography," *Fortune*, July 1, 1991.

22. T. Vollmann, *Cost Accounting for the 1990s, The Challenge of Technological Change* (Montville, NJ: National Association of Cost Accountants, 1986).

23. S. Roach, "Services Under Siege: The Restructuring Imperative," *Harvard Business Review*, September–October 1991.

24. The term was created by R. Coase, 1991 Nobel Prize winner, in his classic "The Nature of the Firm," *Economica*, Vol. 4 (n.s.), November 1937. One of his conclusions, still correct, is that the only economic justification for a firm (as opposed to buying everything in spot markets) is if transaction costs inherent in the latter are greater than insourcing.

25. M. Blaxill and T. Hout, "The Fallacy of the Overhead Quick Fix," *Harvard Business Review*, July–August 1991.

26. *Japan Times*, October 23, 1991.

27. "Work Teams Can Rev Up Paper Pushers, Too," *Business Week*, November 28, 1988; B. Dumaine, "The Bureaucracy Busters," *Fortune*, June 17, 1991.

28. H. Mintzberg, "The Professional Organization," in *Mintzberg on Management* (New York: Free Press, 1989).

29. "Honda Motor Company" (case), Mintzberg and Quinn, *Strategy Process*, 2d ed.

30. R. Guest, "The Quality of Work Life in Japan," *Hokudai Economic Papers*, vol. xii (Tokyo), 1982–83.

31. "Ford: Team Taurus" (case), in Mintzberg and Quinn, *Strategy Process*, 2d ed.

32. T. Stewart, "Brainpower," in *Fortune*, June 3, 1991, presents some high-level executives' views about this point.

Chapter 7. The Intelligent Enterprise: A New Paradigm

1. "Novellus: Thriving—With a Little Help from Its Friends," *Business Week*, January 27, 1992, p. 60.

2. D. Abell and J. Hammond, "Cost Dynamics: Scale and Experience Effects," in *idem, Strategic Market Planning: Problems and Analytical Approaches* (Englewood Cliffs, NJ: Prentice Hall, 1979).

3. "The Cracks at Pilkington," *The Economist*, October 12, 1991, p. 78.

4. P. Drucker, "From World Trade to World Investment," *The Wall Street Journal*, May 26, 1987.

5. "International Logistics Management," *Distribution*, October 1987.

6. R. Shelp, *Beyond Industrialization: Ascendancy of the Global Service Economy* (New York: Praeger, 1981).

7. K. Sauvant, *International Transactions in Services: The Politics of Trans-border Data Flows* (Boulder, CO: Westview Press, 1986).

8. "Services Get the Job Done," *Electronic Business*, September 15, 1988.

9. S. Bell and B. Kettell estimated that 95 percent of daily volume in foreign exchange markets is not connected to trade, *Foreign Exchange Handbook* (Westport, CT: Quorum Books, 1983).

10. J. Bleeke and L. Bryan, "The Globalization of Financial Markets," *The McKinsey Quarterly*, Winter 1988.

11. *Business Week*, April 6, 1992, pp. 64–65.

12. K. Ohmae, "Triad Power: The Coming Shape of Global Competition," *Harvard Business Review*, July–August 1991.

Chapter 8. Managing Knowledge Based and Professional Intellect

1. C. Handy, *The Age of Unreason* (Boston, MA: Harvard Business School Press, 1990).

2. T. Stewart, "Brainpower," *Fortune*, June 3, 1991.

3. J. Newport, "American Express: Service that Sells," *Fortune*, November 20, 1989.

4. Stewart, "Brainpower."

5. H. Itami, *Mobilizing Invisible Assets* (Cambridge MA: Harvard University Press, 1987).

6. R. Teitelbaum, "Reader's Digest: Are Times Tough?" *Fortune*, December 2, 1991.

7. J. Quinn, *Yardsticks for Industrial Research* (New York: Ronald Press, 1959); J. Quinn, "How to Evaluate Research Results," *Harvard Business Review*, March–April 1960.

8. Stewart, "Brain Power."

9. T. Stewart, "GE Keeps Those Ideas Coming," *Fortune*, August 12, 1991.

10. Based on research by Victor E. McGee, in J. Quinn, "Managing Innovation: Controlled Chaos," *Harvard Business Review*, May–June 1985, p. 78.

11. "Intel Corporation © case" (No: PS-BP-256C) developed by G. Cogan and R. Burgelman, Stanford University, 1989 (revised 1991).

12. See "Genentech Inc." (case), in H. Mintzberg and J. Quinn, *The Strategy Process*, 2d ed. (Englewood Cliffs, NJ: Prentice Hall, 1991).

13. "Matsushita Electric Industrial Company" (case) in Mintzberg and Quinn, *Strategy Process*, 2d ed.

14. *The Economist*, November 9, 1991, p. 89.

15. H. Mintzberg, *Mintzberg on Management: Inside Our Strange World of Organizations* (New York: Free Press, 1989).

16. T. Doorley, A. Gregg, and C. Gagnon, "Professional Services Firms and Information Technology: Ongoing Search for Sustained Competitive Advantage," in *Managing Innovation: Cases from the Services Industries* (Washington, DC: National Academy Press, 1988).

17. N. Davis, *Lawrence and Oppenheimer* (New York: Simon & Schuster, 1968); R. Jungk, *Brighter Than a Thousand Suns* (New York: Harcourt Brace, 1958).

18. M. Cohen, J. March, and J. Olsen, "A Garbage Can Model of Organizational Choice," *Administrative Science Quarterly*, March 1972.

19. J. Quinn, "Technology Transfer by Multinational Companies," *Harvard Business Review*, November–December 1969.

20. "The New York Times Company" (case), in Mintzberg and Quinn, *Strategy Process*.

Chapter 9. Managing the Innovative Organization

1. H. Mintzberg, *Mintzberg on Management: Inside Our Strange World of Organizations* (New York: Free Press, 1989).

2. B. Dumaine, "The Bureaucracy Busters," *Fortune*, June 17, 1991.

3. J. Quinn, "Managing Innovation: Controlled Chaos," *Harvard Business Review*, May–June 1985.

4. J. Jewkes, D. Sawers, and R. Stillerman, *The Sources of Invention* (New York: St. Martin's Press, 1958).

5. E. Von Hipple, *The Sources of Innovation* (New York: Oxford University Press, 1988).

6. Jewkes, Sawers, and Stillerman, *Sources of Invention;* A. Koestler, *The Sleepwalkers: A History of Man's Changing Vision of the Universe* (London: Hutchinson, 1959); T. Kuhn, *The Structure of Scientific Revolutions* (Chicago: University of Chicao Press, 1970).

7. R. Kanter, *The Change Masters: Innovation for Productivity in the American Corporation* (New York: Simon & Schuster, 1983).

8. A. Koestler, *The Act of Creation* (London: Hutchinson, 1964).

9. D. Schon, "Champions for Radical New Inventions," *Harvard Business Review*, March–April 1963; J. Quinn, *Strategies for Change: Logical Incrementalism* (Homewood, IL: Irwin, 1980); M. Maidique, "Entrepreneurs, Champions, and Technological Innovation," *Sloan Management Review*, Winter 1980; J. Howell and C. Higgins, "Champions of Technological Innovation," *Administrative Science Quarterly*, June 1990.

10. Moore's Law, defined by Gordon Moore of Intel, stated that the number of components on a semiconductor chip would double each year. In the 1970s and most of the 1980s, it did.

Chapter 10. Managing Intellect in Mass Services

1. J. Quinn, "Managing Strategics Incrementally," *Omega: The International Journal of Management Science*, Fall 1982, pp. 613–27.
2. V. Zeithaml, A. Parasuraman, and L. Berry, *Delivering Quality Service* (New York: Free Press, 1990).
3. J. Kotter and J. Heskett, *Corporate Culture and Performance* (New York: The Free Press, 1992) p. 11.
4. B. Sapporito, "Is Wal-Mart Unstoppable?" *Fortune*, May 6, 1991.
5. M. Barrier, "Walton's Mountain," *Nation's Business*, April 1988.
6. Author's interview with R. Fields, December 1989.
7. L. Armstrong and W. Symonds, "Quality in Services: Strategies," *The Quality Imperative, Business Week* (special issue), October 25, 1991, p. 100.
8. B. Posner and B. Burlingham, "The Hottest Entrepreneur," *Inc.*, January 1988.
9. These include Zeithaml, Parasuraman, and Berry, *Delivering Quality Service*; J. Spechler, *When America Does It Right: Case Studies in Service Quality* (Norcross GA: Industrial Engineering and Management Press, 1991); and L. Schlesinger and J. Heskett, "The Service-driven Company," *Harvard Business Review*, September–October 1991.
10. Particularly Zeithaml, Parasuraman, and Berry, *Delivering Quality Service*, and Spechler, *When American Does It Right*.
11. Armstrong and Symonds, "Quality in Services;" p. 102.
12. Zeithaml, Parasuraman, and Berry, *Delivering Quality Service*; C. Grönroos, *Service Management and Marketing* (Lexington MA: Lexington Books, 1990).
13. M. Oneal, "Quality in Services: Transportation," *The Quality Imperative, Business Week* (special issue), October 25, 1991, p. 117.
14. L. Armstrong, "Quality in Services: Training," *The Quality Imperative, Business Week* (special issue), October 25, 1991, p. 104.
15. B. Dumaine, "The Bureaucracy Busters," *Fortune*, June 17, 1991.
16. J. Newport, "American Express: Service that Sells," *Fortune*, November 20, 1989.
17. Grönroos, *Service Management and Marketing*.
18. S. Walleck, D. O'Hallaran, and C. Leader, "Benchmarking World Class Performance," *The McKinsey Quarterly*, no. 1, 1991.
19. "First Find Your Bench," *The Economist*, May 11, 1991.
20. L. Shostack, "Designing Services that Deliver," *Harvard Business Review*, January–February 1984; G. Rummler and A. Brache, *Improving Performance: How to Manage the White Space on the Organization Chart* (San Francisco: Jossey-Bass, 1991).

Chapter 11. Managing for Service Productivity

1. E. Dennison, *Estimates of Productivity Change by Industry: An Evaluation and an Alternative* (Washington, DC: Brookings Institution, 1989); M. Baily and R. Gordon, "The Productivity Slowdown: Measurement Issues and the Explosion of Computer Power," in W. Brainard and G. Perry (eds.), *Brookings Papers on Economic Activity* (Washington, DC: Brookings Institution, 1988).
2. "Brokerage House Embarks on Journey to Quality Service," *Marketing News*, December 21, 1987, p. 9.
3. J. Goodman, T. Marra and L. Brigham, "Customer Service: Costly Nuisance or Low Cost Profit Strategy?" *Journal of Retail Banking*, Fall 1986, p. 12.
4. V. Zeithaml, A. Parasuraman, and L. Berry, *Delivering Quality Service* (New York: Free Press, 1990).
5. C. Grönroos, *Service Management and Marketing* (Lexington, MA: Lexington Books, 1990), p. 118.
6. Zeithaml, Parasuraman, and Berry, *Delivering Quality Service*, pp. 37–39.
7. J. Quinn and C. Gagnon, "Will Services Follow Manufacturing into Decline?" *Harvard Business Review*, November–December 1987, was one of the first articles to focus attention on these factors in the service sector.
8. T. Peters and N. Austin, *A Passion for Excellence* (New York: Random House, 1985), p. 84.
9. CNN News, May 25, 1987.
10. Source: interview with Richard Liebhaber, Chief Strategy and Technology Officer of MCI, January 1992.
11. B. Schneider, "Imperatives for the Design of Service Organizations," in *Add Value to Your Service*, proceedings of American Marketing Association's Services Marketing Conference, 1987, p. 97.
12. B. Sapporito, "Is Wal-Mart Unstoppable?" *The Economist*, November 9, 1991.
13. T. Peters, "Leadership for Tumultuous Times," visiting lecture, Amos Tuck School, May 7, 1991.
14. R. Larsson and D. Bowen, "Organization and Customer: Managing Design and Coordination of Services," *Academy of Management Review*, vol. 14, no. 2 (1989), detail these uncertainties and some methods of ameliorating them.
15. P. Strassmann, *The Business Value of Computers* (New Canaan CT: Information Economic Press, 1990).
16. E. Giesler and A. Rubenstein, "Measurement of Efficiency and Effectiveness in the Selection, Usage, and Evaluation of Informa-

tion Technology in the Services Industries," Joint Meeting of Institute for Illinois and Industry Information Council, August 31, 1988.

17. L. Schlesinger, and J. Heskett, "The Service Driven Service Company," *Harvard Business Review*, September–October 1991.

Chapter 12. Managing the "Intelligent Enterprise"

1. *Fortune*, news item, April 8, 1991, p. 37.
2. C. Loomis, "Can John Akers Save IBM?" *Fortune*, July 15, 1991.
3. T. Moore, "Goodbye, Corporate Staff," *Fortune*, December 21, 1987.
4. B. Dumaine, "The Bureaucracy Busters," *Fortune*, June 17, 1991.
5. T. Allen, *Managing the Flow of Technology* (Cambridge MA: MIT Press, 1977).
6. Dumaine, "Bureaucracy Busters."
7. T. Peters, "Get Innovative or Get Dead," *California Management Review*, Fall 1990.
8. F. Contractor and P. Lorange, *Cooperative Strategies in International Business*, (Lexington MA: Lexington Books, 1987); K. Harrigan, *Strategies for Joint Ventures*, (Lexington MA: Lexington Books, 1985); K. Ohmae, *Triad Power: The Coming Shape of Global Competition* (New York: Free Press, 1985); J. Lewis *Partnership for Profit: Structuring and Managing Strategic Alliances* (New York: Free Press. 1990); and S. Urban (ed.), *European Strategic Alliances: Cooperative Corporate Strategies in the New Europe* (Cambridge, MA: Blackwell Publishers, 1992).
9. J. Quinn, "Logical Incrementalism," *Sloan Management Review*, 1980, was the first statement of these issues.
10. See J. Quinn, *Strategies for Change*, (Homewood, IL: Richard D. Irwin, 1980).
11. R. Norman, *Management for Growth* (New York: John Wiley, 1977).
12. C. Argyris, "Double Loop Learning in Organizations," *Harvard Business Review*, September–October 1977.
13. E. Wrapp, "Good Managers Don't Make Policy Decisions," *Harvard Business Review*, September–October 1967.
14. J. Quinn, "Managing Strategies Incrementally," *Omega: The International Journal of Management Science*, Fall 1982.
15. F. Gilmore, "Overcoming the Perils of Advocacy in Corporate Planning," *California Management Review*, Spring 1973.
16. R. Cyert, W. Dill, and J. March, "The Role of Expectations in Business Decision Making,"*Administrative Science Quarterly*, 1957, pp. 307–40.

17. H. Mintzberg, D. Raizinghani, and A. Thoret, "The Structure of Unstructured Decisions," *Administrative Science Quarterly*, 1976, pp. 246–75.

18. E. Rhenman, *Organization Theory for Long Range Planning*, (New York: John Wiley, 1973).

19. For an amplification of this approach to goal-setting, see J. Quinn, "Strategic Goals: Process and Policies," *Sloan Management Review*, Fall 1977.

20. R. Cyert and J. March, *A Behavioral Theory of the Firm* (Englewood Cliffs, NJ: Prentice Hall, 1963).

21. L. Sayles, *Managerial Behavior: Administration in Complex Organizations* (New York: McGraw-Hill, 1964), was perhaps the first to comment on this mode of management.

22. P. Soelberg, "Unprogrammed Decision Making," *Industrial Management Review*, Spring 1987.

23. See particularly Chapter 3 in Quinn, *Strategies for Change*.

24. K. Cohen and R. Cyert, "Strategy Formulation, Implementation, and Monitoring," *The Journal of Business*, 1973, pp. 349–67.

25. E. Witte, "Field Research on Complex Decision-Making Processes: The Phase Theorem," *International Studies of Management and Organization*, January 1972.

26. S. Beer, *Designing Freedom* (Toronto: CBC Publications, 1974).

27. This is the core concept developed in Quinn, *Strategies for Change*.

28. Based on personal interviews, 1990, 1992.

Chapter 13. A New Economic and Management Paradigm

1. M. Porter, *The Competitive Advantage of Nations* (New York: Free Press, 1990).

2. J. Quinn and C. Gagnon, "Will Services Follow Manufacturing into Decline?" *Harvard Business Review*, November–December 1987.

3. S. Roach, "Technology and the Services Sector: America's Hidden Competitive Challenge," *Technology in Services* (Washington DC: National Academy Press, 1988); *Technology Focus Series* (New York: Morgan Stanley, 1988–91) and "Services Under Siege: The Restructuring Imperative," *Harvard Business Review*, September–October 1991.

4. Roach, "Services Under Siege."

5. P. Strassmann, *The Business Value of Computers* (New Canaan CT: Information Economics Press, 1990).

6. E. Brynjolfsson and B. Bimber, "Information Technology and the Productivity Paradox," Working Paper, Brookings Institution, February 1991, presents a superb analysis of the issues.

7. Report of "Committee to Study the Impact of Information Tech-

nology on the Performance of Service Activities," National Research Council (Washington DC: National Academy Press, to be released, fall 1992).

8. G. Hatsoupoulos, P. Krugman, and L. Summers, "U.S. Competitiveness: Beyond the Trade Deficit," *Science*, July 15, 1988.

9. D. Aschauer, "Is the Public Capital Stock Too Low?" *Federal Reserve Bank of Chicago Bulletin*, October 1987.

LIST OF TABLES AND FIGURES

TABLES

FIGURES

Figures (*continued*)

INDEX